ESSENTIAL TECHNIQUES

DRAWING & PAINTING

ESSENTIAL TECHNIQUES

DRAWING & PAINTING

MORE THAN 200 TECHNIQUES AND STEP-BY-STEP PROJECTS

amber
BOOKS

First published in 2007 by
Amber Books Ltd
Bradley's Close
74–77 White Lion Street
London N1 9PF
United Kingdom
www.amberbooks.co.uk

Reprinted in 2008

ISBN 978-1-905704-54-5

Project Editor: Sarah Uttridge
Designer: Anthony Cohen

Printed in Thailand by Kyodo Nation Printing Services

10 9 8 7 6 5 4 3 2

Contents

Introduction

People have been drawing and painting for thousands of years, and no matter what your art teacher might have told you at school, it's something everyone can do and enjoy. But it isn't just a satisfying creative pastime.

As you'll discover throughout this book, art can help you see the world around you in new and exciting ways. From architecture to people, natural landscapes to still life, even the everyday becomes extraordinary and is a potential subject for your pencil or paintbrush. No previous knowledge is necessary to get started, although more experienced artists will find plenty here to keep them occupied. Whether you're an absolute beginner looking for a new and challenging hobby, or have always

dabbled and now want to take your interest further, this is the perfect place to develop and improve your artistic skills.

The book is reassuringly straight-forward, setting things out clearly with a large number of visual examples, making even technical ideas and complex principles easy to understand. Each of the more detailed assignments, both within the earlier chapters and the projects section at the back, have full step-by-step instructions, a materials list and photographs to guide you through each stage. To help illustrate various theories and styles, we've used works by some of the world's greatest artists, including Monet, Van Gogh, Constable, Rembrandt, Seurat, Klimt and Whistler. As well as providing useful points of

reference, these will hopefully inspire and enthuse you, too.

The opening chapters of the book cover the basic materials and equipment you need to get started, as well as offering advice on how to set up an art space at home. There's also a comprehensive guide to media and a whole chapter devoted to colour. From there, you'll move on to learn about composition, figure-drawing and painting portraits, before exploring a wide variety of artistic techniques and tricks. The second half of the book is devoted to projects – more than 40 of them – which will help you put what you've learned into practise, expanding and exploring the various techniques as well as developing your own creative style and preferences. Although these chapters are arranged to take you through the Drawing and Painting course, the great advantage in learning this way is that you can work entirely at your own pace, fitting both reading and practical sessions around other commitments, and referring back to the book at any point for help and inspiration. Maybe you're struggling with a piece of work and need some tips or advice on how to take it forward, or maybe you want to start something fresh but aren't sure what to paint, or how to go about it – all the ideas and assistance you'll need are here, whenever you want them.

The book is also fantastically flexible in terms of what you hope to achieve, and the sort of art you most enjoy producing. The projects in particular are hugely varied, covering scale from miniatures to huge canvasses, colour from bright abstracts to black and white sketches, painting indoors and outside, and using a huge range of media, from biros (yes, really!) to gouache. Whether you've always wanted to try portraiture, paint traditional landscapes or have a secret desire to create like a Cubist, there's something here that will inspire and help you realise your artistic goals.

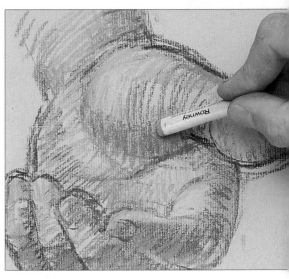

GETTING STARTED

Taking time to set up and organise space
for your art work really does make the hours
you spend creating much more productive
and enjoyable. In this chapter, you'll find
information on the materials and equipment you
need to create a studio at home (however little
room you have available) as well as tips on
storage and making your art projects portable.

Setting up a work space

You are more likely to pick up a pencil or brush if you have somewhere specific to work – even if it is only the corner of a living room.

Few amateur artists have the luxury of a large, dedicated studio space. The lucky ones can convert a spare room, garden shed, conservatory or garage. Most have to make do with a corner of a dining room or part of the living area.

Space and light

Whatever your situation, the basic requirements are enough space and light to work comfortably. You also need somewhere accessible to store your kit and a place to keep finished works safe, clean and dry.

A dedicated studio space would be ideal. You can close the door on work in progress and return to it whenever you like, without tidying up at the end of a session or spending time setting up at the start of the next one. You can also guarantee privacy. Consider your home carefully – is there any unused space, in an attic, perhaps, or a garden shed?

An alternative is to exploit a little-used space such as a guest bedroom, dining or breakfast room. You can leave your work out most of the time, but will need storage spaces where things can be packed away neatly when the room reverts to its primary function. (The set-ups below will give you an idea of the space you need for oil, acrylic and watercolour painting.)

Screening it off

Screens are useful if you have to work in a living or study area – they can be pulled around to mask the clutter.

SET-UP FOR OILS AND ACRYLICS

Oils and acrylics are usually painted on a vertical surface, so you will need an easel. The size will depend on the scale you work at – and your budget. A good studio easel is a costly item, but reasonably-priced models are available, especially if you buy mail order. A sketching easel is suitable for small-scale works, and the metal versions are remarkably sturdy. Your paints and mediums should be within easy reach, on either a table or a trolley – some artists have a palette fixed to the top surface, while others work from a hand-held one. You may need a stool or chair to sit on, though many artists prefer to work standing up.

▶ **A studio easel and a trolley provide a compact and flexible work area. Make sure that there is enough room to step back and assess your progress.**

SET-UP FOR WATERCOLOURS

Watercolours are usually painted on a nearly horizontal surface so the washes do not run. Things happen fast so you must have everything to hand. You need a sturdy work surface, large enough to hold the work and all your equipment easily. A cramped surface impedes the painting process and results in accidents. If you don't want to buy a table easel, you can prop up your drawing board on a book or piece of wood. Paint, palettes and jars of water should be close to hand on your favoured side. Spare brushes can be placed bristle-end up in a jar on the far side of the work surface. Always have plenty of clean rags or kitchen paper for mopping up spills and runs.

◀ **For watercolours you can work on one surface – but make sure it is large enough for your painting, paints, palettes and water.**

Avoid working in a sleeping area if you intend to use oil paint or pastels – sleeping in a room with solvents and dust in the air is not good for your health.

The mobile studio

If you are really pushed for space you can make do with a combination of portable equipment and good storage. Table, portable and box easels fold away and can be quickly and easily set up. A box easel has integral storage compartments and is compact when folded.

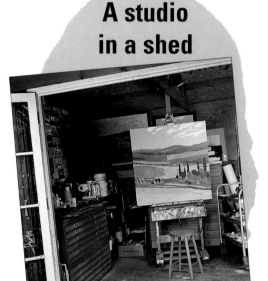

A studio in a shed

Quiet and private, a garden shed can provide the ideal studio space. One drawback is the lack of running water – a nearby garden tap is useful, especially if you work mainly in water-based mediums.

Also, think about heating and lighting. You can run electricity from your house, but this is a major job involving laying armoured cabling underground. Instead, for heating, try using calor gas or paraffin heaters. For lighting, it might pay to replace an existing wooden door with a glass one or, if possible, add windows.

The garden studio above is made from a prefabricated horse loose box. Large French windows were added so that the entire front of the studio opens out into the garden. This greatly increases not only the light but also the space available.

Table easels can be adjusted to various angles and are excellent for watercolour painting, drawing and small-scale work in other media (see Choosing the best easel, pages 22–23).

You will need one or more boxes for your drawing and painting tools. A plastic toolbox with inset or cantilevered storage compartments is a versatile and inexpensive choice. They come in a range of sizes to suit your requirements. In art-supply shops and catalogues, they are sometimes called 'art bins'. A portfolio to protect supports and finished works completes your 'mobile studio'. Your easel, toolbox and portfolio can be stashed away in a cupboard, attic or under the bed when not required.

In the right light

You also need good lighting, so that you can judge colours and save your eyes from strain. Ever since Leonardo da Vinci (1452–1519) recommended them in *Treatise on Painting*, artists have preferred north-facing windows. This is because north light comes reflected from the sky (not directly from the sun) and is, therefore, fairly consistent throughout the day. It doesn't have the yellow cast of direct sunlight, so it is easier to assess colours and their relationships accurately.

Remember, though, that your painting might be viewed in artificial light which will modify the colours. However, artists rarely have any control over the conditions in which a work will be seen, so they still try to 'key' their colours to look right in natural light.

Controlling the light

Leonardo recommended that the artist's north-facing windows should look out on to an external courtyard that could then be covered by a linen tent to control the amount of light. Today it is more convenient to control natural light with blinds and curtains. Translucent roller blinds can be used to soften bright light – or you can tape tracing paper or tissue paper over the glass.

Restricting yourself to natural light limits the hours you can paint, especially in winter. If you can work only in the evenings – or are a night owl by nature – you will need to rely on artificial light. Try using daylight bulbs, available from

THE IDEAL STUDIO

Few artists have an ideal work space, but most of the ideas in this studio can be adapted for less perfect spaces. You could have different aspects of the studio in different parts of your house – a work space in a well-lit room, storage in a darker one. Remember if you use solvents, keep the room well ventilated by opening the window.

WALLS
These should be plain white or a neutral colour. Use them to display finished works, works in progress, sketches and inspirational photos and images from magazines.

STACKING CANVASES
Stack stretched canvases against a wall.

PLAN CHEST
This allows you to store works on paper flat and to keep them away from the light.

HARD FLOORING
Tiles, laminates, vinyl and lino are non-absorbent and easy to clean.

good electrical stores and art-supply shops. The bulbs are coloured blue to compensate for the warmish cast of artificial light. This produces a fairly neutral, consistent light, which is easy on the eyes and excellent for assessing colours and tones. Fluorescent tube lighting gives a similar effect.

Setting up portraits and still lifes

If you work directly from life, you will also need to light your subject. Effective lighting can be supplied by

TASK AND SPOTLIGHTS
An adjustable lamp provides ideal task lighting in a work area. Spotlights can also be set up for task lighting or to provide mood lighting on a subject.

NATURAL LIGHT
A north-facing window is ideal, as the light is consistent and even. If your windows face other directions, use translucent fabric or papers to soften the sunlight.

EASEL
A solid studio easel is best for large canvases. Castors ensure that it can be moved easily.

SHELVING
You can never have enough shelving – for materials, reference books and still-life material that you might want to paint. Adjustable brackets provide the most flexible system.

WORK SURFACE
A board on trestles is a cheap and flexible alternative to a table. You can then have boards of different sizes for different projects. Make sure there is enough space for the artwork and your materials. A drawing board can be propped up on a table easel or on a book.

MATERIALS TROLLEY
Store your paints and mediums on a small shelved unit. It should have castors for mobility. Adapt an existing cabinet or look for suitable trolleys or units in kitchen supply stores.

spotlights, table lamps and long-necked work lights. Experiment, too, with sheets of white card or polyboard to bounce light back on to the subject.

Light or white walls are probably best for your work space as they reflect and enhance the light and are not distracting. However, when very pale colours are used as the background for a still life, they can be a bit stark. Watercolours might work well with a light background; oils, however, often call for a darker one. If you paint many still lifes, it pays to build up a good selection of paper and fabric in different colours and tones to use as backgrounds.

Castors and cups

When space is restricted, mobile units come into their own, allowing you to shift the contents of your studio around to accommodate the requirements of different projects and media. A drinks trolley or a kitchen one makes a handy mobile work station.

Most large easels and some small plan chests are supplied with castors, but otherwise it is relatively easy to attach them. Alternatively, stand the legs of studio furniture in plastic 'cups' that will slide over hard floors – they are available in furniture and DIY stores.

Spills are inevitable in a studio space. A carpet is less forgiving to water, inks, oil paints, acrylics, turpentine and pastel dust than are vinyl, timber, tiles or laminated flooring. If you have to work in a carpeted area, protect the floor with a dust sheet, an old rug or plastic matting.

Organizing your work space

You'll save yourself both time and money if you keep your art materials readily to hand and in good condition. So get organised!

A place for everything and everything in its place is the golden rule for the artist, especially when space is limited. Spend time finding a home for your equipment and you'll be able to work more comfortably and effectively. You will also save money. Remember, art materials are costly, so it is worth making them last. On the following pages, various storage methods are described to help you keep materials and artworks in perfect condition.

Looking after your brushes

Store brushes bristle-end up in a jar or tin, but make sure they are dry first. Dry brushes flat – if they are dried upright, water runs down under the ferrule, loosening the hairs.

If you have a large collection of brushes, group those of a similar size together so that you can find what you want when you want it. You should always separate brushes used for oil painting from those used for water-based media, as traces of oil on a brush can ruin a water-based mix or wash. For long-term storage, put brushes away in a box or tin, but make sure they are thoroughly dry first. Lay them flat and add a few mothballs to ward off insect attacks.

A temporary home

You also need somewhere to put your brushes while you are working on a painting. Acrylic brushes should be rinsed out as soon as you stop using them, because the paint is almost impossible to remove once it has dried. If you have to leave the painting for a short time, plunge the bristles into the water jar – resting a brush on its bristle end won't do it any harm for a few moments.

Other media are more forgiving, so you can leave brushes loaded with paint during a short break. Simply put the brushes on a ridged brush rest or in a piece of florist's oasis, as shown right.

SORTING OUT YOUR ART TOOLS

Keep frequently used pencils, brushes and pens upright in a jar or pot, where they are easily accessible. Alternatively, store coloured and pastel pencils in shallow tins, organizing them by colour – warm to cool, for example. A piece of foam cut to size and laid on top will keep them in place. If you work with a range of media, store them in separate boxes or a set of labelled, small plastic drawers. A plastic toolbox or fishing-tackle box with cantilevered trays is ideal for items such as pencils, erasers, brushes, palettes and nibs. These are sold in art-supply shops as 'art bins', but often at a higher price. When you are actually painting, use a ridged rest or piece of oasis to hold your brushes.

▲ Store pastels by colour in a transparent plastic drawer unit – you can then put your hand on the right stick straight away.

▶ A brush rest is a cheap and useful piece of equipment when painting. The ridges prevent the brushes from rolling off.

▲ Put brushes, pens and pencils upright in pots, tins or jam jars.

▶ A slab of florist's oasis is a useful temporary resting place for oil paint brushes. Simply stab the brushes, bristle-end up, into the oasis.

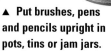

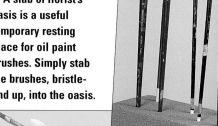

STORING PAPER AND ARTWORKS

The best form of storage for plain paper, or drawings and paintings on paper, is a plan chest. These substantial items of furniture have shallow drawers designed for storing artwork. They are available in a range of sizes and materials. Wooden plan chests are cumbersome and heavy, but lighter and cheaper styles in tubular metal and plastic are available from specialist suppliers, often by mail order. The size you choose will be dictated by the scale you work at.

Interleave your drawings and paintings with sheets of acid-free tissue paper or tracing paper. Pastel and charcoal drawings need to be handled with special care. Fix them using an aerosol fixative, or fixative and a diffuser.

Always spray your work in a well-ventilated place away from other surfaces, ideally out of doors. Prop the drawing so that it is vertical and spray lightly, keeping the spray moving over the surface to get an even coverage.

If you don't have the funds or the space for a plan chest, a portfolio is a good alternative. Consider investing in two, one for finished works and one for pristine paper. They should be stored somewhere dry – in a cupboard, in the loft or under a bed, for example.

Paper should be handled as little as possible, as the edges become grubby

▲ **Use sticky notes to label different types and weights of paper. This avoids having to rifle through the plan chest or portfolio and possibly damaging or marking the papers. And keep sample packs of papers, as they are useful for practising on.**

and tattered with constant handling and fingers leave greasy marks that can disrupt a watercolour wash. For easy identification of each weight and type of paper, place sheets of coloured paper or sticky notes between different batches, then write a description on each one.

▼ **Charcoal and pastel drawings are easily smudged, so fix them (see right) before storing them. Interleave drawings with tissue or tracing paper to protect them.**

▲ **The most convenient way of fixing a powdery medium is with an aerosol fixative, but a diffuser is the traditional method. Bend the diffuser to create a right-angle, immerse one end in the fixative, then blow briskly through the mouthpiece to create a fine spray. Practise on scrap paper first until you can achieve an even coverage.**

STORING CANVASES

Spare canvases can simply be leant against a convenient wall. Place the largest canvas facing the wall with smaller ones stacked against it. For long-term storage, cover the stack with a dust cloth or plastic, or wrap individual paintings in plastic. Protect the corners with corrugated card or buy special corner protectors from art suppliers.

If space isn't a problem, you can construct a simple rack from 50 x 50mm (2 x 2in) timber. Fix some lengths of timber to the floor, so that the canvases rest on them to provide ventilation around the paintings. Canvas boards can be stored against a wall, in a rack or in a plan chest or portfolio.

▲ Remove paintings on canvas from the stretchers to transport or store them. Roll the canvas with the paint on the outside to prevent the paint film from cracking.

▲ Stack canvases with the largest one next to the wall. Lean stretchers against other stretchers or cross pieces, so that the canvas does not get dented.

If you are intending to work away from home, perhaps on location or on holiday, you need to think about how you will transport your brushes. The most important thing is to protect the bristles. A brush roll is a cheap, light and compact way of transporting your brushes. It consists of a rectangle of fabric with pockets into which brushes can be slotted – it is then rolled up and tied with ribbons. You can make one by stitching elastic on to a piece of sturdy fabric, or threading loops of elastic through a split-cane or raffia mat. Brushes can also be carried in plastic brush tubes.

Pin up images

A useful addition to your work space is a pinboard, on which you can keep track of all art-related matters: important exhibitions, and the phone numbers of art suppliers, models or the local adult education centre. You can also display inspirational photographs and images torn from magazines and newspapers – the more you look at them, the more likely they are to trigger an idea for one of your next paintings.

A few shelves for holding reference and sketch books are also useful additions to your working area. Items that are awkward to store, such as a hair-dryer, kidney-shaped palettes and viewfinders, can be hung on hooks underneath the shelves.

Rags and bins

A painter can never have too many rags. They have all kinds of uses: applying paint and blotting it off, wiping up spills and cleaning brushes and palettes. Never throw away waste cotton fabric, such as old sheets or tea towels. Instead, cut or tear it into useable pieces and stash them in an accessible box or bin.

Old paint tubes and rags are messy if left lying around, especially if you work in oils. A pedal bin with a plastic bin-liner is an ideal solution. Paint rags are flammable – empty the bin regularly so that they are out of your house as soon as possible.

Mobile storage

If you have to move your painting materials around – to put them away at the end of every working session, perhaps – a small shelved unit with castors is invaluable. Look for trolleys or similar units in kitchen supply stores.

Keeping a sketch book

Whether you use it to make preparatory drawings, to try out different mediums or to create a visual diary, the sketch book is an invaluable tool for the artist.

Artists have been known to make sketches on old envelopes, shopping lists – and even on the back of the hand! But it is much simpler if you carry a sketch book at all times. In this way you can make on-the-spot drawings and jot down visual ideas whenever and wherever you like – and you always know where to find them when you need them.

The sketch book habit

For most artists, carrying a sketch book is more effective than carrying a camera. True, you can take a photograph in a fraction of a second and it will give you a detailed rendition of a particular scene. However, unless you are a skilled photographer, you cannot use the camera as creatively, as it tends to render everything in the same way.

A sketch book, on the other hand, provides a personal record. In it, you can record not only what you see, but also what you feel. You can emphasize certain elements, and leave out others. If you are struck by a particular facial expression, for example, you can make a quick sketch, capturing the essence of that expression without worrying about detail, colour, texture and so on.

It is a good idea to buy a small sketch book – one which fits into your pocket or a bag that you always carry – and to use it whenever the opportunity arises. Record people and places, and sketch details of what is happening around you. Above all, jot down any ideas you might have for future paintings. Your sketch book – unlike your memory – won't let you down. Once you have made a drawing, it is there forever to provide inspiration.

The quality of the paper in sketch books varies enormously. You can, for example, buy books of handmade paper, often bound with elaborately marbled or fabric covers. These sketch books are beautiful objects in their own right.

The right paper

However, a very expensive sketch book can be quite daunting for the amateur artist who might be afraid to ruin it with poor sketches. Remember also that a sketch book with a delicate, ornate cover will get damaged easily if you intend to carry it around with you.

It is probably better to begin by using an inexpensive book – but avoid very cheap pads that contain thin, shiny paper. These are generally bought from stationers rather than art shops. Usually, the paper is too hard to use with anything except a ball-point or fountain pen.

Most art shops stock sketch books in a range of cartridge and drawing papers, from 95gsm (45lb) sketching paper to the heavier 290gsm (140lb). Also available are pads of assorted coloured and tinted

▲ Large or small, spiral-bound or case-bound, landscape or portrait, there is a sketch book to meet the needs of every artist.

papers, ideal for pastel and coloured pencil work. However, these are not usually made in pocket sizes, A5 generally being the smallest.

Choosing a sketch book

To a large extent your choice of sketch book will depend on what drawing materials you use. Cartridge paper is a good all-rounder, suitable for most drawing tools. However, pen and ink and technical pens are best used on very smooth papers; coarse surfaces are good for chunky mediums such as soft pencil, pastel and charcoal.

▶ In upright sketchbooks, you can attain landscape-format drawings simply by working over the spine.

▼ A sketch book can also be used to keep dried flowers, commercial packaging or anything that stimulates you visually.

Watercolour pads

Like sketch books, watercolour pads come in a range of sizes starting from around 180 x 130mm (7 x 5in). They are made with proper watercolour paper and have a strong backing board for rigidity and stability. The papers range from very rough to smooth hot-pressed. They are available either spiral-bound or as a block which is gummed on all four edges to reduce the need for stretching.

Sketch books come in various shapes and sizes. Some are rectangular and upright ('portrait' format), others are rectangular and horizontal ('landscape' format). The portrait format is perhaps the most versatile, because you can always work across two pages, taking your drawing over the spine for a landscape subject.

Spiral- or case-bound?

The spine of a sketch book can be either case-bound (that is, stitched or gummed) or spiral-bound. The spiral-bound ones don't allow you to sketch across two pages, but they do let you remove pages without ruining the book. This means you can discard sub-standard sketches and mount and frame exceptional ones.

What's more, the spiral-bound books can easily accommodate mounted materials. To make your book really attractive, feel free to include visually interesting items such as pressed flowers and leaves, postcards, tickets, invitations and scraps of fabric – anything, in fact, that may prove useful as a reference, inspiration or as a memory-jogger. Your sketch book is, in effect, a visual diary.

You can also use your sketch book for painting outdoors. Most heavier sketch book papers of around 290gsm (140lb) are fine for light watercolour washes. However, for very wet colour, you should always use a watercolour pad (see above, right).

▲ Carefully worked watercolours that run right up to the edge of the page can look stunning in your sketchbook.

For sketching with acrylic paints, you can buy pads of canvas-textured paper. Oil paints are not really a suitable sketching medium, since they take so long to dry.

Colour notes

Painting out-of-doors can be a delight, but you often find yourself running out of time or stopped in your tracks by a change in the weather. It is difficult to finish the painting at home, because you cannot remember the colours.

The answer is to make colour notes in your sketch book before you start work on the painting. Make a very rough line drawing of the subject in your sketch book. Then you can write the names of the colours on the sketch or, even better, paint an actual blob of colour in the relevant area. These approximate colour guides will provide the reference you need to complete the painting at home.

ONE SKETCH BOOK, MANY STYLES

Use your sketch book to experiment with different drawing styles and mediums. The sketches below – all by the same artist – give some indication of the styles you might like to include in your book. The top picture is a line drawing in pencil, but has blocks of tone dotted across the composition to add variety. The middle picture is also in pencil – but colour has been added with washes of coffee!

The bottom sketch was done in watercolours. Paints might not seem the ideal sketching medium – but you can easily carry around a small watercolour set that contains all you need (see Portable art materials, pages 18–19).

Portable art materials

At some stage, every artist will want the challenge of painting outdoors, but you need to make sure you take the right equipment.

When it comes to deciding what to take when painting away from your home or studio, practical considerations play an important part. Plan in advance and take enough materials to meet your needs while avoiding unnecessary weight or bulk.

First and foremost, comfort is crucial. There is nothing more miserable than trying to work in extreme weather conditions without the right sort of clothing. Depending on your chosen destination, pack a wide-brimmed hat to protect against the sun, or fingerless gloves to help keep you warm.

Are you sitting comfortably?

When using oils or acrylics, working with your painting on your lap or propped up against a handy tree trunk

◀ **Handy equipment for the travelling artist includes a backpack (A), a foldaway stool (B) and a light folding sketching easel (C). (The backpack shown here converts into a stool.)**

might be okay in emergencies, but the frustration and discomfort involved will eventually make a proper easel essential.

For the travelling artist, a box easel is the ideal choice. This combines a materials container and an easel in a compact, portable case with a handle for carrying. The legs are adjustable, so you can choose to stand or sit as you paint.

Sketching easels

Alternatively, a folding sketching easel is lightweight and usually suitable for all but very large or heavy paintings. On soft ground, you can make the easel more stable by tethering the legs with string and metal skewers (just as you would stabilise a tent). If you prefer to work sitting down, a good-quality, modern folding stool or chair is a worthwhile investment.

Whatever medium you're working in, limit yourself to a few colours. This is not simply convenient, it is also a good discipline – colour mixing becomes easier and more automatic, leaving you free to observe and appreciate the subject.

Carry only as much paint as you will need. Even oils and acrylics are available in small (20ml) sizes. It is a good idea to keep the

To paint in watercolours outdoors, you need a sketch pad (D), a pencil (E) for preliminary drawings, brushes (F) and a watercolour set containing pans of paint and a palette area (G). You also need water – why not keep it in a couple of mineral water bottles? For oils and acrylics, you need a palette and paints, clip-on dippers (H) to hold thinners and mediums, perhaps a palette knife (I), and a selection of brushes (J). Canvas paper (K) is a portable, lightweight surface to paint on, and a charcoal pencil (L) can be used for an underdrawing.

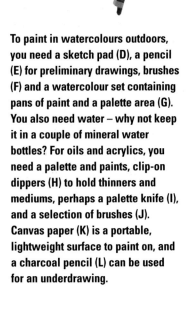

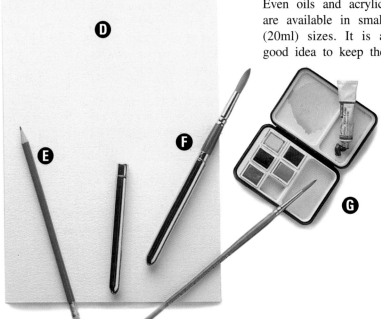

large economy tubes for the studio, and to invest in a few less bulky tubes for painting trips.

Paints of all types can be bought in handy sets – some come in lightweight, attaché-style carrying cases, complete with accessories such as palette, brushes and mediums. The initial choice of colours is that of the manufacturer, but, as you use the set, you can gradually substitute your favourite colours for the ones supplied.

Customised painting sets

Better still, why not make your own customised, portable painting set? This can be a wooden box, designed to carry your usual colours and mediums as well as your favourite palette and brushes.

Watercolourists will find that pads of paper are easier to carry than individual sheets. As the pads have a stiff card backing, there is no need for a board or other rigid surface to work on. Special blocks of paper, which are glued on three sides and do not need to be stretched, are particularly useful if you intend to work with watery washes.

For oils and acrylics, the cardboard-backed pads of canvas-textured paper are ideal for on-the-spot painting. These come with sheets of primed paper in a choice of sizes and grades – fine, medium and

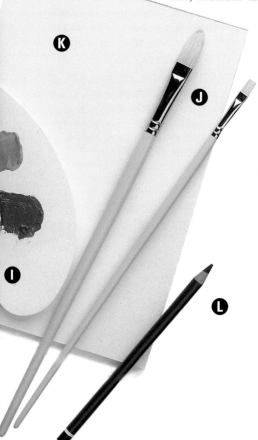

THE COMPLETE WATERCOLOUR SET

As you need only a few lightweight materials, watercolours are particularly well suited to painting outside. You can buy compact, all-in-one sets that fit into virtually any bag and contain everything you need.

As well as a water container, palette, sketching pad and brushes, these sets have pans of colour, which are more practical than tubes because you can see and mix the colours instantly, without having to squeeze out paint and replace caps. Always carry a second bottle of water so that you have one for mixing colours and one for cleaning brushes.

For very small paintings, you can buy tiny watercolour sets – some of which will slip into your pocket.

coarse. Alternatively, use prepared and ready-primed stretched canvases or canvas boards.

Avoid travelling with a traditional wooden drawing board, which is heavy and cumbersome to carry. If you really need a board, try a sheet of lightweight plywood or hardboard instead.

Bottles, boxes and containers

Pliable plastic food containers – the type used for freezer storage – come in a wide range of shapes and sizes and are invaluable to the artist. Use the lightweight lidded boxes for carrying paints, crayons, pastels and other materials.

Pourers and bottles with plastic lids are excellent for holding water, turpentine and liquid mediums. You need one source of clean water or turps for diluting the colours and another for cleaning brushes. If you are travelling by air, remember that it is illegal to take flammable substances, which include turpentine and white spirit, on the plane. In some countries, real turpentine is difficult to come by, so it is worth making a few enquiries before you go.

On any painting trip, you need plenty of clean rags or kitchen paper for cleaning palettes and brushes. Also take clingfilm or plastic bags, so you can

carry a dirty palette home without getting paint everywhere. Alternatively, use disposable paper palettes.

For transporting canvases with wet oils and acrylics, carry paintings face-in, as shown below. To transport drawings and watercolours, cover the surface with a sheet of clean paper, or roll them into a cardboard tube. Remember, soft pencil, pastel, chalk and charcoal smudge easily so drawings should be sprayed with fixative as soon as you have finished.

▼ The trouble with oil paints is that they take time to dry, so it is easy to smudge the colours. A convenient solution is to push panel pins through corks so that both ends of the pins protude. Then cut the blunt ends off the pins with pliers, and use these to attach two paintings, facing inwards, together. You can then carry the canvases around without touching the paint.

Choosing the best palette

Essential to creating good paintings is colour mixing – and to do this successfully, you first need to have the right palette.

Artists' palettes are made from a variety of materials and come in an enormous range of shapes and sizes. Your choice depends largely on the paints you are intending to use. For example, you will need a flat palette for oils and acrylics, and deeper mixing dishes for watercolours.

It is important to work with a palette that is big enough to accommodate all the colours you are likely to need. There is nothing more frustrating than trying to mix on a cramped surface – either you tend not to use enough of each colour or the mixes overlap, creating muddy colours.

Oil paints

The kidney-shaped wooden palette with a hole for the thumb is traditionally used for oil paints. This design has been in use since the advent of the medium in the early fifteenth century. The best wooden palettes are made from mahogany or mahogany veneer, but there are now cheaper options, including plywood and other wood composites.

When choosing a wooden palette, try it out for size, weight and comfort. The ideal palette can easily be held in a horizontal position – usually by using the forearm as support. A badly designed one will be difficult to hold up and will soon make your thumb and wrist ache.

Before using your palette for the first time, seal the wood by rubbing it with linseed oil. This helps prevent the palette from absorbing oil from the paint, causing the colours to dry out. After one or two painting sessions, the palette ceases to be as absorbent and provides an excellent paint-mixing surface. Cared for properly, a good wooden palette will last a lifetime.

Acrylic paints

For acrylics, use a plastic or plastic-laminate palette – these are available at all good art stores. Acrylic paint dries quickly and, if left for several hours or overnight, the paint turns first rubbery, then hard. On a wooden palette the colours will stick fast to the slightly irregular, pitted surface and will be difficult to remove. However, the smooth surface of a plastic palette provides no key for the paint, which can be removed easily by soaking, then peeling it off.

A special 'wet' palette is also available for use with acrylics and is designed to keep the colours moist for as long as possible. The palette works on the principle of osmosis. It consists of a shallow plastic tray with a sheet of absorbent wet tissue placed in the bottom under a thin membrane paper. When the acrylic paint colours are laid out on the membrane, the moisture from the wet tissue is drawn through, so preventing the paints from drying out.

Alternatively, you can make your own wet palette from a plastic or foil dish and some sheets of wetted kitchen paper, with a sheet of greaseproof paper for the membrane.

Watercolour and gouache

Palettes for mixing watercolour or gouache must be deep enough to hold watery mixtures without the colours

INTEGRAL PALETTES

Most enamelled watercolour boxes have lids that open out to form a small palette. They are often divided into two or more recesses and sometimes unfold to provide a larger mixing area. These boxes are particularly handy for outdoor work and sketching.

running together. They are available in a range of shapes and sizes from small round dishes, known as tinting saucers, to much larger, more complex palette trays which have 24 or more recesses for mixing colour.

Watercolour palettes are usually made of ceramic, plastic or enamelled metal. Plastic palettes are light, tough and inexpensive – excellent for painting expeditions and for working outdoors. However, the plastic surface has a slightly repellent effect on water

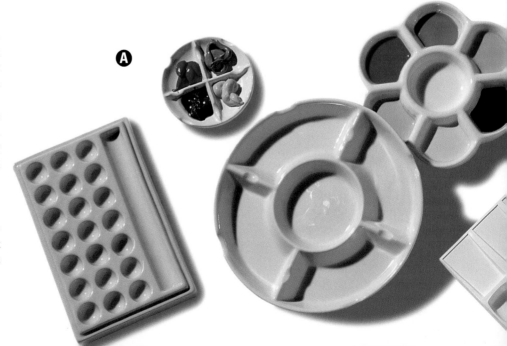

Ⓐ

and the paint tends to break up into globules rather than forming even pools. Although this makes no difference to the colours, it can be irritating and makes it difficult to judge how much colour you have mixed. In addition, some plastics stain easily and soon lose their whiteness. For these reasons, many artists prefer to use ceramic palettes.

Improvised palettes

Lack of a proper palette need not prevent you from painting. For oils and acrylics, you could always improvise with a sheet of plastic, perspex, laminate or glass. The latter can be made safe by binding the sharp edges with tape. One great advantage of a homemade palette is that you can choose a size and shape to suit your needs. It can be as large as you like, perhaps even cut to fit a particular table top.

Other alternative palettes for oils and acrylics are greaseproof paper, old plates and other discarded kitchenware. You can also buy disposable paper palettes in tear-off pads. For watercolour, use old dishes and saucers.

Consider the colour

Be aware that the colour or tone of your palette has an effect on the appearance of the colours you mix in it. For example, on a white palette all your colours will look comparatively dark, whereas on a

Cleaning an oil palette

To clean your oil palette, you need a knife and some diluent – for example, white spirit or turpentine left over in a dipper after a painting.

1 ▲ **Remove excess paint** Scrape off left-over colours with a knife while the paint is still wet.

2 ▲ **Wipe the palette** Dip a rag in diluent and wipe the remaining paint off the palette.

dark palette, your colour mixes will appear paler.

Watercolour palettes are always white, so that they will give an accurate idea of how the colours will appear on white paper. Most oil paintings, on the other hand, are executed in a darker tonal range, and the artist often blocks out the bright white canvas in the early stages of a painting. For the oil painter, therefore, a wooden palette provides a better idea of how the mixed colours will look in the finished painting.

Some artists like to use a sheet of clear plastic or glass as a palette. They can then put a sheet of coloured paper underneath, matching the paper they are using as a support.

Ⓐ **A selection of watercolour palettes**
Ⓑ **Oblong and oval wooden palettes for oils**
Ⓒ **White plastic palette for acrylics**

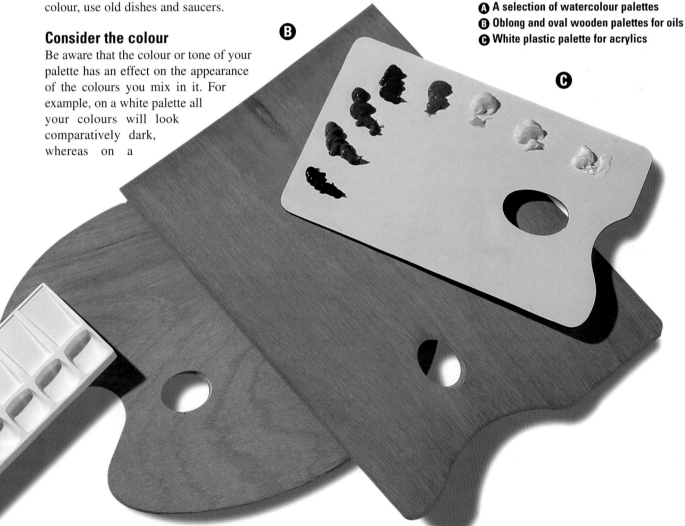

Choosing the best easel

A stable easel, which holds your work rigidly in one position, will avoid the frustration of trying to work with your picture precariously propped up on a table or on your lap. You'll soon find it's a necessity rather than a luxury.

A good easel is an artist's best friend. It will last a lifetime and is one of the most important and permanent pieces of studio equipment, so take time to look around and buy a model that meets all your requirements. Your choice of easel depends on various factors – the available space in your working area, whether you like to work standing up or sitting down, and whether you tend to work mostly indoors or outdoors. It also depends on the medium you generally use and on the scale of your work. For example, watercolours are much easier to use with an easel that can be tilted to the horizontal, so your washes won't run down the paper.

Outdoor easels

Lugging a heavy easel on painting expeditions is no fun at all, so choose a compact, portable model for outdoor work. A sketching easel (see easels E–H, opposite) could be the answer, being both lightweight and foldable. These are made in wood or aluminium, are fully adjustable and can usually be positioned for both watercolour and vertical painting.

Sketching easels can accommodate surprisingly large boards and canvases, but this depends on the make and type. Check the distance between the top and bottom easel grips to make sure that the easel will take the size of support you prefer.

A box easel (see right, below and easel N) is more stable, though slightly heavier than an ordinary sketching easel. However, it is easy to fold up and carry, and also incorporates a box or drawer for holding paints, brushes and other materials.

Easels for indoor work

For large or heavy canvases, a traditional upright studio easel (easels I–L, opposite) is probably your best bet. These can be bulky – some even have castors, so that they can be moved around more easily – but they are reassuringly solid.

If your work space is limited, a radial easel (J) is a versatile alternative. This consists of an upright spine with tripod-type legs. The whole easel can be adjusted, so you can angle your work to suit the light, though not to the horizontal position necessary for watercolour painting. When it is not in use, the radial easel can be folded for easy storage.

A tilting radial easel is also known as a 'combination' easel (K), because it brings together features of both the radial and the sketching easel. It has a central joint, so

◀ **The versatile box easel is ideal for the artist who likes to work both in the studio and out-of-doors. For storage and carrying, the easel folds down to a box shape with a handle for easy carrying (right).**

that it can be adjusted to any position from upright to completely horizontal, and it is therefore an ideal choice for the artist who works in a variety of media.

If your studio space or work area is limited, a sketching easel or a box easel will be just as versatile indoors as outdoors. Alternatively, if you work on a fairly small scale, a table-top easel in wood or aluminium (see easels A-D) might be all you need.

Looking after your easel

Apart from the lightweight sketching easels made from aluminium, most artists' easels are robustly constructed from hardwood, traditionally beechwood. They require little regular maintenance, although the wood benefits from an occasional coat of wax polish, especially when an easel is used outside or in damp conditions. Also, the metal adjusting nuts can get stiff and should be kept lubricated with oil.

THE RIGHT EASEL FOR THE JOB

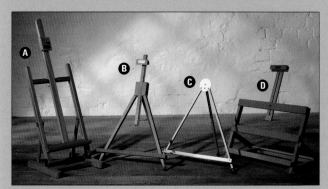

TABLE EASELS

A Sturdy wooden easel with an 'H' frame, which can be tilted to provide the ideal working angle.

B Light, portable tripod-type wooden easel with rubber-tipped non-slip feet.

C Extremely light aluminium easel with adjustable telescopic back leg and rubber-tipped feet.

D Wooden easel, which can be set at four different angles and folds flat when not in use.

STUDIO EASELS

I Sturdy studio easel with an adjustable lower shelf for the canvas or board, allowing simple adjustment of the working height.

J Rigid, adjustable radial easel, which can be tilted backwards and forwards, but not horizontally for watercolour work.

K Combination easel, which can be secured in any position and is suitable for use with all media.

L Artist's 'donkey' or platform easel – a comfortable sitting easel which takes up very little space when folded.

M Simple, popular 'A' frame easel with a metal ratchet on the lower support for adjusting the working height.

N Box easel with a container for paints, brushes and other art materials. Ideal for studio or outdoor work.

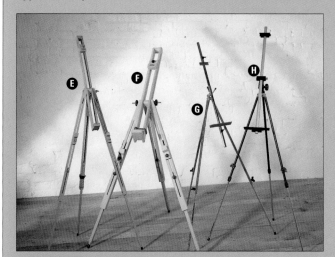

SKETCHING EASELS

E Lightweight easel with an adjustable tilting facility, making it suitable for all media, including watercolour.

F Substantial tilting, sketching easel appropriate for all media.

G Folding, tilting metal easel with telescopic legs and adjustable canvas grip.

H Fully adjustable metal easel with a camera mount fixing, so that it can be used as a photographic tripod.

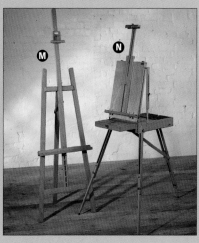

Working on Canvas

Canvas is one of the most satisfying surfaces for oil or acrylic painting because of the way in which it responds to the brush, and it is quite straightforward to prime and stretch it yourself.

Ever since artists first started using oil paints in the fifteenth century, canvas has been the most popular surface to paint on. There is something very special about the way stretched canvas responds to the brush; no other surface matches its springy spontaneity. Unlike rigid supports, the taut fabric 'gives' a little with each dab of colour, and the weave provides a key or 'tooth' to hold the paint. The result is a rich, resonant paint surface.

An added advantage is that canvas is light and easily portable. A finished painting can be removed from its stretcher, rolled up and stored without taking up much space.

Canvas types

Canvas is usually bought in lengths cut off a roll. There is a choice of fabrics, weights, widths and textures to suit your

▼ Pre-primed canvases are ready to stretch and use without further preparation.

Ⓐ Acrylic-primed 350g (12oz) cotton duck
Ⓑ Oil-primed cotton 250g (9oz) cotton duck
Ⓒ Acrylic-primed 250g (9oz) cotton duck
Ⓓ Oil-primed linen
Ⓔ Acrylic-primed linen
Ⓕ Oil-primed coarse linen

pocket. If you do a lot of painting, it might be worth investing in a whole roll and cutting it up yourself – this works out cheaper in the long run.

Flax canvas is made from raw flax, and is extremely strong and hard wearing. Artist's linen is similarly tough, but is finer and has a more even texture. Both flax canvas and linen canvas are made from the stalks of the flax plant and retain the brownish-grey colour of unbleached linen.

Alternatives to linen

Cotton canvas is a popular cheaper alternative to linen. It is densely woven and creamy-white in colour. Compared with linen, cotton is soft and floppy. It may stretch or shrink depending on the moisture in the atmosphere, so it does not remain taut on the stretcher. Wedges driven into the back of the stretcher will normally solve the problem.

Hessian makes a chunky, unusual painting surface. It is inexpensive, but its loose, open weave absorbs a lot of paint unless it is well sealed and primed.

Traditional priming

Like most fabrics, canvas is very absorbent and must normally be sealed and primed before you can paint on it. The prepared surface is sometimes referred to as a ground.

Preparation is particularly important if you are using oils because, over a period of time, the oil paint will rot the fabric. Acrylics can be used on unprimed canvas, but the absorbent surface will soak up a lot of paint. Traditionally, canvas that is to be used for oil painting is sealed with a coat of rabbit-skin size followed by two or more coats of oil-based white lead primer. More recently, household undercoat

is sometimes used instead of lead primer. Rabbit-skin glue has a low adhesive power but it remains flexible when dry, so it will not crack when the canvas is rolled.

Although many artists still like to prepare their canvases in this way, the finished ground is suitable only for oils, not acrylics. Also, mixing the glue and waiting for the glue and primer to dry between coats is time-consuming.

Acrylic primer

This provides a speedy alternative to traditional oil priming. It is the ideal ground for acrylic paints and can also be used with oils. The primer is bright white and can be applied directly to the canvas – there's no need to seal it with rabbit-skin glue first.

▶ This selection of unprimed canvases shows some of the fabrics and weights available.
Ⓐ Linen and cotton blend
Ⓑ 500g (18oz) cotton duck
Ⓒ 370g (13oz) superflax
Ⓓ Superfine linen
Ⓔ 350g (12oz) flax
Ⓕ Fine hessian

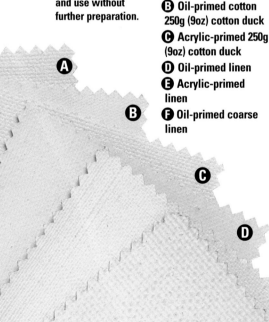

Stretching a canvas

If you cannot find a ready-stretched canvas of the size you want, you can stretch and prime your own. You will need wooden stretcher pieces, available in pairs from art shops.

Assemble the stretcher by slotting the four wooden stretcher pieces together. Then cut a piece of canvas about 5cm (2in) larger all round than the stretcher.

1 Staple the sides Starting at the centre of a long side, staple the canvas to the stretcher. Pull the canvas across the frame and staple the centre of the opposite side. Repeat on the other two sides. Now staple the canvas on each side of the central staple, working first on one side and then on the other. Repeat all the way round.

2 Staple the back Lay the stretcher face down and staple the canvas to the reverse side of the stretcher. Again, start at the centre of each side and work outwards towards the corners. This gives a neat finish and gives the stretched canvas extra strength.

YOU WILL NEED

Assembled stretcher

Piece of canvas to fit over it

Scissors

Stapler and staples

Wooden wedges

Hammer

Acrylic gesso

Small decorating brush

3 Staple the corners Fold the flap of canvas at the corner, making the fold as neat and flat as possible. Staple the canvas in position.

4 Tap in the wedges If there is any slack in the canvas, gently tap the wedges into the slots at the corners of the stretcher. However, do not make the canvas too tight at this stage – the tension can always be adjusted later.

5 Apply acrylic gesso Finally, use a small decorating brush to paint the canvas with two coats of acrylic gesso to prime it. Allow the gesso to dry in between coats.

For a particularly flexible, easy-to-apply ground, try mixing acrylic primer with an equal quantity of acrylic emulsion. Both materials are available from art stores. Acrylic primer is sometimes called acrylic gesso, but take care not to confuse this with real gesso, which is made from chalk and is very inflexible.

Prepared canvases

If you do not want to prepare your own canvas, you can buy a ready-primed length. This can be fixed to a wooden stretcher or taped to a drawing board to make an instant painting surface.

Alternatively, pre-primed canvases stretched over light wooden frames are available in a range of standard sizes. They can be made of linen or cotton duck, and may also contain a proportion of synthetic fibres. Make sure you choose the right texture. Some have a fine grain and are good for detailed work, while others are coarser so that the weave of the canvas may be visible through the paint to produce a more rugged effect on the final painting.

An inexpensive alternative to stretched canvases are canvas-covered boards. These have a good 'tooth' and

are available with very fine or slightly coarser surfaces.

A word of warning. Most ready-made canvases and canvas-covered boards are primed with an acrylic ground, and therefore suitable for use with either acrylic or oil paints. Others are primed with an oil-based primer, and should be used only with oil paints. It is important not to use acrylics on an oil-primed canvas because the oily surface will eventually cause the paints to peel and flake. Always read the manufacturer's label to make sure you are getting the right surface.

Preparing panels

Rigid supports for oil and acrylic painting can be made from a range of readily available materials including wood, plywood and MDF (medium density fibreboard). The secret of success lies in the preparation.

Until the time of the painter Giotto (*c.* 1267–1337), only wood was considered to be a suitable support for easel painting (that is, work intended to be framed and hung on a wall). However, as easel paintings increased in size, the limitations and technical complications of wood became increasingly obvious. Wood is heavy, and to make a large panel several planks must be joined together and battened to prevent warping. The surface then has to be sized and given a finish that will accept the paint.

Painters began to use fabric stretched on to a framework, as this was lighter than wood. Although fabric widths were narrow, they could be joined together to make large supports. Today, artists can choose between a flexible, yielding canvas which is alive to the touch of the brush, or a rigid panel which is firm and can be given a smooth surface. Both types of support have their appeal and advantages; what you choose is entirely a matter of personal preference. Frans Hals (1582/3–1666), for example, sometimes chose canvas and sometimes wood, irrespective of the size of the painting.

Panels must be prepared before they can be painted on, and the nature of the preparation will depend on the medium. Paint bonds to a surface through a combination of its own adhesive qualities and the surface's absorbency and texture. A good oil support must have sufficient roughness or 'tooth' to hold the paint, but must not absorb

▲ **PREPARED SURFACES:**
A Hardboard with muslin applied with acrylic primer
B Plywood with acrylic primer
C Plywood with scrim applied with acrylic medium
D Hardboard, rough side, sealed with acrylic primer

◀ **UNTREATED SURFACES:**
A Hardboard, rough side
B Cardboard
C Medium density fibreboard (MDF)
D Plywood
E Hardboard, smooth side

the oil. If the oil is leached out, the pigment loses its bond and eventually the paint flakes off.

Acrylic differs from oil in that it is not necessary to treat the support before you paint on it. Acrylic can be used on a wider range of supports than any other medium. Nevertheless, it is advisable to have a painting surface that provides a key for the paint. Surfaces must be oil-free, as oil and water are incompatible.

Types of support

If you like painting on panels, you can easily prepare them yourself. Wood, especially poplar, is traditional, but the cheapest and most readily available materials are cardboard, plywood, hardboard and MDF.

Wood If you use wood, make sure it is well seasoned to minimize warping. Battening the back and sizing both sides will also help to stabilize it.

Card Available in different weights and colours, this is ideal for small to medium-sized paintings. It can be used untreated for acrylic paintings, but because it is very absorbent the image will have a chalky appearance that can be quite appealing. If you are using card for oils, it must be sealed with size, an acrylic medium or an acrylic primer. As some cards are an attractive warm mid-tone in colour, you might want to incorporate the colour of the card in your work. In that case, you should seal it with acrylic medium or with PVA.

Hardboard This is a popular support. It is relatively cheap and available in large sheets which can be cut down to the size you need – most timber merchants can be persuaded to supply it cut to your requirements. It has two different surfaces: one side is rough, resembling woven cloth, and the other is smooth. Hardboard is a tough material, but the edges are brittle and larger sizes may need protective battens at the back.

Applying fabric to a panel

YOU WILL NEED

Wooden panel

Scrim

Scissors

Acrylic medium

Decorator's brush

Any panel can be given a woven textile finish by gluing a fabric such as muslin or scrim to the painting surface. This is a cheap and quick way of creating a very acceptable support, similar in texture to canvas.

1 ▲ Cut the scrim Lay the panel on the scrim and cut the fabric to size, allowing a 5cm (2in) overlap all round.

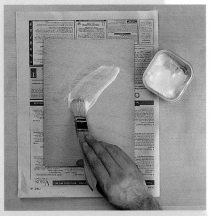

2 ▲ Apply acrylic medium to the board Cover the work surface with newspaper, lay the board on the paper and apply a coat of acrylic medium.

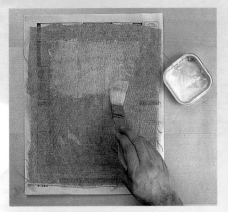

3 ▲ Apply the scrim While the acrylic medium is still damp, lay the fabric over the board. Smooth it out gently and then apply another coat of acrylic medium, brushing it into the fabric.

4 ▲ Turn the board Turn the board over and balance it on a container so that the wet surface is lifted clear of the work surface.

5 ▲ Fold the fabric Fold back the edges of the fabric and paste down with acrylic medium. Make neat folds at the corners. Seal the back of the panel with medium to prevent warping.

Carrying and storing your artworks

Your best drawings and paintings are irreplaceable, so it is important to find practical ways of transporting and storing them to avoid any damage.

Your pictures are probably at their most vulnerable when in transit after a drawing or painting trip. This is especially true of watercolours, drawings and other work on paper, as these might tear or become creased.

The simplest answer is to leave the artworks on the drawing board or pad and cover them with a sheet of clean paper. Alternatively, paintings can be rolled up and carried in a cardboard tube container. These are available in a range of sizes from many office supply stores and stationers, and are also excellent if you want to send drawings, prints or watercolours through the post. To carry wet oil paintings, you can use corks and pins to separate the canvases (see Portable art materials, pages 18–19).

At some point, you might need to show your work – perhaps at an interview or to a gallery – and this is the time to invest in an artist's portfolio. Rather like a large, flat briefcase, a portfolio enables you to transport a number of drawings and paintings easily. It also looks businesslike, especially if the work is presented attractively and in the order in which you want it to be seen.

Wide range of portfolios

Portfolios come in a range of sizes to fit all standard papers, so choose one that is suitable for your requirements. Simple card portfolios are light and inexpensive. They are normally flat and the work is retained by folding flaps, which are fastened with cord or ribbon.

For carrying a large amount of work, try a box-type portfolio secured with a zip, studs, buckles or Velcro. Those made of fluted plastic sheet are tough yet lightweight. Drawings and paintings can also be stored and displayed in transparent plastic sleeves, which fit inside zipped, ring-bound portfolios. Small work will fit into a shallow briefcase or similar compact case.

Artworks pile up very quickly, so try to plan a storage system at home before they

▼ **The range of portfolios includes the box-type (A), the flat card (B) and the ring-bound (C). Soft briefcases (D) are ideal for carrying card portfolios or works on panels. Tube containers (E) are a less bulky alternative to the portfolio.**

A

B

C

D

E

become damaged or dog-eared. A plan chest has shallow drawers designed to accommodate large-scale artworks. For smaller works, an ordinary desk with drawers might be adequate.

Drawings and watercolours should be stored flat. Before putting away artworks in soft pencil, charcoal or pastel, spray them with fixative. Also, secure a sheet of tracing paper over the top of the work with two masking tape hinges. This protects each drawing from loose particles of pigment and dust.

A practical way of storing boards and canvases is to stack them vertically in simple wooden racks – easily made by anyone with rudimentary carpentry skills. It is important that canvases of a similar size are stored together with the wooden stretchers resting against each other. If the wooden edge of one painting leans against the fabric of another, the edges of the smaller painting will make dents or holes in the larger one.

Small dents are sometimes permanent but they can often be remedied by restretching the painting or by brushing the reverse side of the dented surface with water to shrink the canvas.

Roll with it

Alternatively, you can remove the painted canvas from the stretcher altogether and store the painting rolled up. Always roll with the painted surface facing outwards – dried paint will stretch a little, but will not contract. Wrap the rolled painting in paper or cloth to protect it from dust.

MAKING YOUR OWN PORTFOLIO

This portfolio is made from sheets of A3 card – but you can make yours to whatever size you want.

YOU WILL NEED

PVA glue

Glue spreader or scrap of card

Two A3 sheets of thick card, and one strip of the same card, 42cm x 1.5cm (16½in x ⅝in)

Sheet of firm wrapping paper

Scissors

Gummed paper tape

Bowl of water

A2 and A3 sheets of thin coloured card

2m (2¼yd) of ribbon

1 ▲ Cover the card Spread PVA glue thinly over one side of each A3 card, and on one side of the card strip. Glue them to the back of the wrapping paper, with a 1cm (⅜in) gap between the strip and the A3 sheets on each side. Leave a 5cm (2in) border of paper around the edge. Fold in each paper corner and glue it in place, then fold in the borders and glue them to the card.

2 ▲ Strengthen the spine Cut a 42cm (16½in) length of gummed paper tape. Wet the glue on the tape, then stick it along the spine, pushing it down into the valleys on each side of the spine strip. Repeat with three more strips to make the spine really strong.

3 ▲ Prepare the envelope Fold the thin card around the largest sketch you wish to store. Unfold the card and remove the sketch. Then cut away the sides of the two end flaps, tapering the flaps slightly away from the central rectangle.

4 ▲ Finish the inside Strengthen the corners with strips of gummed paper tape. Then glue a rectangle of coloured card to the back of one panel of the portfolio. Glue the back of the envelope to the other panel. Tie the portfolio with coloured ribbon.

Stylish and practical, the portfolio is the perfect place to store your art.

Photographing your artwork

Every painting and drawing you do is unique and irreplaceable – so it really pays to make photographic copies of your work.

Almost all painters – whether they are keen amateurs or high-flying, full-time artists – need to copy their work at some time. Beginners might want to send photos of their paintings to friends and relatives. More advanced artists might want to keep a record of paintings they have sold and, as a consequence, are likely never to see again. Really committed artists might need to send photos of their work to galleries or art publications.

To achieve top-quality reproduction many artists will go to a professional photographer. However, unless you know a friendly photographer, this is not a cheap option. As long as you have a reasonably good camera, you can obtain perfectly acceptable results yourself with the most basic equipment.

What camera?
It is probably best not to use disposable cameras or a very cheap compact. These models have plastic lenses, which give very blurred photos, and they usually have a very basic control of exposure.

A compact camera (the type with a fixed lens, labelled A below) of reasonable quality will do, although it is worth noting that with this type of camera you do not actually look through the lens. As a result, what you see through the viewfinder might differ slightly from what you get in your final photo. If you are shooting something far away, such as a landscape, this effect is hardly noticeable, but when working up close (as you would if you were photographing most drawings and paintings), you need to make a little adjustment.

Adjusting for a compact camera
This is not a big problem. The viewfinder is always above and to the left of the lens – so when you have composed the photo with all the painting in the frame, compensate by moving the camera diagonally up to the left a little.

As this is not an exact science, you should also move back about 10cm (4in), so that you can see some space around the edge of your painting in the viewfinder. But don't get too far away – the smaller the painting is within the viewfinder, the poorer the quality of the final image.

You won't have this problem with a single-lens reflex (SLR) camera, labelled B below. With this type of camera, what you see is what you get. If you are thinking of buying a new camera, consider an SLR – the basic models are cheaper than the more advanced compacts and they have the advantage of interchangeable lenses.

▼ Whether you have a compact camera (A), a single-lens reflex (B) or a digital camera (C), you can take perfectly acceptable photos of your artwork. A digital camera also allows you to produce photos in a variety of sizes (D) on a PC.

HOW TO SET IT UP

It is best to photograph your artworks outside, on a cloudy day. This will provide an even lighting across the whole painting. If there is some sunlight, try positioning a piece of white card on the opposite side of the painting to the sun to throw some light back on to the darker side (see below).

On a very sunny day you might want to try a few shots in a shaded spot. However, if you do this you may get a bluish colour cast and there might not be quite enough light. If you are using an SLR you can attach a warm-up filter to eliminate cold casts, but make sure it's the right diameter for your lens. Don't use a flash, as you will probably get a bright area in the centre of the painting and a dark silhouette around the edges where the flash light falls off.

For minimum camera shake, it is best to set up the camera on something stable (below centre) and set the timer release. Alternatively, try using a cable release – you can attach this to most cameras.

When handholding the camera, if possible set a shutter speed of 1/125th or over to prevent camera shake. Consult your instruction booklet to see if you can change the shutter speeds.

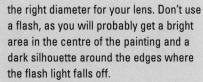

▶ **The easiest way to shoot your artwork is to stand over it and shoot down. This is particularly convenient if you have a zoom lens as you can frame tightly. If you are worried about camera shake, it's best to set your camera on a wall or stepladder (as below). You will have to use the same method when photographing a very large painting – you will not be able to get far enough away by bending over it.**

◀ **For precise framing and minimum camera shake, it pays to set up your camera on something solid – like a wall or a stepladder. Use the self-timer or, as here, a cable release to make sure the camera is absolutely still when you release the shutter. If your artwork is in portrait format, simply shoot it on its side: you can always turn the photo round!**

▶ **If you see that the lighting across your painting is uneven, get a friend to throw some light back on to the dark side by holding a piece of white card out of frame. Uneven lighting may occur if the sun begins to peek out from behind the clouds.**

The digital route

The increasingly popular digital cameras provide another way of photographing your artwork. They really make sense if you have a computer and printer at home, because you can cut out the photo lab altogether. Even if you don't have your own printer though, it is becoming increasingly cheap to get digital prints from a wide variety of shops and even supermarkets.

Film choice

As far as film goes, it's best to choose print film rather than slides. The problem with slides is in getting the exposure right. If you are slightly off, you'll either get a washed-out image or a dark one. Exposure is not as critical with print film since the processors compensate for mistakes when the negative is printed.

The only occasion for which you really need slides of your work is if you are going to have a painting reproduced in a book or a magazine. Most printers prefer to work from slides. However, if you are having your work published, it is probably worth having your paintings photographed professionally.

Prints and processing

For accurate colours, it is best to buy a well-known brand of film rather than cheaper types given away free when you have a film processed. And watch out for colour casts on your prints. If the processors have a machine that is not maintained properly, the reds and yellows in your painting can easily end up as purples and greens in your photos.

Don't be afraid to ask the processors to reprint the photos if there is a strong colour cast. If necessary, show them how the original painting differs from the photos.

Stay clear of black-and-white film – even if you are photographing a monochrome drawing. Most high-street processors do a very poor job of developing and printing black-and-white negatives, because most of their business is for colour films. If you want good quality black-and-white prints, you will have to go to a specialist printer, and that can be costly.

PENCILS, PENS, BRUSHES AND PAPER

As a novice artist, it's all too easy to be over-whelmed by the choice of materials available in art shops. If you're uncertain about the difference between oils and acrylics, or wondering what to do with pastels, this section explains in detail how to choose and use various drawing and painting media, and also offers advice on brushes and paper.

Using Conté crayons

*Less messy to handle than charcoal or chalk,
Conté crayons are versatile drawing tools
that make attractive marks. They are ideal for
sketching as well as for more finished work.*

Nicholas-Jacques Conté (1755–1805), the French artist who invented the modern graphite pencil, also gave the world another popular drawing material – Conté crayons. These distinctive, square-sectioned drawing sticks were patented in Paris by Conté more than 200 years ago.

The square ends of the crayons enable you to use them to produce both broad and fine lines. You can even draw with the side of the stick to fill in large areas of colour quickly and easily. This versatility has been appreciated and exploited by many – not only by famous artists such as Hilaire Germain Degas (1834–1917) and Henri de Toulouse-Lautrec (1864–1901), but also by generations of art students who have been encouraged to use Conté as a clean and manageable alternative to charcoal and chalk.

Conté crayons look rather like pastels but, unlike most pastels, they do not crumble or create powdery deposits. Although some very hard pastels are similar, Conté crayons are generally waxier and harder than most other products on the market. They are also available in pencil form.

An array of colours

The original Conté crayons were made from a few earth pigments, clay, graphite, wax and a little grease. These ingredients produced a limited range of colours: black, white, sanguine, sepia and bistre.

Today, the Conté palette includes not only the original earth pigments, but also a huge array of other colours, giving a selection that compares favourably with the ranges available in paints, pastels and other artists' materials. In addition, there is a tonal set of crayons.

The tonal range

Conté's selection of shades matches the tonal scale, which runs from black to white with a range of greys in between.

▶ **Earth colours:** Traditional earth colours are made from clay and other mineral deposits. Chalk is added for paler tones.

▶ **Tonal selection:** For monochrome drawings and tonal sketches, Conté crayons are available in a range of greys as well as in black and white.

▶ **Coloured selection:** Conté crayons also come in a wide range of colours, which can be bought either individually or in sets.

▼ Conté is available in pencil form. The pencils can be sharpened using a craft knife or scalpel.

▲ Reddish-brown sanguine pigment comes from red clay, the colouring being caused by ferric oxide. This and other earth pigments are used to make Conté crayons.

▶ **Hard pastels:** Some hard pastels have a high wax content and are used in a similar way to Conté crayons.

▲ **For an even, graded effect, overlap two or more colours. A third colour is created where the two colours overlap.**

With this selection of crayons, you can depict any subject by building up gradations of tones instead of blocks of colour.

The best way of judging tones is to try to see your subject as it would look in a black-and-white photograph. Obviously, you can use white and black Contés for the whites and blacks in the subject. Between these two extremes, choose pale greys for light colours, such as yellow, and dark greys for the deeper colours. If you can visualize what kind of grey each colour would be in a black-and-white photograph, you have also understood its tonal value.

Use a mid-toned paper rather than pure white for this exercise. In this way, you can relate the light and dark tones to the medium background tone and both will show up clearly.

Earth colours

The original earth colours, including warm sanguine red and cool brown bistre, are still the most popular in the Conté range. These same earthy pigments have been used for thousands of years. Stone Age cave painters worked with them, as have many artists since then, including Leonardo da Vinci (1452–1519) and Michelangelo (1475–1564). No wonder that works executed with this handful of colours have such an evocative, antique appearance.

Whatever your subject, provided that you restrict yourself to the earth selection and choose a suitable paper, the colour scheme of your Conté drawing will appear harmonious and considered. Earth colours work especially well on tinted papers, particularly those in neutral browns and muted greens and blues.

Making marks with Conté

Unlike traditional crayons, Conté crayons have a sharply squared-off end, which means that you can make a variety of marks simply by turning the crayon round and using a different part of the stick. In this respect, they are very similar to charcoal. And like charcoal, you can achieve different depths of colour and texture effects by using more or less pressure on the crayon as you work.

Fine lines Although they appear quite chunky, Conté crayons can be used for delicate work, too. To make a fine line, draw with the sharp edge of the squared end.

Undulating lines Hold the crayon firmly and use the broad end and sharp edge alternately to get an undulating line of varying widths and textures.

Blocks of colour To block in an area of colour, work with the entire length of the stick. You may find this easier if you break the crayon into shorter, more manageable lengths.

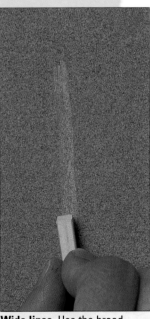

Wide lines Use the broad end of the crayon to draw a wide, regular line with parallel sides. Thick lines like this are well suited to large-scale work.

Introducing marker pens

Whether you're sketching outdoors or working on a finished drawing indoors, marker pens provide a colourful and convenient medium.

If you thought marker pens belonged in the office or the children's playroom – think again! Vigorous, brilliantly coloured drawings can be made with this modern medium, which is especially convenient for outdoor sketching. A set of marker pens is light, compact and clean, allowing you to make full-colour sketches without the need for cumbersome paints, palettes and jars of water.

The only drawback with markers is that they contain dyes rather than pigments, so the colours tend to fade in time when exposed to strong sunlight. You can, however, minimize the risk of fading by keeping your drawings in a portfolio or hanging them well away from direct sunlight.

Types of marker
There is an enormous range of markers to choose from, in literally hundreds of colours and with various sizes and shapes of tip. Art and graphic suppliers sell the best-quality pens, but the types of markers that are sold in stationers and supermarkets are usually cheaper and perfectly adequate for sketching and practice work.

● **Fibre tips** have tips made from nylon or fibre-glass. They are hard-wearing and smooth-flowing.
● **Felt tips** have thicker, slightly more flexible tips made from wool or a synthetic substitute. They flow smoothly and make soft, dense marks.
● **Fine-liners** have tips made from plastic or a similar synthetic material. They are hard and durable and produce thin, spidery lines.

Tip shapes
As well as being made from a variety of materials, felt and fibre tips have a range of tip shapes, varying from fine points to broad, chisel-shaped wedges.
● **Wedge-shaped tips** are the most versatile. By turning the marker as you draw, you can use the edge and the different sides of the tip to make broad, medium and thin lines. You can also fill in areas of flat colour by working quickly in broad, horizontal lines, taking each line over the previous one before it has time to dry.
● **Bullet-shaped tips** produce medium and bold marks, and the rounded tip can be used for stippling effects.
● **Pointed tips** produce thin lines of

▼ **Whether you want to work with fine lines or broad areas of colour, there is a marker pen for you.**

Ⓐ **Wedge-shaped tips**

Ⓑ **Fine-liners**

Ⓒ **Pointed tips**

Ⓓ **Bullet-shaped tips**

Ⓔ **Brush-pen tips**

uniform thickness. They are good for defining outlines and for rendering fine details.

● **Brush-pen tips** are made of elongated, flexible fibres that come to a point, and create a variety of marks that look similar to those made with a watercolour brush.

Two types of ink

Another important consideration with marker pens is whether they contain water-based or spirit-based inks. The water-based inks tend to lie on the paper surface for longer, making it easier to blend colours. Interesting soft, feather-like effects can be achieved by drawing on dampened paper.

The spirit-based colours, by contrast, are readily absorbed into the paper, permanent and waterproof. They tend to 'bleed' beyond the shape drawn by the nib, though for fine-art purposes this doesn't usually matter. They also tend to bleed right through the paper, so when working on a sketch pad, place a sheet of scrap paper beneath the drawing surface.

Spirit-based pens that are drying out can be rejuvenated by tipping a few drops of lighter fuel into the cap before putting it back on the pen. After a few hours, the nib should have absorbed the fuel and, although the colour will be lighter, the pen will last longer.

Papers

It is fun to experiment with different drawing surfaces as each influences the character of the drawn lines, depending on how readily they absorb the marker dyes. You can buy special marker paper which resists colour bleeding. This paper has a hard, non-absorbent surface and is ideal when you want to produce crisp, clear marks and fine details. Alternatively, try drawing on smooth white card or even white scraperboard.

Delicate effects

If you want a more delicate effect, try drawing on ordinary cartridge paper or watercolour paper. The marks produced will be softer and fatter as the colour sinks into the surface and spreads slightly. On the highly absorbent Japanese rice papers, the marker dye spreads rapidly,

Different strokes

Marker pens lend themselves to a surprisingly wide range of drawing techniques. Fine-liners are ideal for stippling or cross-hatching (see top row of apples below). By cross-hatching in colour, you can create great optical mixing effects by overlaying different hues. On the bottom-left apple, look at the way red has been hatched over green to create a brown suitable for the shadowed side. With chisel- and bullet-shaped pens, try making use of the transparency of the inks by laying flat areas of colour over each other (see bottom-right apple). To avoid getting muddy tones, limit the colours you overlay to three or four.

Stippling in monochrome

Cross-hatching in monochrome

Cross-hatching in colour

Building up layers of colour

like ink on blotting paper, producing effects similar to watercolour painting.

Practice is the key to successful marker work. Bear in mind that markers are not a subtle medium, and they do have certain limitations. The colours are bright and brash – they cannot be lightened with water or white paint and mistakes cannot be rectified. Also, the marks cannot be blended on the paper as easily as, say, watercolour or pastel.

On the plus side, a single marker can produce a whole range of lines, tones and textural effects according to how you hold it and the pressure you apply. So buy a selection of pens with different nib shapes and experiment by making marks on sheets of scrap paper.

Soft pastels

Working with pastels is highly rewarding – they are extremely versatile and produce a rich depth of colour not found in other media.

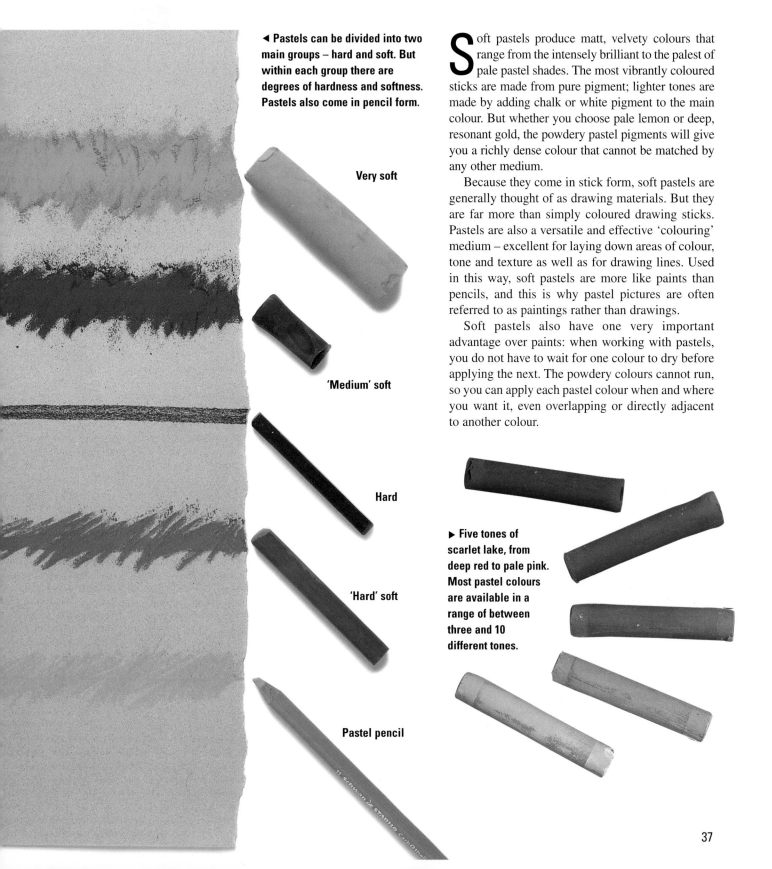

◄ Pastels can be divided into two main groups – hard and soft. But within each group there are degrees of hardness and softness. Pastels also come in pencil form.

Very soft

'Medium' soft

Hard

'Hard' soft

Pastel pencil

Soft pastels produce matt, velvety colours that range from the intensely brilliant to the palest of pale pastel shades. The most vibrantly coloured sticks are made from pure pigment; lighter tones are made by adding chalk or white pigment to the main colour. But whether you choose pale lemon or deep, resonant gold, the powdery pastel pigments will give you a richly dense colour that cannot be matched by any other medium.

Because they come in stick form, soft pastels are generally thought of as drawing materials. But they are far more than simply coloured drawing sticks. Pastels are also a versatile and effective 'colouring' medium – excellent for laying down areas of colour, tone and texture as well as for drawing lines. Used in this way, soft pastels are more like paints than pencils, and this is why pastel pictures are often referred to as paintings rather than drawings.

Soft pastels also have one very important advantage over paints: when working with pastels, you do not have to wait for one colour to dry before applying the next. The powdery colours cannot run, so you can apply each pastel colour when and where you want it, even overlapping or directly adjacent to another colour.

► Five tones of scarlet lake, from deep red to pale pink. Most pastel colours are available in a range of between three and 10 different tones.

▲ The more chalk that is added to the pure pigment, the lighter the tone of the soft pastel. A huge variety of shades of the same colour can be achieved in this way.

Making pastels

Soft pastels have been in use since the early eighteenth century. Until that time their nearest equivalents were hard crayons, usually bound with wax and available in only a few muted colours such as earthy reds, browns and blacks.

Although soft pastels contain exactly the same pigments as paints and other artists' materials, they are a dry medium, requiring no water or any other liquid. Soft pastels are made by mixing the powdered ingredients with enough binder to hold them together. The mixture is then rolled or moulded into sticks and left to dry.

The most usual binders are gum, resin or starch. However, some pigments need a more powerful binding agent than others. For instance, chalky pale shades may be held together with nothing stronger than skimmed milk, whereas others such as cadmium red require a stronger binder. It is the strength and quality of the binding agent that determines how soft or hard a pastel will be.

Hard, soft and very soft

For the sake of simplicity, all artists' pastels can be divided into two main groups – hard and soft. Soft pastels are characteristically chunky and crumbly and are the most

BLENDING SOFT PASTELS

You can use a paintbrush to blend two pastel colours together. Brush gently, as a harsh movement will remove the pigment altogether.

Brush blending

For large areas of colour, a soft tissue or paper kitchen towel blends different shades of pastel quickly and effectively.

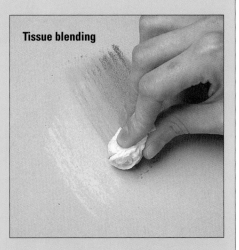

Tissue blending

The quickest and easiest way to blend two areas of pastel colour is simply to rub them together with a clean fingertip.

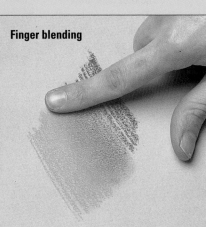

Finger blending

The pointed end of a torchon, a stump of tightly rolled white paper available from art shops, is ideal for blending small, precise areas of pastel colour.

Torchon blending

▲ Keep your pastels clean by storing them in a box of dry rice. The dirt and loose pigment particles on the pastels will rub off on the grains of rice instead of on each other.

popular of the various types of pastel. However, it is worth remembering that even within the category of 'soft' pastels, there are varying degrees of softness. Very soft pastels include those made by Unison, Sennelier and Schmincke, the latter being the softest of all. Winsor & Newton's soft pastels and the Talens' Rembrandt range are slightly harder.

Hard pastels come in the form of compressed sticks, often rectangular in shape. The best known of these is the Conté crayon range, although most manufacturers now have their own product. Hard pastels contain more gum than soft pastels and the colours are usually less intense. Conté crayons are covered in more detail on pages 33–34.

Colour mixing

Unlike paints, soft pastel colours cannot be easily mixed. You will need a different pastel not only for every colour you wish to use in a painting, but for every shade of that particular colour. This is why most pastel ranges are so extensive. Some manufacturers offer as many as 500 different pastels, including several versions of each colour.

Depending on the make, a range of soft pastels can include up to ten versions of any one colour, from very light to very dark. The tonal range is often indicated by a number, although the system varies from one manufacturer to

another. For example, in the Winsor & Newton range, Scarlet Lake 1 is very pale pink and Scarlet Lake 5 is a much deeper, richer colour.

Although soft pastels are used by many professional artists, their enormous colour range makes them an excellent medium for the beginner. Freed from the worry of mixing colours, the artist is at liberty to concentrate on other aspects of the work. In other words, when you use soft pastels, the manufacturer does most of the colour mixing, not you!

Surfaces

The right surface is important. Papers and boards made specifically for soft pastel work have a definite texture, sometimes referred to as the 'tooth', which may be either coarse or velvety.

On a smooth paper, which has no tooth, soft pastels will simply slide around and produce unsatisfactory, weak patches of colour. However, on the

▶ Keep a sheet of sandpaper to hand for maintaining a point on soft pastels. To achieve an even point, apply a little pressure as you turn the pastel slowly.

correct surface with the right amount of tooth, the pastel dust will fill the holes gradually, enabling you to build up several layers of matt, impastoed colour. You will know when your paper has reached its limit, because it becomes difficult to make the colours adhere and the loose pigment stays on the surface of the paper.

Fixing

Soft pastels smudge very easily and your finished picture will be vulnerable until it has been sprayed with fixative. Fixative may slightly darken the colours, so use the spray sparingly. Hold the can about a foot away from the vertical painting and spray slowly and evenly from side to side until the whole surface has been treated.

Care of pastels

Soft pastels are extremely fragile and will easily become damaged if they are not properly cared for. If you drop pastel sticks on the floor or press too hard with them on the paper, they may break, and you can end up with short stubs that are difficult to hold and fiddly to use.

Piles of much-used pastels get very grubby because they pick up pigments from your hands and from each other. Before long, it can become difficult to see which colour is which. An excellent way of avoiding this is to put the pastels into a tray of dry rice when not in immediate use. In this way, the grains of rice get dirty and the pastels stay clean.

When you have finished a session, put the pastels back in their box. If this is not possible, store the sticks between sheets of corrugated cardboard.

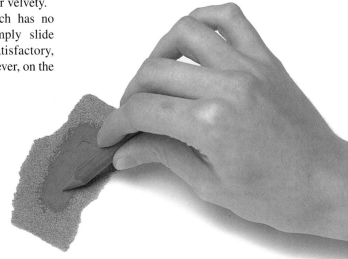

Oil pastels

If you like drawing with bold, vigorous strokes, you will enjoy the effects you can achieve with the lively medium of oil pastels, which are available in a range of bright rainbow colours.

Oil pastels are tough, bright and bold – altogether different from the crumbling sticks of chalky pigment that we know as traditional pastels. Pure pastels are chosen for their soft, velvety colours, whereas oil pastels are much harder and produce thick, waxy lines. In fact, their very name is misleading because oil pastels are not actually pastels at all, having far more in common with oil paints and wax crayons than with pure pastels.

A perfect sketching medium

Oil pastels call for a bold, confident approach. They are excellent for quick colour sketches and drawings in which movement and expressive strokes are more important than a very realistic finish. In fact, because of their chunky nature, oil pastels are not particularly well suited to fine, detailed work. Artists who work on a small scale or with subtle colours are likely to find oil pastels too bright and broad for their purpose, although the pastels can be sharpened with a knife to achieve a finer line.

However, for an immediate effect and for lively, on-the-spot colour sketching, oil pastels are second to none. Unlike most drawing materials, they enable you to work quickly on a large scale in colours that are both bright and strong. In this respect, oil pastels have all the

▶ **Oil pastels produce dense, waxy marks and come in a range of intense colours. Unlike soft pastels, they contain wax and oil and do not break easily or crumble.**

▶ **Oil pastel proved to be the perfect medium for this bold, colourful still-life sketch. These pastels are at their best when applied in strong, loose strokes.**

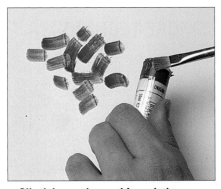

▲ **Oil sticks can be used for painting as well as for drawing. This is done by dissolving the colour with turpentine and applying it to the support with a brush.**

advantages of oil paint, but with the added bonus that they are more portable and more convenient.

For working outdoors, simply slip a sketch book and a few oil pastels into your pocket and you are equipped and ready to go. The pastels can be used without any liquid medium and may be applied directly to sturdy paper, oil paper or primed canvas.

Colour blending

Because of their hard, waxy nature, oil pastel colours are not easy to blend unless dissolved with a thinner such as white

spirit or turpentine. This is normally done on the drawing, so you must first apply the oil pastels to the support. You can then blend the colours with a brush, tissue or finger dipped in the thinner.

An alternative method is to dampen the support with thinner before applying the pastel to it, as shown below left. Note that when blending with thinner, you should work on oil paper or primed canvas; other papers are too absorbent.

As a general rule, blending is more effective when used on a few selected areas of a drawing, or when combined with vigorous, textural strokes. Too

BLENDING OIL PASTELS

Dampening with thinner

Instead of blending oil pastels once they are on the paper, you can wet the support with turpentine or white spirit first and then apply the pastel to the dampened area.

Tissue blending

Roughly apply two colours so that they overlap, then blend these together with a rolled-up piece of tissue or kitchen towel dipped in turpentine or white spirit.

Brush blending

Use a brush dipped in solvent for blending two or more colours together. An oil-painting brush is stiffer and blends more effectively than a soft brush.

Finger blending

Many artists instinctively use a finger to blend dissolved colours quickly. If you like working in this way, make sure you wash your hands immediately afterwards, as some pigments are toxic.

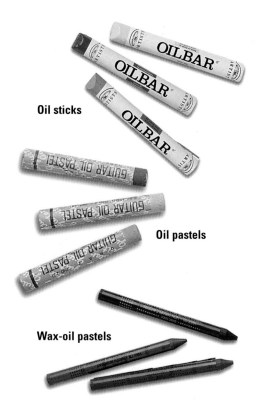

Oil sticks

Oil pastels

Wax-oil pastels

▲ **Depending on the brand, pastels contain varying amounts of wax and oil. The higher the wax content, the harder the pastel.**

much blending can destroy the direct, spontaneous quality of the medium and your picture might start to look smooth and rubbery. An alternative approach is to wait until the blended colours have dried, then to apply bold textural strokes on top of the blended areas.

Overlaid colour

As with all pastels, oil pastel colours can be mixed on the paper by overlaying two or more colours. For example, if you apply yellow over blue, you will get the impression of green. Even though the colours are not actually mixed, they appear to be. Remember, the top colour is the dominant one, so blue on top of yellow produces a bluer green than the other way round.

Oil pastel with oil paint

Oil pastels are compatible with oil paints. Not only can they be used for the initial drawing prior to starting an oil painting, but they are also effective for adding texture and linear detail to the finished painting.

For a softer effect than that given by oil pastels, try oil sticks. The consistency

of the fat sticks of colour comes between oil pastels and oil paint – harder than paint but more malleable than pastels. Oil sticks (sometimes called oil bars) are quite a new invention and, like oil pastels, are excellent for making broad, chunky drawings. Alternatively, you can use oil sticks as a painting medium by dipping a brush in turpentine or white spirit and taking the dissolved colour from the top of the stick.

Oil and water do not mix

An opposite approach to that of using oil pastels with oil paint is to actively exploit the incompatibility of oil and water. First the oil pastel is laid down, then a water-soluble colour such as watercolour, gouache, coloured ink or even thin acrylic is painted over it. The oily marks repel the water-soluble colour, leaving the coloured pastel marks showing through.

This technique, known as resist, can be used to create a variety of marks and textures. It is an exciting way of using oil pastels because the results are sometimes unexpected.

Building up texture

Oil pastels are essentially a drawing material, good for making lively line drawings, with the bold strokes providing texture and colour. However, if you build them up thickly, oil pastels create a dense layer of solid colour and the result is rather like an oil painting.

Once this solid colour has been established, you can then scratch into the waxy surface. Use a scalpel blade or any other sharp instrument to make textures and patterns by revealing the white paper underneath. Another variation of the same technique, known as sgraffito, is to apply one colour over another. By scratching the top layer, you will reveal the colour underneath.

Although they can be used alongside so many other materials, oil pastels are very much a medium in their own right. They provide a powerful means of expression and encourage a bold, overall approach, which is excellent for the less experienced artist who wishes to branch out and experiment. With oil pastels, there can be little subtlety, but you will be pleasantly surprised at the results you will be able to achieve.

MORE TECHNIQUES

Resist Try painting watercolour or other water-soluble colour over an area of oil pastel. The waxy marks repel the paint and show through the painted colour.

Added texture Small strokes of oil pastel applied on top of a blended area of colour can lend contrasting texture to a smooth, flat surface.

Sgraffito Use a painting knife, scalpel or other sharp implement to scratch pattern and texture into layers of thick colour.

Masking Apply colour roughly over the torn or cut edge of a piece of sturdy paper or thin card to give a crisply defined edge to an area of oil pastel strokes.

Using acrylic mediums

Adding mediums to your acrylic colours can completely change the look of your pictures. You can make your paints glossy or transparent – or even create textured and sculptural effects.

▼Thoroughly mix the medium and paint using a clean, stiff brush. If you are working with a palette, the mixing can be done on the flat surface, using either a brush or knife.

Used on their own, acrylics are opaque and can dry with a rather dull finish. However, there are a number of mediums that will alter the appearance and character of the paint, making it glossy, matt, transparent, textural or flat. These mediums are usually added to the wet colour before it is applied to the painting, although one or two can also be used to prime the support and to protect the surface of the finished picture.

Mediums appear cloudy in the pot or tube, but when they dry they become completely transparent and do not therefore affect your colours. However, too much of any medium will make a colour so transparent that the colour underneath shows through. On white paper, for example, a colour mixed with a lot of medium will appear paler.

Retarder and flow improver

If you find the quick-drying nature of acrylics difficult to handle, the answer could well be a retarder, which slows down the drying time of the colours by several hours. Remember, this medium is only effective if you paint fairly thickly – very diluted colours will dry quickly however much retarder you add to them. Use flow improver to help the paint spread more even-

ly and smoothly. This is particularly good for hard-edge painting when you are using masking tape, as the flowing colour remains thick enough not to run under the edge of the tape.

Gloss and matt

Gloss medium gives colours a shiny finish; matt medium produces a flat, unreflective surface. You can buy both in either fluid or gel form – the fluids improve the flow and make the paint easier to apply, the gels create slightly thicker colour. Both fluid and gel mediums increase the paint's transparency without making it thin and watery.

Fluid-type mediums are excellent for mixing glazes – for applying a layer of transparent colour over another colour so that the undercolour shows through. Depending on the effect you want, mix the gloss or matt medium with the glazing colour in a ratio of up to 10:1. Gloss medium is the general favourite for glazing because it produces particularly luminous, brilliant colours.

An alternative to varnishing

Fluid mediums can also be used to seal the canvas or paper prior to painting and used instead of a varnish to protect the surface of a completed painting. In both cases, apply the medium carefully with a

Making paint

Mixing your own acrylic paint is straightforward and should be done just before you start work. If you end up with more paint than you need, you can keep the mixture for a short time in a plastic airtight container.

1 ▶ Mix with powder Using a palette knife, mix dry powder pigment well with either gloss or matt medium to create your own painting colours.

2 ▶ Use it or lose it The mixed colours are ready to use immediately. Like manufactured paints, these colours dry fairly quickly – so mix only as much as you need for one painting session.

ADDING TEXTURES

Here are some of the textures you can make by adding various grains and particles to acrylic medium. The adhesive medium binds the texture-making substances, which can either be left in their natural state or painted.

Dry sand Scatter this on modelling paste for a medium-textured effect.

Sawdust and wood shavings Mix with gel medium for a soft, complex texture.

Fired clay Mix this with gel medium for a fine-textured result.

Grit and gravel Gel medium mixed with these will create a really rough effect.

large brush, using smooth parallel strokes. Take care not to do too much brushing, as you'll produce tiny air bubbles that affect the dried surface.

Impasto effects

Although paint thickened with gel medium will to some extent retain the shape of the brush marks, this will produce only a moderately textured surface. For a more dramatic textured effect you will need to mix the colour with acrylic impasto medium – especially good for knife painting and for covering areas with thick colour quickly.

For a really pronounced impasto, try using modelling, or texture, paste. This can be applied to build almost sculptural swathes of colour, which can be sanded or even carved when dry. Mix the paste with colour prior to painting or, alternatively, apply the paste on its own and

then paint it when dry. Unlike other mediums, modelling paste is white and opaque and might slightly lighten the colour, so you should make allowances for this.

A word of warning: thickly applied modelling paste is not wholly flexible and can crack if used on a non-rigid surface such as canvas. Counteract this risk by mixing the paste with equal parts of gel medium. Also, the risk of cracking is reduced if you build up the paste in layers, allowing each layer to dry before applying the next, instead of working in thick wedges.

Making textures

Some mediums contain tiny particles of various inert substances to create specific instant textures. These include sand, flint, pumice and even tiny glass beads. The glass beads are often used

for creating the effect of frothy air bubbles in water or adding decorative touches to the image.

Special effects

You can easily make your own special-effect mediums by adding gritty or granular materials to any one of the standard mediums (see Adding Textures, left). All acrylic mediums are adhesive, so choose one to give the effect you want – gloss medium for a shiny texture, impasto medium or modelling paste for a thickly applied effect.

For example, to capture the effect of a sandy beach in a seascape, you might mix real sand with a little matt medium. You could then go on to experiment with sawdust, particles of clay and dust, or any other materials you can think of. You will be amazed at the difference a few creative textures will make to your pictures.

Make your own paints

Some acrylic artists never use manufactured paint, preferring instead the more direct approach of mixing powdered pigment with gloss or matt medium. As the mediums have no colour of their own, the pigment retains its full strength and intensity in the painting. The mediums are also flexible when dry, so your home-made paints can be used on canvas or paper.

▲ GLOSS AND MATT
For a shiny paint surface, add a little gloss medium to your acrylic colour (top). Matt medium mixed with the paint (bottom) will produce a more non-reflective surface.

Using oil mediums

For centuries, artists have used traditional natural materials to dilute their oil paints, and these are just as popular today. In addition, there are now other mediums that make painting in oils easier and more versatile.

Oil paint is wonderfully stiff and buttery when you squeeze it from the tube – perfect for textured effects but too thick for most other purposes. Fortunately, oils are easily diluted. The traditional method is to use a combination of oil and turpentine. You can also try oil mediums, which can be added to the paints to alter their consistency and give exciting effects.

Oil and turpentine

Real turpentine comes from pine trees and is one of the oldest solvents for diluting oil paints. Because the solvent thins the oil in the paint, the colours dry with a matt finish and, if a lot of solvent is used, it tends to dull the colours. For this reason, turpentine is usually used in conjunction with an oil to replace the lost sheen. Linseed oil is the most popular, although there are alternatives to both linseed oil and traditional turpentine.

Ideally, use a double dipper like the one below for the oil and turpentine. This small container clips on to the edge of the palette and is designed to minimise the risk of spills. Mix the colour on the palette, adding turpentine and oil with a brush until you have the consistency you want. If you need a large amount of diluted colour, mix it separately in a jar rather than on the palette. Note: avoid using a turpentine substitute or white spirit as an inexpensive alternative to real turpentine for thinning paint. Both these solvents tend to deaden the colours and produce a cloudy patina on the paint surface.

Painting 'fat over lean'

Oils should be applied 'fat over lean'. In other words, start by blocking in the subject with very thin colour diluted with turpentine. Gradually add more oil colour and less turpentine to the paint as the picture progresses.

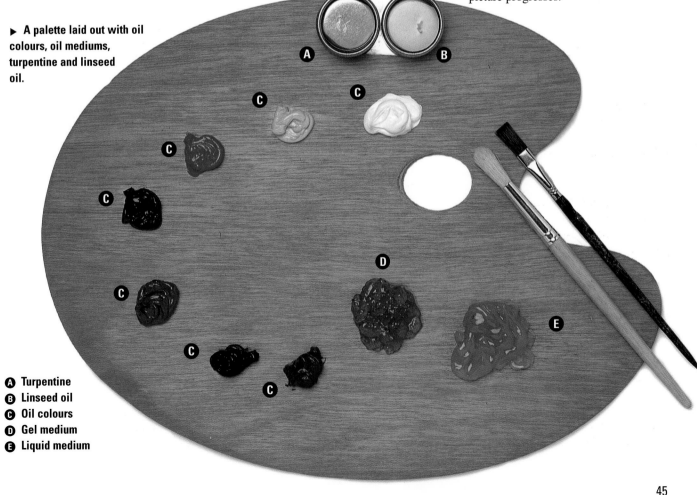

▶ **A palette laid out with oil colours, oil mediums, turpentine and linseed oil.**

Ⓐ **Turpentine**
Ⓑ **Linseed oil**
Ⓒ **Oil colours**
Ⓓ **Gel medium**
Ⓔ **Liquid medium**

MIXING OIL MEDIUMS WITH PAINT

TURPENTINE AND LINSEED OIL

Use a double clip-on dipper for the oil and turpentine. Dilute the colour by loading the brush from the dipper and adding to the paint.

GEL MEDIUM

Squeeze gel medium directly on to the palette. Mix in the colour using a knife or a stiff brush. The mixture generally becomes stiffer if left to stand.

LIQUID MEDIUM

Pour the liquid medium on to the palette or into a container. Many mediums dry quickly, so don't use too much. Add to the colour, mixing with a knife or brush.

Using this method, the underpainting dries quickly without holding up the rest of the work, and the finished surface has a rich, glossy colour.

Other mediums

There are various specialist mediums designed to alter the paint for specific purposes. Depending on the product, a medium can make oil colours thicker or thinner, improve the flow, create a matt finish, or speed up the drying time of the paint. Some mediums are simply ready-mixed versions of traditional ingredients; others contain synthetic materials.

Colour thickeners

Thick mediums come in tubes, in gel or paste form. They can be squeezed on to the palette alongside the colours and added to the paint as required. For a very

thick consistency, use a paste, but gels are best used where expressive brushwork is required. Mix the paint with the gel or paste and leave to stiffen before use. These mediums can also be mixed with a solvent to make the paint flow more easily.

Liquid mediums

Oil paint diluted with turpentine alone dries with a dull, matt finish, but if you add a little liquid medium, the paint will dry with a smooth, shiny surface. Most liquid mediums are also suitable for glazing – they dilute the colour to make it more transparent without affecting the glossy nature of the paint. Alternatively, buy a glazing medium made specifically for the purpose.

Despite their name, 'liquid' mediums are not necessarily completely liquid in consistency. Although some are quite

runny, others are more like jelly. Small amounts of the latter can be poured directly on to the painting palette, but very liquid mediums are best kept in a separate container.

Trying out the mediums

If too much of any medium is added to an oil colour, it will inevitably alter the opacity and strength of the colour. Only by trial and error with a particular product will you find out exactly how much of the medium you can introduce without spoiling the particular result you are aiming to achieve.

Also, it is important to bear in mind that mediums are essentially additives which change the nature and chemistry of the paint. If you overdo them, you might reduce the durability of the completed painting.

▶ GLAZING
Mix the paint and glazing medium to the consistency of single cream and apply this to a dry undercolour. Some colours, such as lemon yellow, are naturally transparent and work particularly well in glaze mixtures.

Watercolour mediums

If you would like to experiment with watercolour, try mixing it with some of the special additives that change the character of the paint.

The fluid nature of watercolour means that it is ideal for creating washes of translucent colour and delicate tones. However, this is by no means the end of the story. You can actually change the consistency of watercolour by adding one of several mediums to the paint. In this way, your colours become more versatile and you will be able to invent many different textures and surfaces. For example, watercolour mixed with the appropriate medium can be used with masking tape, painted in stiff peaks and even applied with a knife.

Gum water and gum arabic

Gum water and gum arabic are useful additives that enhance both the colour and texture of watercolour. A little of either medium mixed with the paint will give a rich gloss to the picture

WATERCOLOUR MEDIUMS

Choose a watercolour medium to make the colour thicker or thinner; to improve the flow; to slow down or speed up the drying time; to get a glossy finish; or to paint impasto textures.

- **A** Thickening paste
- **B** Gum water
- **C** Gum arabic
- **D** Glycerine
- **E** Ox gall liquid
- **F** Drying medium

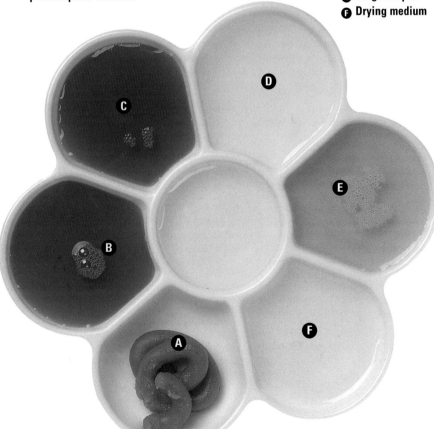

USING GUM ARABIC

To achieve a glossy sheen, add a little gum arabic to the diluted watercolour with a brush, then try the following experiments.

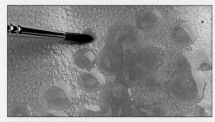

MOTTLED PATTERN

Drops of water applied with a small brush will dissolve dry, thickened colour and disperse the pigment particles to create this attractive mottled texture.

SGRAFFITO

Use a fork or other sharp tool to scratch patterns into wet, thickened colour. The white paper or underlying colour will show through the paint.

SPATTERING

Using a toothbrush, flick clean water on to dry, thickened colour. Wait for a few seconds until the water has had time to dissolve the colour, then blot the excess.

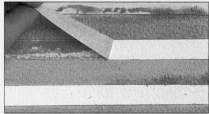

MASKING TAPE

Press strips of tape firmly down on the paper and apply the thickened colour. When the colour is dry, carefully peel back the tape to reveal the crisply painted stripes.

THICKENING PASTE

Stiffer than gum arabic, thickening paste is particularly suitable for impasto watercolour and other highly textured effects. As it is often translucent rather than transparent, too much of the paste can affect the colour of the paint and produce a cloudy effect. Once watercolour paint has been thickened with this medium, it can then be applied with a painting knife as well as with a brush.

MIXING
Blend the paste and colour together well using a stiff brush. If the mixture is too firm for your purpose, add a little water.

IMPASTO
Use the flat blade of a painting knife to apply thick layers of colour and to create wedges of overlapping paint.

SGRAFFITO
Pronounced ridges and other scratched patterns can be made using a fork, comb or other implement on the wet colour.

BRUSH MARKS
Thick colour retains the marks of a stiff brush so experiment with different types of brush stroke – dabs, swirls, and so on.

STIPPLING
Pat the wet colour with the flat blade of a painting knife to create raised peaks of colour in a coarse, stippled effect.

surface. Both mediums can be spattered or sprayed on to an area of dry colour to create a speckled or mottled texture.

Gum arabic is less fluid and more viscous (sticky) than gum water. When watercolour paint is mixed with gum arabic, it can become stiff enough to hold the shape of brush marks. The thickened colour allows you to create other surface textures such as combing or stippling. However, too much gum arabic will make the paint jelly-like and too slippery to be workable.

Thickening paste

For a heavy impasto effect, try adding thickening paste to your watercolours. The resulting mixture can be so stiff that it looks quite unlike traditional watercolour paint – in fact, many purists disapprove of the additive for this reason. However, it is always fun to experiment, and watercolour applied with a painting knife is certainly an intriguing idea. Also, if used discerningly on selected areas of a painting, thickening paste can add textural interest and enhance the surface of the paint without detracting from its more classical qualities.

Thickening paste comes in tubes and looks similar to equivalent mediums made for oil and acrylics. Take care, when purchasing the medium, to buy a product that is made specifically for watercolour.

Flow improvers

Ox gall medium is the best known of the 'flow improvers', which are used to disperse colour evenly, particularly in washes and wet-on-wet techniques. It is a brownish-yellow liquid originally made from the gall bladders of cows and is normally added to the water rather than to the paint. Although still available, real ox gall has generally been replaced by synthetic alternatives.

In addition to ox gall, a number of other proprietary mediums are available to improve the flow of watercolour and to disperse the pigment evenly.

Drying mediums and retarders

If you have ever tried painting wet-in-wet on a very hot day, when the colour dries as soon as it touches the paper, you will appreciate the value of glycerine. A few drops of this heavy, honey-like liquid added to the watercolour will keep your painting moist and workable for considerably longer by delaying the natural drying time of the paint.

Conversely, watercolour paint dries surprisingly slowly in damp and humid conditions. This can be frustrating, especially if you are waiting to apply colour to a dry surface. Happily, you can speed up the drying time by using a proprietary drying medium. Alternatively, a few drops of alcohol added to the paint will also have the same effect.

'Painting' with graphite

With water-soluble graphite, you can combine the fluid finish of watercolour with controlled line work, as well as developing a range of tones.

◄ Just a small amount of water will transform a graphite drawing into a monochrome painting with a watercolour look.

Water-soluble graphite pencils, are very versatile drawing tools. When used dry for sketching and drawing, they behave exactly like ordinary graphite pencils. However, water-soluble pencils are capable of more than just straightforward mark-making on paper. If you brush a little water over an area shaded with soluble graphite, it dissolves to create a grey wash. Depending on the wash strength of the pencil (they are available in various grades), or on how much graphite was laid down in the first place, the wash can be very pale or velvety black. You'll find that your brush picks up a lot of graphite as you work, so keep rinsing it in water and wiping it clean.

Dark and light

Another way in which you can use a water-soluble pencil is to dip the lead directly into water and then draw with it. This technique makes very dark marks, ideal for emphasizing details or filling in deep shadows. Hold the pencil almost upright so that the water can flow down more easily.

As with all watercolour painting, you should work from the light areas of the picture to the dark ones. If the brush picks up too much graphite and gives too dark a tone on the paper, you can rescue this by going over the same area with clear water to lift off excess graphite.

It is best to use watercolour paper with water-soluble pencils. Stretch the paper first to prevent it from cockling (blistering or puckering) or, if you don't intend to use lots of water, simply fix the paper to the drawing board with masking tape to keep it flat and smooth.

FIRST STEPS

1 ▶ **Make an initial sketch** Using a medium water-soluble pencil, draw in the line where the worksurface meets the tongue-and-groove background. You can then use the vertical boards as a measuring guide when you draw the folds of the soft tool bag and the angles and smooth curves of the tools.

2 ▼ **Fill in tone on the bag** Begin adding medium tone with hatched lines to define the folds of the bag. In the recesses of the folds, where the shadow is deepest, press harder with the pencil to give a darker tone.

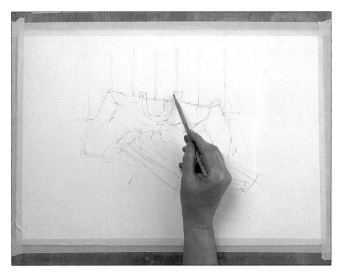

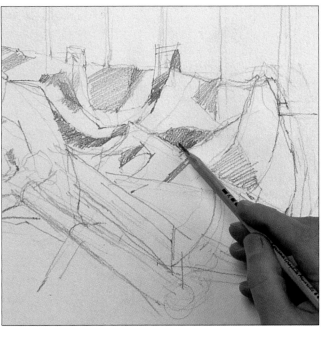

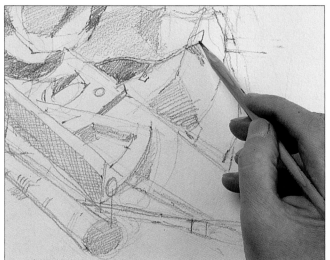

4 ▲ **Concentrate on details** Complete the surface of the file with lines of cross-hatching. Shade in some very dark tone where the bag handle folds over. Define the zip and tag on the bag with hard, fine lines.

3 ▼ **Develop the tools** Darken the shaded surfaces of the tools, such as the inside of the plane handle. Indicate the pattern on the hammer handle and begin to show the rough surface of the file with diagonal hatched lines.

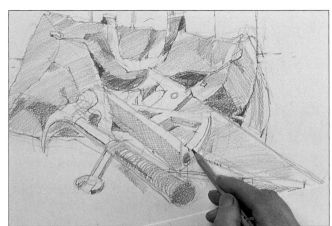

5 ▲ **Tidy up the drawing** Shade light tone over the saw and indicate some of the teeth. Follow the form of the hammer handle with curved lines and show its cast shadow. To complete the shading on the bag, hatch in medium tone and then change to a soft pencil to strengthen the darkest shadows. Firm up the hard lines of the tools.

ADDING WATER TO THE DRAWING

Once you feel that the overall tone of the drawing is correct, you have reached the exciting stage where you can begin to 'paint' with the graphite.

6 ▲ Begin using water Load a little water on to a soft round brush and use the side of the brush to wash over the bag, working from light areas to darker ones. The water smooths out the graphite shading to create a more uniform tone.

7 ▲ Shade the background boards Using the paper palette method described in Expert Advice below, brush a very pale wash of graphite over the tongue-and-groove boards behind the tool bag.

8 ◄ Develop the tone further Brush water over the saw and the hammer handle. Using the tip of the brush, paint water over the folds of the bag to give a dark watercolour effect. For the black interior of the bag, dip the lead of a very soft water-soluble pencil into water and shade with this.

EXPERT ADVICE
Using paper as a palette

Instead of brushing water directly over your drawing, you can pick up pigment from a patch of graphite shaded on to a spare piece of paper. In this way, you can control the depth of colour more easily, especially if you want a very pale wash.

9 ▲ Continue with the wet pencil lead Emphasize all the darkest folds of the bag with the wetted tip of the very soft pencil. Returning to the brush, stroke water lightly over the rough surface of the file. Picking up graphite from a paper palette, develop the medium-toned shadows on the bag, and paint cast shadows under the chisel and hammer.

A FEW STEPS FURTHER

The drawing now shows various levels of tone, some achieved with a pencil used dry, some with a wash of water and the darkest with a wet pencil lead. You can add interest to the picture with some extra detail drawn with a wet pencil and brush.

10 ▶ **Draw the fine lines** Using the medium pencil dipped in water, draw fine, dark lines to strengthen the stitching on the bag, the edges of the zip and the edges of the handles. Accentuate the rivet on the saw handle and the pattern on the hammer handle.

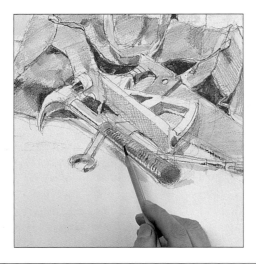

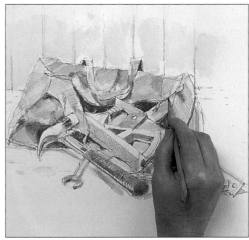

11 ▲ **Add finishing touches** Using a wet brush and a little graphite, very lightly show the knots in the wooden worksurface. Firm any edges, if necessary, with a wet pencil – for example, the top of the saw blade, the plane handle or the zip.

THE FINISHED PICTURE

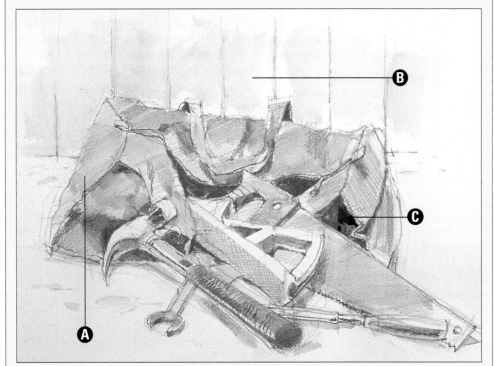

A Mid tones
The areas of medium tone, such as on the tool bag, were created by brushing water over dry graphite shading.

B Palest tone
The light wash on the tongue-and-groove background was achieved by using a wet brush tip to pick up graphite rubbed on to a piece of paper.

C Dark tone
Very black shadows in the creases of the bag were drawn in with the tip of a very soft water-soluble pencil dipped in water.

Drawing with fibre-tipped pens

Interpret the fascinating geometric pattern and sharp, spiky leaves of a pineapple with the crisp, decisive lines produced by a fibre-tipped pen.

Drawing with a pen requires a different technique from drawing with a pencil, charcoal, pastel or other softer medium. A pen gives a well-defined line that cannot easily be erased or altered, so you need to be decisive in your approach from the beginning.

There are many different types of pen available to the artist, ranging from drawing pens with fine tips for graphic designers to dip pens hand-made from goose quills and bamboo. Each has its own character and its own advantages and disadvantages to the artist, some pens being more suitable for precision work and others for freer interpretations of a subject.

The pineapple in this project was drawn with a fibre-tipped pen rather than a dip pen and ink. You'll find a wide range of fibre-tipped pens to choose from at any art shop. Ideal for line illustrations, cartoons and quick sketches, as well as finished drawings, these pens come in a variety of tip sizes, graded in numbers from the very fine 005 and 01 to the thicker 08 and 10. Versatile brush pens are also available if you want more flexibility. When working with a fibre-tipped pen, remember to replace the cap each time you finish using it, or it will dry out.

Use cartridge paper when drawing with a pen – you'll find the nib moves easily over its smooth surface.

Showing tone in pen

While you can show tone with a soft pencil or a stick of charcoal simply by shading with the edge or pressing hard, you'll need a different approach with a fibre-tipped pen as it creates lines which are all of a uniform thickness. One way to convey gradations of tone is to draw hatched lines either close together (for dark areas) or further apart (for paler areas). To create an even darker tone, add lines of cross-hatching as well. Alternatively, change to a pen with a thicker tip for areas of deep shadow.

◀ This pen drawing of a pineapple combines well-defined outlines with subtly drawn areas of tone to give a highly realistic finished image.

FIRST STEPS

1 ▶ **Make a sketch** Holding one of the pens vertically, compare the height of the pineapple to the height of its leaves – the proportion is about half and half. Using an 01 pen, begin to sketch the pineapple, some of its leaves and the paper bag underneath it. Draw the body of the pineapple as a smooth oval, marking diagonal lines across it to help you interpret the regular growth pattern on the skin.

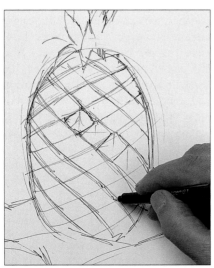

2 ◀ **Map out the pattern** Notice how the pattern on the pineapple forms a diagonal grid. Sketch in the crossing diagonals, curving the lines slightly to show the pineapple's rounded shape.

EXPERT ADVICE
Trying out the pattern

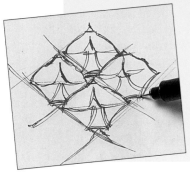

Practise sketching a small section of the pineapple's pattern before you begin the drawing. Each segment is based on a simple diamond shape. Build it up with a short, flat base, a point at the top and curves at the sides. Draw a horizontal line across the shape – the small spike sticks up from this with two lines below it.

3 ▲ **Develop the leaves and pattern** Draw more leaves, checking that they emerge symmetrically from the top of the pineapple by lightly marking a centre line through the fruit. Hatch in a little dark tone where the leaves are in shadow. Begin to draw some of the distinctive segments inside each diamond shape on the pineapple.

HOW TO DEVELOP TONE

As the pineapple is in shadow on the right, you will need to develop darker tones on this side of the fruit. With fibre-tipped pens, the most effective way to achieve gradations of tone is with hatching and cross-hatching.

4 ▶ **Shade with a thicker pen** Change to an 07 pen and fill in the darkest areas of shade on the leaves and where they cast shadows on the pineapple. Return to the 01 pen to hatch in light tone across the shaded right-hand side of the fruit. Create texture with cross-hatching and add the spikes visible along the right-hand edge.

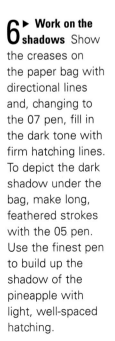

5 ◀ **Define the segments further** Use an 05 pen to work on each segment individually, emphasizing its features. Then change back to the 01 pen to hatch in a little light shading on the left side of the pineapple.

6 ▶ **Work on the shadows** Show the creases on the paper bag with directional lines and, changing to the 07 pen, fill in the dark tone with firm hatching lines. To depict the dark shadow under the bag, make long, feathered strokes with the 05 pen. Use the finest pen to build up the shadow of the pineapple with light, well-spaced hatching.

7 ▲ **Return to the leaves** Render areas of tone on the leaves with parallel marks made with the 05 pen, keeping the look crisp and well-defined. Work the lines close together for dark tones and further apart for medium tones. Add the softest tones to the leaves with the 01 pen. These hatched lines also suggest the fibrous nature of the leaves.

A FEW STEPS FURTHER

Apart from a few minor tonal adjustments, the illustration of the pineapple is finished. In spite of being built up entirely with line work and cross-hatching without any really solid shading, it is a very realistic image.

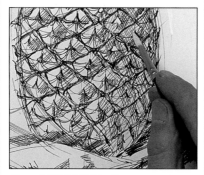

8 ▲ Add highlights If you want to add a few highlights to the drawing, you can blank out some of the pen lines with an opaque white liquid called Bleedproof Designer's White. Pick up a small amount on a No.5 round brush and dab it on to the tips of the spikes to make them catch the eye. You can also remove the early construction lines around the pineapple by painting over them with this liquid.

9 ▲ Darken the overall tone Outline the segments on the pineapple's skin with the 07 pen. Changing back to the 01 pen, darken the pineapple's right side, especially at the upper and lower edges, with more cross-hatching.

THE FINISHED PICTURE

A Regular pattern
The distinctive pattern on the skin of the pineapple was built up gradually, using a diamond-shaped grid as a guide.

B Graded tone
Variations in tone on the surface of the pineapple were achieved with hatched and cross-hatched lines drawn either very close together or further apart.

C Light shadow
Long, fine lines made with a sweep of the wrist created a patch of light tone to represent the shadow cast by the pineapple on to the horizontal surface.

Using mixed media

Once you feel confident using a range of drawing and painting materials,

try combining two or more of them in a single image.

▼ **Isolated areas of
bark pattern can
have a fascinating
abstract quality.**

Certain media, such as pastels and water-colour, or charcoal and chalk, work well together because their different qualities enhance or complement one another. By using a combination of different media and techniques, it is possible to create optical and textural effects that will broaden the range of your work. It is exciting to experiment to see the results that can be achieved and to decide which suit your style.

PROJECT 1

Making studies of found objects is an absorbing exercise that will develop your powers of observation and your ability to draw well.

These tree branches have interesting surface patterns that lend themselves well to a mixed media approach. Try homing in on a small area of the subject and enlarging it on the page.

1 ▶ Draw the outlines Decide which parts of the branches you are going to concentrate on and lightly sketch their outlines using a 6B pencil. Map in the 'snake-skin' pattern on the right-hand branch.

In the three projects that follow, the aim is not to create finished pictures but to make a series of quick studies from nature by experimenting with mixed media. You can combine different drawing media, a mixture of painting media, or even a combination of both. The idea is to use your creative imagination to interpret patterns and textures with a range of materials that you feel are compatible with the subject.

2 ◀ Work on the right-hand branch
The base colour of the right-hand branch is a bleached yellowish-white. Recreate this using pastels, applying strokes of cadmium yellow, white and flesh tint on top of each other, and then blending them together with your finger to create a thick, even layer of colour. Leave the dark patterns untouched for the moment.

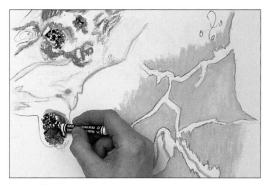

3 ▲ Work on the left-hand branch Add colour to the left-hand branch, using overlaid strokes of flesh tint, cadmium yellow and light brown. Mix light brown with black for the dark areas, and with white for the light areas. Blend white pastel into the pencil outlines to soften them.

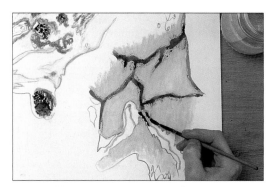

4 ▲ Add lines with watercolour Returning to the right-hand branch, fill in the dark lines with sepia watercolour, using a No.3 round brush. Go over the edges of the drawn lines slightly – the surrounding pastel resists the paint, which dries in feathery streaks. Use the same method to add small, random marks to the pastel areas between the dark lines. Leave to dry.

5 ▲ Complete the left-hand branch Return to working on the left-hand branch. Mix a dilute wash of sepia and ivory black and brush this over parts of the branch, leaving some areas of bare paper to indicate bleached wood. While the paint is still wet, draw lines and whorls with the 6B pencil, pressing quite hard so that the paper is slightly indented.

6 ◄ Complete the right-hand branch Close observation of the branch on the right shows long, vertical, slightly wavering lines over the pale areas of bark. Finish off the sketch by drawing these lines over the blended pastel areas with the 6B pencil. This extra definition gives a subtle indication of texture and detail to the bark, and makes the study more realistic.

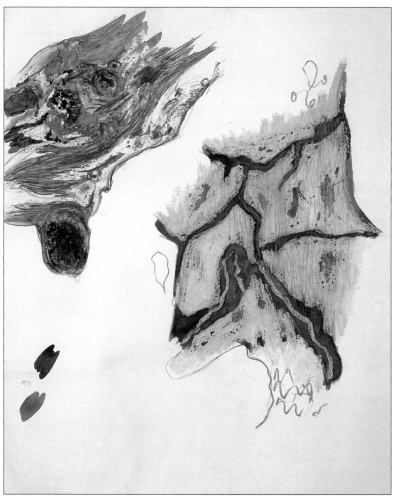

7 ▲ The finished study Although this mixed media exercise is a study rather than a finished image, it conveys a strong sense of form and pattern, based on direct observation from nature. The use of watercolour with pastels conveys the natural, organic appearance of the bark.

PROJECT 2

An irregular fragment of tree bark with a rough, peeling surface is the inspiration for this study. To create a realistic image, a sheet of paper is first placed over the bark and rubbed gently with a soft graphite stick so that the texture comes through – a technique known as 'frottage'. The image is then built up in colour, using watercolour, soft pastels and coloured and graphite pencils.

▲ The intricate texture of this bark is recreated using four different media.

1 ▶ **Use the frottage technique** Lay a sheet of paper over the tree bark and gently shade with a 6B graphite stick until the texture of the bark is revealed. Use small, localized movements with the stick rather than long sweeping ones, and don't press too hard.

2 ▶ **Soften the marks** Use the corner of a putty rubber to soften the textural marks made in step 1 and lift off some of the graphite so that it doesn't mix with the watercolour wash that is to be applied at the next stage. Do this very gently, with short dabbing motions, so that the texture of the bark is still visible – if you pull the eraser right across the paper, the marks will disappear.

3 ▲ **Add a watercolour wash** Apply a thinly diluted wash of sepia and ivory black watercolour paints over the bark, using a No.12 round watercolour brush. The bark has a silvery sheen in places – suggest this by applying thin washes of Chinese white to these areas while the previous wash is still slightly damp.

4 ▲ **Start to suggest texture** Define the rough surface of the bark and the warmer brown tones using a pastel stick in burnt umber. Use the tip of the pastel to make short vertical lines and the side of the pastel to make broader, horizontal blocks. Then do the same with a sap green pastel.

5 ▼ **Continue building up the texture** Work on top of the pastel marks, using coloured pencils to add small lines and marks that suggest the cracked and peeling texture of the bark. Here, coloured pencils in Vandyke brown, golden brown and copper beech (which provide dark, light and medium shades) are being used, along with touches of scarlet lake and cedar green.

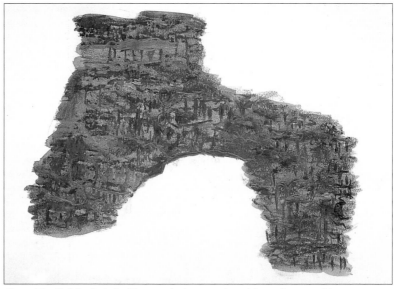

6 ▲ **The finished study** The study is completed by using graphite once again, this time in the form of a 6B pencil. Press hard with the pencil to suggest the edges of the flaking pieces of bark.

PROJECT 3

Using a piece of tree bark once more, this three-dimensional interpretation involves working over a thick layer of PVA glue with pastels and acrylic paint. These bond with the dried surface of the glue to create random, mottled patterns that magically suggest the rough texture of the bark. The final details are added using graphite and coloured pencils.

▶ **This chunky piece of bark** has a tactile, sculptural quality that offers a special challenge.

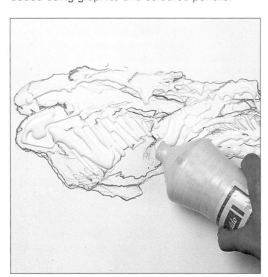

1 ▲ **Draw the bark and apply the glue** Use a 6B pencil to draw the bark, varying the pressure to create light and heavy lines. Observe which areas have the heaviest texture and pour PVA glue over these parts of your drawing, using the bottle as though it were a drawing tool. Let the glue form ridges that stand proud of the surface.

2 ▲ **Create a 3-D surface** Recreate the bark's gnarled texture by using a flat hog's hair brush to move the glue around on the paper. Make stabbing marks in the surface of the glue or dab the brush with a stippling motion, leaving some areas raised. Allow to dry overnight.

3 ▶ Apply pastel colours
Check that the glue is completely dry. Using burnt umber for the dark areas and raw umber for the light areas, apply pastel to the patches of bare paper between the glued areas. Then rub with your fingers to spread the colour over the surface of the glue. The pastel blends into the glue to create mottled patterns.

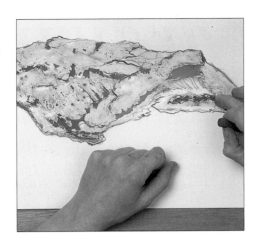

4 ◀ Add acrylic colour Squeeze a small amount of burnt umber acrylic paint from the tube, pick it up on the tip of your finger and then rub it gently over the areas where the bark is dark in tone. Apply the paint thickly for the darkest parts and skim lightly over the surface where the colour is lighter. The paint settles into the indentations on the glued surface, once again creating interesting mottled patterns.

5 ▶ Add linear details Finish off by working over the surface with a 6B pencil and a 6B graphite stick, making random lines and hatchings that suggest the cracks and fissures in the bark. Add coloured lines too, using coloured pencils in Vandyke brown (dark) and golden brown (light). Apply the dark brown to light areas of the bark and vice versa.

Master Strokes

John Constable (1776–1837)
Tree Trunk

Constable's love of nature shows in this masterly painting of a tree trunk, which is so realistic that it has a photographic quality. His rendition of the bark is done in the single medium of oils, with which he skilfully interprets every fissure on the surface.

The interpretation of the tree trunk shows beautifully observed detail on the bark.

The less detailed background helps the viewer to focus on the subject of the painting.

6 ▲ The finished study In this interesting three-dimensional study, the richly worked surface not only describes the form of the subject but also gives it life and character.

Pens for drawing

The range of pens available to the artist is vast and inspiring, ranging from traditional dip pens made from quill, bamboo or reed to fibre-tipped pens in many shapes, sizes and colours. Here we review the choices available.

Your choice of pen is very personal and most artists have a favourite. However, it is worth knowing what is on the market because you might have special requirements from time to time.

Dip pens are the most basic type. As their name suggests, they are loaded by being dipped into ink and have to be recharged at intervals. At the other end of the scale is an ever-expanding range of innovative markers and brush pens which come in a vast array of colours.

Traditional dip pens

These are made from quills, bamboo and reed. Quill pens are cut from the flight feathers of birds such as swans, ravens, ducks or geese, and usually produce a slightly scratchy line. They are particular-

ly popular with calligraphers. Bamboo pens are very tough and vary in size depending on the piece of bamboo used. Reed pens are more flexible than bamboo pens, but tend to chip easily. Both reed and bamboo pens are still used in Japanese and Chinese art today.

Metal dip pens

The metal pen has been traced back as far as Roman times, but it wasn't widely used until the nineteenth century, when technical innovations made it possible to mass-produce steel nibs. From this time, steel nibs became more popular than quill, bamboo and reed. Most metal dip pens consist of a shaft or handle into which a separate metal nib is slotted. It is worth experimenting with some of the

many different nibs available to discover the marks they are capable of producing and to find out which suits your needs and your style of drawing.

Script pens Old-fashioned script nibs consist of a shaped piece of metal with a slit cut in it down which the ink can flow. Some have fine or rounded points, while others are chiselled for italic lettering. They are ideal for sketching.

Mapping pens These have slender, straight nibs with very fine drawing points. They are specially designed for detailed work such as technical drawing and map-making.

Lettering pens The nibs used for lettering pens are available in various shapes, which are designed to produce the special serifs, flourishes and ribbon shapes used

VARYING THE LINE WIDTH

Technical pen
The fine lines produced by a technical pen are ideal for delicate drawings with a lot of detail. Use hatching for darker areas.

Brush pen
With the flexible tip of a brush pen, you can adopt a more fluid approach, using both thick and thin lines in a sketch.

Marker
A marker with a chisel tip makes thick, bold lines that can fill shapes such as the flowers' stalks with a single stroke.

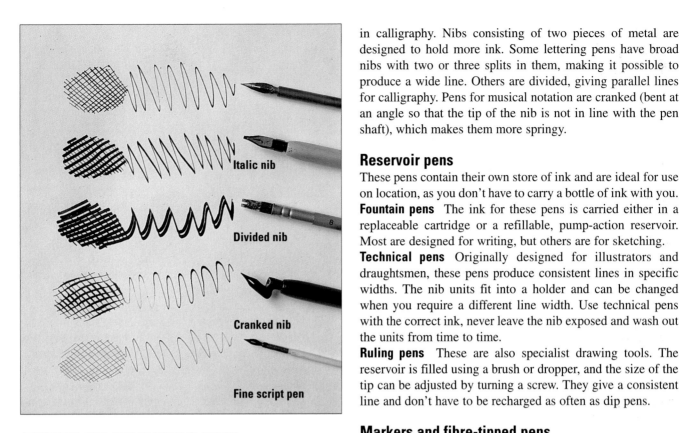

Italic nib

Divided nib

Cranked nib

Fine script pen

TYPES OF DRAWING PEN

- **A** Ballpoint
- **B** Fineline ballpoint
- **C** Chisel-tipped marker
- **D** Brush pen
- **E** Fibre-tipped pen
- **F** Three chisel-tipped markers
- **G** BiC ballpoint pen
- **H** Technical pen
  with nib units

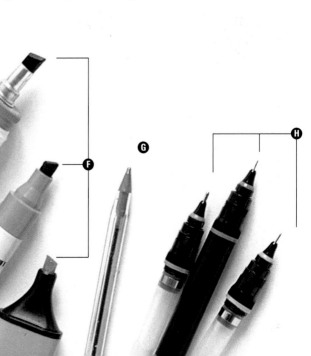

in calligraphy. Nibs consisting of two pieces of metal are designed to hold more ink. Some lettering pens have broad nibs with two or three splits in them, making it possible to produce a wide line. Others are divided, giving parallel lines for calligraphy. Pens for musical notation are cranked (bent at an angle so that the tip of the nib is not in line with the pen shaft), which makes them more springy.

Reservoir pens

These pens contain their own store of ink and are ideal for use on location, as you don't have to carry a bottle of ink with you.
Fountain pens The ink for these pens is carried either in a replaceable cartridge or a refillable, pump-action reservoir. Most are designed for writing, but others are for sketching.
Technical pens Originally designed for illustrators and draughtsmen, these pens produce consistent lines in specific widths. The nib units fit into a holder and can be changed when you require a different line width. Use technical pens with the correct ink, never leave the nib exposed and wash out the units from time to time.
Ruling pens These are also specialist drawing tools. The reservoir is filled using a brush or dropper, and the size of the tip can be adjusted by turning a screw. They give a consistent line and don't have to be recharged as often as dip pens.

Markers and fibre-tipped pens

This category includes a wide and colourful range of pens, some of which are designed for professional applications, while others are intended for everyday use.
Markers Chisel-tipped felt pens, or markers, leave a broad, transparent line and can be used to build up layers of vibrant washes. Most manufacturers also produce markers with bullet (rounded) tips in the same colours. Some ranges include double-ended markers, with a chisel tip at one end and a bullet tip at the other. They dry quickly and can be blended if you work fast, or you can use a special blender to slow down drying. There is also a huge range of general-purpose markers with medium to fine tips, ideal for adding colour to sketches.

Most markers are fugitive – they fade over time if exposed to the light – so they are best kept for sketches rather than for images that will be displayed. Solvent-based markers should always be used in a well-ventilated space.

Fineliners These allow you to work with more precision, although the tip will eventually become blunt. Some fineliners are available in specific line widths.

Brush pens The tip on a brush pen is longer and more pliable than on other markers, and some ranges have a huge choice of colours. By varying the pressure, you can produce fine, medium or bold strokes. Some double-ended pens have a brush pen on one end and a fine fibre tip on the other.

Ballpoint pens

The first ballpoint pen was invented in 1938 by a Hungarian journalist called Laszlo Biro, who was inspired by the quick-drying, smudge-proof ink used for commercial printing presses. The thicker ink would not flow from an ordinary nib, so he devised a pen with a tiny ball-bearing in its tip. Biro is often used as a generic term to describe ballpoint pens. One of the most popular ballpoint pens today is the BiC, launched by the French Baron Bich in 1950. Ballpoint pens are cheap and convenient, and can be a useful addition to your sketching kit.

Rollerballs These pens work on the same principle as ball-points, but the ink in them is more like that used in cartridge pens or fibre-tipped pens. It dries quickly by evaporation and does not create blotches as ballpoints sometimes do.

Inks

The main distinction between inks is whether they are water-proof or water-soluble. Waterproof ink allows you to lay a wash over a line without dissolving it, whereas a water-soluble ink will spread and run. Indian ink is the best-known drawing ink – it is black, permanent and waterproof. Coloured waterproof drawing inks are dye-based and not lightfast, so are best used in sketchbooks where they won't be exposed to light for long periods. Waterproof inks should not be used in fountain pens, as they will clog the mechanism.

Liquid watercolours and acrylics Like coloured inks, these can be used with dip pens and are available in a wide array of shades. Liquid watercolours are soluble once dry, while liquid acrylics are not.

Liquid acrylic

Indian ink

Liquid watercolo[ur]

Waterproof drawing ink

Bamboo pens

- **I** Selection of nibs for a dip pen
- **J** Divided nib for parallel lines
- **K** Mapping pen
- **L** Cranked nib for music notation
- **M** Script pen
- **N** Ruling pen
- **O** Sketching fountain pen
- **P** Selection of coloured fibre-tipped pens
- **Q** Bullet-tipped pen
- **R** 3mm (⅛in) chisel-tipped pen
- **S** Fineliner

The versatile paint brush

Using a brush is the simplest and most conventional method of applying paint. It is also the most versatile, as you'll see from the effects shown in this chapter.

A single brush has many uses. With this one tool you can fill in large areas of colour, or you can paint delicate lines. You can create a whole range of exciting marks, textures and patterns on any surface you choose.

Artists' brushes come in a variety of shapes, each designed for a specific purpose. For example, brushes with square-cut bristles are often used for painting areas of flat colour, while brushes with fine points are good for detail and for painting tapering lines. A brush with a full head of bristles generally holds more paint than a flattened or fine brush, which means that you don't need to dip it in the paint quite so often.

◀ The flat, square cut broad brush (top) is ideal for backgrounds and areas of flat colour; the finer, tapered brushes are better for detail work and highlighting.

A variety of effects

Any paint brush can be used in a variety of ways to create many different marks. The marks you make depend upon whether you use the side of the brush or the tip, how much pressure you apply and the sort of movement you make as you paint. Many artists use one type of brush for everything and even create beautiful paintings using the same brush – sometimes until it wears out!

Experiment with whatever brushes you have to see what effects you can create. Discover, too, how many different marks you can make with a single brush. Your confidence will soon increase and you'll begin to develop your own painting style, which is as unique to you as your handwriting.

▲ Strong, swirling brush strokes are used to astonishing effect in Van Gogh's immortal *Sunflowers*.

▶ This detail from *Sunflowers* reveals the thick, juicy texture of the oil paint, a technique known as *impasto*.

PLAYING WITH TEXTURES

Invent your own textures, using the brush and paint in as many different ways as you can. Try painting with a dry brush, dipping only the tips of the bristles into the paint, so that patches of the paper show through the colour. Instead of laying conventional horizontal brushstrokes, why not try stippling the colour using a vertical stabbing motion to create a stubbly paint surface? The possibilities for making textures with paint and a brush are almost endless.

Paper and canvas have textures of their own and it is worth experimenting with both thick and thin colour on a variety of painting surfaces. Many artists like to see the weave of canvas or the texture of rough paper through the brushstrokes and deliberately use thin or sparse colour to create this effect.

Dry brush

Stippling

Paint dabs

Horizontal dashes

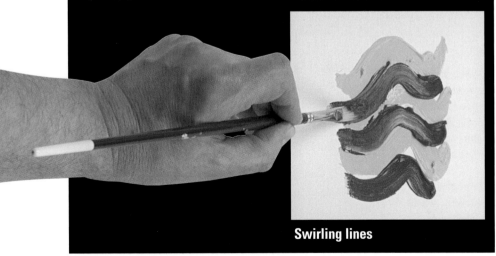

Swirling lines

Magic brushmarks

If you lack confidence in your brush-work, why not start by making the brush do the painting for you? You can simply use the shape of the brush bristles to create a shape on the paper. For example, take a round brush, dip all the bristles in the paint, lay the side of the bristle head on the paper and you have a perfect petal shape. Paint these in a circle and you have a daisy.

The same shape can also be used to paint buds and leaves. Add a few stems and stalks using the point or thin side of the bristles and you have a complete plant. Carry on painting flowers and leaves in this way and before long you will have created an effective and colourful garden landscape, without either drawing the shapes or filling them in. It's easy!

Swirling brushwork

Oil and acrylic paints can be used undi-luted, straight from the tube. The buttery, succulent colour holds the shape of the brush strokes and you can build up beautiful textures and patterns in your pictures.

For inspiration, look at the famous paintings of sunflowers by Vincent van Gogh, or the lovely waterlilies and flowers in the giant garden paintings of French Impressionist Claude Monet. Van Gogh often used thick, unmixed colours, following the shapes of the flowers with his expressive brush-strokes. Monet frequently painted flowers and leaves with single brush strokes of pure colour, building these up to create an impression of a garden more real and convincing than any amount of detail could have produced.

▶ **This Japanese print, entitled *Winter Landscape with Countryfolk*, shows how both lines and washes can be made with a well-pointed brush to create images of great charm.**

▲ Letting the brush do the painting: striking effects with the simplest of strokes.

Dots and dabs

A spontaneous and fun way of painting is to apply colour in tiny dabs or dots, especially if you use two or more colours. For example, paint an area of yellow and red dots, then stand back to look at the effect. You will discover that the reds and yellows appear to merge together to give the impression of orange. Try 'mixing' other colours in this way: blue and yellow to create an impression of green; blue and green to make turquoise and so on.

Painting lines

The type of line you produce depends very much on how you hold the brush and how hard you press down on it as you paint. A lot of pressure causes the bristles to splay out to give you a fat line. To paint a fine line, hold the brush lightly, so that just the tips of the bristles touch the paper. If your brush has square-cut bristles, turn it so that you are working with the narrow side of the bristles.

For a tapering effect, start lightly, then gradually thicken the line by applying more pressure. For undulating lines, vary the pressure, or try twisting and turning the brush as you paint. A single stroke can convey a surprising sense of movement and rhythm.

Going oriental

In China and Japan, the same brushes and brushstrokes are used for lettering as for painting. This is why the term 'calligraphic' is often used to describe the decisive, flowing lines found in much oriental art. This deft brushwork,

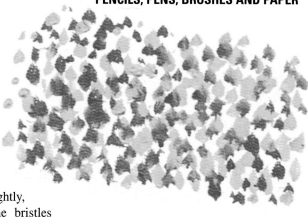

▲ Small, separate dots and dabs of colour appear to merge in the viewer's eye and create exciting and vibrant effects.

often painted over delicate washes, enables artists to capture an entire landscape with just a few strokes of paint or ink. Blossoms and bamboo leaves look so lifelike that they appear to sway in the breeze.

Traditionally, Chinese and Japanese artists used oriental brushes with bamboo handles, designed originally as writing tools. However, any pointed soft-bristled brush – the type normally used with watercolour – works well with this technique.

Brushes

It's worth building up a collection of different brushes as they will help you achieve a wide range of exciting paint effects.

Artists' brushes come in an enormous range of shapes and sizes, corresponding to the various purposes they are intended for. They may be made from several different kinds of natural bristles or from synthetic fibre, and the difference in price between the different types of bristle can be considerable. The choice is wide, but in the end the decision as to which to buy and use is a personal one, often depending on trial and error. Initially, it is a good idea to experiment with one or two brushes at a time to see how you get on.

WHAT TO LOOK FOR

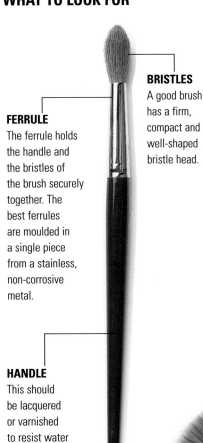

BRISTLES
A good brush has a firm, compact and well-shaped bristle head.

FERRULE
The ferrule holds the handle and the bristles of the brush securely together. The best ferrules are moulded in a single piece from a stainless, non-corrosive metal.

HANDLE
This should be lacquered or varnished to resist water and for ease of cleaning.

Small and large

Most artists' brushes are available in a range of sizes, usually numbered. For example, a standard watercolour brush range can start with a tiny No.0000, used only for the very finest work, going up to No.20 and even larger. However, it is worth remembering that each brush manufacturer has a slightly different system. Hence a No.2 brush made by one manufacturer is not necessarily exactly the same size as a No.2 brush produced by another. The size of some flat brushes may be expressed in terms of total bristle width instead of numbers – 25mm (1in), 51mm (2in) and so on.

Types of brush

Each type of brush is designed to make a specific kind of mark. Choosing a brush depends very much on the effect you want to achieve, but if you have one or two of the following basic brush types they will be all you need to begin with.

Round This is a brush with a rounded ferrule. It is a popular, general-purpose brush with a full bristle head that holds a lot of paint. Large rounds are useful for laying washes and wide expanses of colour. The point can be used for painting lines and detail.

▲ **Brushes are available in many sizes. These sable rounds range in size from the finest No.0000 to the much larger No.20.**

Flat or chisel headed This brush has a flattened ferrule with a square-cut bristle head. The wide bristles are good for applying paint in short dabs and for laying flat areas of colour, while the narrow edge of the bristles is useful for making thinner lines. A flat with very short bristles is sometimes referred to as a 'bright'.

Filbert Somewhere between a flat and a round, a filbert has a flattened ferrule but with tapered bristles. It is a popular and versatile brush, combining the functions of other brush types.

Fan The attractively shaped fan brush, or blender, as it is also sometimes known, has widely splayed-out bristles and is used primarily for blending colours together smoothly.

Flat

Filbert

Round

Fan

Watercolour brushes

Watercolour brushes are usually softer than those designed for use with oil and acrylics. The very best-quality watercolourbrushes available are sable brushes. These are made only from the tail-end hairs of the sable, a small, fur-bearing animal that is found in certain regions in Siberia. This is why pure sable brushes are so expensive. To reduce the cost, manufacturers sometimes mix sable with other natural hair. This is usually ox or squirrel hair, but occasionally goat, camel or even mongoose hair is used.

Why are sable brushes so good to work with? For a start, they combine strength with suppleness, and this allows you to paint in a lively yet controlled way. They also wear well, and will keep their shape. If properly cared for, a sable brush can last a lifetime.

However, manufactured bristles have improved enormously in quality in recent years. They fall into two main categories. Soft brushes are made especially for watercolour paints and have a texture and pliancy which aims to match the qualities of natural hair. Stiffer, general-purpose nylon brushes are made mainly for use with oil and acrylics, but are occasionally used by watercolourists to give a textured surface.

Caring for watercolour brushes

Each time you use a brush, rinse it in water. Either hold your brushes in your free hand while you work, or lay them down on a flat surface. Never leave them standing head down in water, because this will bend the bristles. Once this has happened, it can be difficult to restore a brush to its proper state.

At the end of a painting session, wash each brush thoroughly in warm soapy water, then rinse well under running water. Gently shake the bristle head back into its natural shape. If necessary, reshape the bristles with your thumb and index finger. Store brushes upright with the handle end downwards.

Special brushes

You may come across various eye-catching and exotic-looking brushes in the art shop. Though they may appear unusual and have intriguing names – rigger, oriental, mop and spotter – these brushes are very practical and invaluable for creating specific effects.

Rigger So-called because it was originally used to paint fine ship's rigging in marine paintings, the rigger has long, tapering bristles. Today it is used more generally for all linear work, but especially for lettering, poster writing and also calligraphy.

Oriental brushes Recognizable by their cane or bamboo handles, these brushes produce the characteristic, flowing lines which give Japanese and Chinese paintings their distinctive quality. The bristles taper to a fine point and the brushes can be used for painting fine lines as well as for creating broad strokes and laying washes.

Spotter Miniature paintings and all fine detail can be executed with a retouching brush, or spotter. This is a small round brush with short bristles, good for all precise work.

Wash brushes There are several large brushes that are designed specifically for laying flat washes. Most artists use a soft, flat brush; others prefer a large round, or a mop. The mop brush has a large, rounded head and is especially good for laying textured washes such as sea and sky.

Brushes for oil and acrylic

Brushes made for oil and acrylic paints

igger

able rounds

ynthetic rushes

Mop

WATERCOLOUR BRUSH MARKS

Rigger

The long bristles of a rigger are designed for linear work.

Flat or chisel headed

A flat brush can give broad or narrow lines of paint.

Round

Use the whole brush for painting large areas, and the tip for details.

69

ACRYLIC BRUSHMARKS

Round

The oval marks made by a round brush echo the shape of the bristle head.

Flat or chisel headed

The rectangular profile of a flat brush produces regular dabs of acrylic colour.

Filbert

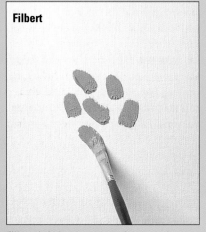

Filbert bristles curve gently to a point and give strong, tapering strokes.

Fan

Use a fan-shaped brush for delicate blending effects with acrylics.

are stiffer than those used for water-colour painting. However, watercolour brushes can also be used with oils and acrylics, especially if you are painting areas of thin colour or painting detail.

Oil painting brushes are traditionally made from a natural bristle, usually hog's hair. There are also excellent synthetic brushes now available and some artists actually prefer these, finding them easier to clean and harder-wearing.

Certain synthetic brushes have been specially developed for use with acrylic paints, but as a general rule, both natural bristle and synthetic brushes can be used with either oil or acrylic paints. One word of warning, however: oil and water do not mix. Brushes which you have already used with oil paints should be carefully cleaned before you go on to use them with acrylics, which are water soluble.

Care and cleaning

Whether you are using oils or acrylics, paint should never be allowed to dry on the brush. At the end of every painting session, clean your brushes carefully by first wiping off excess paint with paper or kitchen roll. Brushes used with oil paint should then be rinsed in turpentine or white spirit, wiped clean and washed in warm water and household soap. Rub the soapy brush in the palm of your hand to loosen

the paint that has accumulated round the ferrule. Rinse the brush well, then shake it to remove the water. If necessary, carefully reshape the bristles then leave the brush to dry in a jar, with the bristle end up.

Acrylic brushes should only be cleaned in warm water and soap. Because acrylic paint dries so quickly, it is a good idea to keep brushes moist during the painting session when you are not using them. Do this by laying brushes in a dish of water with the handles resting on the side of the dish.

If you let acrylic paint dry on the brush accidentally, you can rescue it by soaking the bristles overnight in methylated spirits. This will soften the paint, which can then usually be washed off with soap and warm water.

Other handy brushes

Once you have experiment-ed with the range of recog-nized artists' brushes, you might like to try other kinds. Small house-deco-rating brushes are excellent for painting flat areas of colour and can save time if you like working on a large scale. Avoid very cheap ones – they tend to moult and you may waste any time you would have saved picking loose bris-tles off your painting. The very best decorating brush is still much cheaper than the equivalent artists' brush. Other useful brushes include a stencilling brush with a flat end to create stippled colour; a sash brush for painting large areas; and an old toothbrush for spattered effects. A fitch is a cheaper alternative to a sash brush.

Synthetic

Hog's hair

Sash

Stencilling

Decorating

Fitch

Using coloured paper

Applying watercolour to toned paper breaks with tradition but, as these quick sketches show, the results can be both striking and instructive.

A watercolour painted on coloured paper is quite different from a classical watercolour picture on white or pale cream paper. White paper intensifies the transparent colours without changing them. On coloured paper, the underlying support shows through the paint and can alter the colours.

Underlying colour

The colour of the support will modify the painted colours in precisely the same way as if that colour had been added to the paint on the palette. Yellow paper, for instance, will push red towards orange and blue towards green.

One useful characteristic of tinted paper is the unifying effect it can have

on the finished painting. While some artists create harmony in a painting by including a little of one particular colour in every mixture on the palette, others find that they can achieve a similar effect simply by painting on coloured paper. This is because the underlying paper colour effectively mixes with each of the painted colours to create a general, unified colour theme.

Testing colours

It is helpful to make a colour test to find out how the painted colours will appear when applied to a particular paper. You can do this by cutting a small strip from the paper you intend to use for your painting. On this test strip, try out the

colours from your usual palette, as well as any of your favourite mixtures, before introducing them into the paintings.

Colour and tone

It is easier and quicker to establish light and shade on toned paper than it is when working on white paper. For example, the seated figure in the watercolour painting below is lit by an overhead window, which creates strong highlights and dark shadows. To bring out these contrasting tones, the artist chose medium-grey paper – a tone that is approximately halfway between the dark shadows and white highlights.

Having established this paper as the mid-toned colour, it was then a

WORKING ON MID-TONED PAPER

To discover the benefits of using tinted paper in a tonal study, try making a quick monochrome watercolour sketch of a figure on a sheet of medium-grey paper. Treat the paper tone as the mid tone in the picture – this stands for the limbs, the face and the clothing. Then add the background and shadows with washes of darker grey, and put in highlights with simple strokes of opaque Chinese white. Use broad brush strokes to avoid detail, relying on the tonal contrasts to build up the form.

▼ **Highlights have been picked out in Chinese white watercolour, which shines out against the grey paper.**

1 ▲ Block in the background Using a No.4 sable brush, wash Payne's grey over the background. Paint around the figure, and dot in one or two of the darkest shadows.

2 ▲ Add dark tones Change to a 25mm (1in) flat brush. Establish shadows on the chair and figure in a dilute Payne's grey that is slightly darker than the background wash.

relatively simple matter to add the shadows and a few highlights that show up clearly against the medium grey of the paper. To accentuate the tonal contrast, the artist simplified the tones, using Payne's grey for the shadows and Chinese white for the highlights.

Tinting your own paper

What happens if you cannot find paper in the colour of your choice? You can make your own tinted paper by applying a watercolour wash to a sheet of white paper or even over another colour. This will allow you to choose exactly the right tone and colour for the purpose.

The paintings that follow are both made on paper that has been tinted by the artist. An evening landscape (opposite) is painted over a multicoloured wash. In the second watercolour (see page 74), a washy blue makes an attractive background for the darker blue of the painting.

▼ These strips of coloured paper, each painted with the same colours, show the considerable effect that background colour can have on the appearance of watercolour paint. Grey paper, for example, tends to mute the colours. On red paper, the yellow and orange almost disappear.

LOCAL COLOUR

Brightly coloured paper can give dramatic results, but it is important to choose the right colour for the subject. The main colours in this still-life arrangement of a basket of fruit are yellow, orange and brown. By selecting a bright yellow support, the artist was able to leave patches of unpainted paper to represent the local colour of the yellow fruit as well as to show the highlights. So, by choosing an appropriate colour, you will find the paper does most of the work!

Keep the painted colour to a minimum, using thin mixes that allow the yellow paper to glow through the transparent paints. Add just a few deeper patches for the shadow areas. This way of working creates an overall warmth and harmony in the finished painting.

1 ▲ Paint outlines Using a No.4 round sable brush, outline the fruit and basket in dilute orange mixed from cadmium red and cadmium yellow.

3 ▲ Put in the dark tone Paint the pattern on the cloth in dilute burnt sienna. Mix a wash of raw umber and burnt sienna to complete the shadows on the fruit and basket. Suggest the basket texture with the brush's narrow edge.

2 ▲ Deepen the tone Paint the shadow on the basket and the dark areas on the fruit, using a 25mm (1in) flat brush. Add burnt sienna to the mixture and block in the background.

▼ The bright yellow support complements the paint colours and gives an overall golden glow to the finished picture.

TINTING PAPER WITH A MULTICOLOURED WASH

An interesting way of tinting paper is to use more than one colour. Choose colours that will become an integral part of the painting. Here, four bands of colour are washed across the paper to represent a sky tinged with pink, and a line of foliage reflected in water. A simple landscape is added, but this method would work equally well for a more complex scene.

1 ▲ **Lay the background** Working on a slightly tilted board and using a large, flat brush, paint the background in broad overlapping stripes of dilute cadmium yellow, ultramarine, cadmium red and sap green.

2 ▲ **Add grey** Allow the background to dry. Using dilute Payne's grey and a 25mm (1in) flat brush, paint ripples on the water and dab in clouds. Suggest trees and reflections with short vertical strokes.

◄ **All that is needed to finish off this simple impression of a landscape are minimal horizontal and vertical brush strokes, using Payne's grey over the sap green band.**

TINTING PAPER WITH A SINGLE WASH

If you think pure white paper will look too stark, a solution is to tint it with a toning pale colour before beginning to paint. In this watercolour sketch, the artist decided to tint the paper with a dilute blue wash, which provides a harmonious background for the buildings and figures all of which are overpainted in a darker tone of the same colour.

1 ▲ Tint the paper Using a large, flat brush and starting at the top of the paper, apply a dilute wash of ultramarine in broad, overlapping strokes. Work on a slightly tilted board.

2 ▲ Paint the buildings Allow the wash to dry. Using a No.4 round brush, paint the buildings in a stronger wash of ultramarine. Use the tip of the brush for the fine lines.

3 ▲ Fill in the foreground Finally, use the same colour to paint the fountain in the foreground and to add the figures as solid strokes of colour.

▲ **The pale blue tint harmonizes with the painted linework and, at the same time, adds substance to the background.**

Specialist papers

Bored with the same old cartridge and watercolour papers? Take your pick from a variety of surfaces from around the world.

Papers made from banana skins, rice and even tea leaves might sound unlikely supports for the artist. But these and many other exotic papers from countries all over the world can be used with almost any medium to give unusual and beautiful results.

There is a fascinating range of textures and surface patterns – from gossamer-like tissue made in Japan to the thick, chunky papers of India and Nepal. Many papers are still made by hand using traditional techniques.

Choosing a paper

Unlike conventional artists' supports, these papers are not necessarily made specifically for painting or drawing. They are also used by bookbinders and other craft workers. It is therefore important to make sure that a particular paper is suitable for your needs.

For example, some papers are very porous and need sealing with size so that the paint does not soak in. Size is available at good art stores and is simply brushed on to the paper and left to dry. Other papers, such as many Japanese ones and the Thai tissue paper overleaf, are quite fragile and will not withstand

robust drawing, wet washes or thick colour. It is often obvious by simply looking at and feeling the paper whether it will be up to the job. If you are not sure, do a test on a small sample of the paper.

There are also important aesthetic considerations. Some of the most striking papers are those in which real flowers, leaves and other recognizable objects are clearly visible. While these are often very beautiful in themselves, they are not necessarily suitable for

▲ Coloured inks work particularly well on khadi paper, as Elda Abramson's *Tulips* shows. The rough texture of the paper is visible through the transparent washes and seems to add vigour to the painting.

▼ There is a huge range of papers on the market, including khadi papers from India, Lotka papers from Nepal and Thailand, and Kozo papers from Japan.

KHADI AND TISSUE PAPERS

Among the best-known imported papers are the khadi papers from India. They are made from khadi, the handspun cotton yarn that has been produced in rural India for thousands of years. They are generally robust and take most media. Some of the best tissue papers come from Japan and Thailand (see bottom). These are often too fragile for drawing media and need to be handled with care.

PASTEL ON KHADI PAPER
This cold-pressed paper from Northern India is ideal for soft pastel. The paper is thick and card-like and the rough surface holds the pastel pigments well.

WATERCOLOUR ON THAILAND TISSUE
This flimsy, off-white paper is made from the lokta plant and is photographed here on a dark surface in order to show the fibres and mottled pattern. The surface is very absorbent and the watercolour washes bleed slightly, giving a soft edge and a blurred image.

artists because the decoration may be too dominant and can interfere with the drawn or painted image.

Hand-made papers

The character of a paper is determined by the manufacturing process and by the kind of fibrous plant material used to make the pulp. Additional materials are often introduced to add colour, texture and surface pattern.

The first manufactured paper was papyrus, made from the fibres of the papyrus reed that grew abundantly in Ancient Egypt. Papyrus is still produced and it is one paper that is guaranteed to last for centuries – papyrus scrolls have been found in Egyptian tombs dating from 2700BC! Today, however, it is expensive and difficult to source.

Other handmade papers are made from cotton or linen rag (which are literally off-cuts and seconds from the clothing industry) as well as various wood barks, mulberry wood, hemp and any other suitable fibres that can be pulped and pressed or moulded into sheets.

Delicate papers

The indigenous crops and trees determine the sort of papers made in each region. So papers from a particular country tend to be made from the same basic materials. For example, the delicate lokta papers from Nepal and Thailand are made from the bark of the lokta shrub which grows abundantly in the Himalayas and other regions, and Japanese kozo papers come from the inner fibres of the native kozo, a type of mulberry tree.

Added materials

In papers made from traditional cotton rag and natural fibre, the colour and texture comes from various materials added during the manufacturing process. These include banana leaf, recycled jute sacking, sugar cane and algae. The black specks found in some paper may well be recycled tea leaves, added after the workers' tea break! Brighter coloured papers are made by adding dyes to the paper pulp during manufacture.

Japanese papers

The range of Japanese papers is enormous. Many are made especially for painting, drawing and printmaking. Others are too fragile to be used in this way, but are wonderful for collage.

Decorative papers include the translucent ginwashi, which has delicate strands of short fibres embedded in each sheet; crumpled momi papers, which may be pearlized or flecked with real gold and silver; and the see-through lace papers, made by the falling-water process, which involves vigorously spraying each freshly made sheet of paper to create a distinctive lacy pattern.

Handmade paper from overseas is a comparatively recent arrival on the art scene. This is partly because a lot of imported paper comes from remote areas, and this used to make quality control and regular delivery difficult. Availability and uniformity could not be relied on and, with some exceptions, artists generally preferred machine-made products that were consistent, affordable and easy to obtain. During the last few decades, however, the picture has changed dramatically. Handmade paper from all over the world is now readily available and appreciated by artists for exactly those qualities that once made it unpopular – its distinctiveness and irregularity.

Swatches and sizes

Some imported papers can be found in general art shops; the more unusual ones are only available from specialist suppliers. The latter sometimes provide specimen swatches and offer a mail delivery service.

As they are often made especially for the international market, many papers are available in standard sizes from A2 to A5 as well as in several traditional paper sizes. Indian atlas, a khadi paper measuring approximately a metre by a metre and a half, is probably the largest available handmade paper in the world.

COTTON PAPERS

There are many papers made with cotton yarn and rag – what you see here is the tip of the iceberg! Seek out your own exotic papers and experiment to discover the exciting effects that can be achieved using your favourite colours and drawing tools. These papers can be used with most media – although many are not strong enough to support thickly applied oils or acrylics.

PEN AND WASH ON PAPER WITH HUSKS
Surprisingly, the pen nib rides smoothly over this irregular, textured paper – probably because the paper is very compact and the surface has a slight sheen.

GOUACHE ON BANANA FIBRE PAPER
Apply the gouache thickly to cover the slightly porous, rough surface of the paper. The paper takes the paint well and the natural beige colour enhances the bright pinks and reds of the painting.

ACRYLIC ON COTTON RAG PAPER
This off-white paper has an attractive, woven look and a rough surface. Acrylic can be applied directly on to the paper – however, for a large painting, it's best to seal the surface with size first.

COLOURED PENCILS ON ALGAE PAPER
It is hard to believe that the green, hair-like lines in this paper are actually algae. However, they complement the coloured pencil lines beautifully and the paper is easy to work on.

COLOURS

Colour is everywhere, and has a far greater effect on our psyche than most people realise. As an artist, you'll not only learn to see colours differently but also to use them for specific effects in your work. This section will help you understand the principles of colour theory and, on a practical level, how to mix shades from a basic palette of primaries.

The power of colour

Colour is the painter's most versatile tool. It has the power to excite, control space, create atmosphere, express emotion and represent the illusion of reality.

I t was not until after the invention of the camera in the mid-nineteenth century that artists recognized light as the prime factor in the way we see colour in the world around us. Before then, the 'local' colour was most often taken as the first consideration: sky is blue, grass is green – but is it that simple? If you look at the sky on a sunny day, it's much bluer overhead than it is on the horizon, where it is paler and also has some yellow in it. Colour is dependent upon light, and we need to understand how it works.

The theory of colour

White light (sunlight), passing through a raindrop, splits into the colours of the rainbow spectrum. When these are fanned into a circle to make the colour wheel (see overleaf), the principles of colour mixing can be seen. Red, yellow and blue are known as the primary colours: they are pure colours and cannot be mixed from any others. The other three (orange, green and violet), are called secondary colours because they are formed by an even mixture of their two immedi-

▲ Franz Marc's (1880–1916) *The Yellow Cow*, complete with blue patches and red foreground, makes the point that colour can be used to great effect expressively, as well as realistically.

ate primary neighbours in the circle.

This can be extended to make tertiary colours by mixing any of the primaries with either of its secondary neighbours. For example, blue and green will produce a colour generally called turquoise.

The colour wheel

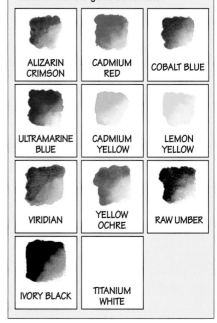

COOL COLOURS

BLUE

GREEN

VIOLET

YELLOW

RED

ORANGE

WARM COLOURS

The colours in one half of the wheel (red, orange, yellow) are specified as 'warm' and appear to advance from the page, while those in the other half (blue, violet and green) are 'cool' and seem to recede. This factor can be used in landscape painting for example, where trees in the distance can be made to recede by making them more blue-green than those in the foreground. Colours opposite each other on the colour wheel are described as complementary. Placed side by side they react against each other and fight to dominate the visual space. Artists use this to create vibrancy and contrast in pictures.

A BASIC PALETTE

There are certain colours which, when mixed together, can form the backbone of your art. The colours listed below are all good 'mixers' in any medium. If you have viridian, two blues and two yellows, you can mix most greens you are likely to need. Practise mixing pairs of all the colours without white.

Be careful when using black on its own, since it can 'deaden' a painting if overdone (remember, it is not really a colour!). Raw umber mixed with ultramarine is a good substitute.

ALIZARIN CRIMSON	CADMIUM RED	COBALT BLUE
ULTRAMARINE BLUE	CADMIUM YELLOW	LEMON YELLOW
VIRIDIAN	YELLOW OCHRE	RAW UMBER
IVORY BLACK	TITANIUM WHITE	

In fact mixed colours are often named after gemstones or flowers they resemble. These are the sort of labels you will see on tubes of paint in an art shop.

Black and white

You will notice that the circle does not contain either black or white. When light falls on an object, the object will absorb some of its wavelengths and bounce back others which make up the colour we see. Black soaks them all up and white bounces them all back, so black is the absence of any colour and white is all the colours rolled into one.

Brown

And what of brown? An object seen as brown is absorbing very few of the spectrum of light wavelengths (just those at each end of the rainbow) and bouncing all the others back. By mixing the three primaries together or the three secondaries in different proportions, a whole range of browns can be made.

Warm versus cool

Colour temperature is also part of the equation (see the colour wheel), while colour can also be said to be opaque or transparent, dark or light, translucent or impasto, flat or textured, matt or gloss, vibrant or dull.

► Claude Monet (1840–1926) used colour to convey passing impressions of light and atmosphere – in this case a group of waterlilies which seem to dissolve into the water around them.

Pick and mix

▼ Seurat's (1859–91) pointillist technique can be seen in his painting *Young Woman Powdering Herself*. Tiny dots of paint mingle to create myriad subtle colours.

Developing skills in colour mixing takes practice and familiarity with your preferred medium, but it is vital if you want to interpret a subject effectively.

One of the most important concepts to grasp when learning to paint is that the tonal range of the paint palette is nowhere near as broad as that of natural light. The brightest and lightest colour you can put down on paper is pure white, but this can never match the intensity and brightness of white light. There is a similar challenge when trying to match the depth of dark tones and colours.

Working order

In practical terms, if you are painting in oils, it is best to start with the darker colours and gradually work up to the lighter ones. Keep in mind that the brightest object in the picture cannot be brighter than pure white.

If you are using watercolours, remember that the lightest areas are created by leaving the paper unpainted. In contrast to oils, you should put in the darkest tones and colours last.

Mix and match

Mixing colour to try and match what you see is a subtle process. You will need to observe your subject carefully and make small adjustments to represent the 'local' colour accurately. As you build up your picture, you might want to mix colours that are tonally lighter or darker, warmer or cooler, more intense or softer and 'muted'. You might also choose to make the colours more transparent or opaque.

Grass greens

Try mixing some colours to represent a stretch of grass. Mix a green using ultramarine and cadmium yellow as a base. For the shadowed areas, you could add more blue to lower the tone and make a cooler green. Or, for a warmer shade, you could add one of the umbers.

Where the grass is lighter, you might mix in some lemon yellow and perhaps a little white to raise the tone; but you may find that the colour has now lost its 'greenness'. In this case, it may be better to start again, using viridian mixed with cadmium yellow or lemon yellow as an alternative base.

With two yellows and two blues plus viridian, there are countless combinations that make a basic green. Even so, if you are working with a limited palette, it is not always possible to mix a perfect match. Even if you added another twenty colours, some shades might still not be achievable. The best you can aim for is what is called a 'visual equivalent' – a range of tones and shades of a given colour (sometimes described as colour 'values') that is broadly parallel to what you see in reality.

Optical mixing

There are further ways of creating different colours, other than adding extra shades to a basic colour. The most notable of

▲ **Degas (1834–1917) relied on optical mixing in many of his pastels, particularly in his nude studies. In this painting, *After the Bath*, the pastel marks in different colours merge visually to produce the convincing flesh tones.**

these is to place small spots of different colours close together, so that when viewed from a distance they are seen by the eye as a single colour – an effect called 'optical mixing'.

This technique, generally known as 'pointillism', was developed by Georges Seurat, a nineteenth-century French painter. He and his followers used only the colours of the spectrum plus white. By carefully intermingling painted dots of these colours, they found that they could create innumerable colours and tones, provided that the viewer stood an appropriate distance away so that the optical mixing process could take place.

Limited technique

The pointillist technique has its limitations. If it is used for a small painting, the dots have to be very tiny so the desired effect is achieved when the painting is viewed close-up. Also, being a rather 'scientific' approach, it is not particularly expressive or personal.

Glazing and scumbling

Paint used thinly can be transparent, allowing the colours underneath to show through. This enables another type of optical mixing, called 'glazing', to take place. Dark colours are usually laid over lighter ones once they are dry (for example, blue can be laid over yellow to make

FINDING THE PERFECT MATCH

This exercise suggests how you can practise mixing paints to match specific colours as exactly as possible.

Collect together some scraps of different coloured papers, preferably plain rather than patterned. Make sure you include two or three scraps torn from printed paper such as wrapping paper, postcards or magazines. Other papers you could use include sugar paper, copying paper or letter paper. A couple of your pieces of paper should be in different shades of white.

Acrylic paint is the best medium to use for this exercise. You can use oil paints, but the drying time will slow down your progress.

1 Make a collage Tear or cut some random shapes from your selection of papers and stick them down on the left-hand side of an A3 sheet to make a small, abstract collage. Overlap the shapes, but don't make the collage too complicated.

2 Match the colours Now paint a version of the collage on the right-hand side of the paper, trying to match the colours (and shapes) you see as exactly as you can. Notice that pastel shades are much easier to match than raw, pure colours, especially those produced by printing inks. Remember, too, that the appearance of colours can be changed by those placed next to them.

green). The results are less easy to control than with direct mixing, but it is worth practising the technique to see the effects that can be achieved.

The opposite of glazing is 'scumbling'. Here, an opaque colour (usually containing some white) is put over a darker one in broken patches by rolling the brush. This allows the darker colour to show through and optically mix with the lighter one.

▼ **Camille Pissaro (1831–1903), like some of the other Impressionists, began using small brush strokes of various colours placed next to each other in an attempt to make them more vibrant. This is shown to great effect in his oil painting *The Flood at Eragny*.**

White on white

Drawing white objects against a white background will help you to develop your skill in using shading to render shape and volume.

This all-white still life may seem a daunting prospect at first, but you will find it a worthwhile exercise in both observation and the use of tone. It is important that the objects you are painting are strongly lit from one side so that they cast dark shadows in a single direction only; this simplifies the composition and allows the white flowers and china objects to stand out against the background.

Softer, subtler shadows on the rounded objects themselves convey their shape and also differentiate them from the white fabric backdrop.

Grading shadows

You will discover how to give a sense of depth to your picture by grading the shadows from dark – in the folds of the cloth behind the vase and on the leaves of the tulips – to light in the foreground. Accurately judging the density of the shading will help your composition by making the china objects 'sit' realistically on the horizontal surface.

You will find darker shadows can be drawn most successfully with a soft 4B graphite pencil. You should switch to a B pencil for finer details, such as the tulip petals.

Negative shapes

By shading the background you create dark positive shapes, which form light negative ones in front of them. You will find the final effect is much more convincingly three-dimensional than if you give each object a hard black outline.

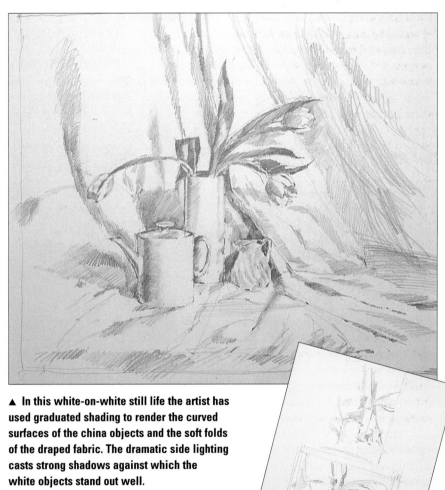

▲ In this white-on-white still life the artist has used graduated shading to render the curved surfaces of the china objects and the soft folds of the draped fabric. The dramatic side lighting casts strong shadows against which the white objects stand out well.

YOU WILL NEED

Sheet of cartridge paper

Graphite pencils: 4B and B

Putty rubber

▶ It's worth making a couple of preliminary thumbnail sketches to decide on the best format for your picture. Here, the artist has chosen a landscape image to show more of the fabric folds, which help to balance the composition.

FIRST STEPS

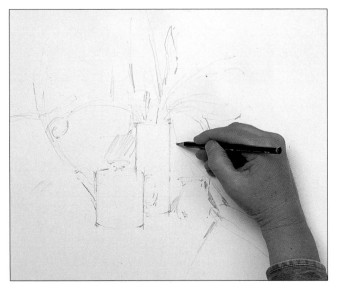

EXPERT ADVICE
Sharpening your pencils

It is best to use a craft knife rather than a pencil sharpener to sharpen your drawing pencils. In this way not only will you make a sharp tip but you can bare a long expanse of lead and use the side of it for shading.

1 ▲ Sketch in the shapes Lightly sketch in outlines of the teapot, vase and jug to establish their positions in relation to each other. Use light lines to indicate the edges of the shadow areas and the shapes of the tulips. Use the 4B pencil, which is easy to rub out, as these lines will be removed later.

HOW TO DEVELOP THE DRAWING

Pause to look at your drawing so far: all the elements are in place and the relative areas of light and dark have been indicated. Notice how the background shadows have created the outlines of the china objects as negative shapes. Now you can go on to work on the details.

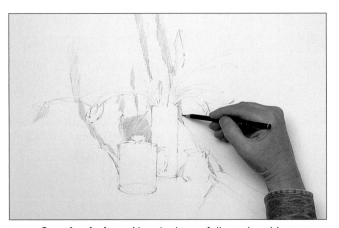

2 ▲ Start the shadows Next look carefully at the objects to see where the strongest shadows fall. Start blocking these in, using the side of the 4B pencil lead to give a dark, soft effect. Begin with the area behind the teapot, then render the shadows cast by the flowers and the fabric folds.

3 ▶ Fill in the shadows Continue filling in the background shadows. Using the tip of the pencil, draw the shadow made by the teapot with soft, even hatching strokes, then fill in the dark area between the vase and jug. Hold your pencil well away from the lead tip so that you can move your hand freely.

4 ▲ Shade the objects Start shading the objects themselves to render their rounded surfaces. Change to the B pencil, as you want this shading to be lighter and finer than the background shadows. To achieve a straight edge for the shadow on the vase, mask off the left edge with a piece of paper while shading. This will leave a narrow white strip of unmarked paper, representing the band of light (reflected from the white fabric) on the edge of the vase.

5 ▼ Strengthen the shadows Add shading to the teapot and jug, making this stronger on the left, furthest from the light source, to give the objects a realistically rounded appearance. Change back to the 4B pencil and continue defining the jug by strengthening the shadow around it.

6 ▶ Draw the leaves Now start working on the tulips. Begin with the leaves: parts of them are tonally darker than the background shadows, so shade these more heavily.

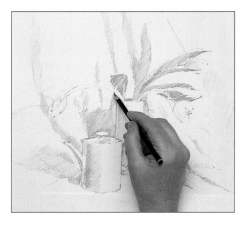

7 ▼ Adjust the balance of tones Strengthen the background shadow behind the teapot lid. Whenever you change one element in your picture, always stop to look at the whole composition, to make sure the relationship of tones and shapes is still harmonious.

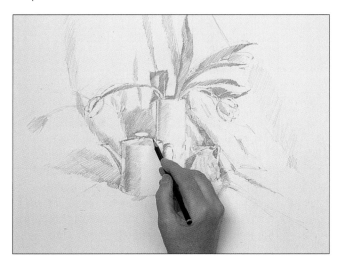

8 ▲ Draw the flowers Draw the flower heads with the B pencil to achieve more delicate shading. Remember to keep your pencil well sharpened so that you have a fine point to work with.

9 ▲ Shade in the folds Finally, add a little more shading to the shadows in the folds of the fabric to diffuse the edges and give them a gently rounded shape, remembering to use the edge of your pencil. This completes the picture, but if you feel you would like to develop it further, you could draw some more of the softly folded fabric.

A FEW STEPS FURTHER

You can extend your drawing by adding more folds to the foreground and to the right of the picture. This will help frame the objects and make a pleasing composition. It will also help to define the horizontal surface on which the china objects stand, locating them in space and giving them extra solidity.

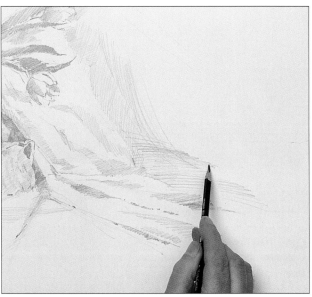

10 ▲ Add more folds Add shading to represent the folds in the fabric in the foreground. Use the 4B pencil, but remember to keep the shading very light as the shadows are much paler in this area than in the background.

11 ▲ Enlarge the picture area Extend the picture to the right by adding shading to show where the folds of fabric 'break' from the vertical to the horizontal plane. This will help to develop the perspective of your picture.

TROUBLE SHOOTER

CORRECTING HIGHLIGHTS WITH A PUTTY RUBBER

The lightest tones in this drawing are created by letting the white paper show through. If you shade over an area and then decide it should have a highlight, use a putty rubber to erase the pencil marks. One of the advantages of this type of eraser is that it can be moulded to a fine point, enabling you to make adjustments very accurately.

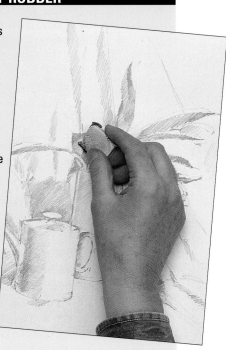

12 ▲ Indicate the table edge Continue to develop the folds to the right of the picture. Next add a line of shading along the bottom of the picture to indicate where the fabric falls over the edge of the table. This will help define the edge of the picture and enhance its three-dimensional effect.

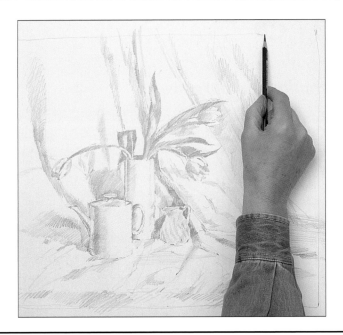

13 ◄ **'Frame' the picture** Use the putty rubber to remove any of the early construction lines that are still visible and clean up the paper. Now the picture is finished, you can 'frame' it by drawing a pencil line to confirm the composition and define the area you are including. This line would be the guide for a mount if you wanted to mount and frame your picture. Note that the artist has deliberately cut off the shadow of the flower-head on the left and some of the folds on the far right. You do not have to include every element of the picture; often you can improve the composition by cropping off details at the edges.

THE FINISHED PICTURE

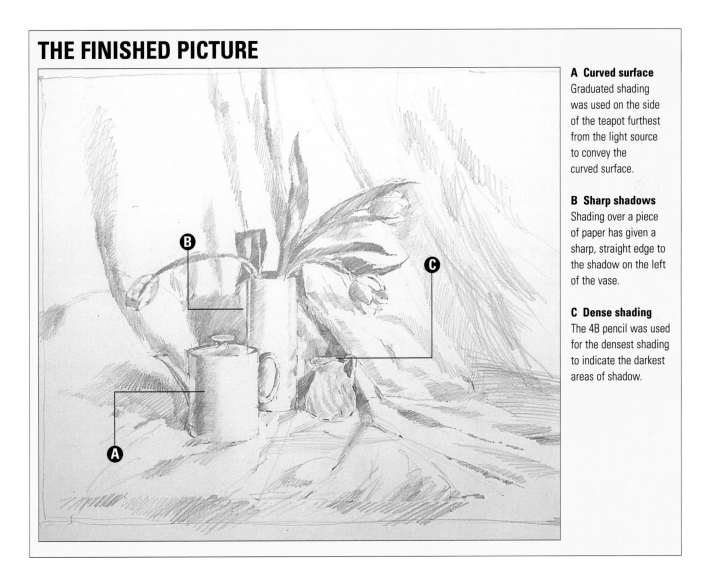

A Curved surface
Graduated shading was used on the side of the teapot furthest from the light source to convey the curved surface.

B Sharp shadows
Shading over a piece of paper has given a sharp, straight edge to the shadow on the left of the vase.

C Dense shading
The 4B pencil was used for the densest shading to indicate the darkest areas of shadow.

Mixing orange

In the first of three sections covering the secondary colours, we look at the secrets behind rendering a variety of oranges.

The basic rules of colour mixing are taught in primary school. There, painstakingly scribbling one coloured pencil over another, we discovered that red and yellow make orange. Easy!

As orange is a secondary colour, it can be mixed very simply by combining the two primary colours next to it on the colour wheel – red and yellow. In terms of paint, the equivalents of these primaries are cadmium red and cadmium yellow.

The range of oranges

However, cadmium red and cadmium yellow alone will probably not provide you with all the oranges needed for painting a wide range of subjects. Instead, you should experiment with the many other reds and yellows available to the artist.

We tend to associate orange with the bright, acidic colour of the fruit – but think also of the variety of mellow tints in autumn leaves or the earthy colours of sand and brickwork. As this still life arrangement shows, 'orange' is a very general label used to describe a wide range of colours.

Experimental mixing

Depending on the brand and type of paint, there are up to 20 yellows on a manufacturer's colour chart. Counting the earth colours, the yellows include lemon, cadmium yellow, chrome yellow, aurora, aureolin, Naples yellow and Indian yellow, as well as yellow ochre and raw sienna. The range of reds is equally wide and includes cadmium red, vermilion, scarlet, rose madder, permanent rose, alizarin, Venetian red, Mars red and Indian red.

In theory, by combining every available yellow with every available red, you

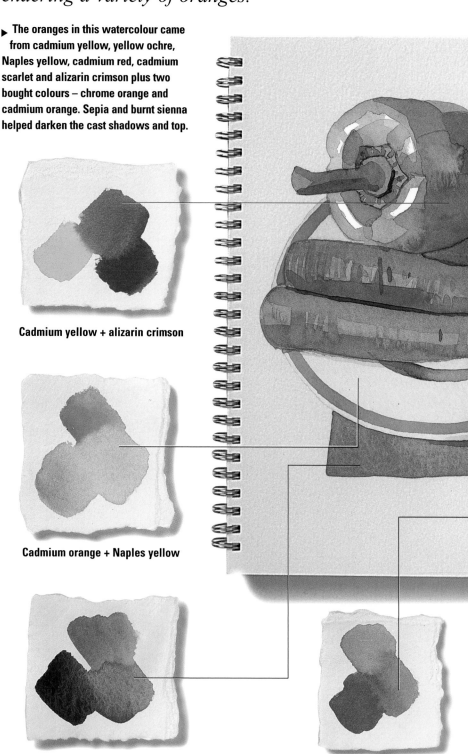

▶ The oranges in this watercolour came from cadmium yellow, yellow ochre, Naples yellow, cadmium red, cadmium scarlet and alizarin crimson plus two bought colours – chrome orange and cadmium orange. Sepia and burnt sienna helped darken the cast shadows and top.

Cadmium yellow + alizarin crimson

Cadmium orange + Naples yellow

Yellow ochre + burnt sienna

Cadmium orange + cadmium red

**Cadmium orange +
yellow ochre**

Chrome orange

**Sepia + cadmium yellow +
cadmium red**

Cadmium orange

Cadmium scarlet + cadmium orange

could have a palette of hundreds of different oranges at your fingertips. In reality, many of these mixes are so similar that you can't differentiate between them. And as no artist is likely to need such a range of oranges, confine your mixing experiments to the yellows and reds normally on your palette.

Practical mixtures

On the working palette of almost any painter you will find at least two or three reds and two or three yellows. Typically, these will be: a bright yellow, usually cadmium; an earthy yellow such as yellow ochre or raw sienna; and also a cooler colour, for instance lemon. In the painting on the left, the artist chose Naples as the cooler yellow because it is very effective at neutralizing, or 'knocking back', a strong red or orange.

The same palette will probably also contain cadmium red and a cool red such as alizarin crimson. You might also add a third red that falls somewhere between them in colour temperature – for example, cadmium scarlet. A warm earth colour, such as Venetian red, Indian red or burnt sienna, is also useful.

Note that by varying the proportions of any mixture you will get a different result. For example, cadmium red and cadmium yellow will produce a range of results from yellowish-orange to deep reddish-orange.

Bought colours

In addition to those colours you can mix yourself, there are also a few manufactured oranges. The most common are cadmium and chrome orange, both of which are strong and bright. The former is slightly lighter but considered to be more permanent.

A bought orange is by no means essential. However, it can also provide a consistent starting point for certain standard mixtures. For example, portrait and figure painters commonly use orange mixed with white as a pale flesh tone.

Note that mixing bright yellow with bright red sometimes produces a slightly duller orange than you would expect. To avoid this, try to choose pigments with a degree of natural transparency. For example, yellow mixed with alizarin crimson will give you a brighter orange than when mixed with cadmium red, which is a more opaque pigment.

Mixing green

By mixing and modifying the manufacturers' greens it is possible to expand your palette well beyond the range available otherwise.

For many artists – especially those interested in the natural world – green is probably the most important colour on the palette. Rural landscapes, flowers and plants, as well as many still-life subjects, call for a variety of greens.

A common misconception
However, the great versatility of the colour green is often underestimated. Beginners sometimes believe that, because green is mixed from blue and yellow, all things green must therefore be painted from equal mixtures of these two colours.

Many first attempts at landscape painting are disappointing for this reason – simply because the artist has failed to distinguish between the different greens in the subject.

Experiment first
One way to overcome this difficulty is to experiment with green mixtures before starting to paint. Look at the subject and pick out as many different greens as you can. Where there are highlights and shadows on a green area, take note of the light and dark tones these create.

Try your hand at mixing the greens you have detected on a separate sheet of paper. The process will initially be one of trial and error, but you will be surprised at the extraordinary range that can be achieved by mixing and modifying the colours on a very limited palette.

Mixing greens
Start by exploring the possibilities of a pair of colours, and see how many different shades of green you can get. For instance, by varying the proportions of ultramarine and cadmium lemon, you can obtain colours ranging from lime green to deep blue-green. Repeat the experiment, substituting yellow ochre for lemon yellow, and you will create an equally varied range extending from golden green to deep olive.

Modifying a green
Bought greens are also useful – in this fruit-and-vegetable still life, the artist made full use of them. However, they can be very strident – so more often than not you'll need to modify them with other colours. Again, it is useful to experiment and to extend your repertoire before

▶ Although it's possible to obtain greens by mixing blues and yellows, it's often best to use bought greens and, where necessary, modify these with other colours.

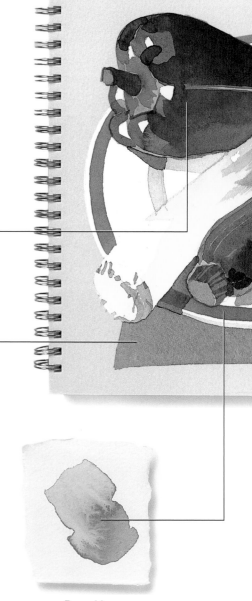

Payne's grey + sap green

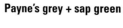

Payne's grey + terre verte

Emerald green

Viridian   **Ultramarine + terre verte**

Cadmium lemon + sap green   **Yellow ochre + emerald green**   **Olive green**

painting. Choose a strong shade, such as emerald, viridian or sap green, and make some test samples. Modify the tone by adding varying amounts of a neutral colour such as raw umber or Payne's grey. This will give you a choice of rich and interesting dark greens. Avoid using black as this can deaden the colour.

Alternatively, any green can be modified or toned down by adding a little of its complementary – red. Try using different reds in varying quantities to produce a range of muted greens and neutrals.

Bought greens

Five manufactured greens were used in this painting. If you have not used these pigments before, now is the opportunity to try out the new colours.

● **Emerald green** is more brilliant than any green you could mix yourself. It is useful for capturing man-made colours, such as the bright green band around the plate here. The clear emerald stands out beautifully from the natural greens of the fruits and vegetables.

● **Terre verte** is the oldest known green. Made from natural earth pigments, it works well when painting vegetation and other organic forms. Here, it is used with a little ultramarine for the blue-green broccoli. The table top and shadows are painted in a mixture of terre verte and Payne's grey to create a cool, neutral and unobtrusive background.

● **Olive green** varies depending on the manufacturer, but it is generally a muted natural green, good for foliage and vegetation. Here, it is used with plenty of water to put a glaze on the shadowed side of the rosy apple.

● **Viridian** is very powerful and needs careful handling. It can easily take over and dominate your picture. Used in small quantities and modified by other colours, it is a useful ingredient in mixtures. Otherwise, viridian is best restricted to specific areas. Here, it is mixed with varying amounts of water for the light, medium and dark tones of green on the leaves of the leek.

● **Sap green** is a warm, leafy green and is often used for painting grass and foliage, especially in spring. Here, it is mixed with cadmium lemon for the green apple and with Payne's grey for the dark green pepper.

Mixing purple

Discover how to create rich variations on a theme by mixing bought purples with blues, reds and neutrals.

Purple is rare in nature. The earliest purple pigment came from the shells of the 'purpura', a large whelk found on the shores of the Mediterranean. The Phoenicians are reputed to have ground several million purpura shells to make enough purple to dye their emperor's clothes. The colour they used was known as 'royal purple' and it is still produced today.

Nowadays, purple is a far more accessible colour, but even today real purple pigments are comparatively few in number. The majority of manufactured purples and violets are actually combinations of existing blues and reds.

Purple mixtures

Many artists find it unnecessary to buy ready-mixed purple. Instead, they prefer to make their own by mixing various blues and reds to get the colour they need. Fortunately, it is possible to mix a range of good purples yourself. The brightest of these are achieved by using a cool red, such as alizarin crimson, rose madder or magenta. The addition of white to these mixtures will give various shades of mauve and violet.

If you have ever tried to mix purple using cadmium red, you will know that the result is not a bright colour at all, but a muted brownish-purple. This is because cadmium red contains yellow, which gives the mixture a brown bias.

Mix your own

To discover the potential of the colours on your basic palette, try making some simple two-colour mixtures. Start with alizarin crimson and ultramarine, combining these colours in equal proportions. The result will be a strong, bright purple.

By varying the proportions of the ultramarine and alizarin crimson in the mixture, you can then go on to produce a range of purples with either a red or a blue bias.

Do some more tests, this time substituting cerulean blue for ultramarine. Because cerulean is a cool, pale blue, the resulting purple will be less bright and slightly more opaque.

It is worth repeating similar experiments, using a number of different blues and reds. The resulting mixtures will

▶ **The purples in this still life include bought colours used alone and mixed with reds, blues and neutrals (such as Payne's grey or raw umber). Don't forget to try mixing red and blue as well – such as the alizarin crimson and Prussian blue used here.**

Winsor violet + Payne's grey

Winsor violet + phthalo blue

Mauve

Winsor violet + raw umber

Winsor violet

**Cadmium scarlet +
violet carmine**

**Purple madder alizarin +
Winsor violet**

**Alizarin crimson +
Prussian blue**

vary enormously and not all of them will be purple. Some will be brown or muddy grey. Only by trial and error is it possible to have control over your palette and the colours it can produce.

Shadow colours

Purple is frequently used for painting shadows. If you look carefully at those that initially appear to be grey or brown, you will notice that they often contain traces of purple and violet. In this water-colour still life, the thrown shadows are mixed from the purples and violets used on the fruit and vegetables, toned down with neutral colours, such as Payne's grey or raw umber.

You can try mixing your own shadow colours by adding raw umber, Payne's grey or another neutral to any of the purples and violets below. Adding a little of their complementary colour, yellow, can also tone down purple and violet.

Bought purples

Our artist chose four manufactured purples for this still life, modifying these to acquire all the colours needed for painting the fruit and vegetables:

● **Mauve** may have a red or blue bias, depending on the manufacturer. The mauve used for the plate in this painting has a definite red tinge and stands out distinctly from the other colours. It is used here as a dilute wash.

● **Winsor violet** is a transparent colour with a powerful staining capacity. A little goes a long way, so use it sparingly. It is shown here unmixed; modified with Payne's grey and phthalo blue to obtain cool purples; and mixed with raw umber to create the neutral tone of the table top.

● **Purple madder alizarin** is a rich nat-ural colour somewhere between brown and purple. It is popular with landscape artists for painting the warm tones of foliage and trees. Purple madder alizarin is mixed with a little Winsor violet for the dark shadow on the persimmon fruit.

● **Violet carmine** is a clear, transparent purple, used here with cadmium scarlet to depict the cool orange-violet of the persimmon fruit.

Cobalt violet is another bought purple you could try. It is not used here but it provides an attractive warmish purple that cannot be mixed from other colours.

▲ This 1871 painting by James Abbott McNeill Whistler (1834–1903) is often called *Portrait of the Artist's Mother,* but Whistler actually gave it the title *Arrangement in Grey and Black No.1*. He explores the many subtle shades within his chosen limited range, and at the same time produces an unusual but moving portrait.

Mixing greys

You might think that grey is simply a mixture of black and white,
but you'll find that greys are actually much more subtle than that.

Making grey is not just a matter of mixing black and white. A painting with this type of grey in it would become lifeless because the grey would really be a tone, not a colour. This is valid in a monochrome work where only black and white are used, but for colour painting you will be dealing with a more exciting range of greys.

So what exactly is grey? It is important to remember that black is not a colour, but the absence of colour – in other words, the absence of light. So a grey object should be described as 'dark white' rather than 'light black', because you can't actually see black.

This concept is easier to understand if you look at some white objects placed in strong natural light or against a white window frame. Away from the light, the shadowed areas could be described as grey, and on a curved form it is immediately noticeable that there is more than one shade of grey. In addition, because the white colours are likely to be

▶ In *Eleven a.m.* by Edward Hopper (1882–1967), dark and mid-toned greys on the walls and furnishings of this interior contrast with the pale grey shadows on the white skin of the naked woman. The overall greyness of the room contributes to the atmosphere of solitude in the painting.

slightly different, you will see that there is also more than one *colour* of grey. This variety of grey colours might be exaggerated by colours reflected from the surroundings and the colour of the light source. Grey shadows are similarly affected (see pages 97–98). So, if you were trying to paint all these possible greys, you would struggle to be accurate using only black and white.

Mixing greys

Distinguishing subtle colour changes (hues) in greys takes practice, and a little colour theory might help here. Each of the primary colours (red, blue and yellow) is neutralized by its complementary colour (green, orange and violet). If you mix a primary colour with its complementary in varying quantities, shades of brown and grey will emerge.

Try the exercise on the right to experiment with mixing a range of greys using various combinations of warm and cool blues and reds. Once you have tried this, do the same exercise using blue and yellow pairs instead of blue and red pairs – this will provide a range of greens, the cool and warm primary mixes giving 'greyer' greens. Adding a

MIXING GREYS

Try the following experiment on a white painting surface, using oils or acrylic paint. Mix two small dabs of each pair of primary colours listed below, then mix in small touches of each of the grey-making yellows in the last column to make warm and cool greys.

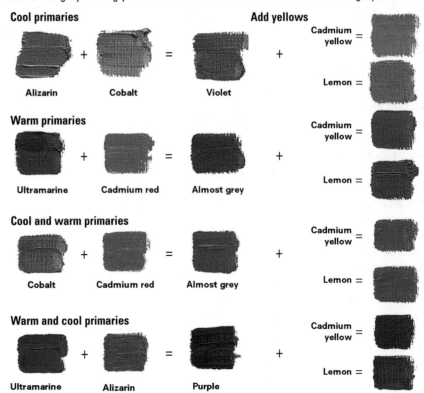

Cool primaries

Alizarin + Cobalt = Violet

Add yellows

+ Cadmium yellow =

Lemon =

Warm primaries

Ultramarine + Cadmium red = Almost grey

+ Cadmium yellow =

Lemon =

Cool and warm primaries

Cobalt + Cadmium red = Almost grey

+ Cadmium yellow =

Lemon =

Warm and cool primaries

Ultramarine + Alizarin = Purple

+ Cadmium yellow =

Lemon =

little extra of either of the two blues (warm or cold) to any of the above colour combinations will add to their 'greyness'. You should be able to make at least eight discernably different greys, from warm brownish greys through the more neutral green-greys to cool blue-violet greys.

Tones

The addition of white will, of course, give lighter shades of each of these greys. To darken them, you don't need to use black – try adding a mix of raw umber (and/or burnt umber) and ultramarine or viridian. This will affect the colour of the grey as well as the tone, but more greys will be discovered! Greys are very useful in painting landscapes, which often have more green-greys in them than actual greens. Notice, too, how often greys occur in interiors.

▼ **The Italian painter Georgio Morandi (1890–1964) exploits the variations of the colour grey in his series of mystical still life paintings – below is *Still Life* (1946). The soft neutral hues give a feeling of tranquility.**

Exploring a range of greys

Gather together a range of white and perhaps a few grey objects. Choose some different whites – enamel, for example, is usually bluer than china, which tends to be more creamy in colour.

1 Set up a still life Place the items on white, grey or even black paper against a white painted wall in a strong light by a window.

2 Make a painting Look hard at the objects to work out the colour bias of the different greys – are they greenish, blueish or pinkish? Start painting, using the pure colour greys you found in the mixing exercise on the previous page. Add white or darker colours (no black) to adjust tones.

3 Discover the greys When the painting is dry, take a strip of white paper and make half a dozen holes in it about 1cm (⅜in) across and 5cm (2in) apart. Move this around over the surface of the painting and you'll discover how many different colours of grey you have made.

Colour in shadow

Shadows are rarely black or solid. They are full of complex colour and light reflected from surrounding surfaces.

When you look carefully at shadows, you will generally find that they are neither black nor opaque. Their tone and colour, and the quality of their edges, vary depending on the direction and intensity of the light source. The more you study shadows, the more varied, nebulous and complex they appear. While some are crisply defined and velvety dark, others are vibrant and suffused with luminous colour, or barely discernable at all.

In painting you will come across two types of shadow: cast shadow and shading. A cast shadow is the area of darkness projected by an object, either on to the surface it is sitting on, or on to the other objects and surfaces nearby. Shading is the area of darkness on an opaque object that you can see on the side facing away from the light source.

Graded shading

The gradations of shading around an object help us to understand and model its form, while cast shadows are useful in painting because they define the surface on which an object is placed. In landscape painting, shadows provide clues to the position of the sun, the time of day and even the season of the year.

In the nineteenth century, there was an awakening of interest in the theory of colour. The Director of Dyeing at the Gobelins tapestry workshop near Paris, Michel-Eugène Chevreul (1786–1889),

▲ Twelve of Monet's haystack studies show a winter setting. In *Haystacks: Snow Effect* (1891) he has painted cool blue shadows, creating a chilly scene in spite of the warmer tones of the sun-tinged snow.

discovered two phenomena involving complementary colours – simultaneous contrast and successive contrast. These effects are concerned with the ways in which different colours affect each other when placed side by side.

Impressionist shadows

The Impressionists painted outdoors, working directly from the subject. They sought to create a spontaneous and authentic rendering of the world by carefully observing and replicating the effect of natural light on objects.

They noticed how colours appeared to 'dance' from one area to another as they were reflected from adjacent surfaces. With an understanding of Chevreul's theories, they were able to see that the complementary colour of an object was present in its shadow, together with reflected colours. By including the complementary, the Impressionists were able to enliven their shadows so that they became as

Shadows in art

• There are no shadows or gradations of tone in ancient Egyptian wall paintings or on Greek vase painting.

• Leonardo da Vinci (1452—1519) disapproved of harsh shadows, exploiting a technique known as *sfumato* to achieve subtle transitions between one tone or colour and another. He made analytical drawings of light falling on objects to aid his understanding of shadows.

• In the seventeenth century, Caravaggio (1573—1610) and his followers favoured stark realism and the heightened drama of sharply defined shadows

• Cast shadows were often used by the Old Masters to create optical illusions. By carefully rendering the shadows on columns and niches, they were able to deceive the viewer into thinking that they were seeing a three-dimensional surface.

• In Japanese art, shadows were usually ignored because they interfered with the clarity of the image and the narrative.

• In the nineteenth century, the Fauves dispensed with shadow and shading in order to focus on pure colour and decorative surface.

• The Cubists deliberately distorted and exaggerated shadows to create an ambiguous image.

▲ In *Haystacks at Sunset, Frosty Weather* (1891) Monet has created a scene that is suffused with a rosy glow from the setting sun; the dappled shadows in the foreground are a soft grey.

vibrant as other parts of the painting. Shadows in Impressionist paintings are complex areas of broken and layered colour. Their luminosity mirrors the complexity of natural light.

Snow scenes

Coloured shadows are a particularly important feature of Impressionist paintings of sunlit snow scenes. The colour in these shadows can be very complex indeed, including several different tones, reflections from nearby objects and the reflected blue of the sky. The German romantic poet, Johann Wolfgang Goethe (1749–1832) published a book entitled *The Theory of Colour*, in which he describes the ever-changing colours of shadows on snow: 'During the day, owing to the yellowish hue of snow, shadows tending to violet had already been observable; these might now be pronounced decidedly blue, as the illuminated parts exhibited a yellow deepening to orange. But as the sun was about to set, and the rays began to diffuse a most beautiful red colour over the scene around me, the shadow colour changed to a green, in lightness to be compared to a sea-green, in beauty to the green of the emerald.'

In summer landscapes, the Impressionists used purplish-reds for the shadows of trees, and muted violets for the shadows of rocks or shadows falling across

dusty roads. The famous artist Claude Monet (1840–1926) explored the colours of light and shadows in his series paintings. The first of these was the *Haystacks* or *Grain Stacks* series, which he began in 1890.

Monet would go out to paint in the early morning or just before sunset, taking paints, easels and several partially completed canvases, often carrying his equipment in a wheelbarrow. He would work first on one canvas, then on another as the light changed, finding the canvas that most resembled the scene in front of him. In this way, he was able to record precise shifts of light and tone, and subtle nances of colour throughout the day and through the seasons. He was trying 'to convey the weather, the atmosphere and the general mood'.

You can use the discoveries of Monet and his fellow Impressionists in your own work. When painting a subject, study the shadows with care, looking for reflected colour and for the complementaries in them. Try exaggerating these phenomna to add vigour to your work.

Colours for skies

When you've perfected the sky, your whole landscape will come together – so it's well worth practising to get it right.

▲ **This atmospheric sketch in oils,** *Sky Study, Clouds,* **is the result of one of Constable's numerous 'skying' expeditions. He believed that skies were supremely important, painting them again and again.**

Trying to capture the ever-changing moods of the sky seems rather daunting at first – where do you start? The sky changes constantly, as the sun rises and sets and as atmospheric effects such as clouds, rain and mist move across it. But if you watch the sky regularly and make notes, practise using different media and familiarize yourself with colours and techniques, you'll soon have the confidence you need to render skies skilfully and convincingly.

Sky sketches

The great landscape painter John Constable (1776–1837) sketched the sky constantly, working in oils directly from the subject – a process he called 'skying'. On 23 October 1821, Constable wrote to his friend Archdeacon Fisher, emphasiz-ing the importance of the sky in land-scape painting: 'That landscape painter who does not make his skies a very material part of his composition, neg-lects to avail himself of one of his greatest aids.... The sky is the source of light in nature, and governs everything.'

Follow Constable's example and study the sky as often as you can. Make notes about the location, time of day, season and weather conditions. This process will help you to understand what you are seeing when on location, and will enable you to reproduce sky effects in your work.

Sky relationships

The sky is the backcloth to the land-scape and should relate logically to the rest of the painting. If the sky is bright blue, the landscape should be sunny. Think about where the sun is and create shadows that are appropriate: small or non-existent if the sun is overhead, long and clearly defined if the sun is lower in the sky. If the sky is overcast and leaden, the tones in the landscape will be muted and shadows absent or indistinct.

Linking sky to landscape

A toned ground laid over the entire support will subtly modify the sky and the landscape and pull the two areas together. If you add tiny dabs of sky

colour to the landscape, as delicate touches or highlights, this will help to mirror the way in which light is constantly reflected from one area to another in nature.

The colour of the sky

The colour and brightness of the sky depends on factors such as the amount of cloud cover present, the quantities of dust and water droplets in the air, and the position and strength of the sun. The sky is at its deepest blue between showers of rain, while on a beautiful summer's day it is often bright but not very blue because of the dust particles in the air.

To check the precise colour and tone of the sky, hold something blue or white up to it. You will find that generally the sky is brightest and whitest close to the sun, and that it often becomes paler again as it approaches the horizon.

The way you reproduce the sky will depend very much on the medium you are using and the style of your painting. In a cloudless sky, you need subtle gradations of colour and tone. You can achieve this with watercolours by laying a graduated wash, or with oils by work-

▲ A range of greys mingle with browns in this Constable study; the paint was applied loosely and the ground shows through.

ing wet-on-wet to create subtle blendings. You can create skies of great depth and luminosity by applying layers of glazed and scumbled colour. You can even use a rich impasto, applying and smearing the paint with a knife – a painting such as the well-known *Starry Night* by Vincent Van Gogh demonstrates the truly dramatic potential of the impasto technique for skies.

Special effects

Sunrise, sunset and special effects, such as rainbows, provide colourful spectacles – and each occasion is different. At sunrise and sunset, the sky is suffused with reds, oranges and yellows, which flow gradually into one another.

To describe these subtle transitions, use blending and wet-on-wet techniques. Clouds at sunset create emphatic shapes which are best painted wet-on-dry, or wet-on-damp in watercolour.

In the picture opposite, the artist Eugène Boudin (1824–98) has painted a sunny day on the beach at the seaside

KNOW YOUR SKY COLOURS

Cerulean blue
This warm blue has a slightly greenish tinge, useful near the horizon.

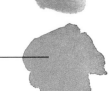

Prussian blue
A cold shade for rainy weather, Prussian blue also contains a hint of green.

French ultramarine
This deep shade is a warm violet-blue, perfect for sunny days.

Cobalt blue
Cobalt blue provides a good balance between warm and cold.

Payne's grey
A blue-grey, ideal for moody skies and storm clouds.

resort of Deauville in northern France. The clouds scudding across the sky give us a sense of the sea breeze.

The sky dominates the composition, occupying almost three-quarters of the canvas. The paint layer consists of thin veils of colour, which have been skimmed over the canvas so that the light itself seems trapped in a delicate web of atmospheric colours. The brush-work is soft, loose and informal, the most solid paint applications being reserved for the deep, intense blue of the sky at its highest point.

Sky moods

Despite the apparent simplicity of the subject, Boudin's painting is pervaded by a marvellous sense of space, light and airiness. If you visualize this sunny scene under a brooding, stormy sky, or gilded by the setting sun, you will see that by simply changing the sky you can create an entirely different picture.

▼ One of Eugène Boudin's many beach paintings, *Deauville, 1893*. You can almost feel the blue sky and bracing air of a breezy day by the seaside.

MIXTURES AND DILUTIONS

The colours you choose depend on the key of your painting, the effect you are trying to create and the appearance of the sky itself. So, for an intensely blue sky, you could use French ultramarine at the highest point, graduating through pure cobalt blue to cobalt blue muted with vermilion at the horizon.

Mix...

A range of warm greys can be very useful when painting cloudscapes.

 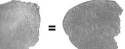

Payne's grey   yellow ochre   warm greys

Add a little vermilion to cobalt blue to create atmospheric muted violets.

vermilion   cobalt blue   muted violets

...and dilute

Cobalt blue is a very useful sky colour. In watercolour, it can be diluted to create a range of tints. With other media, you can achieve a similar effect by adding white.

varying strengths of cobalt blue watercolour

A colour for all seasons

Nature's annual cycle has always provided inspiration for artists, challenging them to respond to its changing colours and moods.

▲ In this watercolour painting, *In a Shoreham Garden* (*c.* 1829) by Samuel Palmer (1805–81), the white blossom tinged with pink typifies a spring scene. The deeper yellows and greens around the central tree act as a foil to the white, throwing it forwards in the picture.

In 1530, a German painter called Albrecht Altdorfer painted a picture of pine trees and rocky hillsides. It had no figures in it and told no story, thus beginning a long obsession that artists have had ever since with landscape and nature as subject matter for pictures.

Some of the early landscape painters, such as Claude Lorrain (1600–1682), idealized nature in a romantic way. J.M.W. Turner (1775–1851) created dramatic scenes of extreme weather conditions. Gradually, as painters tried to be more truthful, working directly from nature became more popular. John Constable (1776–1837) and later the Impressionists recognized that the way the light changes, both during the day and with the seasons, has a marked effect on the colours in a landscape.

Watching the changes

In order to observe and record the changing colours and tones of each season for yourself, it is useful to paint four different versions of the same scene at about three-monthly intervals. A garden is an obvious choice, because it shows distinct colour changes as flowers bloom, berries ripen and leaves fall.

A more subtle approach would be to select a view where the changes occur within the colours themselves as the light varies with each season. You might decide to observe some brightly painted buildings by the sea, for example, or in a wooded landscape.

To achieve the strongest contrast between the four versions of the scene, try to paint on days when the weather and atmosphere are most typical of the seasons. Work in the early morning in spring, when the light is crisply bright, or when it is hot and sunny in summer. Evening light is dramatic in autumn, while a frosty atmosphere sets the scene for a winter painting. Remember to

place yourself in exactly the same spot each time, whether you are painting directly from observation or taking photographs to use as reference.

Colours of the seasons

There are certain paint shades that will help you to portray the essence of each season when used with a basic palette. A word of warning, however – too many colours in your palette can be a hindrance rather than a help. Be selective and try working with just one extra colour from those mentioned below for each of the seasons.

Spring This season brings crisp, clean yellows, greens and blues into a landscape. These shades suggest the use of pure colours directly, without too much

mixing, and are particularly appealing to the watercolourist. Look out for long mauve and violet shadows cast when the sun is very yellow and low in the sky. Notice the fresh, light appearance of colours in sunlight at this time of the year, and try to paint them without using too much white.

Summer The heat-haze of summer will soften the colours in a distant landscape creating atmospheric blues, whilst reds, purples and violets really come into their own as rich, dominant hues in the foreground. The greens of the foliage and meadows become warmer – mix these shades using the deeper yellows, such as chrome yellow and transparent gold ochre, with either of the blues from your basic palette. Cerulean blue is a useful

▲ The strong blues and warm greens and yellows in the foreground of this Scottish landscape, *The River Goil, Argyllshire, 1913*, by George Houston (1869–1947), conjure up a bright summer's day. The hills and sky behind fade to a soft, hazy colour in the distance.

addition to widen the options for painting water and skies, and to mix the chalkier greens on the horizon.

Autumn We often think of autumn as being a 'golden' season and you should certainly explore the range of warm colours from the deep yellows (ochre, raw sienna and burnt sienna) and the coppery reds (Venetian red and Indian red), through to the rich browns (burnt umber). The 'season of mists and mellow fruitfulness' also provides soft shadows and a damp atmosphere, offering the artist a selection of subtle mauves and generally warmer blues and greens.

Winter In winter, sharp tonal colour contrasts are revealed, especially when snow has fallen. Greys, dark blues, greens and browns predominate, but these are often complemented by small patches of very bright colour such as red or orange berries. Winter encourages you to practise mixing warm and cool greys without using black. Useful additions to a basic palette might be Payne's grey in watercolour or phthalo blue in oils.

The seasons indoors

Seasonal colour can also be explored in still life by bringing together natural forms and objects at different times of the year – for example, fruits of the harvest in late summer, or pine cones and the pale green Christmas rose in winter.

The seasonal theme has inspired some contemporary artists to make abstract compositions, reflecting moods and rhythms through shape and structure as well as through colour. Alan Davie's *Music of the Autumn Landscape* (1948) and Ivon Hitchens' *Autumn Composition* (1932) are paintings which use warm greens and browns in a still-life format.

▲ Steely grey and teal blue in the leaden wintry sky and the shadows on the icy ground cool down the warmer ochre shades in this Impressionist painting, *Frosty Morning in Louveciennes* (1873), by Alfred Sisley (1839–99).

▼ The browns, russets and ochres of autumn are just starting to take over from summer's greens in *An Autumn Landscape with a View of Het Steen in the Early Morning* (c. 1636) by Peter Paul Rubens (1577–1640).

Colour for colour's sake

When great artists at the end of the nineteenth century turned away from naturalistic painting, a whole new world of colour opened up.

The end of the nineteenth century saw many radical changes in painting. One of the most important was the use of decorative rather than realistic colour. 'Who cared if a landscape actually was green?' thought many avant-garde artists; they would paint it red if it tallied with their sense of beauty or emotional feelings. This philosophy was one of the major steps on the road to abstract art, where the artist's internal world becomes more important than the external one.

Gauguin's legacy

Paul Gauguin (1848–1903), with his use of bright, flat areas of colour, was one of the most important artists in this development. But perhaps the most influential painting was by one of Gauguin's disciples, a young French artist called Paul Sérusier (1863–1927).

While visiting Gauguin in 1888, he made a little painting (right) on the wooden lid of a cigar box that was to have far-reaching consequences. He claimed to have created it 'under the dictation' of Gauguin. With abstract yellow blobs and light blue for wood, the scene shows trees reflected in a river.

The Talisman

Sérusier came back to Paris describing Gauguin as his talisman to his friends, and the painting is commonly referred to as 'The Talisman'. He and his friends, including Maurice Denis (1870–1943), Pierre Bonnard (1867–1947) and Edouard Vuillard (1868–1940), the three of whom shared a studio, started painting in a similar style.

Colour, rather than being truthful to appearance, was the guiding force. In 1892 they formed a group called the 'Nabis', a Hebrew word meaning prophets. As apostles of Gauguin, they were both progressive and traditional, painting like their master but without the black brush-marked outlines. They

believed in a work of art as a decorative object, using the expressive power of planes of intense colour. In 1890, Denis formulated a famous theory: 'Remember

▲ **Paul Sérusier's *The Talisman* (1888), in which a river scene is rendered in bold blocks of colour, inspired a generation of artists.**

that a picture – before being a warhorse or a nude woman or an anecdote – is essentially a flat surface covered with colours assembled in a certain order.'

Reaching under the surface

While the Impressionists wanted to convey the objective appearance of scenes, the Nabis deliberately distorted colour and composition for dramatic effect. Denis was relatively conservative in the style and subject matter of his painting, but Bonnard and Vuillard forged a revolutionary path.

They kept the loose brushwork of the Impressionists to create mosaic-like patchworks of glittering colour. They were also great fans of Japanese art, with its simplicity of form. Bonnard, in

particular, flattened perspective so that tables tilt alarmingly towards the viewer. Figures are closely cropped and seem to become part of the busy background pattern. Look, for instance, at *Breakfast*, opposite.

Bonnard and Vuillard also painted non-naturalistic theatre sets for the many experimental plays of the time. Even their paintings for private patrons took the form of large-scale, vertical, decorative panels. Absorbent canvases helped to give their paintings a matt appearance in which blobs of colour melted into one another.

In the 1890s, Bonnard was rather in the shadow of Vuillard. But as the Nabis were absorbed into the establishment, Vuillard became increasingly slick at

▲ In Maurice de Vlaminck's *Landscape with Dead Wood* (1906), the colours have been simplified and exaggerated to create a dance of energy and excitement.

painting bourgeois French lifestyle. Bonnard, by contrast, developed his use of colour. In the early 1900s, he returned to broken touches of glowing colour. His many pictures of his wife in the bath show how effectively he used colour to portray form.

Possibilities of colour

The Nabis never quite realized their own radical aims. In 1905, they were eclipsed by a group of artists known as the Fauves (literally the 'wild beasts'). The movement's central figure, Henri

Matisse (1869–1954), transformed interior scenes into a colourful pattern.

Matisse and Bonnard were good friends and in tune with each other's work. Matisse bought and kept Bonnard's *Soirée in the Salon* in 1911, while Bonnard purchased Matisse's *Open Window, Collioure* in 1912. Like Bonnard, Matisse flattened perspective so that his paintings were as shallow as a pane of glass.

Ideal colours

But Matisse went much further. Whereas Bonnard kept a sense of light and shade, Matisse dispensed with modelling. He created wonderful designs by simplifying his subject matter down to exciting, distorted shapes. The same went for the colours. He would merrily change them to fit his ideal of beauty. If his scheme was red, then wallpaper, tablecloth and surroundings were all red, with touches

▼ **Bonnard's expressive use of colour is evident in** *Breakfast* **(1932). Blues and lilacs are emphasized in the shadows and are played off against their complementaries, orange and yellow.**

Playing with colour

Select a scene: indoors or outdoors, still life, landscape or portrait – it doesn't matter. Whether you are working in oils or watercolour, keep all your colours by you but leave out black and white. Exaggerate the colours in your subject as you paint, letting imagination rather than natural appearance govern your choice. Listen to what Gauguin said to his disciple Sérusier: 'What colour do you see that tree? Is it green? Then use green, the finest green on your palette. And that shadow? It's blue, if anything. Don't be afraid to paint it as blue as you possibly can.'

Take a tip from Bonnard as well. Keep a warm and a cool palette and mix the colours for each separately, so you have one predominantly red plate and one based on blues. Bonnard's pictorial ideas often developed out of his responses to the colours on his palette – try letting your paints be your guide rather than your tool. He kept a plate to record the palette used for each painting – a useful memory jogger if you have enough old plates at home!

of cool complementaries serving to accentuate the warm glow.

Restless vitality

While Matisse used colour to create a sense of harmony and balance, his fellow Fauve, Maurice de Vlaminck (1876–1958), used it to instil a feeling of restless vitality. He favoured hot, fiery reds and oranges and would often apply paint straight from the tube. 'I try to paint with my heart and my loins,' he said.

The Nabis, and Bonnard in particular, may have laid down the rules of the game, but it was the Fauves who scored the goal and took decorative colour to its logical conclusion.

Expressive colour

Play up the colours you see in this still-life arrangement and make them the main feature of the composition. Use pastel pencils for their vibrant hues.

This collection of antique artist's equipment – two empty pigment jars, a mortar for grinding powder pigments and a small wooden box – has a dusty grey patina of age and is not, at first glance, particularly colourful. But the artist has studied it closely and found hints of colour that can be played up, even in the shadows on the table.

Colour accents, such as the dried-on paint stains are exaggerated, too. The result is a bold and vibrant image that is not just a mundane copy of the subject but expresses the artist's immediate response to it.

Pure pigments

Pure, vibrant hues are essential for this vivid colour treatment. Most of the drawing is executed with pastel pencils, with touches of loose powder pigment.

Pastel pencils have the soft, easy delivery and rich colour effects typical of all pastels, but they also offer a sharpness of definition that is not as easy to obtain with soft pastels. They can be honed to a fine point or used

▲ **The combination of pure, bright colours and expressive marks injects life and vitality into this group of inanimate objects.**

side-on to deliver broad strokes.

Raw powder pigments can be bought from larger art-supply stores and their sumptuous colours are very seductive. Here, they are used as a drawing medium – the artist dipped a stump into the powder and used it to describe lines and to smudge on colour. If you can't find raw powder pigment, grind soft pastels to a powder instead.

FIRST STEPS

1 ▼ Draw the set-up Draw the items with a stump dipped in graphite powder. Check the elliptical rims. Firm them up with a French grey pastel pencil and add cast shadows.

YOU WILL NEED

Piece of 190gsm (90lb) buff-coloured textured drawing paper 37 x 48cm (14½ x 19in)

Medium-sized stump

Graphite powder

17 pastel pencils: French grey; Orange earth; Burnt carmine; Burnt sienna; Red earth; Burnt umber; Zinc yellow; May green; Hooker's green; Brown ochre; Crimson lake; Spectrum blue; Titanium white; Lilac; Geranium lake; Purple; Pale pink

4 artist's pigments: Cobalt blue; Red ochre; Primrose yellow; Emerald green

Soft eraser

Craft knife (for sharpening pencils)

2 ▼ Fill in the background Use an orange earth pastel pencil to fill in the background with long, sweeping strokes. Keep the lines quite open overall, but make them a little denser close to the objects, where the shadows are darkest. Briefly indicate the shadows and reflections on the mortar and jars.

3 ▲ Block in the shadows Fill the cast shadows with a burnt carmine pastel pencil, hatching with the side of the point. Use a light touch and fade out the colour towards the edges of the shadows. Soften the hatched lines slightly with the stump. Add touches of burnt carmine to the jar and mortar.

4 ◄ Bring in local colour Fill in more of the background with strokes of orange earth. Define the planes of the wooden box with shades of brown: burnt sienna for the top, red earth for the long side, and burnt umber overlaid with burnt carmine for the shadow end. Suggest dried-on stains of yellow paint on the mortar and jars by rubbing on some zinc yellow with the side of the point.

DEVELOPING THE PICTURE

Now that the main shapes of the group are in place, and the shadows indicated, begin to work up the various hues and tones, looking for hints of colour that could be played up.

5 ▼ **Introduce more colours** Dip the tip of the stump in some cobalt blue powder pigment and suggest the blue stains on the rim of the jar and its stopper. Start to build up the patina of paint stains on the mortar with small patches of colour, using pastel pencils in May green, Hooker's green and brown ochre. Hatch May green over the inner parts of the cast shadows to warm them up and make them resonate.

6 ▲ **Work on the red jar** Fill in the red-stained glass jar with crimson lake pastel pencil, blending the strokes in places with the stump. Suggest patches of dried-on dark paint by rubbing on red ochre powder pigment with the stump.

Express yourself

Rely on tone

Try another version of the still-life group – this time black on white. Use a 6B pencil to draw the items, then create soft tones with graphite powder applied with a stump. Pull out the highlights with a putty rubber. The main feature is now the arrangement of lights and darks, rather than the impact of bright colour. The tonal progression on the jars and mortar helps to show their rounded forms, while the box has three clearly defined facets in light, medium and dark tones.

▲ Artist's powder pigments can be applied to a painting with a stump to provide patches of vivid colour. Use a palette with deep wells to help prevent traces of powder contaminating the pure pigment colours in the adjacent wells.

7 ▼ **Add more definition** Use the tip of the stump dipped in cobalt blue powder pigment to define the bases of the mortar and jar. Rub over the darker parts of the cast shadows with burnt carmine and Hooker's green pastel pencils to give these areas more body.

8 ▲ **Develop the forms** Fill in the stopper of the red jar with burnt carmine. Strengthen the shadow inside the mortar with brown ochre. Overlay this with strokes of spectrum blue to suggest reflected light within the shadow.

Master Strokes
Edward Burra (1905–76)
Dishes and Pears

This painting by English artist Edward Burra is a beautifully balanced arrangement of circles and ellipses that overlap and echo one another. His technique of applying layer upon layer of watercolour produces rich, dense blocks of colour. The predominantly muted shades are enlivened by the red apple and the Prussian blue and gold bowl in the centre.

The slant of the table's back edge gives the composition a sense of perspective and looks more dynamic than a straight-on view would have done.

Strong contrasts of light and shade convey the rounded forms of the fruits and dishes and suggest their solidity.

The circular shape of the pear is enclosed within the larger curve of the bowl and echoes its fluid line.

9 ▶ Suggest the paint stains Strengthen the shadows of the jar and stopper with burnt carmine pencil and cobalt blue pigment. Using the stump, rub some primrose yellow pigment on to the right-hand jar and the glass stopper.

10 ▲ Develop shadows and highlights Add emerald green pigment and orange earth pencil to the yellow jar. Pick up reflections on the jars and bowl with a titanium white pastel pencil. Add touches of emerald green pigment to the red jar and cast shadows with the stump.

11 ▲ Unify the image Now work over the whole image with a lilac pastel pencil, applying small patches to the bowl, the jars and stopper, and the wooden box. Also use it to outline the cast shadows.

A FEW STEPS FURTHER

The drawing is now almost complete. The touches of lilac you have just added make the objects resonate with light and help to tie the composition together. All that remains is to add a few final colour accents.

12 ▼ Complete the glass stopper Add the smear of blue paint on the top and rim of the glass stopper by rubbing on some cobalt blue pigment with the stump.

EXPERT ADVICE
Making a point

The best way to sharpen pastel pencils (and any other type of pencil) is with a craft-knife blade. This gives you more control over the shape of the point than a pencil sharpener does and also prolongs the life of your pencils – the colour strip sometimes snaps in a pencil sharpener.

13 ▼ **Add colour accents** Add bright accents to the red jar with a geranium lake pastel pencil and darken the shadow side with strokes of crimson lake. Lighten the top of the lid with titanium white and purple blended together. Define the rim with purple.

14 ▲ **Add the final highlights** Work some pale pink hatching over the light parts of the right-hand jar, the stopper and the bowl to add touches of warmth.

THE FINISHED PICTURE

A Overlaid colours
Thin layers of pastel colour were built up and smeared in places with a stump to suggest the patina of age on the traditional artist's items.

B Luminous shadows
The shadow hues were deliberately heightened. Broken strokes of pastel give them luminosity and also prevent them looking too solid.

C Harmonious design
Strong complementary colour contrasts – especially the yellow and purple on the right bottle – bring the picture alive.

COMPOSITION

Whatever your subject and whichever medium
you use to capture it, the way you compose,
or put a picture together, is vital to the finished
result. In this chapter, you'll learn about
perspective, contrast and the connection
between art and geometry. There's also a
practical look at sketching and painting
landscapes plus, for portraiture, tips on
the best way to pose your sitter.

Keeping your balance

Composition is a vitally important factor in picture making. Take a closer look here at both the traditional and a revolutionary approach.

One of the major difficulties with painting has always been how to make the flat surface look three-dimensional. After Albrecht Dürer had clarified the laws of perspective by constructing a simple machine to demonstrate them in about 1525, possibilities for artists to push deeper into the picture space opened up considerably.

Rectangular construction

Before then, it was generally accepted that a picture would be set in quite a shallow space, with the main characters in the story occupying the foreground as actors do on a stage. Paintings were constructed within a rectangle and were planned rather like an architectural design to give stability and a sense of order. Like architecture, painting was a 'high art' and in Renaissance times was also closely linked with science.

Leonardo da Vinci was probably the last great practitioner of both art and science, but all artists of that period applied some mathematical principles to their compositions. The one who best illustrates the artists' serious concern with geometric composition, was Piero della Francesca, who died in 1492.

Long and short division

When we come to explore the geometry of composition further, on page 117, we will see how symmetry can be avoided and a rectangle 'balanced' in a different way by applying the rules of the Golden Section. Piero's tempera painting of *The Flagellation of Christ* (above) has a very

▲ Renaissance artist, Piero della Francesca, used various geometric devices to construct his painting *The Flagellation of Christ*.

GEOMETRY

Piero della Francesca relied heavily on the triangle to keep the viewer's attention within the rectangle of the painting, pulling the eye in from the corners. If you look closely at *The Resurrection* (below right), you will see that he uses an equilateral triangle standing rigidly on its base at the bottom of the picture with its tip at Christ's chin, between his forked beard. He repeats the triangle shape several times to reinforce the structure. You can see a second triangle resting on the top of the tomb and slanting up through the outside of the arms, with its tip at the top of the head. A third triangle has the same base, but the right-hand diagonal starts at the back of the neck and through the ear of the soldier with the lance and follows the line of Christ's knee, inner arm and a point directly between the eyes, to peak at the tip of the flagpole.

In addition, if you imagine where Christ's standing foot would be behind the tomb, this spot is the tip of a number of upside-down triangles formed by the legs and arms of the soldiers. Can you see, too, another, 'suggested' triangle, the three points of which are all outside the painting itself? Starting from somewhere above the top of the flagpole, the right-hand side of the triangle can be followed down through the sky and the line of the trees; on the left, the edge of the little hill points the way down.

Stability is added to the whole piece by the strong verticals, like the tree trunks, and the horizontals. These give symmetry to the composition.

▲ Marc Chagall's (1887–1985) *The Violet Cockerel* is a circular composition. People and animals float illogically around the focal point formed by the clown's bunch of flowers.

◄ Chagall's *Village in Blue* also has a basically circular structure, but the composition is balanced by two strong right-angled triangles, at top left and bottom right.

unusual composition. By placing a strong vertical shape (the column) in the centre, Piero divides the painting into two separate pictures – the one on the right in close up and the one on the left in the middle distance. But notice how he positions the figure of Christ just over a third of the way in, following the rules of the Golden Section (see opposite).

Slanting lines

In addition, Piero deploys his usual triangular construction (as shown on the previous page), using the slanting lines of the ceiling and roof to lead you into the action. The two halves of the picture are pulled together by the long horizontal divisions linking certain features, sometimes in a rather contrived way (look at the hems on the cloaks of the men on the right).

Contrast

This painting is also an excellent example of the use of 'contrast' as an important tool in composition, in this case using light and dark tones. These are not evenly distributed, but they balance each other overall.

Partly because of the influence of photography on art, the last hundred years have seen artists deliberately breaking the 'rules' of geometric composition. Marc Chagall, for example, painted fantasy pictures with no logical proportions or scale. Everything is topsy-turvy and people, animals and objects often swirl around a central focal point, as though the picture isn't big enough to contain them. In *Village In Blue* (above), they randomly collide with the edge of the canvas or extend beyond it.

Many of Chagall's paintings rely on the geometric structure of a circle.

Notice, too, in *Village in Blue* the strong, balancing right-angled triangles at top left (along the line of the mule's neck) and bottom right (slanting down through the rooftops to the baby's groin).

Holding attention

Whereas Piero's compositions produced static images, Chagall was concerned with vitality. Although outrageous, his zany compositions hold your attention and that, remember, is the basic aim.

ADDING AND SUBTRACTING

Try your hand at 'live' composition. Collect together lots of different objects. Try to vary their shapes as much as possible – tall and short, thin and fat, regular (geometric) and irregular – to achieve good contrast.

1 Arrange the still life On a table top, arrange a still life of four or five of the objects. Start by trying to organize them into a triangular composition, using a tall object for the apex. Begin drawing, working quickly with long strokes of the arm to emphasize angles and directions, particularly following the lines of perspective.

2 Change your composition After about ten minutes, take one object away and add two more. By drawing over the top and rubbing out afterwards, you can watch and control your changing composition.

3 Repeat the process Repeat the changeover of objects every ten minutes or so to keep widening the possible options.

The process in this exercise is more important than the end product. Think about verticals, horizontals, diagonals and other geometric connections in the still life arrangements you put together. Try to incorporate the rules of the Golden Section (see opposite), and above all, keep your balance!

YOU WILL NEED

Large sheet of white cartridge paper

Charcoal or a very soft pencil

Putty rubber

Blueprint for a painting

Like a play or film, a picture must be put together so that its component parts make a balanced, harmonious whole to hold the attention of the viewer. This important skill is called 'composition'.

Traditionally, artists have used the rectangle as the framework for paintings. When used horizontally, it is referred to as having a 'landscape' format, and when used upright as having a 'portrait' format (although, of course, you could paint a landscape in the 'portrait' format or use other shapes instead).

Getting the right fit

The shape and size of the rectangle has to be right for what you want to fit into it. If it is too small, the image looks squashed and this makes the viewer want to see past the edges; too large, and the eye wanders about trying to find something to hold its interest. Good composition is achieved when all the elements of the picture (colours, shapes, tones, textures and, vitally, the spaces between them) relate to each other in a balanced way.

The focal point

Imagine that you have just moved into an empty house and you are arranging the furniture in the living room. You will probably set out the armchairs and sofa so that they face the television, or perhaps a fireplace. These are 'focal points', and the angles and relative distances that you create in positioning the furniture is an important consideration.

Alternatively, the chairs might be arranged to face each other for conversation, in which case the focal point is actually a space.

In a painting, the focal point is the point to which the viewer's eye tends to be drawn most strongly. This is usually the main subject of the work – for example, the face in a portrait, or the

THE GEOMETRY OF COMPOSITION

This information is by no means essential to composing a successful picture, but you may find it interesting. Absorb as much, or as little, of it as you like.

Euclid noted that a sequence of numbers (3, 5, 8, 13, 21, etc) gave a series of ratios which Renaissance artists called the 'divine proportion', otherwise the 'Golden Section' or 'Golden Mean'. If a line is drawn by combining any two successive numbers (say 5 and 8, making 13), and divided into the two component lengths (i.e. one of 5 and one of 8), then the ratio of the smaller part to the larger (5:8) is the same as the ratio of the larger part to the whole (8:13).

▶ **The Golden Section**
The diagram shows how a focal point within a rectangle is created by using the 'Golden' proportions. Giovacchino Toma (1838–91) used this principle for the main focal point in his painting *Luisa San Felice In Prison*, below.

This principle was used as the basis for many Classical buildings because the balance created by these divisions, either vertically or horizontally (or both), is very satisfying. In paintings, the points where the verticals and horizontals of the 'Golden Mean' intersect within the rectangle are often used as the focal point (or points) of the image. This is about a third of the way in and a third of the way up (or down).

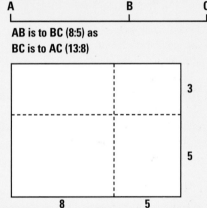

AB is to BC (8:5) as
BC is to AC (13:8)

Composition in practice

To understand the importance of composition, you will need to explore a little, observing how different elements relate to each other. Try these exercises.

1 Take a sheet of white paper and some coloured papers (say red and green). Cut up the colours into rectangular shapes of various sizes and practise arranging them in different ways on the white sheet, overlapping some of them if you like. Try to organize a focal point and to achieve a good balance between shapes, spaces and colours. Look at how your arrangements visually affect the rectangle. Is there a sense of space; are there 'busy' areas and 'quiet' ones; is there any sense of 'movement' or 'tension' between shapes? Try the same exercise with other colours, or with black and grey.

2 Find a reproduction of a well-known painting for this exercise. Using tracing paper, draw lines to connect up the main directions formed by the various objects, light, shadows and forms within the painting. Notice how diagonals are used to hold together different areas and create 'routes' for the eye to follow.

3 From a sheet of white paper measuring 8 x 5cm (3 x 2in), cut out a rectangle from the centre to leave a frame about 1cm (⅜in) wide all round. Hold this at arm's length and move it slowly around the room or the garden. The view you see inside the frame is your composition. Notice how a very small shift of the frame can make for a much more balanced composition.

▲ Renaissance painters used the formal geometry of vertical, horizontal and diagonal lines to form triangular compositions within the rectangle. The portrait shown here, the *Madonna of the Goldfinch* by Raphael Sanzio (1483–1520), shows the principle clearly.

church tower in a village scene. In more complex images, where no one element is more important than another, the artist has to guide the viewer's eye around the picture by the way the various elements are arranged. As in the living room, the balance of these and the 'dynamic' that is set up within the rectangle are what composition is all about.

Things to avoid

There are no firm rules, but some things are best avoided. Dividing the surface in half by placing a tall object in the centre, or positioning the horizon line exactly half-way up, makes the picture 'boring'.

Similarly, same-size objects equidistant on either side of the centre line, or a continuous row of trees running right across the middle of the picture, make for dull compositions. As a rule of thumb, remember to compose 'through' the picture as well as across the surface.

▼ The compositions of Pieter Brueghel (the Elder) (*c.* 1515–69) are full of incident and usually contain lots of different focal points with plenty of space for the eye to wander about in. Notice the position of the flying bird in his painting *Hunters in the Snow*. Is it the first thing that caught your eye?

A sense of perspective

With a basic knowledge of perspective, you will find it much easier to recreate the often complex three-dimensional world around you on a flat painting surface.

Try this simple experiment: take two paperback books of the same size and hold one in each hand vertically at arm's length in front of you, level with your eyes. Gradually bring one of them towards you, moving it slightly across so that it overlaps the one in the outstretched hand. The book furthest away now appears to be about half the size of the other one. This effect, which is called foreshortening, demonstrates the first principle of perspective: distant objects appear smaller than those close to.

It wasn't until the early fifteenth century that Filippo Brunelleschi, a Florentine architect, devised precise mathematical rules to work out the scale of objects at different points in space. His discovery brought a new sense of reality into art, which had a great effect on its subsequent history – painters could now give objects depth on a flat surface.

How perspective works

The first thing to establish when looking at a scene is your eye-level – if you are sitting down, this will be lower than if you are standing. Assuming the ground is flat, the eye-level is also the horizon line.

Now look at any parallel lines that recede into the distance and you will see that they appear to taper towards a single point on the horizon. Look at a railway track from a bridge to see this effect.

▲ In *The Avenue at Middelharnis* (1689), Meindert Hobbema (1638–1709) used receding verticals to create the illusion of space in a landscape. The parallel lines of trees converge downwards towards a vanishing point on the horizon, as though the viewer is standing on the road.

If the parallel lines in the scene are below your eye-level (the base and top of a fence, perhaps), they will run upwards. If, however, the parallel lines are above eye-level (like the treetops in the painting above), they will run downwards.

The following exercise demonstrates how the principles of perspective affect what we see. Take a felt-tip watercolour pen (not an indelible one) and stand or sit in front of a window. Closing one eye, draw a horizontal line on the window, level with your eyes. Then trace on the window the outlines of the main objects you can see. Try to keep your head still, drawing only what is within range. The result will be a drawing in perfect perspective. The window, in this case, has become what is called the 'picture plane'.

One- and two-point perspective

On the left-hand side of the diagram on the right, the viewer is looking at two boxes placed on a flat surface below the eye-level (EL) directly in front of the line of vision so that they are exactly parallel (Row 1). The receding lines 'vanish' to a single point on the horizon (VP1), while the horizontal lines forming the other two sides of the boxes remain parallel to the picture plane.

When the boxes are moved along to the right of the viewer (Row 2), but drawn from the same position, the receding lines on the long sides vanish to the same point as before, but the lines that were horizontal now line up with a new vanishing point far to the right (VP2). This is known as two-point perspective.

Further to the right, the two original boxes are placed upright. Two others are added, one on top of the other (Row 3). Standing upright, the boxes happen to be exactly the same height as the eye-level – the tops of each box therefore lie along a straight line. The box balanced on top is

One- and two-point perspective

This diagram illustrates how perspective alters according to the position of the objects relative to a given viewpoint.

above the eye-level, so its upper edges incline downwards to the two vanishing points. Notice how the boxes in this row rapidly reduce in height as they recede. This effect also means that the vertical centre line of a given plane appears to be closer to the vanishing point than the front edge. In the diagram of the house below, this effect is shown by the dotted line running from the highest point of each roof to the base of the house.

Bear in mind that the vanishing points do not have to be within the picture; in the diagram below, one is and one is not. Also, parallel lines never actually meet, even though they look as if they will, so the vanishing points are at infinity. Perspective implies the location and

scale of objects, creating an illusion of space. In the diagram above, you 'read' the boxes as being about the same size. But if you measure them, you will see that they are actually very different in size on the paper. The brain operates an 'adjustment' factor so that the scene appears realistic.

Without any extra information, the actual size of the boxes is undefined. If the viewer is standing, the boxes could be packing cases in a warehouse. But the viewer could equally well be a child looking over a table-top at some matchboxes. More clues are needed to identify the scale: if a bowl and spoon were added in the right scale, you might assume that the boxes contained breakfast cereals.

Drawing buildings

To help you draw a roof peak correctly, draw diagonal lines on the house wall from A to A and from B to B. Then draw a vertical line from the base of the house through the point where the lines cross. The peak lies somewhere on this line, depending on the slope of the roof. The ridge of the roof runs down towards the vanishing point on the right. To practise two-point perspective, try drawing doors and windows on to the house.

Key
EL   Eye-level
VP   Vanishing point
(The left-hand vanishing point is off the page.)

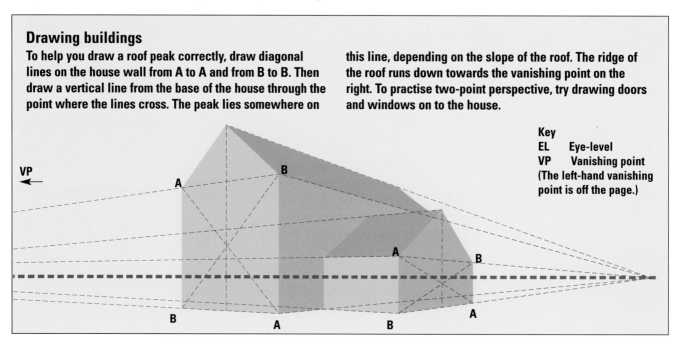

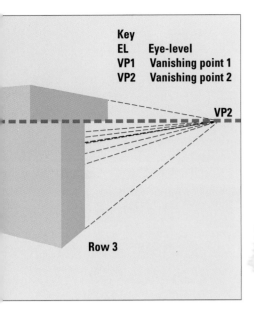

Key
EL — Eye-level
VP1 — Vanishing point 1
VP2 — Vanishing point 2

VP2

Row 3

▼ The battle scene in *The Rout of San Romano* by Paolo Uccello (*c.* 1396-1475) is one of the earliest examples of linear perspective. The strange foreshortening of the soldier's corpse in the left foreground shows the difficulties in applying what was, at that time, a very new idea.

Getting it in perspective

Try this exercise to practise drawing a selection of rectangular objects, such as books and small boxes, in perspective. It will help if you draw 'sight-size', that is the size at which you actually see the objects. You can work this out by using a pencil as a measuring tool. Hold the pencil up at arm's length, locate the tip at one corner of an object and move your thumb along to the point on the pencil that lines up with the other corner. Draw a line of this length on to your paper.

You could also make a small viewfinder from a piece of perspex in the same proportions as your paper. Draw vertical and horizontal centre lines on it to help you assess the angles of the receding lines.

1 Set up the objects at random Place the objects at random angles on a table, with one or two on top of each other or standing upright. Position the biggest ones furthest away and the smallest ones nearest to you.

2 Draw the objects in perspective First establish your eye-level line on the paper, then make a careful line drawing of the objects. Draw those lying straightest first and remember to check the size of the spaces in between objects. As you draw each item, follow through all the receding lines to their vanishing points with the ruler. You will almost certainly be dealing with more than two of these vanishing points and some may extend beyond the page.

3 Put your skills to the test Show the drawing to a friend and ask if he or she can tell which are the largest and smallest books.

Choosing the best format

There are many ways to frame a scene – make sure you choose the best one before you start drawing.

One of the first decisions to make when planning a drawing is whether it should have a horizontal (landscape) format or vertical (portrait) one. In this scene of a tree-lined road in France, the artist saw the possibilities of both formats (right).

The vertical format was ideally suited to capturing the height and grandeur of the trees. These strong verticals help to create a rather dramatic mood. The artist, however, decided to use the horizontal format. This enlarges the scope of the view and the inclusion of the farm building helps to provide a balanced composition. The strong horizontals of this building make for a more serene, peaceful mood.

Whether you choose a horizontal or a vertical format, plan to offset the centre of interest in the composition. A useful rule of thumb is to divide your paper into thirds each way, either by eye or by marking it lightly in pencil, and then place the focal point at the crossing point of two of the dividing lines. The focal point of the drawing below – the distant hut with the cyclist in front of it – is positioned in this way.

▼ In the horizontal format, the farmhouse on the left balances the verticals of the trees, helping to create a tranquil, rural image.

Piece of Hot-pressed
watercolour paper

7B pencil

15 coloured pencils:
Light turquoise; Apple
green; Lemon yellow;

Olive green; Sap green;
Pale grey; Venetian red;
Yellow ochre; Dark grey;
Prussian blue; Aubergine;
Burnt sienna; Viridian;
Vandyke brown; Burnt
orange

FIRST STROKES

1 ▼ **Sketch the composition** Using a 7B pencil, sketch the
main elements of the scene – the trees, buildings, road and
cyclist. Notice how the negative sky shapes formed between
the trees are roughly triangular. Also, look at how different
parts of the scene relate to each other – the roof of the long
building lines up with the distant tree-tops, for example.

CHANGING THE EMPHASIS

Quick pencil sketches are a great way of working out the best
format and composition for your drawing. The vertical format
emphasizes the height of the avenue of trees, conjuring up a
cathedral-like image. The horizontal format provides a 'quieter'
image – the eye is still pulled down the road but it also has a
place to rest on the farm building on the left. (Also try making
use of a viewfinder).

2 ▶ **Establish dark and light tones** Add more spiky branches to the tree at the end of the avenue, tapering them off from the trunk towards the top of the paper. Hatch in the shaded parts of the trunks and also the shadows cast on the grass and road.

3 ▶ **Begin with the light colours** Complete the tonal pencil shading on the trunks and vegetation on the right of the picture. Now, using a light turquoise coloured pencil, fill in the sky, including all the shapes between the trees. Move on to the sunlit areas of foliage, using an apple green pencil. As with watercolour painting, you are working from light to dark, so that you gradually build up depth of colour.

ADDING COLOUR TO THE SCENE

Once you have roughed in the main shapes and tonal areas, work up the rest of the drawing in coloured pencil. Blend shades if necessary to capture the essence of the colours.

4 ▲ Introduce darker greens Put more apple green on the tree-tops and highlight the distant trees with a touch of lemon yellow. Now look for the areas of darker green in the distant trees and colour these with olive green and sap green, working over some of the graphite pencil tone.

EXPERT ADVICE
Giving form to the trees

Shade in the tree trunks using mainly horizontal hatching lines. The eye reads them as curving around the trunks, which helps to suggest the cylindrical shapes. By leaving one side of the trunks pale where they catch the light, you can convey their form and solidity.

5 ▲ Continue with dark greens Using vigorous strokes of sap green, hatch in the shadows on the grass and foliage to the left and right of the road. Changing to the olive green, hatch across the tree-tops and trunks. Block in a mid tone across the road with a pale grey pencil.

6 ▶ Work on the building and road
Hatch the roof on the building with diagonal strokes of Venetian red and work loosely over the wall below it with yellow ochre and dark grey. Use Prussian blue for the figure on the bicycle, then strengthen the cast shadows on the road with Prussian blue, aubergine and dark grey.

7 ▲ Colour doors and windows Shade the hut doors in burnt sienna, dark grey and viridian, and the doors and windows of the building in Vandyke brown and burnt orange. Hatch over the trees with the 7B and olive green pencils, suggesting leaf texture with dashes of olive green. Use dark grey to put tone down the ochre wall and to strengthen the far left tree.

A FEW STEPS FURTHER

The drawing now successfully evokes the atmosphere of a sunny and tranquil rural scene. A touch of detail on the roof and treetops will add texture and interest.

8 ▼ **Complete the roof** A suggestion of terracotta roof tiles will give the left-hand building more character. Using the 7B pencil and Vandyke brown, draw the lines of tiles and their rounded ends.

9 ▲ **Hatch in more leaves** To enhance the effect of mottled colour in the tree-tops, use the olive green pencil to hatch dark clumps of leaves amidst the foliage. Press firmly to achieve a deep, rich shade.

THE FINISHED PICTURE

A Blended colours
To find the correct shade for the wall of the building, a darker colour was worked over a lighter one to tone down the brightness.

B Dappled effect
The shadows falling across the road create an interesting pattern on what would otherwise be a broad area of plain colour.

C Focal point
The eye is drawn down the avenue of trees towards the focal point – the brightly coloured doors in the distant building.

Placing the horizon

Think carefully about where you place the horizon in your landscape painting – it has an enormous effect on the atmosphere of your composition.

The location of the horizon defines the proportion of sky to land, and has a crucial effect on the mood and sense of space within a landscape picture. Without really thinking about it, we know that the horizon line is probably the most important element in a landscape painting. In fact, if a single horizontal line is drawn anywhere on a rectangular support, most people will 'read' it as the horizon.

A low horizon

Flat, open landscapes such as plains and fenland have a broad, spacious feeling. The horizon is far away and wide, and the sky is large and important. Seascapes have a similarly open feeling. In these regions you can see weather fronts approaching and watch the shadows of clouds crossing the landscape. To recreate these conditions in a picture, place the horizon line low.

The shape of the canvas also affects the mood of the composition. A wide landscape format allows the eye to travel slowly from side to side, so it is ideal for broad, open panoramas. For his painting *Deauville,* 1893, Eugène Boudin chose a landscape format and placed the horizon low in the picture area. There is a large sky, and the clouds and the people on the beach diminish in scale towards the horizon, creating an airy, spacious feel.

Contrast this with *Poplars on the Banks of the Epte* (right) by Claude Monet (1840–1926). Here the artist has combined a very low horizon with an upright format. The tall, slender columns of the poplars and the sinuous zig-zag line of their canopy draw the eyes upwards. The viewpoint (that is, the viewer's eye-level) is an important aspect of landscape composition. If you are high up – standing on a wall, for example – you can see further than if you are sitting down, and the horizon will appear to be

▲ *Poplars on the Banks of the Epte* (1891) was painted by Claude Monet in the autumn, so the warm colours of the turning leaves emphasize the sinuous curve created as the trees follow the river bank, and increase the illusion of depth in the picture.

further away. This work was painted from a boat, and the low viewpoint means it is dominated by the sky and the towering, silhouetted trees. Although the trees get smaller as they recede into the distance, they and their reflections break the edges of the picture, drawing attention to the picture plane.

A high horizon

By contrast, a high horizon leaves little room for the sky and produces a contained and rather intimate landscape. In nature you can experience this effect in mountain valleys; towering crags crowd in upon you, casting deep shadows and limiting your view of the sky. Wooded landscapes and forests can also produce this slightly claustrophobic atmosphere.

In *Red Vineyards at Arles* (below), Vincent Van Gogh (1853–90) has taken an exaggeratedly high viewpoint, so we can see all the activity in the vineyard. A high horizon tends to flatten the picture, and the artist exploits this quality to create a graphic, almost decorative painting. Van Gogh has also created a rather ambiguous sense of space – the trees and human figures diminishing in the distance contrast with devices which emphasize the picture plane; bright colours, strong outlines and vigorous brushmarks which do not change in scale.

Experimenting with horizon lines

The horizon is just one aspect of the internal geometry (organization) of a landscape painting. The final impact of the composition will depend on how you organize the other elements such as space, tone, colour and format. Choose a landscape and make thumbnail sketches of it, placing the horizon at different levels. You will find that each treatment demands a different internal geometry.

● If you place the horizon low in the picture area and create a thunderous sky, the painting will have a dramatic, threatening mood.

● Introduce trees on either side of the scene and the image will feel more enclosed.

● Place the horizon high within an upright format – the landscape will advance towards the viewer.

● Introduce a sweeping path or a river to lead the eye towards the horizon and you immediately create a sense of recession.

● Try placing the horizon right in the middle – you may have been told that this is 'wrong', because an even, symmetrical image can be boring, but it can work very well.

A high horizon creates an enclosed, intimate feeling and allows the artist to show greater detail in the foreground.

A central horizon can be unnaturally stable, but the right tonal balance between the areas adds dynamism.

A low horizon is ideal for showing dramatic skies to their best advantage, and to create a sense of spaciousness.

◄ Vincent Van Gogh used a high horizon in *Red Vineyards at Arles* (1888) to give him the space to show a landscape drenched in the red, orange and golden tones of a glorious sunset.

Sketching landscapes

Simplicity is the key to sketching outdoors. This allows you to work quickly, capture fleeting light effects and end up with the essence of the scene.

The landscape artist frequently has to contend with changing light. This means working quickly to record as much information as possible before the scene alters completely. In addition, materials and equipment must be portable – often a handful of water-colours and a small sketchbook.

Working on a small scale does not necessarily mean painting with a small brush or recording minute detail. On the contrary, the changing landscape allows no time to depict every branch on the tree, or every cloud in the sky.

The minimum of brush strokes

The best approach to landscape sketching is to use as large a brush as is practical, and to simplify what is in front of you. A sweeping expanse of grass or water can often be described in one or two strokes of colour; a tree or bush may be painted with a single brush mark.

The watercolour sketches here appear effortless because they contain very little detail. However, this impression is misleading. It is often more difficult to describe a scene in half a dozen strokes than it is to include every detail. You will need a little practice to gain the necessary skill and confidence.

Wet and wild

Working wet-on-wet, for instance, is a vital skill – it lets you work quickly (before the paper dries) and is ideal for capturing mist, clouds and reflections. However, to control the runs of colour, you must be able to judge the dampness of the paper.

If you have problems eliminating details, look at your subject through half-closed eyes. This excludes much of the detail and some of the local colour from your vision. You see only the main shapes and tones which, in turn, helps you to simplify the composition. Try to be selective – include only those elements in the subject that you either like or are essential to the painting. Is it the tones or colours that attract you? Make up your mind firmly and execute your ideas quickly.

Simplification need not be limited to sketches. Once you have mastered economic brushwork and minimal colour, there is no reason why these techniques should not be used in finished paintings. Many artists prefer to take this broad approach in all their work.

Scaling up

As a first step, try working on a large sheet of paper. You will then need to scale up the size of your brushes and strokes in proportion to the support. For example, use 50–75mm (2–3in) brushes on a sheet of A1 paper. These will seem ludicrously large compared with your usual brushes. But, for simple, suggestive marks and a 'no detail' approach, they are perfect.

▼ **Working wet-on-wet can create visually stunning sketches. Here the technique was used for the mist over the mountain tops and the beautiful silvery surface of the water.**

CAPTURING THE MOMENT

CHASING THE SUN

This sunset was as transient as it was beautiful. The artist had to work quickly to capture it, as the colours and the tonal relationship between the sky and the landscape were rapidly changing. The hills are rendered in Payne's grey and ultramarine; the sky is cerulean with cadmium orange and vermilion bleeding into it to capture the colour of the sun.

 Palette: Cerulean, cadmium orange, vermilion, ultramarine, Payne's grey

A 'SNAPSHOT' SKETCH

Again, the light was changing rapidly in this scene. The clouds were scudding across the sky creating ever-changing shadows and patches of pale sunlight. As a result, the artist mixed up the washes of green, yellow and grey before starting to paint. The artist describes the resulting sketch as a watercolour 'snapshot', a moment frozen in time.

 Palette: Payne's grey, ultramarine, raw sienna, indigo, burnt sienna

SPONTANEOUS CLOUDS

On this damp day at the seaside, the paint took forever to dry. However, the artist used this to his advantage. Working wet-on-wet, the colours of the sky and horizon immediately ran together to create the hazy effect of low clouds hanging over water. The rest of the sketch is painted wet-on-dry, with flecks of white paper left untouched to represent highlights.

 Palette: Cerulean, Payne's grey, ultramarine, raw sienna, indigo

Composing the sitter

To attain a good figure study or portrait, choosing the best pose for your model should be taken as seriously as applying the paints.

When composing a sitter it's vital to consider not only the pose of your model – but also how that pose relates to the format of your support, the background, lighting and your viewpoint.

You might want to create a particular mood, or recreate a classical composition, or perhaps you want something quite informal, such as the black-and-white

pictures here. First, think about how the figure relates to the shape of your support. If the figure is small in relation to the size of the canvas, the subject will seem remote and inaccessible. The distance between the artist and the subject creates a similarly distant relationship between viewer and subject. Conversely, if the figure is closely cropped within the picture area, the per-

son appears accessible – almost within physical reach of the viewer.

Another device for creating a sense of familiarity is to ensure that the viewer's attention is held within the composition. The directions of the arms, hands and head can be arranged to form a circular or enclosed shape that retains the eye within the painting. Poses where the face looks out towards the frame

AN INFORMAL AIR

In his 1882 painting of Charlotte Dubourg, Henri Jean Fantin-Latour has taken care to chose a pose and composition that counteract the otherwise formal nature of this commissioned portrait.

A EYE POSITION
Instead of looking directly out from the canvas, the subject averts her gaze to create a less formal mood. The angle of the head to the right balances the angle of the legs to the left.

B ENCLOSED COMPOSITION
The arms help create a loose circular shape at the centre of the picture (even though the hands do not quite meet). This creates an enclosed composition that holds the eye of the viewer within the picture area.

C ASYMMETRICAL POSE
The arms and legs are directed at an angle to offset the upright, centrally placed face and torso.

of the picture work against a sense of intimacy, as do poses in which arms and hands point outwards.

Eye contact

One simple way to create a formal figure or portrait painting is to have the sitter looking straight at you. This creates direct eye contact and establishes a relationship between viewer and subject in the finished painting.

For a more informal painting, make sure the sitter's attention is focused elsewhere. In these sketches, the sitter either looks downwards or slightly to one side. The result is natural and spontaneous – more like a candid photograph than a deliberately posed model.

A comfortable pose

It is as important for the sitter to be at ease with the pose as it is for the artist to like what they see. An awkward position will almost certainly look unnatural in the painting. So make sure the chair is comfortable and has enough cushions.

A pose inevitably changes as the sitter relaxes. The sitter will be unaware of this gradual slump, so wait a few minutes before starting, to allow the model to settle into position. Also consider how easy the facial expression is to hold.

Frequent breaks are essential. In life classes, the model usually takes a 15-minute break after 45 minutes, but an inexperienced model may need more. Don't get so involved in your painting that you forget the needs of the sitter!

FULL LENGTH

Here, the pale shapes of the face and limbs form a pleasing oval that helps lead the eye around the picture. Note also how the figure provides a strong diagonal, with the pale tone of the face at top right balanced by the foot at bottom left.

THREE-QUARTER LENGTH

Accentuated by the arms of the chair, this pose forms an even stronger diagonal than the picture above. The artist has emphasised this diagonal by taking the study across a double page. And the model's gaze – down and to the left – encourages us to wander along the length of the diagonal.

Ask your subject to tell you when it is time for a rest. Apart from the discomfort, sitting for a portrait can be boring. Playing music is a good idea provided it does not affect your concentration.

Resuming the pose

Finding exactly the same pose after a break is impossible because the folds and creases of clothing can never be coaxed back into the same place. Accept this and try to get the model into as similar a position as possible.

Many artists like to keep the painting 'on the move', particularly in the early stages. For these painters, the constant redrawing necessary to accommodate small changes in the clothing helps to keep the image alive and spontaneous.

Alternatively, if you want a still subject, try using a digital or Polaroid camera to capture the pose before the first break. This way, you can continue working on the clothing as it was at the start. And before a break, use masking tape or chalk to mark the position of feet, hands and elbows on the floor and chair.

If you're doing a proper portrait rather than a loose figure study, pay attention to the background. You may need to intro-

HALF LENGTH

Sometimes it pays to break the rules. Here the model is looking out of the composition rather than into the other page. The result is unusual yet dynamic – and it creates a sense of solitude. (Compare this to the more conventional, 'looking in' composition in the three-quarter length box.)

HEAD AND SHOULDERS

The model's pose here is very similar to the three-quarter length one but close cropping throws the focus on to the face. Unusually for a portrait, the artist has used landscape format. This creates a large black area on the left to balance the pale tones of the face and arms on the right. In between is a strong diagonal formed by the edge of the model's hair and arm.

duce a special backdrop or perhaps move the sitter around. Models often have their own preferences, wanting to be portrayed in personal settings, perhaps in a particular room or against a favourite colour.

The background

A busy or patterned background inevitably detracts from the sitter. This is not necessarily a bad thing, but it does need careful planning, such as choosing colours and lighting that prevent the figure from becoming entirely dominated.

In these sketches, the artist was interested in showing the importance of shape and rhythm in the composition. The fair-skinned model was asked to wear a sleeveless black top and the artist chose a plain black background to create maximum contrast. Reversing the tones – placing a dark-skinned model against a light background would create a similarly dramatic effect.

Finally, don't overlook the lighting, which always plays a crucial part in the composition of portraits.

Composing a group

Whether you are painting a group for posterity or for pure enjoyment, you need to compose the figures in a way that is both meaningful and visually pleasing.

In terms of composition, a group of figures provides much more flexibility than a single-person portrait – and as a result offers a wonderful opportunity to create exciting, innovative designs.

Quick poses

Basing a series of studies on a group of figures can teach you a great deal about how lines, shapes and tones work together in a composition. Ask friends or family members to pose while you make quick studies. Alternatively, take photos and work from these.

The studies here were done with brush and ink. This has a wonderful fluidity, but you might want to choose charcoal as it is a more forgiving

▲ In *The Misses Vickers* (1884), John Singer Sargent creates a pleasing composition by balancing the elliptical shape of the two sisters on the left with the vertical formed by the sister on the right.

medium. Charcoal also enables you to draw swiftly and to put down line and tone with equal ease.

With each separate study, rearrange the poses and figures. You can also change the composition by moving yourself around the group, viewing it from different angles, eye levels and distances. Then compare the results and assess which compositions work, which ones don't – and why.

Arranging the group

People tend to arrange themselves into cohesive groups quite naturally, especially if they are family or friends. So start by asking your sitters to relax together while you sketch or take photos. Then start to 'fine-tune' the poses, moving a hand here, tilting a head there, until you arrive at an arrangement that is comfortable for your sitters and makes a good design. Remember, your picture

COUNTERBALANCE

Here, an oblique viewpoint creates an asymmetrical design in which the figures are concentrated mainly in the right half of the image. The left side is relatively empty, but the large, dark shape of the table counterbalances the 'weight' of the figures and equilibrium is maintained. The high viewpoint and the pensive gazes of the figures give the image a mood of detachment.

SPOT THE MISTAKES

This set-up demonstrates the old adage that 'to fail to prepare is to prepare to fail'. No thought has gone into the models' poses; there is no interaction between them, and the composition is unbalanced. Time spent studying and reorganizing your sitters will help you avoid the compositional mistakes listed here.

There's a large area of 'dead' space in the middle of the composition.

A clash of hands and arms looks messy and confused.

This sitter's face is turned away from us and his arm creates a barrier – nothing invites us into the picture.

This sitter's pose, with arms defensively folded, is very closed. He seems adrift – both socially and compositionally.

should convey the relationship between the people in the group *and* form a pleasing pictorial composition that holds the viewer's attention.

The value of a viewfinder

It is a good idea to look at your subject through a camera or cardboard viewfinder. Placing a border around your subject isolates it from its surroundings, allowing you to see it as a picture; you will find it much easier to examine the interplay of shapes, lines and tones and to judge how the figures relate to the edges of the frame.

Move the viewfinder forward and back, and from side to side, until the image is framed in a pleasing way. Mentally divide the picture area into thirds, vertically and horizontally: the most pleasing positions for focal points are near where the dividing lines cross. In the two-person study opposite, for instance, the two heads fall near to the top two cross points while the girl's hand and knee are close to the bottom-right cross point.

Watch out for any jarring elements that spoil the balance of the composition, and for areas where hands are

STEPPING STONES

In this composition, the light-toned heads placed against the dark background act as visual stepping stones, moving the eye around the image. The sharp tonal contrast between the central head and the dark shadow on the backdrop forms a natural focal point: the eye is pulled to it both by the direction of gaze of the other figures and by the diagonal lines created by the table and the boy's raised arm.

RHYTHM AND BALANCE

This set-up is similar to the error-filled one on the left, but it shows how even minor adjustments can vastly improve a composition. Here, the whole feel is more open and inviting and the sitters are alert and interacting. The balance is better, with the boy in the white T-shirt positioned just off centre. He no longer uncomfortably overlaps the girl in front. The composition flows rhythmically from the girl's head, down her arm, across the table, up the central figure's right arm and down his left to the right-hand figure. There is a small, pleasing 'quiet' area off to the top left, but no vast empty spaces.

awkwardly placed, arms hang limply or background objects appear to sprout from people's heads. Look at the angles of arms, legs and heads – do they form rhythmic lines that lead the eye from one figure to the next? Have you included a quiet, restful area to offset the active shapes of the figures? Is there enough tonal contrast? Again, the counterchange of light shapes against dark, and dark shapes against light, leads the eye and enlivens the composition.

Background shapes

Remember that the background is part of the 'jigsaw' of shapes that make up the whole picture. Are the negative shapes around the figures interesting and varied? Do the colours and tones in the background complement those of the figures? For example, light clothing and hair are generally more effective against a dark background, and vice versa.

As well as thinking visually, keep in mind the mood you want to set. By putting the sitters in different positions – facing each other, back to back, hands touching – you are inevitably suggesting something about their relationships.

BODY LANGUAGE

Two people can be harder to compose than three – they often create a static half-and-half composition. Here, however, there is enough variety in the poses to give the image energy. We sense that the subjects are close; she is leaning forward into his space, and he responds with an open pose and eye contact. The picture is warm and relaxed, yet underpinned by a well-balanced design.

PORTRAITURE

Drawing the human form is a daunting prospect for many artists, but with practise and a little knowledge, it's an easily-improved skill. This section provides step-by-step guides to drawing figures and faces, including potentially problematic features such as hands and eyes. You'll learn some basic human anatomy, how to capture a likeness and, in case of a subject-shortage, the art of the self-portrait.

Looking at anatomy

Combine your talent for art with a little knowledge of science and you'll find that your figure-drawing skills will improve immensely.

▼ The muscles on the plaster cast are well defined and produce a drawing which shows clearly how they are grouped together. The most important muscles for the artist are indicated on the cast.

To draw the figure convincingly, it really pays to have some knowledge of anatomy. After all, if you are familiar with the body's internal structure, you are much more likely to get its external form right. Of course, you don't have to visit mortuaries and operating theatres, as the likes of Leonardo da Vinci and Rembrandt did. Instead, simply practise drawing this anatomical plaster cast.

For the beginner, this type of cast is ideal. First and foremost, unlike a real person, it stays still. Furthermore, it can be a bit intimidating to ask someone to sit nude until you are confident about your figure-drawing skills. (If you're thinking of buying one of these casts, take note: they are costly and only available at specialist art shops.)

Visible form

The basis of anatomy is that, while the skeleton provides the basic framework of the body and determines its proportions, the muscles, which overlay the bones, create the visible form of the figure. The skeleton and muscles work together to produce the vast variety of movements that humans are able to make.

When you move on to a life model, the muscles are unlikely to be quite as pronounced as this cast. However, in most slim, strong models, the muscles will create discernible forms. And with practice, you will soon be able to see exactly how the muscles change in form as the body moves. This, in turn, will help you analyse and capture the overall pose of your model.

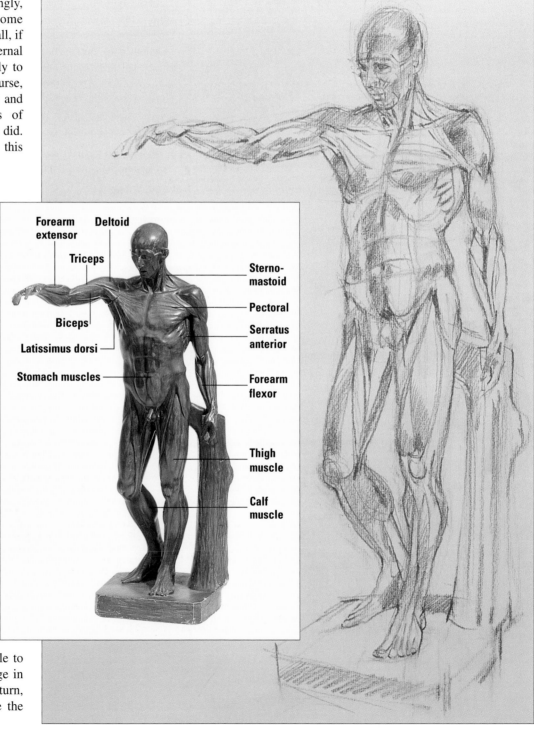

Forearm extensor
Deltoid
Triceps
Biceps
Latissimus dorsi
Stomach muscles
Sterno-mastoid
Pectoral
Serratus anterior
Forearm flexor
Thigh muscle
Calf muscle

LOOKING AT BONE STRUCTURE

It is important to bear in mind the structure of the skeleton when you work on a figure drawing. The pose of a figure depends on the position of the head, spine, shoulders, pelvis and limbs in relation to each other, and this is easier to ascertain if you can visualize the skeleton beneath the flesh.

As you work through the steps in this project, refer to the skeleton shown here and try to relate the muscles on the anatomical model to the bones they cover. And note that some bones, such as the kneecap, will be visible through the skin.

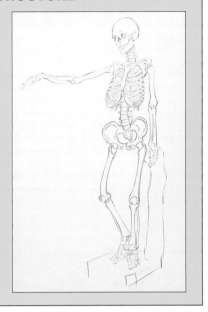

FIRST STEPS

1 ▲ **Sketch the figure** Using a sepia Conté pencil, sketch the main lines of the figure. As you work, check the proportions of the figure and the angles of the head, torso and limbs. A few guidelines – across the chest and running down the length of the torso and legs – will help you get the stance correct. Indicate the tree stump and stand.

**EXPERT ADVICE
Checking the pose**

Before beginning your anatomical drawing, make sure you get the stance of the figure right by making a quick sketch of the main lines of the body. Here, the weight is taken by the left leg and the pelvis is tilted at an angle towards the bent right leg.

2 ▶ **Work on the head** Indicate the facial features, the jawline and the indented line above the brow. Emphasize the prominent muscle – known as the sterno-mastoid – that runs down the side of the neck, from the base of the skull behind the ear to the inner end of each collarbone.

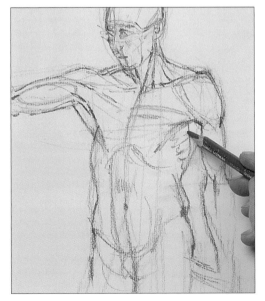

3 ◀ **Develop the upper body** Just below the armpits, show the ends of the latissimus dorsi muscles, extending around the back from the spine. On each arm, draw the oval biceps, the triceps behind them and the triangular deltoid above. Mark the pectoral muscles on the chest and, below them and to the side, the strap-like serratus anterior muscles.

4 ▶ Describe the limb muscles On the hanging forearm, draw the muscles running from the elbow to the wrist. These comprise the flexor on the inside, which bends the arm, and the extensor on the outside, which straightens it. Define the powerful muscles at the front of the thighs – these connect the pelvis to the shinbone. Indicate the position of the kneecaps with tentative circles. Then draw the calf muscles – note how one calf muscle is seen side-on and one protrudes from behind the shin.

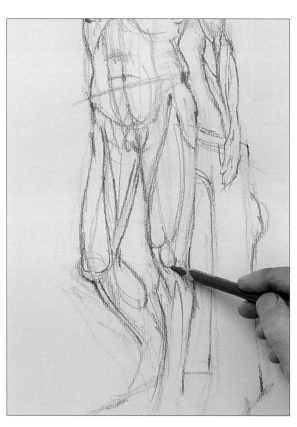

5 ▼ Draw the feet Indicate the bony structure of the feet with lines radiating out from ankle to toes. Bring the tree stump into focus by firming up its outline.

ADDING TONE TO THE BODY

The main muscles on the body are now clearly visible in outline. To help show the contours of the muscle groups, add tone to your drawing by shading with the Conté pencil.

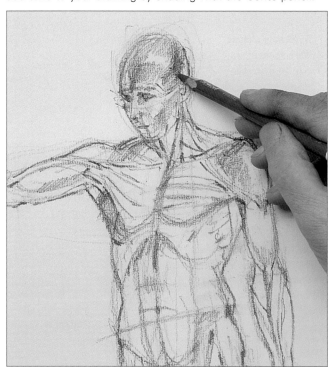

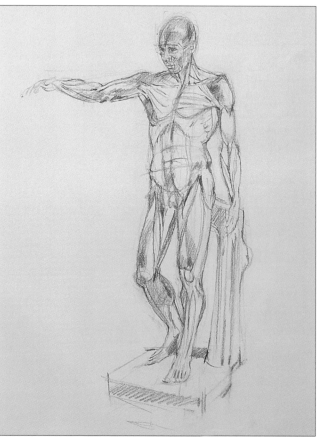

6 ▲ Shade the upper body On the figure's right side, render the dark tones under the biceps and in the armpit. Shade the front of the left shoulder. Darken the shadows under the pectoral muscles and below the rib cage. Then shade mid and dark tones over the face and cranium.

7 ▲ Shade the lower body Complete the flexor and extensor muscles on the right arm. Add definition to the stomach muscles and darken the shadow at the groin. Render a mid tone under the outstretched arm and on the leg muscles. Hatch in some shading on the stand and tree stump.

A FEW STEPS FURTHER

If you want to use your drawing as a reference for future figure studies, define the muscles a little more strongly in places, so that each muscle group will show up clearly.

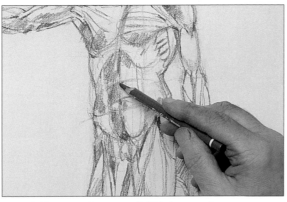

8 ▲ **Add tone to the stomach** Work over the serratus anterior muscles to emphasize the serrated effect at their edges. Shade more tone on to the regular blocks of muscles down one side of the stomach.

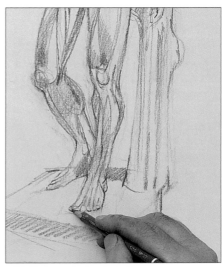

9 ▲ **Define the feet** Give the structure of the feet a little more detail, defining the toenails, the heels and the ankle bones. Shade the shin of the left leg.

THE FINISHED STUDY

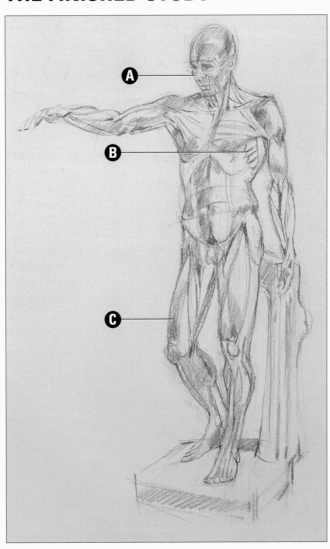

A Head proportions
As the cast has no hair, you can clearly see that facial features occupy only a small area in the bottom half of the skull.

B Muscle shapes
The outlines of the muscles have been clearly defined, so that it is easy to see how they overlap to build up the structure of the body.

C Body contours
Through subtle shading, the muscles take on a three-dimensional appearance, which helps to suggest the rippling contours of the body.

Drawing portraits

If you have ever wanted to record the likenesses of the people around you, but have felt uncertain about how to tackle the subject, now is your chance to try a simple, effective approach.

Help is at hand for all those who would love to draw their friends and family but find the prospect rather challenging. This subject can be simplified to make portraiture just as accessible as other genres.

The aim of this project is to enable you to portray the head from three different viewpoints. You will need some coloured papers, a handful of soft pastels and a willing sitter. The first portrait starts off as an egg, and nothing could be much simpler than that!

Visualizing facial structure

A face is composed of small surface areas or 'planes'. The planes facing the light are pale, whereas those facing away from the light are darker. If you find this difficult to visualize, try to imagine what your subject would look like if he or she were made of folded paper, rather like an origami model. Instead of rounded cheeks and other features, the face would be composed of angled planes.

Bearing this in mind, you can begin a portrait by establishing the subject in bold planes of light and dark, without worrying too much at this stage about whether the picture looks realistic.

Skin colour

Skin consists of both warm and cool colours. Light areas are generally warm, containing oranges, pinks and yellows; shadows are darker, often containing cooler browns, violets, blues and greens. You can apply this general rule

▲ **With an understanding of the basic structure of the face, you can achieve a realistic and characterful portrait.**

to all portraits, making adjustments to the colour proportions to accommodate particular skin types and racial differences if necessary.

Human skin is made up of several translucent layers that change appearance according to the light. As no single opaque colour will capture this quality effectively, you will need to overlay two or more colours to get a realistic effect. Soft pastels are excellent in this respect, because they can be overlaid easily so that the undercolours show through the pastel strokes.

PROPORTIONS OF THE HUMAN FACE

When working on the initial stages of a portrait, it is useful to remember that the human face is basically shaped like an egg. If you divide the egg into two approximate halves, the eyes fall more or less on the dividing line. If you then draw another line dividing the lower half in two, you will find the position of the bottom of the nose.

Divide the lower section into two halves again and the dividing line determines the approximate position of the mouth.

Obviously, every face is different, and you may have to adjust these proportions to suit your particular subject. However, as a general rule, an egg divided into equal sections provides a useful starting point.

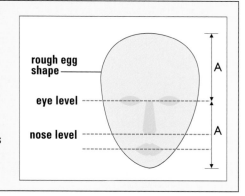

rough egg shape — eye level — nose level — A, A

PROJECT 1

FULL-FRONTAL FACE

For this front-view portrait, restrict yourself to just two colours. This will allow you to concentrate on the main features and on the broad areas of light and shade on the face.

As you can see from the portrait, the features are clearly visible because the subject is lit from one side with the other half of the face being thrown into shade. Front lighting on a full face tends to make the features appear flatter than they really are, and is therefore avoided by many portrait artists.

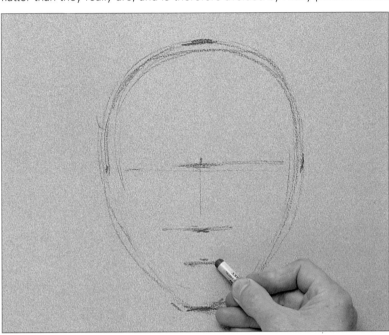

1 ▶ **Start with an egg shape** Using charcoal or a dark grey pastel, lightly sketch a basic egg shape – obviously, your subject's own head will be different, but the egg provides a useful starting point. Using the diagram on the previous page as a guide, sketch in a few horizontal lines to help you position the main features.

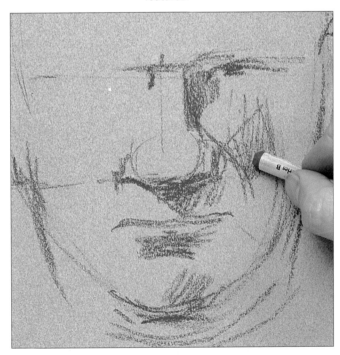

2 ▲ **Draw the facial features** Adapt and define the features, adjusting the drawing so that it begins to ressemble your sitter. For example, here the nose is broadened to suit that of the subject. Pick out the main shadows on the face and block these in using hatched lines.

3 ▲ **Adapt the shape of the head** As you progress, keep checking the proportions of the subject, paying as much attention to the spaces between the features as to the features themselves. Adjust the shape of the basic oval to match the outline of the face you are drawing.

6 ◄ **Add the highlights** Finally, choose a pale orange pastel for the highlights on the face. Look carefully at the subject to see where tiny patches of light are reflected on the prominent areas – forehead, nose, cheeks and upper lip and draw these in fine, cross-hatched lines.

4 ▲ **Add the shadows and hair** Carry on with the dark tone, picking out the rest of the shadows on the face. Don't forget the shadows under the eyebrows. These are important because they set the eyes in the face, avoiding a staring look. Sketch in the hair, treating this as a solid area of tone.

THE FINISHED SKETCH

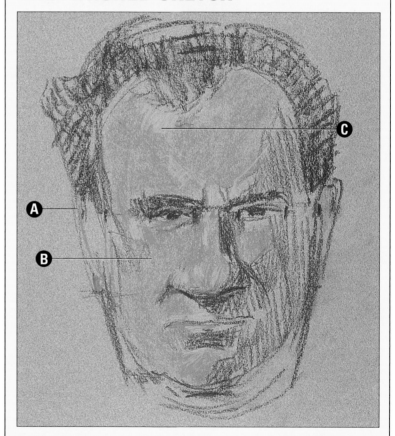

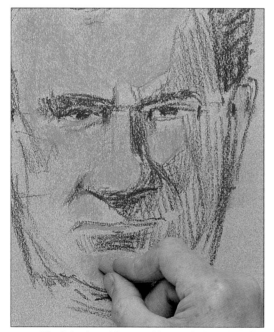

5 ▲ **Block in the mid-tones** Use a dark pink soft pastel to block in the rest of the face, this time picking out the warm medium tones which cover most of the illuminated side of the head. Again, simplify the planes into large, chunky shapes on the forehead, cheeks and chin, and on the front and side of the nose.

A The basic shape
The egg shape showing the position of the features was developed to form the outline of the face. The same dark tone was used to indicate the shaded side of the face.

B The mid-tone
A warm, dark pink pastel was used for the middle tones. Applied as blocks of colour, it shapes those areas of the face which are not in shadow.

C Pale highlights
Prominent areas of the face catching direct light are picked out and cross-hatched in very pale orange pastel.

145

CREATING REALISTIC SKIN TONES

Skin colours can be mixed by building up layers of soft pastels. A predominantly warm mixture might contain small amounts of a cooler colour; a cool tone might contain some warm colour. The colours here are just a few of the warm and cool pastels which can be built up to create realistic skin colours. Experiment with these and other shades to develop your own portrait palette.

Cool colours

From left to right: Indigo; Violet; Hooker's green; Grey; Ultramarine; Cobalt

Warm colours

From left to right: Indian red; Pale orange; Burnt sienna; Raw sienna; Pink; Yellow ochre

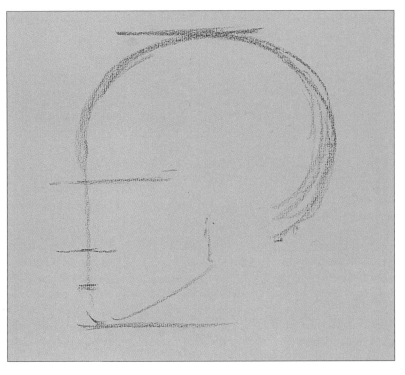

PROJECT 2

PORTRAIT IN PROFILE

Unlike a full-face portrait, a profile – or side view – of the face often benefits from being lit from the front. In this way, the features and expression of the subject are sharply defined, particularly when seen against a plain background as in this pastel study.

The following very general guidelines will prove useful when making the initial drawing. Start by sketching in the back of the head as an arc and the face as a straight, vertical line. As a rule of thumb, the distance from the face line to the back of the head is approximately the same as the distance from the mouth to the top of the head. Also, the jaw line usually falls about halfway between the line of the face and the back of the head. The ear is positioned just behind the jaw line.

YOU WILL NEED

Sheet of grey-green pastel paper

Charcoal or dark grey soft pastel

3 soft pastels: Dark pink; Mid brown; Pale pink

1 ▶ Draw some guide lines As with the full frontal view, it is best to start with a few light guide lines. Use charcoal or a dark grey soft pastel to sketch the cranium and to position the facial features.

2 ▲ **Establish the broad shadows** Position the ear, then develop the drawing, making sure that the features are all correct in relation to each other. Start to block in the main shadow areas, using parallel cross-hatched strokes.

3 ▲ **Block in the warm skin tones** Use a dark pink soft pastel to block in the warm tones on the jaw, forehead, cheekbones and nose. Work a little mid brown soft pastel into the dark shadow areas.

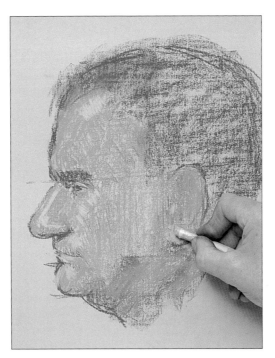

4 ◄ **Add the hair and highlights** Using the charcoal or dark grey soft pastel, block in the hair as a lightly rendered area of flat colour. Finally, use a pale pink pastel to pick out the highlights on the raised areas of the face – the nose, ear, forehead and cheekbone as well as around the mouth and chin.

THE FINISHED PROFILE SKETCH

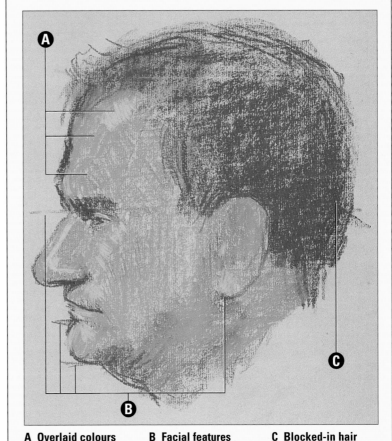

A Overlaid colours
The skin was applied as overlaid cross-hatched planes, using three basic colours – pale pink, dark pink and brown.

B Facial features
The nose, mouth, eye, jaw line and ear were positioned once the overall shape of the head was established.

C Blocked-in hair
The hair was blocked in over the basic structure of the back of the head as a flat shape of overall dark tone.

PROJECT 3

THREE-QUARTER VIEW

The final portrait depicts a three-quarter view of the head – the position between a full face and a profile. This view presents the subject informally and naturally, and is extremely popular with portrait artists for that reason.

Brilliant red paper paves the way for a sizzling colour scheme. Although much of the paper is eventually covered by layers of pastel, flecks of red show through the strokes to brighten and warm the skin tones of the finished picture.

Because colour plays such a dominant role in this picture, the initial approach differs slightly from the first two studies. Here, the flesh colours of the face are established before the outline is drawn. However, you should not find this way of working difficult, as the principles are exactly the same: careful construction and simplified planes of light and shade.

YOU WILL NEED

Sheet of red pastel paper

6 soft pastels: Orange; Medium grey; Pale grey; Dark grey; Brown; Pale yellow

Master Strokes

Jean Fouquet (*c.* 1425–80)
Gonella, the Ferrara Court Jester

A celebrated painter in fifteenth-century France, Jean Fouquet produced this characterful portrait of a court jester in 1445, while he was travelling in Italy. He has portrayed the jester's wrinkled, expressive face and aging features honestly, yet sympathetically. The artist has also perfectly captured the jester's subtly humourous expression with a slight smile playing about his lips. Fouquet's work has an almost sculptural sense of form and he has modelled the face with translucent flesh tones and sensitive line work.

One skin tone blends imperceptibly into another to create the curves and furrows on the old man's face and the shaded areas around his eyes and mouth.

Features such as the jester's hair and beard are painted in impeccable detail and help to bring him to life as a personality.

1 ▲ **Start mapping out the face** Keeping your strokes light and loose, start by drawing the palest areas of the face with an orange pastel. Use a medium grey pastel to suggest the eyes and the deeper shadows.

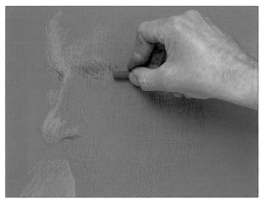

2 ▲ **Suggest the shadow areas** Establish the shirt and outline of the chin in pale grey. Using the side of the medium grey pastel, lightly block in the main shadows, allowing the red paper to show through. Hatch the shadows on the shirt and under the eyebrows in dark grey.

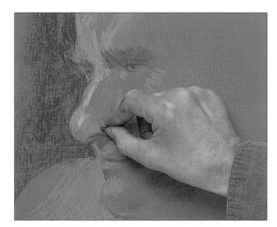

3 ▲ **Establish the background** Block in the background with the side of the dark grey pastel, redefining the outline of the face. Use brown to emphasize some of the shadows and creases. Overlay hatched strokes of pale yellow, orange and pale grey for the light flesh tones.

4 ► **Extend the background shadow** Strengthen the deep background tone with the side of the dark grey pastel, taking the heavy shading out towards the edge of the picture.

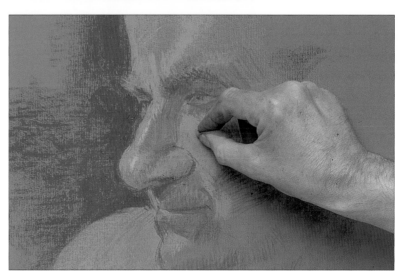

5 ◄ **Develop the light and dark areas** Block in the pale patches on the side of the face and on the throat with the orange pastel. Strengthen and define the broad facial shadow, using the medium grey pastel. Extend the shading towards the back of the face and into the neck.

6 ▲ **Strengthen the skin colours** Working with small hatched lines, develop the face by strengthening and building up the planes of colour and overlaid pastel strokes. Introduce some areas of brown to add more warmth to the existing grey shadows.

7 ▼ **Add the hair** The hair is treated as a single dark mass with patches of denser tone in the shadow areas. Here, the deep shade around and behind the ear is emphasised in dark grey, using heavy opaque strokes.

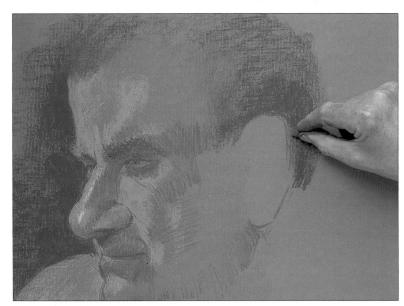

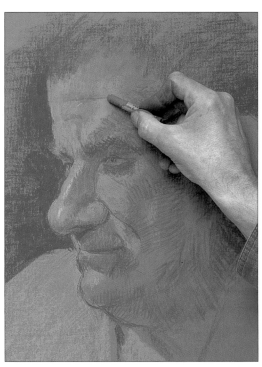

8 ▲ **Draw the wrinkles** Finally, lightly sketch in the position of the forehead creases and the lines around the mouth, using the brown pastel. These marks should not be too pronounced, so try to keep the strokes light and feathery.

THE FINISHED SKETCH

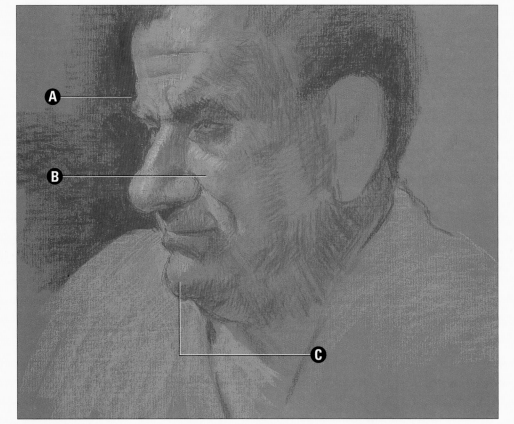

A The background
The dark background emphasizes the pale highlights on the skin and gives a crisp, well-defined edge to the face.

B Hatched skin colours
Layers of pastel colours were built up to create a variety of subtle skin tones from cool, greyish shadows to pale orange highlights.

C Red undercolour
The red paper shows through the pastel strokes, providing a warm, unifying undercolour to the other colours in the portrait.

Introducing figure drawing

With these few simple rules as a guide, you'll find that drawing the human figure is much more approachable than you might have thought – it's all a matter of keeping things in proportion.

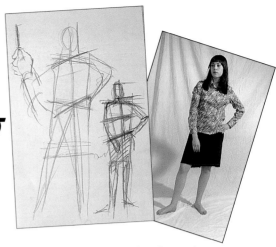

▲ Before beginning your drawing, make plenty of thumbnail sketches from the figure – these will help you to get the feel of the project.

First of all, try to forget that you are drawing a human being. If you look at the figure as you would examine a still-life group, you will find that it seems easier straight away. Forget about producing an accurate likeness, and concentrate instead on understanding and drawing exactly what you see.

Simplify the form

You will find it easier to see objectively if you try to visualize your subject as a series of abstract shapes – spheres and ovals for the head, for example, cylinders for the limbs, and softened cubes for the torso and pelvis. One of the wonderful things about the human body is its flexibility, so notice the way that one part moves against another. If you can't work out how the body is held in a particular pose you can check it by adopting the pose yourself – this is a marvellous way of really getting a 'feel' for what is going on under the surface.

The proportions of the figure

In a standing figure, the height of the head fits into the rest of the body approximately seven times. The legs are about the same length as the head and trunk together, and the navel is placed about three heads down. With the arms by the side, the hands reach halfway down the thighs. These proportions provide a useful starting point, but you will find that individual sitters are often different from this average.

The head fits into a seated body approximately four times. This rule of thumb is useful if you are drawing a seated figure for the first time.

1
2
3
4
5
6
7

CHECK ANGLES AND PROPORTIONS

To produce a convincing figure drawing, it is important to render key angles and proportions as accurately as possible. You can measure and plan both of these very easily by using a pencil or pastel and your thumb as a measuring tool.

Measuring proportions
Hold your pencil vertically with the sharpened end down. Extend your arm fully, close one eye and look at the model. Align the top of the pencil with a key point – say the top of the model's head – and slide your thumb down until it aligns with another important point, such as the base of her neck. Keeping your arm fully extended, move the pencil to the measurement you want to check.

Checking angles
The slope of the shoulders or pelvis is often the key to a pose, but can be difficult to judge by eye. Use a pencil to check these important angles. Extend your arm and align the pencil with the line of the shoulders, for example. Maintaining that angle, transfer the pencil to your drawing and mark the angle on the support – this will give you the correct slope of the shoulders.

PROJECT 1

A STANDING POSE

Ask the model to stand with her hand on her hip and her weight on one leg – this will automatically cause one hip to swing out and the shoulder to dip to counterbalance that swing. Try the pose yourself to get the feel of it.

FIRST STEPS

1 ▶ Determine the key verticals and angles
With the help of a sanguine Conté crayon, check the key lines and angles: the centre of the face and torso, and the slopes of the shoulders and pelvis. Note, too, the centre of gravity running down into the weight-bearing left leg. Draw in these key lines with the Conté crayon. Once these are right, the pose will look balanced and convincing.

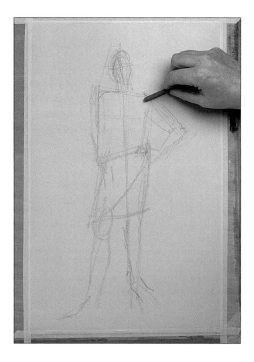

2 ▲ Check the proportions Use the Conté crayon to check the proportions of the figure, using the rule of thumb method. Bear in mind that your model might be slightly different. Check your drawing by making light marks to align with the top of the head and the chin, then use your pencil to transfer this dimension to the paper seven times to locate the feet.

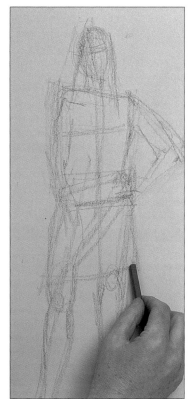

3 ◀ Continue sketching the figure
Using the same sanguine Conté crayon, continue refining the broad outlines of the drawing. Apply the chalk very lightly, measuring, drawing and redrawing until you are satisfied that the stance and proportions are correct. Don't worry about building up lots of lines – these will all be absorbed into the final drawing.

DEVELOPING THE DRAWING

Once you have established the broad shapes and proportions, start to develop the figure in pencil. The Conté sketch provides a useful underpinning for the subsequent drawing.

4 ◀ Start to refine the drawing Change to a 4B or 6B graphite pencil, or a Mars Lumograph EB, which is blacker and waxier. Indicate the hairline and the facial details. Because the head is tilted, the lines of the eyes and lips slope slightly. Use the pencil to measure the angles of the left forearm and upper arm. Draw the arm, then compare the negative space between the arm and torso on your drawing to that of the model.

5 ▶ Simplify shapes
Continue refining the drawing, studying the model carefully. Places where the body bends, such as the waist, shoulders, elbows and knees, are important. The knee can be rendered as a simple oval.

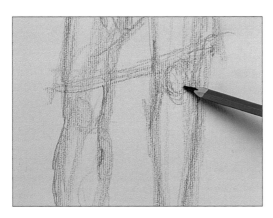

THE FINISHED PICTURE

6 ◀ Add surface detail When you are happy that the underlying figure is accurate, start to add surface details, such as the folds and creases in the fabric. Use rough, rapid hatching to show how the fabric of the model's blouse falls under her breast, and strengthen the fold where her skirt is pulled across her thighs. The curve at the wrist and the crease at the elbow describe her garment, and at the same time emphasize her rounded arm.

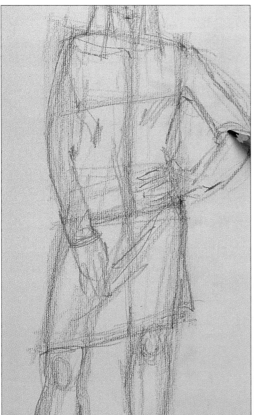

7 ▶ Add tone Half-close your eyes so that you can see the areas of darkest tone as well as the highlights. Apply loose hatching to the darkest areas – on the skirt and on the shaded areas on the legs, for example. These touches of dark tone will make the figure appear more solid and three-dimensional.

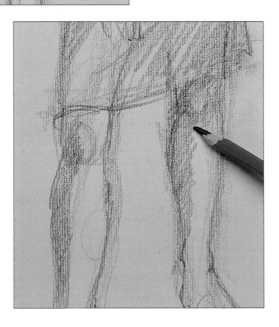

A Crayon underdrawing
Using a coloured crayon for an underdrawing helped to establish the figure and provided a useful guide for the more detailed pencil drawing. The combination of black and sanguine is visually pleasing.

B Loose hatching
Loosely hatched pencil marks were used to describe the dark skirt and the shading on the figure.

C Tinted paper
The buff colour of the paper was chosen by the artist because of its close similarity to a natural skin tone. This is why certain areas of the paper could be left unworked as highlights.

PROJECT 2

AN ALTERNATIVE POSE

Studying a wide variety of poses is vitally important in figure drawing to get a feel for the proportions and movement of the body. Working with a seated figure gives you the opportunity to examine a whole different set of angles and proportions.

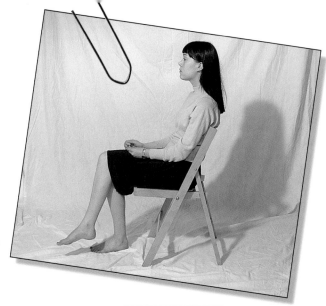

FIRST STEPS

1 ▼ **Establish the main outlines** With a sanguine Conté crayon, lightly lay in the main outlines of the figure. As you work, use a pencil to check the slope of the body, the head, the legs and the chair. Note that, during a long pose, it is inevitable that the model will shift slightly. In the early stages, you can modify your drawing accordingly, but as the drawing progresses, it is best to ask the model to hold one particular position as much as possible – you can discuss what she finds most comfortable.

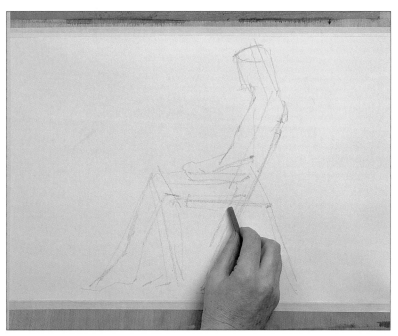

2 ▶ **Refine the drawing** Once you have checked the accuracy of the drawing, you can start to emphasize the important lines. Vary their weight, using heavier, darker lines where there is shadow: on the back of the model's calf and where her back rests against the back of the chair, for example.

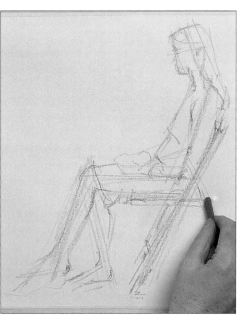

YOU WILL NEED
Piece of buff-coloured Ingres paper
Conté crayon (studio stick) in Sanguine
Staedtler Mars Lumograph EB pencil

DEVELOPING THE DRAWING

Now that the outlines of the seated figure have been broadly established, you can start to add detail in pencil. As in the previous study, the Conté sketch provides a useful basis for the subsequent drawing.

3 ▲ **Develop the drawing in pencil** Change to the EB pencil. Refine the face, adding the details with a few deft touches. Don't overwork the drawing; you will find that the black pencil lines applied over the sanguine Conté crayon begin to show up very quickly.

4 ▼ **Draw the hands** Study the folded hands carefully, then draw them quickly and economically with a light, energetic line. Draw the outline of the model's jumper and skirt, adding the folds at her elbow, on her back and under her breast. Add touches of dark tone under her skirt and in the angle of the chair.

6 ▲ **Darken the hair and folds** Add dark tones to the hair with hatched lines. Use long, flowing strokes of the pencil to give emphasis and texture to the strands of hair falling on to the model's shoulders. Study the figure carefully and add more folds to the jumper.

5 ▲ **Add tone and detail to the skirt** Continue working across the entire drawing, outlining the legs and adding some dark tone to the hair and the skirt. Notice the way the hatching follows the folds on the skirt. It is important to include the chair as it explains the model's pose, so draw its legs and add the shadow cast by the upright on the seat.

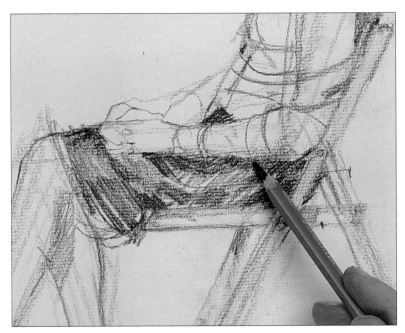

7 ▲ **Add dark tones to the skirt** Using the EB pencil, hatch the shadow cast by the model's arm on to her skirt. The contrasts of tone on this part of the skirt help to model the roundness of the thigh.

8 ▶ Hatch the cast shadow Holding the EB pencil loosely, start to hatch the shadow cast by the model and the chair. Use light marks that follow the way the shadow falls across the floor and then sweeps up the draped sheet behind. Cast shadows anchor the figure firmly to the horizontal surface and also add an interesting shape to the study.

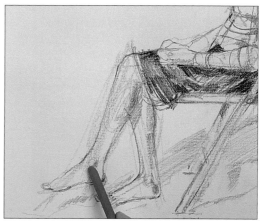

9 ▲ Add warm tone to the legs and hands Use the sanguine Conté crayon to add warm shadows on the ankles and down the back of the calf. Add another touch of tone on the underside of the folded hand.

THE FINISHED PICTURE

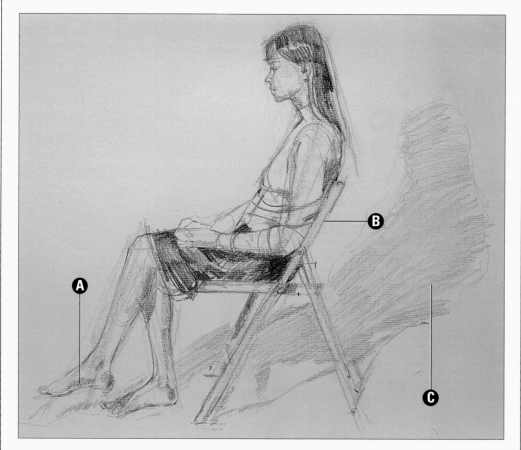

A Sanguine underdrawing
The warm tones of sanguine Conté crayon are ideal for any figure study, especially when combined with a warm, buff-coloured support as here.

B Explain the pose
In a figure drawing, it is important that the viewer can understand the pose. The chair was drawn in some detail to make it clear that the model was supported not only by the seat but by the back.

C Cast shadows
The cast shadows were drawn to set the figure in space and anchor it firmly to the ground. They also improved the composition by providing an interesting shape to balance the main figure.

Drawing the head

Although each person's head is unique, there are certain fundamental principles of figure drawing that can help you improve your portrait skills.

There are many aspects to consider when you are drawing a portrait – how to establish the shape of the head, how to convey an individual's facial features and how to build up a sense of form through shading. If you master these concepts, you will find it easier to create a good likeness.

Skull structure

A knowledge of how the underlying bone structure of the skull determines the shape of the head and facial features is extremely helpful when you are drawing from life and trying to analyze your model's main characteristics. The form of the skull is initially evident on the surface of the face in the appearance of the cheekbones, the jaw and chin, the ridge of the nose and the dome of the cranium. The skull's structure also determines the relative positions of the facial features.

Certain proportions tend to be similar in most people. For example, the distance from the top of the head to the eyes is roughly equal to the distance from the eyes to the chin. The distance from the eyebrows to the bottom of the nose is more or less the same as from the bottom of the nose to the chin. The gap between the eyes is approximately the width of an eye. However, you should always check an individual's proportions by measuring with your pencil.

▶ Where the form of the head can be seen clearly, as on this model with a shaven head, it is easier to relate the visible features to the underlying structure of the skull.

DRAWING FACIAL FEATURES

Although everybody's features are unique, there are common characteristics to look out for when you are drawing them. The classical features represented in these plaster models are based on the sculpture *David* by Michelangelo (1475–1564). The models are available from the British Museum in London.

EYE
The eye is simply a ball set inside a bony socket in the skull. Shading above the eye suggests the protruding brow bone. Lids are shown by pairs of curved lines around the iris.

NOSE
A simple but helpful way of visualizing the nose is as a cylinder emerging from a sphere with a quarter sphere on each side for the nostrils. Shade around the nose and inside the nostrils to define them.

MOUTH
The mouth is made up of lobes: three on the upper lip (a circular central area and a lobe on either side), and two on the lower lip. The chin forms a circular form below it. Emphasise the line where the lips close together.

EAR
The ear can be broken down into an outer rim of cartilage ending in the large lobe and, inside this, a protruding semi-circular piece of cartilage. Add shadows in and around the ear to define these features.

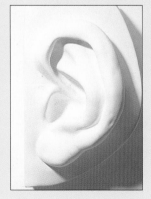

FIRST STEPS

1 ▲ **Establish the proportions** Using a sanguine Conté pencil, draw the outline of the head and shoulders. Measure proportions with your pencil and lightly mark in a curved line at the level of the eyes and another down the centre of the face to help place the nose. Sketch in the features and begin to develop them (see left).

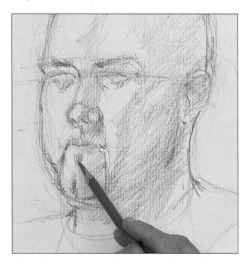

2 ▲ **Work up some details** Begin modelling the head with long, light hatching lines on the right of the head, neck and jaw. Lightly shade in the lips, marking a heavier line where they meet. Darken the beard and eyebrows, and the shadows under the nose.

MODELLING THE HEAD

Give the head a more solid feel by adding and refining areas of tone. Remember the head is lit from the left, so most of the shading will be on the right-hand side.

3 ▲ **Work on the eyes** As you develop the eyes, check that they still sit well on the curved guide line you drew in step 1. Emphasize the upper lids and hatch a little shading above them to indicate the shadow under the jutting brow-bone. Draw the irises and put in the pupils.

TROUBLE SHOOTER

SENSITIVE LIPS

Avoid the temptation to draw lips with strong outlines and then shade them in afterwards. They will look more sensitively drawn if you use shading alone to define them. The top lip is shaded more heavily than the upturned lower lip, which catches the light.

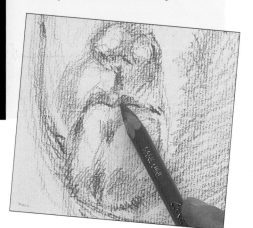

The underlying structure

Underpinning the soft flesh of the face is the bony structure of the skull. Keep the shape of the skull in mind when you are drawing a portrait, as it helps you make sense of the features of the head. In both the three-quarter view and the side view shown here, you can see how the skull is based on a sphere and an egg-shaped oval. The facial area is quite small compared to the whole skull.

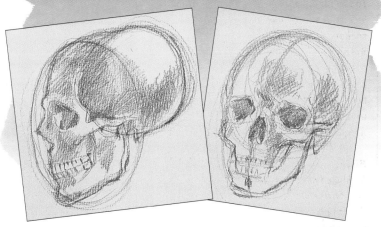

4 ▶ **Develop the mouth and ear**
Work up some dark tone on the far right of the head, which is in the deepest shadow. Define the lips more clearly, but don't give them heavy outlines (see Trouble Shooter). Using a combination of shading and line work, define the outer areas and recesses of the ear.

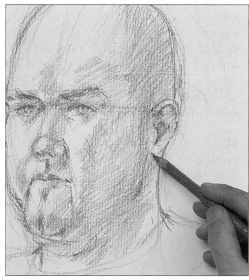

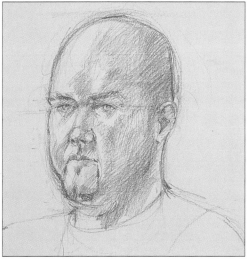

5 ◀ **Work on final details** Go over the outline of the head once more to firm up the shape. Make two emphatic marks for the nostrils and darken the beard. Lightly extend the shading on the right of the head and face, covering the whole cheek area except for a highlight under the eye.

A FEW STEPS FURTHER

Now that the head is worked in a lot of detail, a little more definition on the upper body will give a better balance to the portrait. Don't overdo it, though – the main point of interest is the head.

6 ▶ Sketch the T-shirt Lightly suggest the logo on the T-shirt and draw the silver chain and cross. Add light tone to the shoulder on the right with some well-spaced hatching lines.

7 ▲ Put in the last facial details Sharpen the Conté pencil well and work over all the features, putting in details that you might have missed, such as the dots at the inner corners of the eyes. Complete the moustache and beard with short hatched lines.

THE FINISHED PICTURE

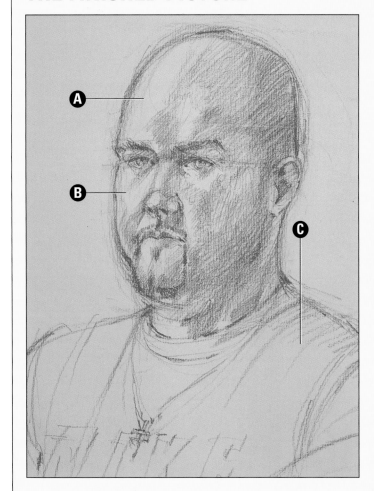

A Egghead
The distinctive egg-shaped form of the head can be seen quite clearly in this portrait, reflecting the underlying structure of the skull.

B Informative pose
The three-quarter view of the head, with strong lighting from the left, gives good contrasts of tone and shows the shapes of the features distinctly.

C Head and shoulders
The upper body, though only sketchily drawn, is necessary to anchor the head and put it in context, adding to the character of the portrait.

Sketching a group of people

If you carry a sketchbook around with you, you can make rapid drawings wherever you are and capture the many ways people move and interact when in a group.

Getting models and friends to pose for you is a marvellous way to learn about drawing the human figure, but the most interesting sketches are often those made from everyday life. These spontaneous sketches are full of movement and atmosphere, interesting poses and expressive gestures.

Sketching in public

Find a quiet corner where you won't be jostled. Equip yourself with a newspaper, a cup of coffee or a glass of beer so that you blend into the background – your subjects probably won't notice what you are doing. Keep your materials simple – a small sketch book, a pencil or pen, a pencil sharpener and an eraser are all you need. Study the scene carefully and then start to draw, looking for the telling details – a profile, a gesture, a fold of fabric. Work quickly and don't worry about the accuracy of your lines. The pages of your sketchbook are the best place to experiment and find out what you can do.

Part of the skill of successful sketching is training your visual memory. You cannot be sure that your subjects will hold a pose for more than a few seconds, so you will have to rely on your memory to complete a sketch. If you practise regularly, you will soon discover that this becomes easier.

You may find, too, that even when people are moving about a great deal, they often return to the same pose, so you can sometimes go back and refine your drawing. It is especially useful to bear this in mind when drawing people at sports matches – both players and spectators.

SKETCHING IN A CAFÉ

The size of sketch book you use will depend on the circumstances. If you are in a crowded environment, it makes sense to work in a small sketch book, but in a quiet corner of a café, like the one in this exercise, a large sketch book is practical. A large page also allows you to make several small studies of individual figures and to include plenty of detail if you wish.

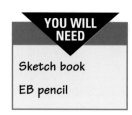

YOU WILL NEED

Sketch book

EB pencil

1 ▶ Start the sketch
Using a black, waxy EB pencil, or another drawing medium that you feel comfortable with, begin sketching the first figure. Work freely and loosely, looking for details, such as the angle of the head or a hand clasping a glass.

2 ◀ Add the second figure Draw the figure of the man, noticing in particular the distance between him and the first figure you sketched. The EB pencil gives a great variety of tones from velvety black to grey. Make a mental note of the glasses and other items on the table – these details may be useful at a later date.

3 ▼ **Draw the third figure** Draw the girl seen in profile on the left of the group. With practice, you will be able to establish a figure with just a few lines. Don't worry about the composition – simply record what you see.

4 ▲ **Sketch the background** It is worth adding details from the background, if you have time. The coat stand adds an important vertical element and the curling hooks at the top have a decorative quality. Complete the sketch by adding hatched tone on the back of the figure in the foreground.

CREATING A PICTURE FROM SKETCHES AND PHOTOGRAPHS

Even the most basic sketch can conjure up a particular moment, a gesture, a look. Wherever possible, make sketches of individuals and details from the background, too. This will supplement your other material and help you to commit the scene to memory. The more reference material you have, the better.

Master Strokes

Edward Burra (1905–76)
Dockside Café

The English painter, Edward Burra, was drawn to the kinds of characters found in seedy locations such as this café in Marseilles. Both the figures and the background are painted in lively detail.

The dock workers and barmaids in the café are painted in a stylized way that verges on caricature. Small details add a theatrical touch.

The location is as important to Burra as the characters in it and it is drawn with the same precision, warmth and humour.

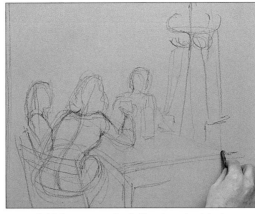

1 ▲ **Start the drawing** Study your reference material and decide what format suits the composition best. Working lightly with a black pastel stick, position the three main figures. Look for their centres of gravity and the rhythms of their poses. Indicate the location of the spine on the foreground figure.

2 ▲ **Add the coat rack** Still using the black pastel, sketch the coat rack – an important vertical element that marks the right-hand edge of the picture. Working with fluid gestures, develop the figures, thinking about the forms of the bodies underneath so that you can effectively suggest their solidity.

YOU WILL NEED

Large piece of mid-grey pastel paper

11 pastel sticks: Black; White; Naples yellow; Venetian red; Raw umber; Magenta; Olive green; Oxide of chromium; Ultramarine; Pink; Flesh tint

5 pastel pencils: Black; White; Naples yellow; Venetian red; Cadmium yellow

3 ▼ **Add some tone and detail** Change to the black pastel pencil. With loosely hatched marks, suggest the dark tone on the back and arm of the foreground figure. This dark area is an important element of the composition. Add touches of detail to the man's face.

4 ▲ **Develop the other figures** Still using the black pastel pencil, develop the head of the girl in profile. Draw the sweeping lines of the chair-back and use hatched lines that loop across the back of the foreground figure to suggest the bulk and weight of the torso.

5 ▼ **Add white pastel to the wall** Break a small segment off a white pastel stick and use this piece on its side to work colour over the background. The grey paper showing through the white pastel will give this area a vibrant and luminous quality which would be absent in an area of solid white. Take the white around the head in profile, using it to 'cut back' into and refine the silhouette.

6 ◄ **Finish the wall** Use a white pastel pencil to take the white of the wall around the heads and shoulders of the seated group. The contrast between the figures and the bright background is an important aspect of the composition, and the 'negative space' of the white wall will be a key element of the finished picture.

DEVELOPING THE PICTURE

The composition is now broadly established. Stand back and review your progress so far. Check the drawing in a mirror – because the reversed image is unfamiliar, it is easier to spot inaccuracies. Make any necessary adjustments and then start to add colour.

7 ► **Add colour to the hair** Using white and Naples yellow pastel pencils, start to indicate the wavy texture of the foreground figure's hair. A few rapidly drawn lines are an excellent shorthand to depict this area.

8 ► **Develop the flesh tones** Add some touches of Venetian red and cadmium yellow pastel pencil to give variety to the curly hair. Use a Naples yellow pastel stick for the flesh tones on the illuminated side of the man's face and Venetian red for the warm tones on the shaded side. Apply the same colours to the arm in the foreground. Don't press too hard – the lightly worked colour breaks over the textured paper, giving the image a pleasingly luminous quality.

9 ▲ **Add more local colour** Using pastel sticks, work over the entire image. Apply light strokes of raw umber for the table and the blouse of the left-hand figure; Venetian red for the terracotta plant pot; magenta for the wine bottle and the coat on the stand; olive green for the man's shirt; oxide of chromium for the plant; and ultramarine for the other coat on the stand. Use a black pastel stick to add some detail to the wine bottle.

10 ▼ **Fill in the top surface of the table** Use the Naples yellow pastel stick to block in the light tone of the table-top. Apply the colour lightly.

11 ▲ **Finish the table** Use the same Naples yellow pastel stick to complete the legs of the table, as well as the backs and seats of the chairs.

A FEW STEPS FURTHER

All the main elements of the picture are now in place and the colours have been broadly established. Although the picture was composed later from sketches and photographs made on location, the image retains the energy of a sketch made on the spot. You could take this painting much further, but it would lose some of its immediacy – pastel is easily overworked. However, a few more details will add impact.

12 ▶ **Add colour to the red coat** When working with pastel, it is difficult to blend colours. If you want to create a range of tones, you need to use pastels in various tints and shades of each colour. Therefore, add more magenta to the coat on the stand, and use a touch of pink for the highlights.

13 ▶ Develop the light and shade

Add strokes of flesh tint where the shoulders of the figure on the left catch the light. Use a sepia pastel to add a warm but dark tone to the side of the table – this increases the sense of depth in this area of the picture.

14 ▲ Add final details
Use a black pastel pencil to add touches of detail that strengthen the drawing of the profile of the girl on the left. Avoid the temptation to overwork the drawing.

THE FINISHED PICTURE

A Negative space
Don't be frightened of large 'empty' areas. Here, the large area of white wall became an important shape within the finished painting.

B Paper texture
The regular texture of the paper gave it tooth so that it held the pastel. It also broke up areas of pastel, creating passages of luminous broken colour.

C Tinted paper
The artist used a mid-grey paper to provide a useful base tone to underlie the entire painting and hold it together.

Drawing hands

Drawing hands is a useful skill, as convincing hands make all the difference to portraits and to figure-drawing in general. The best way to begin is to try some studies, such as the ones shown here, so that you can observe hands closely.

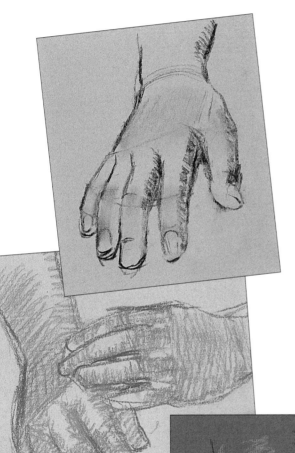

Hands play a vital role in figure studies. Not only can they convey movement or gesture, but they can also reflect the age, gender, lifestyle and personality of the subject. This is why a portrait that includes the hands is usually more interesting and compelling than one that does not.

Sadly, the hands are often overlooked, neglected or, like the feet, drawn too small in relation to the rest of the body. The aim of this project is to help you appreciate the importance of the hands, and it encourages you to find simple ways of capturing their apparent complexity. Don't worry if you have no model because, even when drawing, you have a hand to spare which can either be observed directly or reflected in a mirror.

Tones and colours

Keep the colours simple. No more than three or four pastel colours are used in each of these studies – just enough to indicate the lights, darks, warms and cools in broad terms. Also, choose a tinted paper, as this gives you an extra colour and also provides a medium tone against which both dark and light pastel tones will show up clearly.

The studies

Each of the four studies here looks at a different aspect of drawing hands, starting with a charcoal sketch showing the basic outline and proportions of the back of an outstretched hand. The other three are colour studies in soft pastel showing a pair of hands, the palm of the hand, and a closed fist.

▲ **Hands are so flexible that you will find endless poses for them. Here, four different views show hands from various angles.**

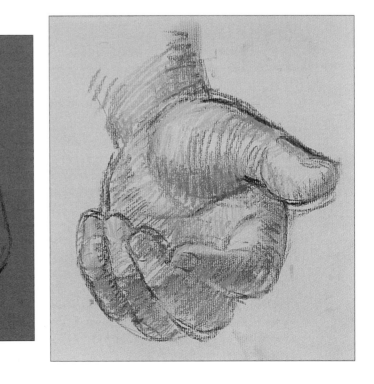

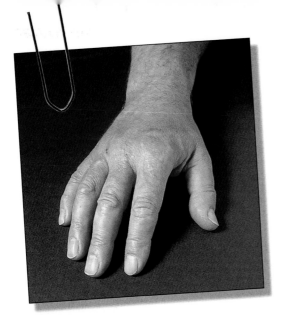

PROJECT 1

THE BACK OF THE HAND

Lay your hand, palm downwards, on a flat surface (it will be easier to see and draw if you use a mirror). Look carefully at your fingers. These taper at the tips, but will probably be surprisingly even in width. Note that each finger has three joints, including the knuckle. If you join each set of joints to form a curved line, you will end up with three arcs running almost parallel to each other. These provide a good general construction guide.

▲ **This basic position is a good starting point for your first hand-drawing, enabling you to observe the shape and length of the fingers.**

1 ▶ **Sketch the outline** Use charcoal to plot out the shape of the hand lightly. Pay particular attention to the width of each finger – you will find this easier to gauge if you also concentrate on accurately drawing any spaces between the fingers.

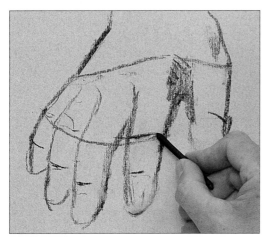

2 ▲ **Use construction lines** To help find and check the correct position of each finger joint, draw arcs to connect each row of joints.

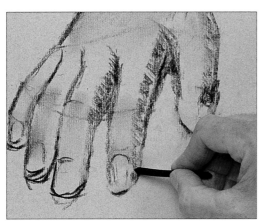

3 ▲ **Hatch the shadows** Indicate the shaded sides of the fingers with neat parallel strokes, following the curved forms.

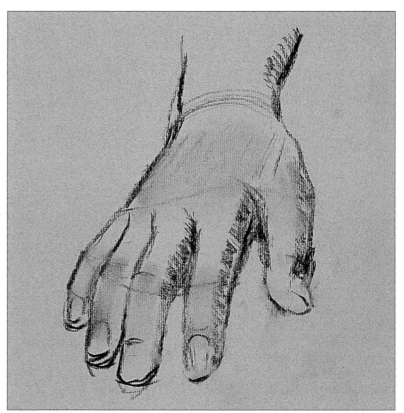

4 ▲ **The finished study** The completed hand is well proportioned and has a convincing shape. Notice how the fingers are basically narrow cylinders and how the lines of dark hatched tone indicate the roundness of the forms. The middle finger is the longest and straightest, with the other fingers bending slightly towards it.

PROJECT 2

A PAIR OF HANDS

For this pose, you will need to borrow a willing pair of hands. If this is not possible, use the reflection of your own hands in a mirror. Take a good look, then work from memory. From time to time, stop drawing to reposition your hands and check your work.

When you are drawing two hands, they must look the same size. Ensure this by first drawing the outlines as two mitten-like shapes. If the mittens look roughly the same size, then go ahead and construct the fingers and the rest of the hands within these outlines. Just two pastel colours, a mid blue and a mid brown, are used here in order to establish the relationship between the warm and cool flesh tones.

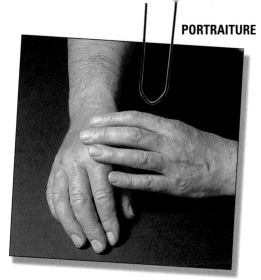

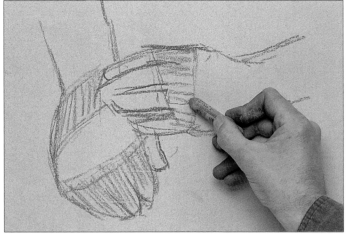

YOU WILL NEED

Sheet of grey-blue paper

2 soft pastels: Cobalt blue; Medium brown

1 ▶ Start with cool outlines
Using a cobalt blue pastel, draw the hands in outline. Use light cross-hatching strokes to suggest the broad shadow planes across the knuckles and the backs of the hands.

▲ **If possible, find a willing sitter to pose for this hand study. You can then concentrate on making the hands equal in size and proportion without having to keep moving one of your own hands.**

2 ▲ Introduce the warm tones Change to a medium brown pastel for the warmer tones in the hands. Introduce the brown into the shadowed areas, working over the initial blue pastel hatching.

3 ▲ The finished study Continue to work with parallel hatched and cross-hatched marks, using the direction of the strokes to describe the planes and curves on the backs of the hands, wrists and fingers. The brown and blue pastels, as well as the grey-blue paper, indicate the warm and cool tones of the skin.

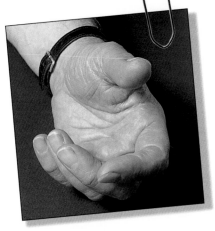

◄ When the hand is at rest, the fingers tend to curl up, forming a rounded shape. This viewpoint shows a foreshortened thumb.

PROJECT 3
OPEN HAND

In this relaxed position, the fingers of the hand are curled up and only partially visible. We are looking slightly down the thumb rather than seeing its full length. This viewpoint makes the fingers and thumb appear shorter than they actually are – a phenomenon known as 'foreshortening'. This does not present a problem provided you draw what you see rather than what you know to be there.

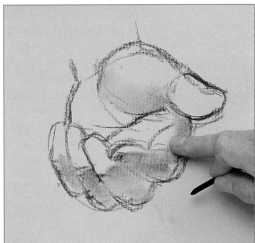

1 ▲ Make an outline sketch Use charcoal for the initial outline sketch, making sure the shapes and proportions of the fingers and thumb are correct in relation to each other. Lightly mark in the shadows on the underside of the fingers and rub these back slightly with your finger.

3 ◄ Add the paler areas Change to a cool, dull pink for the lighter areas. Again, work in directional strokes that follow the forms to indicate the curves of the hand. Add a touch of crimson to show the creases in the palm of the hand.

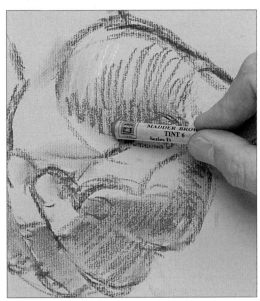

2 ▲ Indicate the shaded areas Develop the shadows with a red-brown pastel, using the charcoal underdrawing as a guide. Make crisp, hatched lines that follow the curved forms of the thumb and fingers.

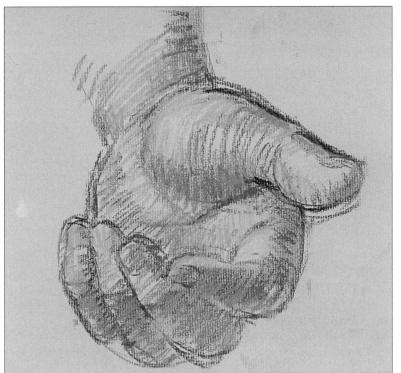

4 ▲ The finished study The foreshortened effect in this drawing is clearly evident. The outlined shape of the open hand is compact and round, rather than long and narrow as we know a hand to be, and as it would appear if it were viewed from above.

Master Strokes
Albrecht Dürer (1471–1528)
Hands of an Apostle

Dürer was primarily known for his woodcuts and engravings, and was a brilliant draughtsman. He paid meticulous attention to detail, a quality very evident in this sensitive portrayal of hands held up in prayer. This realistic brush drawing is worked on a slate blue background, the paper forming a mid tone between the black and white. The contours have been described with small hatched and cross-hatched marks, leaving the blue paper to show features such as the veins and the folds of skin around the knuckles. Bright highlights on the front edges of the hands imply strong illumination from the left of the picture.

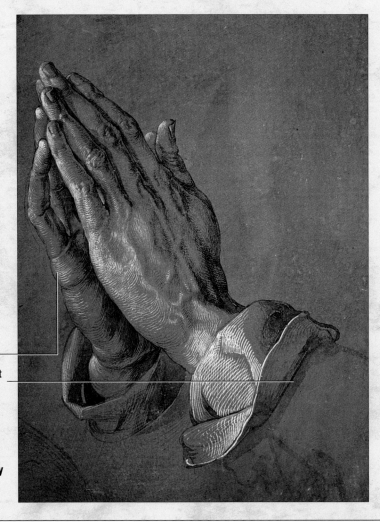

Tiny hatched lines are worked around the contours of the fingers, palms and backs of the hands to build up their curved forms. The lines are white in the light and black in the shadows.

A little dilute black paint suggests the shadow of the turned-back cuffs and part of the sleeves. There is no more detail beyond the cuffs, so the viewer's attention is fully on the hands.

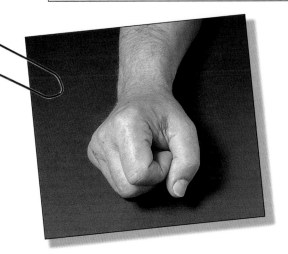

▲ This hand study is drawn in a different way from the others. The form is created by building up colour, tone and contours before drawing the actual outline.

1 ▶ **Start with the skin colour** Use a light brown pastel for the flesh colour of the hand. Work loosely and thinly, allowing the strokes to follow the curves of the fingers.

PROJECT 4

CLOSED FIST

Try making a pastel study of your closed fist, this time starting without the usual preliminary outline drawing. It is not as difficult as it sounds. Simply begin by establishing the skin colours and the internal contours, then gradually work outwards towards the outline.

YOU WILL NEED

Sheet of blue paper

4 pastel colours:
Light brown; Dark brown; Orange-pink; Very pale orange

EXPERT ADVICE
Trying out the colours

Before you begin your drawing of hands, first try out your chosen pastel colours on the tinted paper to make sure they contrast sufficiently. The paper and pastels should provide a good range of flesh tones and colour temperatures.

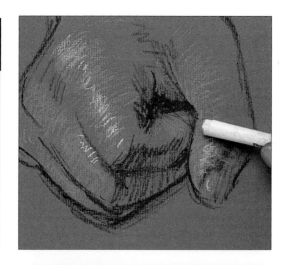

4 ◄ Add the highlights Finally, add the highlights along the tops of the fingers and the thumb. This is done in a shade of very pale orange – an almost white tint.

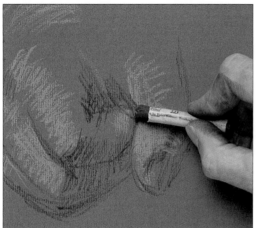

2 ▲ Add the shadows and outline Use thin hatched strokes of dark brown to render the shadows. With the same colour, draw the outline of the closed fist and fingers.

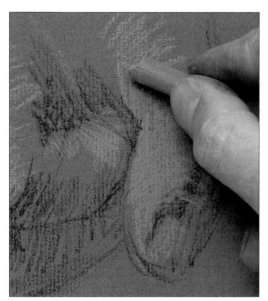

3 ▲ Work in a medium warm tone Changing to an orange-pink pastel, work into the fist, using this warm, rosy tone to link the existing dark and light areas. Do this by overlapping the existing colours with the new colour.

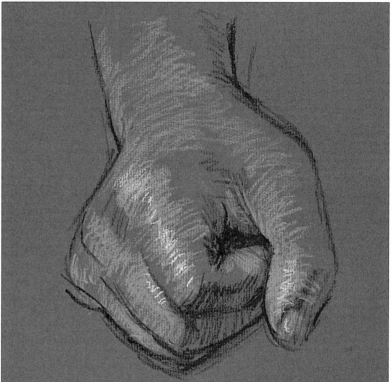

5 ▲ The finished study The flesh tones of warm pink, orange and brown contrast with the cool tone of the blue paper, which shows through the skin colours to represent the shadows. The dark brown outline, added during the later stages of the drawing, defines and contains the internal colours and the contours of the fist.

Drawing a child

Find out how to draw successful portraits of your own and your friends' children that will provide lasting memories of their early years.

Pencil drawings are a wonderful way to capture those precious moments of childhood that are over all too soon. But drawing a child needs a different approach from drawing an adult friend or model. Very young children find it difficult to sustain a pose for long, so you will have to work fast and loose if you intend to draw from life.

To make a more considered study, with accurately rendered detail and shading, it is probably better to work from a photo – as the artist did here. However, there is a danger that pictures worked from photos can be rather static so, ideally, spend some time sketching

your subject in life – looking in particular for subtle changes in the child's expression.

Holding a pose

Slightly older children can often be encouraged to hold a pose for longer periods if they are engaged in a favourite activity. One of the best times to draw a child is when they are 'glued' to the television, or lost in a book.

▲ **A light, sensitive touch with a graphite pencil conveys the soft, rounded limbs and delicate features of this young girl.**

The pencil drawing here is of a six-year-old girl. By posing her playing the recorder, the hands become an important focal point and they help balance the face. The slight tilt of her head prevents the portrait from being too symmetrical.

CHANGING PROPORTIONS

Children's faces and bodies alter with each passing year as their limbs become less chubby and their faces lengthen and gain definition. Be aware of these changing proportions when you are drawing – babies and toddlers have surprisingly large heads compared to their bodies, whereas adolescents gradually approach adult proportions.

In this diagram, the figures of three children of different ages are compared to an adult in terms of how many times the head fits into the body. A baby's head takes up a quarter of its total height, while the adult head fits into total body length on average between seven and seven-and-a-half times. The proportions of a six-year-old and a ten-year-old fall in between these extremes.

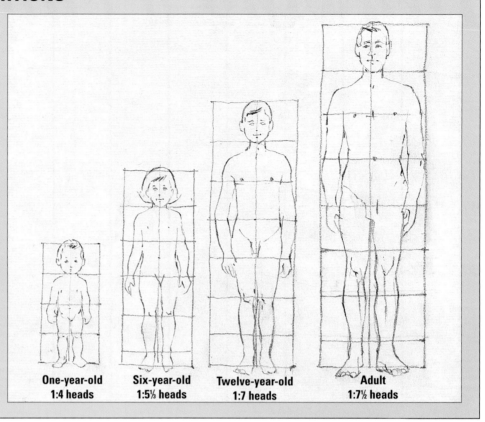

| One-year-old | Six-year-old | Twelve-year-old | Adult |
| 1:4 heads | 1:5⅓ heads | 1:7 heads | 1:7½ heads |

FIRST STEPS

1 ▼ **Make a sketch** Draw the girl's head as a slightly tilted oval – to help you place her facial features, mark crossing guide lines that follow the angle of the head. Outline the shoulders and arms and rough in the position of the hands on the recorder. Lightly mark in the eyes, nose and mouth.

2 ▲ **Add definition** Define the eyebrows and the nose, marking nostrils on each side of the ball shape that forms the nose tip. Draw curved lines to show the segments of the recorder. Work a little light shading on the face to the left of the recorder, then hatch darker tone on the underside of the hair. Begin to add texture to the hair with curved strokes.

3 ▼ **Develop the fingers** Shade lightly over the left side of the face, which is in shadow. Now work on the lower part of the picture, strengthening the shoulders and arms. Draw the fingers carefully – look at how they are placed at intervals on the recorder holes and notice how the little finger of the right hand curls up.

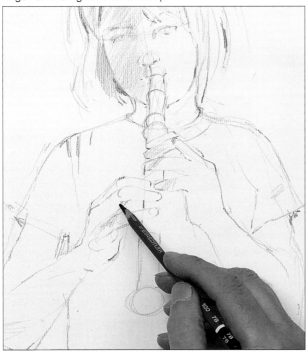

4 ▼ **Work up some shadows** Hatch shading around the fingers, curving the lines to indicate their rounded forms. Add more shading on the left side of the neck and on the arms. These shaded areas begin to give a three-dimensional feel to the limbs.

Looking at head size

In this photo of a boy aged three-and-a-half, the comparatively large size of the head is obvious – the domed skull dwarfs the shoulders. The features are close together, so that the facial area forms only a small part of the whole head. Make sure you show these proportions in your drawings.

BRING IN DARKER TONES

At this point, it is a good idea to extend the tonal range by establishing some darker tones in the drawing. Work shading on the recorder and on the left side of the hair.

5 ▲ **Put dark tone on the hair** Sharpen your pencil with a craft knife and redefine the eyes around the iris and lids, taking care to keep the drawing subtle. Put in light shading at the corners of the nose and mouth. Now use more vigorous strokes to work dark tone over the left side of the hair.

6 ▼ **Develop the features** Lift the corners of the mouth into a smile. Shade the irises and emphasize the pupils, then put a small shadow under the inner corner of the right eye. Work up the dark colour of the recorder showing between the fingers. Loosely indicate strands of hair on the right, then add more shading under the chin on this side.

7 ▼ **Work on the T-shirt** Bring out the contrast between the light and dark sides of the face by shading once more across the darker left side, strengthening the nostrils and the shadow on the nose. Begin hatching areas of tone across the T-shirt to give the impression of folds in the fabric. The band of dark tone on the right shows the shadow cast on to the T-shirt by the girl's arm.

8 ▲ **Complete the T-shirt** Continue working medium and dark tones across the T-shirt to complete the shadows created by the folds. Moving back to the girl's face, very slightly darken the shading on the left of the face, leaving a pale edge to define the face against the dark hair.

A FEW STEPS FURTHER

It is important to avoid being heavy-handed when drawing a portrait – so to add any more definition to the features, keep a light touch.

9 ▲ **Refine the features** Add shadow to the left side of the nose – the dark edge helps isolate this plane of the face from the gentler contour of the cheek. Fill out the fringe, then put in some subtle final touches on the eyes.

10 ▶ **Deepen tones**
Darken the shading on the arm, using curved lines to describe its rounded form. Strengthen the deep shadow on the T-shirt just below the arm. Put more definition into the fingers, darkening them at the joints.

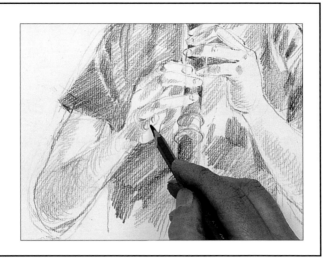

THE FINISHED PICTURE

A Oval face
The face of the young girl retains its babyish chubbiness, so the outline around the jaw and cheeks was kept very soft and smooth.

B Light and dark
The portrait was lit from the right. The resulting contrast between light and dark on the face gives the drawing added interest and avoids the flattening effect that a front-lit, full-face portrait can give.

C Fabric folds
The folds and creases in the T-shirt were simply described with different blocks of tonal shading.

Foreshortened figure

Take a new angle on figure drawing with this charcoal study of a young man observed from a low viewpoint.

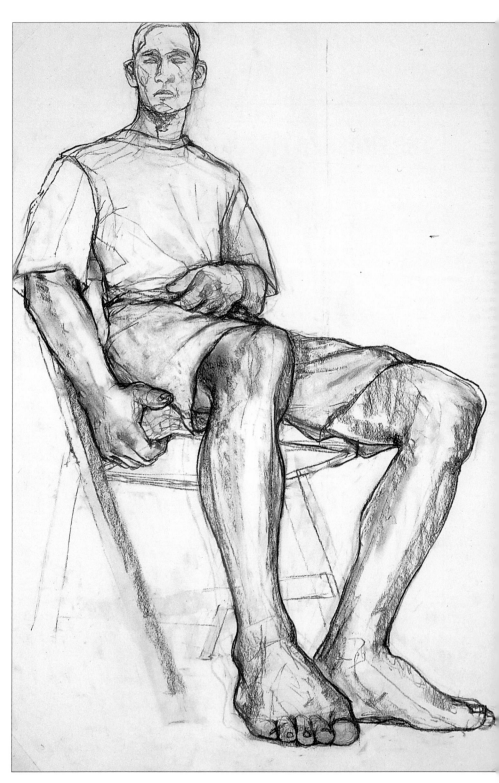

Figure studies tend to be drawn from a conventional viewpoint with the artist working on the same level as the model. However, you can create unexpected results by positioning yourself above or below your model so that the figure is foreshortened. Seen in this way, a figure appears to take on quite different proportions. You can even exaggerate the foreshortening effect to increase the drama of the picture.

A loose style

This drawing was worked in charcoal, which encourages a free, bold approach. Make the initial drawing quickly, putting down the pose as you see it rather than giving it the proportions you might expect. Then work over your first marks, firming them up as necessary.

Don't worry about making mistakes. With charcoal, you can change your lines easily by erasing them with a putty rubber or just your finger. It doesn't matter how often you do this – the faint marks that remain add a dynamic feeling to the drawing.

▶ **Working on a piece of paper almost a metre high encouraged the artist to use the charcoal in a bold, gestural way.**

STARTING WITH SKETCHES AND PHOTOS

SETTING UP A FORESHORTENED POSE

For this study, the artist set up the model on a chair placed on a table while she drew from a kneeling position in front of him. This created a foreshortened effect with the feet and legs seeming very large in comparison to the upper body. Ask a friend to sit for you and adopt similar poses. View your model from different sides and use sketches and photos to help you decide on a composition for the final drawing. (A Polaroid or digital camera is handy for instant results.) Look out for any unsightly or off-putting negative shapes created by the limbs of the figure or, indeed, the limbs of the chair. Also make sure your model can hold the pose comfortably.

FIRST STEPS

1 ▼ Sketch the body Outline the body, using a stick of willow charcoal. See how the feet look larger than life, while the left forearm appears compressed.

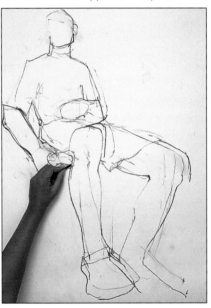

2 ▼ Redefine the hands Check the proportions of the hands by measuring with a pencil or by using linking lines (see Trouble Shooter, overleaf). Make changes as necessary. Here, the artist redefined the sitter's left arm and hand.

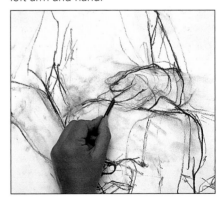

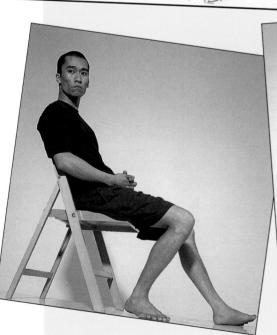

3 ▶ Draw features
Keep checking the accuracy of your initial drawing as you move from one area to another. Here, the head and shoulders have been moved up to reflect the correct position. Change to a charcoal pencil to draw the facial features. Mark in the hairline and draw the ears. Outline the triangle of shadow under the chin.

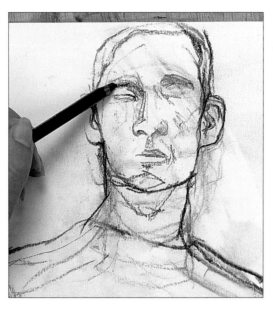

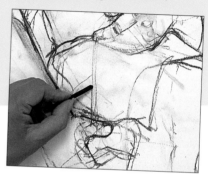

TROUBLE SHOOTER

CHECKING THE POSE

As you draw, constantly assess the relative positions of the limbs. Link one area to another with a lightly drawn charcoal line – here the artist draws a vertical from the end of the top hand to check its alignment with the bottom hand. If the angle of the line is wrong, correct the drawing as necessary.

4 ◀ Rework the legs
Pick up the willow charcoal again and work over the original drawn lines of the shorts and legs – reposition them if necessary. Define the contours of the calf muscles and ankles. Begin work on the toes of the right foot. Using a short length of charcoal on its side, apply a little tone to show shadow around the kneecap.

5 ▼ Develop the toes Darken the shadows between the toes on the right foot. Draw the nails and joints and mark in the tendons. Add tone on the ankle bone and up the leg.

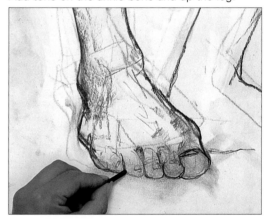

DEVELOPING THE FOREGROUND

To convey a sense of scale in the composition, begin to work into the lower part of the body in more detail, so that the eye is attracted here initially before moving up towards the head.

6 ▶ Work up the right hand Rough in the chair to anchor the figure in space. Firm up the outline of the right arm, then draw veins on the back of the hand and show the curled fingers. Using the short stick of charcoal, shade along the edges of the arm, across the hand and on the inner edge of the right leg. Add a dark smudge of charcoal in the crook of the right knee.

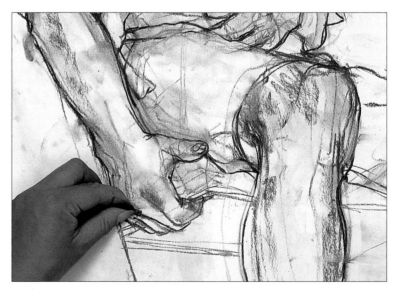

7 ▶ **Add more detail to the feet** Shade the edges of the left leg and foot to build up their three-dimensional form. Finish drawing the left foot, showing the curve of the arch and the shadow under it. Define the toes and nails and the line of the ankle bone.

8 ▼ **Block in the shorts** Tidy up the outlines of the legs and the shadows on them. Block in the shorts with the side of the short stick of charcoal, marking fabric creases. Smooth the texture with your fingers, then lighten the tone by using a putty rubber to erase pigment around the creases.

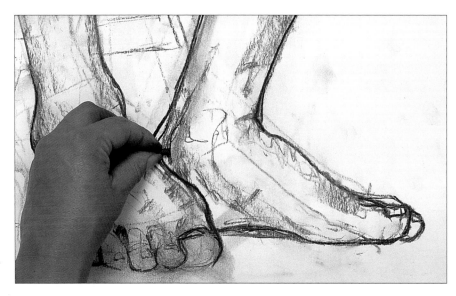

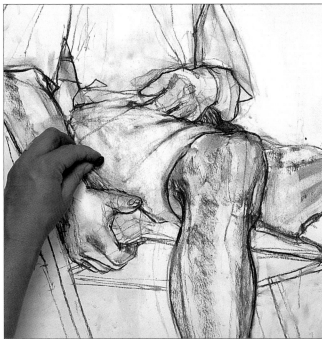

EXPERT ADVICE
Using board clips

Strong metal board clips offer a quick and easy alternative to masking tape for securing large pieces of paper to your drawing board.

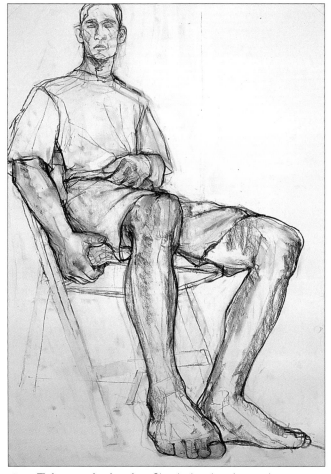

9 ▲ **Tighten up the drawing** Check the drawing and rework outlines if they have been rubbed away as you worked. Mark in more folds in the T-shirt and darken the shadows on the left hand. Using the charcoal pencil, add definition to the features, blocking in the shadow under the chin and emphasizing the shape of the cheekbones.

A FEW STEPS FURTHER

Now it only remains to deepen the tone in some areas and to put in a few emphatic final details. Create some highlights by erasing pigment with the putty rubber.

10 ▾ **Darken the toes** Using a compressed charcoal stick, work a darker tone over the toes and smudge with your finger. Add dark shadows under the toes, then go over the outlines of the toes and nails.

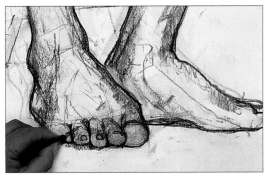

11 ▴ **Build up contrast on the legs** Add dark tone with compressed charcoal to the left hand and arm. Extend more dark tone across the legs, smudging in places with your finger. Lift out a highlight down the right shin with the putty rubber. Fix the drawing with spray fixative.

THE FINISHED PICTURE

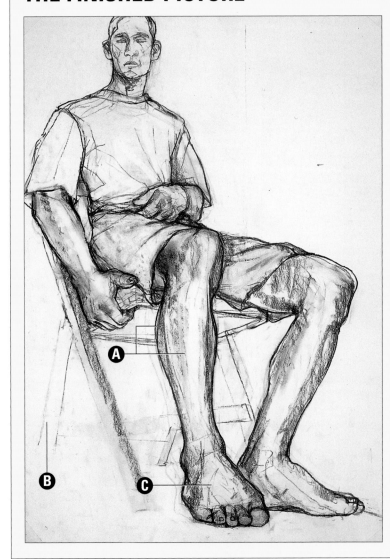

A Rich blacks and soft greys
The full potential of charcoal was exploited in this drawing. The outlines are strong and dark, but where the pigment was rubbed, it has become paler and softer, ideal for subtle tonal work.

B Lightly drawn chair
The chair was drawn very simply and lightly to make sense of the model's pose without distracting from the main focus of the composition.

C Big feet
As well as being large in comparison to the head and chest, the feet were worked more emphatically. This helps to increase the impression of recession.

An eye for detail

There's more to depicting eyes than accuracy – you should also try to invest them with a sense of life that says something about the sitter's character.

When we look at a person we usually notice their eyes first, and the old saying that the eyes are 'the windows of the soul' does have some truth. Perhaps more than any other facial feature, the eyes convey a person's character and emotions, and they are a vital element in any portrait.

Eye anatomy

Although eyes vary in shape, size and colour from one person to another, the underlying anatomical structure is the same. The eyeball is basically spherical and the visible portion of its surface is small in relation to the area that is hidden behind the eyelids.

When drawing or painting eyes, beginners often make the mistake of leaving white showing all around the iris, giving the sitter a rather manic stare! In fact, the upper lid covers a small portion of the iris (the coloured area) and so, for most of the time, does the lower lid, except when the eyes are looking up.

Always draw both eyes in tandem – don't finish one and then start on the other. The eyes work as a pair, so draw them as a pair.

Start by sketching

As with all the facial features, it is best to begin drawing the eyes by sketching the overall shape with very light, tentative strokes; hard, dark outlines tend to make the eyes appear 'pasted on'. Start by indicating the spherical shapes of the eyeballs, then sketch in the lids that

ANATOMY OF THE EYE

The eyes are spheres that 'sit' inside the circular cups of the eye sockets; use your fingertip gently to feel the roundness of your eyeballs through your upper eyelids. Note how the covering eyelids follow this form. The distance between the eyes varies between individuals, but as a general rule the distance between the two inner eye corners is about one-eye's width.

The upper lid folds over the lower one at the outer corner.

The upper eyelid obscures the top curve of the iris.

The upper lid has a more pronounced curve than the lower one.

The bottom lid has a discernible top and bottom edge – however, it is not as thick as the top lid.

wrap around them. Indicate the rims of the eyelids, and then place the pupils and the irises.

Light and shade

Once you are happy with the basic construction, you can start to refine the contours and develop the tones, keeping in mind the structure beneath. Observe how the lights and shadows – on the lids, the white of the eye and on the surrounding skin – help define the spherical shape of the eye. Often the eyelids cast a shadow on the surface of the eye, while a shadow cast by the brow bone accentuates the depth of the eye socket.

The sparkle that gives life to the eyes comes from the moisture on the surface catching and reflecting light. The iris is also illuminated from within as some of the light that passes through the pupil bounces back. To capture the sparkle of the eyes you must observe carefully the subtle modulations of tones and highlights. For example, the brightest highlight on the eye will sparkle more if the whites of the eyes are toned down slightly (see right).

Eyelashes

Build up the form of the eye and the area surrounding it at the same time, so that the eye becomes an integral part of the face and does not appear 'stuck on'. Avoid overstating the eyelashes. Even though you know that they consist of many fine hairs, don't try to paint every single lash – unless you are working on a large scale or in close up (as on the right). Usually it is best to use just a few curving irregular lines with dry brush strokes.

CLOSED EYES

You can create a very restful portrait by depicting your sitter with the eyes closed. This emphasizes the spherical form of the eyes so make sure you capture this with close observation of the tonal variations. Also note how in this front-on view of the closed eyes, the eyelashes become much more prominent.

Most importantly, remember that you are not simply drawing a pair of eyes – you are drawing a pair of eyes that is unique to one individual, and accuracy is vital if you are to achieve a convincing likeness. Observe the eyes of your sitter closely: are the eyelids narrow or hooded? What about the shape and thickness of the eyebrows and their distance from the eyes? How does the arch of the upper lid differ from the curve of the lower one? Don't forget to look at the eyes in the context of the whole face, constantly measuring and comparing the sizes and positions of the eyes in relation to the other features.

Also note that the eyes of Oriental people are different. They have an extra layer of fat attached to the eyelid muscle, flattening the surface from the eyebrow to the eye socket. Their tear ducts point down almost vertically and they don't have an upper eyelid crease.

▼ **The surface of the eyeball is highly reflective; as light falls on it, a highlight appears on the iris, giving the eyes their lively quality. Notice here how the whites of the eyes have been toned down to a bluish-grey, against which the bright highlights really sparkle.**

Tackling spectacles

Depicting spectacles requires a sureness of touch. The trick is to suggest their presence rather than reproduce them in precise detail. Select only the important lines, tones and reflections that shape and define the spectacles – put them in with a minimum of detail so that they don't detract attention from the sitter's face. In the painting (top), a few small strokes of off-white suggest reflections from the glass of the lenses. In the drawing, the reflections have not been put in, but the viewer still 'reads' glass. If the spectacles cast shadows on to the face (as they do in both pictures here), put them in but, again, underplay them.

YOUNG AND OLD, SMILING AND FROWNING

When drawing eyes, watch out for the differences between the eyes of children and older people. In children, the eye sockets are more open and the flesh is tight, so the eyes are less likely to be in deep shadow. The opposite applies in older people. Also pay attention to how the eyes change when the facial expresssion changes.

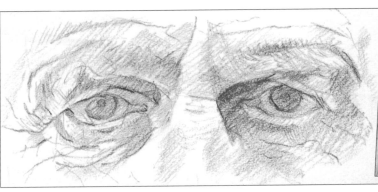

▶ Children's eyes are large, round and clear, and bigger in proportion to the face than adults' eyes. Because the skin and muscles are firm, there is very little shadow around the eyes.

◀ As we age, the skin around the eyes begins to sag and wrinkle and the eyelids droop. With advanced age, the eyes appear to sink deeper into the sockets.

▶ In a smiling face, the eyes often appear larger and more rounded. The space between the eye and the eyebrow is greater, the upper eyelids are well defined and the eyebrows are more arched.

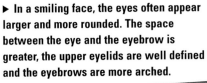

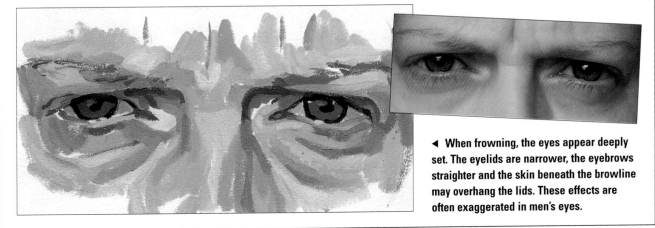

◀ When frowning, the eyes appear deeply set. The eyelids are narrower, the eyebrows straighter and the skin beneath the browline may overhang the lids. These effects are often exaggerated in men's eyes.

Capturing a likeness

Practise your portraiture skills with this oil painting of a young man. With accurate drawing and subtle colour handling, you'll get an excellent likeness.

Many artists can come up with perfectly acceptable head-and-shoulders studies. But how many can really record what is unique about the person they are painting?

Being able to capture a likeness is not easy. You have to be prepared to take time really looking at your subject in depth and, of course, to practise converting your observations into an accurate painting.

The making of this oil painting reveals many secrets behind conveying the essence of a person. But remember, there is no better practice than painting from life – so when you feel confident enough, ask a friend to sit for you.

Preparing the canvas

A fine linen canvas was used for the support in this study. If preparing your own canvas you will need to do so several weeks before you want to begin work on the painting. First, the canvas must be stretched over wooden stretchers, then sized with either rabbit-skin glue or PVA and left to dry overnight. Next, a lead-white oil primer should be applied, and this can take about three weeks to dry.

▼ A subtle range of coloured neutrals set against a toned ground is used to capture the flesh tones of the sitter.

Finally, knock back the stark whiteness of the ground with a thin, turpsy mixture of Payne's grey and yellow ochre oil paint applied with a No.20 filbert brush, then leave for a day or two to dry. The resulting mid tone cancels the glare of the white primer and allows you to see the effects of the lights and darks immediately. It also serves to unify the painting.

Plan the composition

Before you begin your initial drawing, study your sitter closely and adjust the pose and lighting until you are satisfied with the result. View your subject through half-closed eyes, which allows you to see the general distribution of light and dark areas. These are just as important in a portrait as in any other subject, but are often neglected.

The three-quarter view used for the step-by-step focuses on the head and shoulders. This angle provides scope for an interesting composition and avoids symmetry. Using charcoal, which is easy to correct, start by establishing the line of the nose, noting where it passes between the eyes. This acts as a centre point for the drawing, from which you can assess the distance to the eyes. Once you get the eye-nose relationship correct, work outwards to the rest of the head.

Rendering the eyes

Getting the eyes right is one of the keys to capturing a good likeness of your subject. However, eyes are often overworked and drawn out of proportion to the rest of the head – the eyes are generally smaller than we assume them to be.

Make the eyes of a piece with the rest of the study. Don't paint individual lashes, as this makes the eyes look over-defined. A dark line along the upper eye is usually sufficient, with perhaps a couple of lashes picked out.

Dabs of paint

Don't be tempted to paint the iris with one blob of colour – instead, work it up gradually with dabs of paint. Start with a neutral grey, then add just a bit of colour to about one quarter of the eye – this will have the desired effect. The whites, too, look far from uniform. Remember that the eye is a sphere, so the whites appear to vary in tone as the eye curves.

FIRST STEPS

1 ▼ **Make a sketch** Sketch the head using a thin stick of charcoal. Start by locating the nose, then position the eyes. These are the key relationships around which the rest of the drawing will be constructed. Knock back the charcoal lines with a rag to avoid contaminating the paint.

◄ Tone down the brightness of the white-primed canvas with a thin mix of yellow ochre and Payne's grey oils.

2 ▶ **Begin painting**
Using a No.4 filbert, paint the eyebrows with a mix of Payne's grey and flake white. Mix a basic flesh tint from white, lemon yellow, cobalt blue and alizarin crimson for the side of the nose. Pick out highlights on the side and tip by increasing the white in your flesh mix. For the top of the nose, make a pinkish mix of cobalt blue, yellow ochre, alizarin and white. Add viridian to this mix for the nostrils and lips.

3 ◀ **Start on the eyes**
Work back into the painting with charcoal, defining the nose and spectacles. With the No.4 filbert and a mix of cobalt blue and transparent red oxide, indicate the eyes and the shadows around them. Add more of the pinkish mix from step 2 to the nose – notice how flecks of unmixed yellow ochre enliven the paint surface on the bridge of the nose.

4 ▲ **Paint the face** Mix cobalt blue, lemon yellow, spectrum violet and white to create browns for the forehead. Dab on the pinkish mix, too. Add viridian to the forehead mix and darken eyes and spectacles. Mix varying proportions of spectrum violet, lemon yellow and white to paint the shaded side of the face. Paint the lips using the same rich browns – the lower lip is lighter in tone.

EXPERT ADVICE
Pot luck

Use a washer/dipper tray to help you complete this oil painting. The large compartment can be used for the turpentine and the small one for the linseed oil.

5 ▲ **Add light tones** Block in the shadow under the near cheekbone with the brownish mix from step 4. Make a pale mix of cobalt blue, alizarin crimson, lemon yellow and flake white for the light area where the top of the cheekbone catches the light.

6 ▲ **Add cool tones** Take some of the basic flesh tint down into the neck. Mix flake white, raw umber, lemon yellow and cobalt blue and use this for the cool tones on the lit side of the face. Mix a dark tone from Payne's grey, ultramarine, transparent red oxide, burnt umber, viridian and white. Paint the moustache and beard, the line between the lips, and the shadows under the lips and nose.

DEVELOPING THE PICTURE

At this point, use a painting knife to scrape the colour from your palette to provide a clean working surface for new mixes. Begin to put the head into context by working on the clothing and background.

7 ▶ **Start on the T-shirt** Paint a light flesh tint on the near eyelid. Describe the whites of the eyes, using white with viridian and white with lemon yellow and spectrum violet. Block in the background with a mix of white, cobalt blue and cadmium orange. For the neck, mix flesh tones from spectrum violet, lemon yellow and white. Block in the T-shirt with cobalt blue/yellow ochre/ white and cobalt blue/white.

Master Strokes

Sir Anthony van Dyck (1599–1641)
Study of a Man Wearing a Falling Collar

One of the greatest Flemish painters of the seventeenth century, van Dyck had a refined style that is evident in this study for a portrait. The sitter's florid complexion, especially strong across the nose and cheeks, is brilliantly conveyed with rosy tones. Darker tones under the chin suggest plump folds of flesh. The head is viewed slightly from below, which tends to exaggerate the man's supercilious expression.

Touches of warm red lightly scumbled over the cool, dark-toned background echo the highly coloured flesh tones of the face.

Very loosely defined with simple brush strokes, the white lace collar is included as much to anchor the head in space as to be an informative part of the portrait.

8 ▶ Work on hair and eyes Mix a brown from transparent red oxide, ultramarine and flake white and use this to paint the hair. Paint shadows under the eyelids and in the eye socket, using alizarin crimson, lemon yellow and spectrum violet. A dot of red in the corner of the eye gives it a lively appearance. Use transparent red oxide mixed with a touch of cobalt blue and flake white to edge the eye.

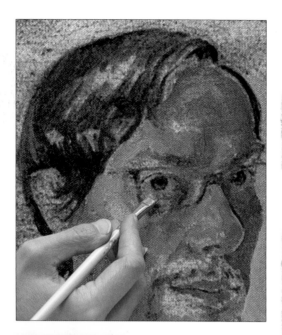

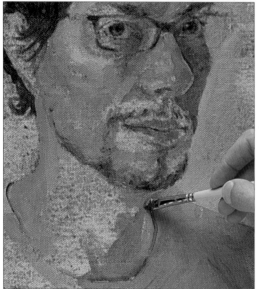

9 ◀ Complete the eyes Develop the tones around the eyes, making very fine adjustments without overworking this area. Use the brown from step 8 to suggest upper and lower lashes – don't draw a continuous line around the eyes, as this will make the sitter look startled. Darken flesh tones on the neck and indicate the shadow around the T-shirt neckline.

10 ▶ Paint the ear Check the size and location of the ear by measuring and finding alignments with your brush. The ear has a rich blood supply, so use warm flesh tones mixed from cobalt blue, alizarin crimson, lemon yellow and flake white to paint it.

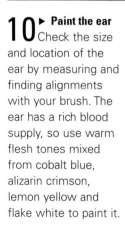

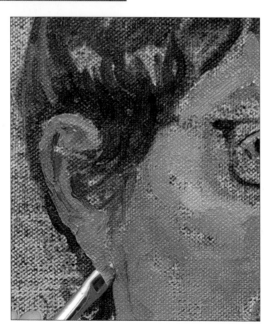

Express yourself

Charcoal study

Before starting with oils, it pays to do a drawing to familiarize yourself with your sitter. This can be a quick sketch or, as here, a more considered work. In this charcoal study, linear marks define the features and blended areas build up the form.

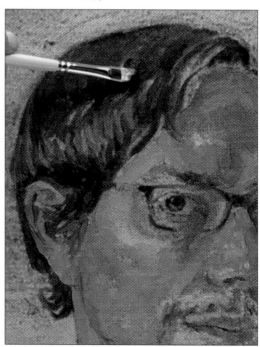

11 ▲ Add texture to the hair Work into the hair with various mixes of alizarin crimson, viridian and white to vary the tones, and to suggest its sheen and the way it reflects light. Allow your brush to follow the way the hair lies.

12 ▼ **Add more colour to the neck** Work into the neck with mixes of lemon yellow/cobalt blue/alizarin crimson and spectrum violet/lemon yellow/white, cleaning your brush on a tissue or rag between mixes. Arrange light and dark areas, and warm and cool ones, so that you build up a three-dimensional impression of the neck. If an area looks flat when it should be rounded, adjust the tones very slightly.

13 ▼ **Soften the hair** At this stage, the junction between the hair on the right of the head and the background is too harsh – use a rag to soften it.

14 ▲ **Pull tones together** Study the subject and the image carefully and then work across the painting, adding touches of light and dark tone to knit the various passages together and make them read as a whole. It is not necessary to cover up the ground completely – by showing through subsequent patches of paint it creates a unifying effect.

A FEW STEPS FURTHER

The portrait has now come together – probably more quickly than you expected due to the unifying tones already provided by the ground. Just a few characterful details need to be added. A little more background colour will suggest the solidity of the figure and the space behind it.

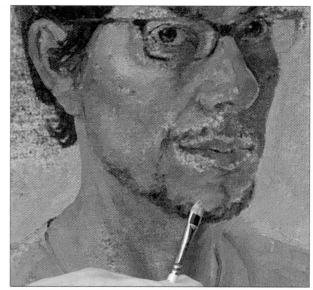

15 ▲ **Add the highlight on the chin** Use a warm mix of cobalt blue, alizarin crimson, lemon yellow and white for the highlight on the chin.

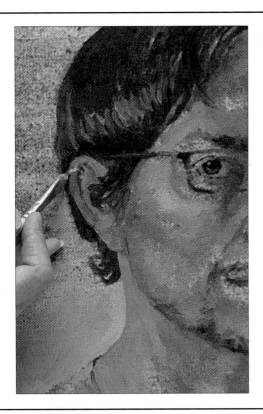

16 ◄ **Put in the silver earring** Indicate the distinctive earring with a buttery mix of white and lemon yellow, adding just a touch of spectrum violet to knock it back. Don't be tempted to overwork this detail.

17 ▲ **Suggest the background** Scumble in an indication of the light background with a mixture of white and cobalt blue knocked back with cadmium orange and yellow ochre.

THE FINISHED PICTURE

A Dabs of colour
The eyes were built up from subtly graduated dabs, not just one blob of colour.

B Subtle spectacles
The spectacles were just suggested with touches of colour rather than painted with a harsh drawn line – this prevents them from becoming too dominant.

C Warm versus cool
Warm tones on prominent features, such as the nose, forehead and ears bring these areas forward, while cool shadows under the chin and cheekbones sit back in space.

D A toned ground
A thin wash of warm undercolour shows between the patches of paint and knits the image together.

Self portrait

If you can't find a willing model to sit for you, the obvious answer is to draw a portrait of someone who is always available – yourself.

▲ By using water-soluble coloured pencils, the artist was able to combine lively shading with soft washes of colour.

I f you are new to portrait drawing, you might feel uncomfortable about asking someone to sit for you until you have had more practice. Instead, an excellent way to find out more about the human face in your own time is by studying your reflection in a mirror and drawing from this.

For a full-face portrait, set up a mirror in front of you, about 30cm (12in) beyond your drawing board, so that you can see your head and shoulders comfortably and clearly. Alternatively, to view yourself from different angles, place two mirrors so that one reflects the image from the other.

It is natural to frown slightly as you look hard at your features and concentrate on capturing them on paper. Try to avoid doing this by consciously adopting a relaxed expression.

Light and colour

For this self portrait of the artist, the lighting was set up on the left, illuminating this side of the head and throwing the right side into shadow. This helped to emphasize the three-dimensional form of the features, as well as give an interesting contrast of tones.

The lively colour on the face was achieved by gradually building up the flesh tones with layers of coloured pencil. Two useful shades for flesh tones – warm brown and rose pink – are used for this study. They can be blended with a little water where required.

193

YOU WILL NEED

Piece of cartridge paper, 50 x 40cm (20 x 16in)

6 water-soluble coloured pencils: Warm brown; Rose pink; Light blue; Dark grey; Cobalt blue; Indian red

Putty rubber (for erasing mistakes)

No.1 brush and jar of water

FIRST STEPS

1 ▼ Sketch the head Use a warm brown water-soluble coloured pencil to sketch the head and shoulders. Measuring the proportions with the pencil, mark guidelines to position the eyes, nose tip and mouth (see right). Sketch the features and indicate the main shadows.

2 ▼ Strengthen the shadow Still using the warm brown pencil, shade the upper lip. Darken the shading on the right side of the face, taking it down to the shirt.

STRAIGHT ON OR AT A SLIGHT ANGLE?

A front view of your face (left) is easier to observe in a mirror and your features are positioned symmetrically. Notice how the eyes come about halfway down the head. The tip of the nose is about halfway between the eyes and chin, and the mouth halfway between the tip of the nose and the chin.

You can also try drawing yourself with your head slightly turned (right). This may be more pleasing in terms of composition, but is a more awkward position to achieve with a single mirror. You need to sit at an angle to the mirror or to turn your head frequently. The same guide lines for positioning the features apply, although the lines need to be curved to follow the form of the head.

BRING IN MORE COLOURS

Now that the structure of the face and the main tonal areas are mapped out, introduce more colours to build up a realistic flesh shade and define the features. Some of the colours can be blended into a wash with water.

4 ◄ **Define the eyes** Darken the shadow above the nose, under the chin and on the right of the face with the warm brown pencil. Define the spectacles, shading lightly over the right lens. Develop the eyes, colouring the irises with a light blue pencil, then use the same colour to shade loosely over the shirt and add cool shadow to the white hair.

3 ▲ **Introduce a warm pink** Extend the warm brown shading to the left side of the neck and very lightly shade the left side of the face, including the glass of the spectacles' lens. Then change to a rose pink pencil to warm up the flesh colour on the face and neck.

5 ▲ **Shade a dark background** Using a dark grey pencil, work lively shading across the background. Minor adjustments to the head outline can be made at this stage. The dark colour throws the head into relief and forms a strong contrast to the artist's white hair. Hatch a few textural lines over the right side of the hair.

6 ◄ **Brush on some water** Emphasize the pupils with the dark grey pencil, then change to a cobalt blue pencil to liven up the colour of the shirt. Now dip a No.1 brush into water and wash over the background to soften the dark grey pencil lines. Clean the brush, then use it to blend the two shades of blue in the shirt.

7 ▶ **Warm the tone** Using an Indian red pencil, warm up the tone on the right of the face. A little tone at the corners of the mouth lifts it into a smile. Shade lightly across the face with warm brown and rose pink, leaving highlights of white paper. Redefine the features with the warm brown pencil.

A FEW STEPS FURTHER

The lively rendering of the artist's face is now complete. There is always room to add a few more details to the features, but don't overwork them and risk losing the spontaneity of the drawing.

8 ▶ Shade a darker background With the dark grey pencil, deepen the tone around the head, fading the colour out towards the edges. Add texture to the eyebrows with a few jotted marks in warm brown and dark grey. Extend the shirt with light blue hatching.

9 ▲ Add final definition Use light blue again to add depth to the irises. With Indian red, put in the final definition on the eyes, including the inner corner of the eye on the right. Darken the pupils with dark grey.

THE FINISHED PICTURE

A Hair texture
Just a few loose lines in light blue and dark grey were drawn on the shaded side of the white hair to suggest its texture.

B Sensitive detail
The facial features, especially the eyes, were sensitively drawn with a sharp coloured pencil. They show the artist's character without becoming too dominant.

C Blended flesh tones
Layers of brown and a warm pink were worked lightly over one another, visually blending to give a warm and lively flesh colour to the face.

Creative portrait

Use a combination of conventional and unusual materials and techniques to produce a colourful, decorative portrait.

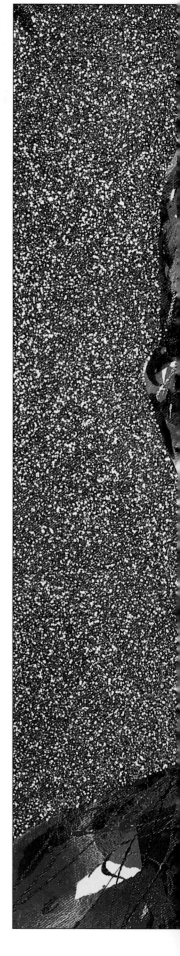

Make preparatory notes and sketches, observing, for example, the undertone of the skin – some people have a warm, pinkish tone to their skin, like the model on the left, while others may have a cool-ish tinge, which is exaggerated under some lighting conditions. This will give you a clue to the palette you might use. Make this study some time before you put brush to canvas. When you tackle the project, these visual memories will come into play.

A useful way of freeing yourself from working too literally is to make a digitised print from the colour photo (see above, right). If you don't have computer equipment, go to a print bureau. Ask for the photo to be scanned at a low resolution (72 dots per inch or less) and blown up to twice the size. This will break up the photo into a mosaic of shapes and colours, and provide a good starting point for a colourful interpretation of the subject.

The idea behind this painting is simple – the artist wanted to be creative and free in his approach, while at the same time retaining a likeness of his sitter. To get the best from an exercise such as this, choose a subject you know really well – a relative or a friend. By all means, work from a reference photo rather than from life – but don't copy the photo slavishly.

The idea is to let your imagination have free reign, using the subject as a jumping-off point. Allow yourself to take pleasure in the colour and consistency of the paint, the way it moves on the surface or drips from a brush or stick. Try to retrieve the pleasure you gained as a child from paint and mark-making. On the other hand, keep in mind that the image you produce should resemble the subject and capture something of his or her personality. So stand back and review the progress frequently and, if the image has moved too far away from accuracy, drag it back with a few judicious touches. It is a tricky balance but this painting proves it can be done.

Immerse yourself in the subject

Before you begin, make a close study of the reference photo or the subject. Familiarize yourself with the proportions, colouring and expressiveness of the face and the way in which these reflect mood. The more you immerse yourself in your subject, the more you see and understand.

A layered approach

The step-by-step project is painted in three distinct stages, using three very different media and techniques. Working in layers and introducing unusual materials will help you to approach the subject with fewer preconceptions.

Use washy acrylic for blocking in the underpainting. It dries fast, allowing you to get the main elements of the composition in place quickly. Then place the painting on the floor and drip household gloss paint over it to create a tracery of lines. In the final stages, apply oil paint in dabs to pull the image into focus. This complexity creates a sense of depth and encourages the eye to linger and enjoy the painting. Finally, add glitter to the background – this will make the head really stand out.

▶ **A combination of traditional artist's acrylic and oil paints, together with less conventional materials – household gloss paint and glitter – results in a painting that is both entertaining and descriptive.**

YOU WILL NEED

Medium cotton duck on stretchers 54 x 43cm (21 x 17in), primed with an acrylic primer

2B pencil

5 acrylic paints: Cadmium yellow; Magenta; Alizarin crimson; Ultramarine; Violet

5 household gloss paints: Magenta; Cadmium red; Phthalo blue; Cadmium yellow; White

Jar for mixing gloss paint

Old paint brush or stick to drip gloss paint

Turpentine or white spirit

8 oil paints: Alizarin crimson; Lemon yellow; Ultramarine; Titanium white; Vermilion; Yellow ochre; Burnt umber; Burnt sienna

Rag for cleaning oils from brush

Brushes: 50mm (2in) hake; Nos.6 and 10 flat bristle brushes

Mixing palettes or dishes

Silver glitter

FIRST STEPS

1 ▲ **Establish the underdrawing** Using a 2B pencil, draw a rough egg shape for the head and start to plot the main features. Don't worry too much about achieving complete accuracy – a few minor distortions might say something about your response to the sitter.

▲ A wash of alizarin crimson (left) overlaid with ultramarine (centre) creates a deep purple shade (right) for the shadow tones.

2▶ **Block in yellow acrylic** Load a 50mm (2in) hake brush with dilute cadmium yellow acrylic paint. Using the digitized image as a guide, start to apply patches of bright colour on the blond hair and the light areas of the face and neck.

3▶ **Apply magenta acrylic** Still using the hake brush, apply magenta acrylic to stand for the cool reds and pinks in the digitized image. Work magenta over the pullover, too. The broad shape of the hake brush gives a range of thick and thin marks, while the pliant bristles give the marks a fluent, calligraphic quality.

4▼ **Add a warm red** Still working with dilute acrylics and taking your lead from the digitized print, apply alizarin crimson over the crown of the head and on to 'hot' areas, such as the ears and around the eyes, defining their forms.

5▲ **Introduce a dark tone** Load the hake brush with fluid ultramarine acrylic and tap the end of the bristles on to the support to make lines charged with colour. Use these to refine the drawing, defining key features such as the mouth and jawline.

6 ▶ Develop the dark tones Continue applying the fluid ultramarine paint to the face and pullover, allowing it to bleed into the still-wet reds and yellow. This method of working gives rise to random blending and pooling of colour, and these 'happy accidents' should be welcomed. Notice how the blue blends with the two reds to produce mauves and purples.

7 ▲ Paint the background Load the brush with violet and introduce this colour into the shadow areas – around the eyes, across the head and down the right cheek. Apply a thin wash of violet over the background. Leave the painting to dry thoroughly.

Master Strokes
Frank Auerbach (b. 1931)
Head of Gerda Boehm

This highly individual interpretation of a woman's head is painted in the Expressionist style by London-based artist Auerbach. Worked in oils, it demonstrates the artist's characteristic use of impasto, in which the paint is applied very thickly and retains the marks of the brush or painting knife.

Many aspects of the picture – the colours, the shape of the head, the thick, black outline – appear distorted. The aim of the artist, however, was not to produce a natural-looking likeness, but rather to convey the character of his sitter as he personally saw it. And, of course, in the thick, luscious brush strokes there is – as in the step-by-step project – an enjoyment of paint for its own sake.

On the face, greens and yellows have been loosely combined on each brush stroke to give a marbled effect.

Small peaks and narrow trails of oil paint were created where the brush was dragged across the support and lifted at the end of some of the strokes.

© Frank Auerbach

8 ▼ Drip gloss paint Using an old paint brush or a stick, mix magenta, cadmium red and phthalo blue household gloss paints in a jar to make a warm brown. Thin the mix to the consistency of single cream by adding a few drops of turpentine or white spirit. Place the canvas on the floor, load the brush or stick with colour and drip on lines of paint to 'draw' features such as the eyes, the curve of the jaw and the strands of hair.

EXPERT ADVICE
Dripping paint

Dripping thinned paint from an old brush or stick is ideal for breaking up areas of flat colour, such as on the boy's pullover, as it introduces a linear element. Move your brush around just above the surface, making expressive, swirling marks.

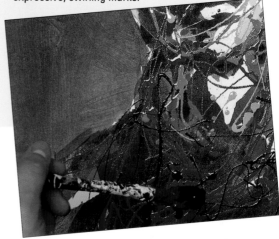

9 ▼ Drip more paint Working as before, drip more gloss paint over the image, spattering it in places. First use a tangerine mixed from cadmium yellow and magenta, then a violet mixed from magenta and phthalo blue. Follow this with white, then phthalo blue. Allow the paint to dry overnight.

DEVELOPING THE PICTURE

The process of applying dripped paint required broad gestures and played up the abstract and decorative aspects of the composition. Now it's time to pull the image into focus by applying a mosaic of flesh tints in oils.

10 ▲ Apply oil paints Mix alizarin crimson, lemon yellow and ultramarine oil paints to create a dark tone; using a No.6 flat bristle brush, apply dabs to the right eye socket. Mix light flesh tones from titanium white, vermilion and alizarin crimson; white and vermilion; alizarin crimson and lemon yellow; white, alizarin crimson and ultramarine. Start to build up the right cheek, dab by dab.

11 ▼ **Apply warm tones** Mix a warm pink flesh tint from alizarin crimson, white and lemon yellow, then apply touches down the nose and on the lips. Add more white and take this colour on to the cheeks.

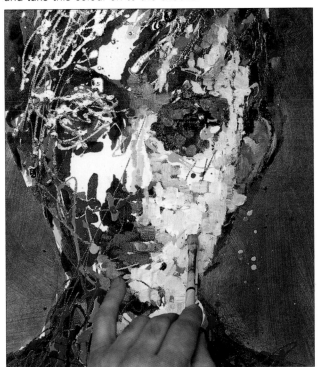

12 ▼ **Develop shadows** Build up the shadowed side of the face with various mixes of yellow ochre, burnt umber and burnt sienna, wiping the brush on a rag between mixes. Mix more dark skin tones from a mix of burnt umber, vermilion, ultramarine and a touch of white, and a mix of ultramarine and alizarin crimson.

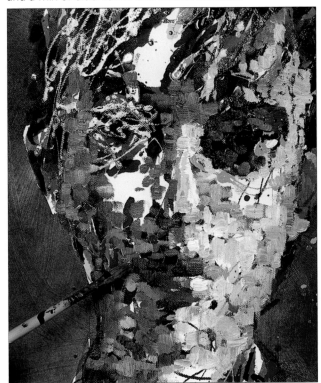

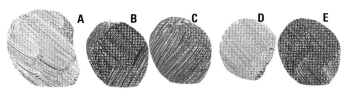

▲ The flesh tones were created with a wide variety of colours and tones, including white with a hint of ultramarine (A); white with a touch of vermilion (B); burnt sienna (C); white, ultramarine and alizarin crimson (D); ultramarine and alizarin crimson (E).

Express yourself

Coloured-pencil study

This coloured-pencil study of the boy has the same lively quality as the step-by-step painting. The artist held the pencils at an angle, allowing him to make thick, grainy lines with the side of the lead. Holding the pencil in this way also encourages a free and uninhibited drawing style – long flowing lines and scribbled areas of tone are easy to render.

13 ▼ **Paint the eye sockets** Continue to sculpt the right side of the head with controlled, blocky brush marks, using the same dark tones as in step 12. Develop the right eye socket.

14 ▲ **Paint the right eye** Using touches of burnt umber, burnt sienna and the flesh tint from step 11, block in the eye. Simply put down the patches of light and dark, and warm and cool, as in the digitized print, and an eye will emerge.

A FEW STEPS FURTHER

The image now works as a good description of the subject. When you stand back, the separate dabs of colour resolve in the eye to create pearly skin tones. The background, though colourful, lacks texture by contrast with the rest of the image, so consider adding interest here.

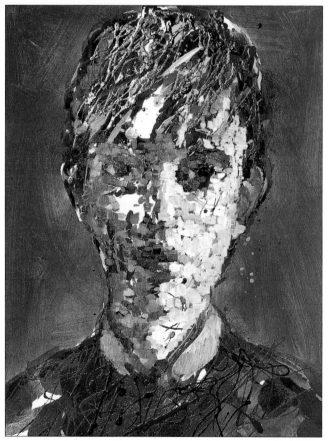

15 ▲ **Complete the flesh tones** Continue building up the flesh tones, keeping the brush marks loose and avoiding the temptation to 'fill in' all the gaps. The technique is most effective when the mosaic of oil paint forms a broken film that allows the underlayers to show through.

16 ▲ **Apply gloss to the background** Using a No.10 flat bristle brush, apply magenta gloss paint all over the background, working carefully around the head.

17 ◄ Apply glitter

While the magenta gloss paint is still wet, sprinkle a layer of silver glitter over the surface. Tip the support to shed any loose glitter. Work very carefully to avoid getting glitter on the face, or this will spoil the effect.

THE FINISHED PICTURE

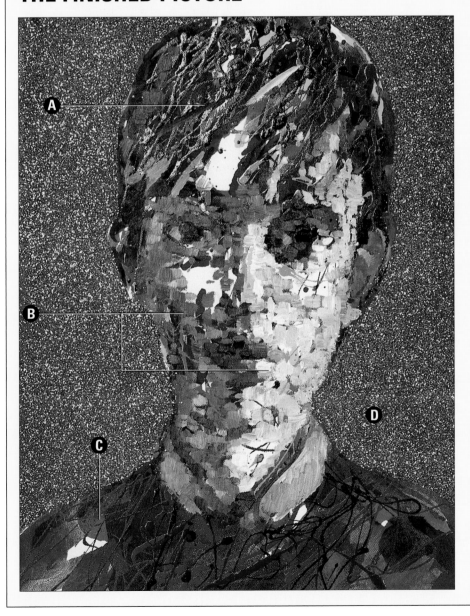

A Strands of hair
Dribbled gloss paint suggests the springy texture of hair. Washes of bright acrylic can be glimpsed through the shiny strands.

B Mosaic of paint
Dabs of oil paint in a wide range of flesh tones form a mosaic of small squares that, when seen from far enough away, really capture the advancing and receding planes of the face.

C Complex layers
Washes of semi-transparent acrylic paint have the luminosity of watercolour. Seen through dribbles of gloss paint, they create a sense of depth.

D Sparkling finish
Glitter adds a surprising but highly decorative touch, and ensures that the painting catches the light and sparkles.

TECHNIQUES

From creating a sense of movement in your
figure-drawing to experimenting with texture,
this chapter is an invaluable resource, packed
with practical projects and challenges to stretch
and enhance your existing range of artistic
skills. Whether you're stuck in a creative rut or
concerned your pictures aren't quite all they
could be, the answer may well lie in learning
a new technique.

Sketching the figure

Here we look at how to create a sense of movement in your figure drawing – even when the subject is stock-still.

How do artists make their figures come to life? In life drawing, the model is usually standing, lying or sitting. Yet the best figure drawings and paintings have a sense of motion and rhythm, even when the pose is a static one.

Working quickly

There are various ways of achieving this elusive feeling of movement, the most effective of which is quite simply to work quickly. Rapid sketches are invariably more animated than finished drawings and paintings. They are gener-

ally done on the spot, often with lively lines and splashes of colour applied with a quick flick of the wrist and, inevitably, this spontaneous approach creates a sense of life and action.

Line drawings have an inherent sense of movement that tonal or shaded drawings often lack. This is because hatching and other types of shading needed to emphasize the form of the figure often work against a sense of motion and rhythm – they make the drawn figure appear solid and therefore more static.

A sure-fire way of conveying an idea of motion in a drawing is to concentrate

on the outlines and contours of the subject, making the lines as fluid and natural as possible. The pencil drawing of the walking figure below was done quickly and without looking at the paper at all. What's more, the artist barely lifted the pencil off the paper during the process.

Responding to the subject

This is an unusual approach, but it's one that often works because it forces the artist to respond directly to the subject without having to worry about the drawing technique. Such drawings or paintings may not always be

---

WALKING FIGURE

To achieve a convincing walking motion, the artist looked at the moving model rather than the drawing. She hardly took the pencil off the paper – instead she simply left it trail off in places. This way of working often produces – as here – a drawing of real beauty and sensitivity that an exact image would lose.

▼ Breaking up the outline of a figure adds to the sense of movement. Here, the back of the left thigh (on the right) is drawn with one line – suggesting the stretching of the hamstring – but the front of the other thigh is 'lost' altogether.

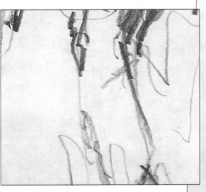

▲ Gestural strokes define the form of the back in a much more expressive way than shading or cross-hatching.

▲ Half finishing the foot suggests a fleeting movement. If it had been fully drawn, the model might have looked as if she were holding a pose rather than walking.

MOVING FIGURES

When drawing the moving figure, try to pick out one instant in the complete action. If necessary, ask your model to repeat the process until you have a clear mental image of it. Alternatively, ask her to hold a pose in the movement for a few seconds.

▲ **SUPERIMPOSED MOVEMENT IN SEPIA INK**
The model is stopped midway as she stands up from a sitting position. Using a small sable brush, our artist recorded three stages of this action to produce an animated sequence of figure drawings.

◄ **SPINNING FIGURE IN CHARCOAL**
The subject was moving around continuously as the artist used a few deft lines to capture the model's swinging arms and the swirling motion of her skirt.

anatomically accurate, but they will certainly be lively and interesting.

The figure stretching upwards (see opposite) was also done without taking the drawing tool – in this case a pastel stick – off the paper. In this image, however, the artist was concerned with accuracy as well as expressing motion and so dragged the pastel slowly across the surface. This continuous, flowing mark echoes the sinuous pose of the model and captures her slow, graceful movement.

It's quite possible to communicate a sense of rhythm and movement even when working from a figure in a static pose, such as lying down or sitting. You can achieve this simply by drawing or painting in a spontaneous way, using lively marks. However, a figure in action offers even more scope for introducing movement into your work. To get the most natural-looking pose, ask your model to carry out a number of different actions and then to freeze in mid-movement. The resulting poses may be difficult to maintain for more than a moment or two, but this is all you need. In fact, your work will benefit from being done quickly.

Repetitive movement

If, however, the model's mid-movement pose looks stiff and unconvincing, it is also possible to sketch from a moving model. The walking figure on the previous page was done in this way. It helps if the action is repetitive, as is the case when someone walks. You can then see the part of the pose you want to draw time after time.

STATIC FIGURES

Using a variety of materials, our artist explored some of the different ways in which an impression of motion can be introduced into a still figure. Test some of these ideas for yourself. Work quickly, using just the materials you have to hand. Above all, try to ignore detail. The secret lies in working spontaneously – in responding to the rhythms of the model's pose rather than attempting to produce an accurate representation of the figure.

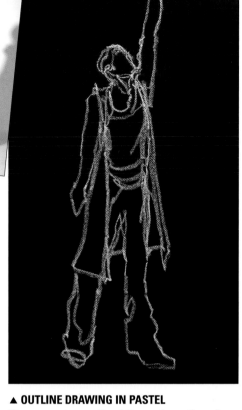

▶ FORESHORTENING IN CHARCOAL

The legs loom forward in this drawing because of the close, low vantage point. The ladder accentuates the foreshortening and the strong upward direction of the drawing.

▲ OUTLINE DRAWING IN PASTEL

Here a continuous line follows the outline of the figure, emphasizing the stretching motion of the pose and giving the whole sketch a sense of movement.

▼ TONAL DRAWING IN CHARCOAL

This pose may be static physically, but it is very active visually. The varying angles of the legs and arms lead the eye around the picture and this effect is enhanced by the use of charcoal. The artist used her fingers to create lively, directional smudges, which describe the dark shadows without destroying the rhythm of the pose.

▶ ARBITRARY COLOUR IN PASTEL

Using red for the flesh tones and to outline the trousers is not exactly true to life, but it helps capture the exuberant spirit of the pose. The artist was sitting on the floor and the low viewpoint has helped create an explosive sensation, as if the figure is about to shoot upwards.

Drawing with a grid

Make a grid to help you position objects on paper and create a balanced outline. Then shade in the composition using a charcoal pencil for a bold effect.

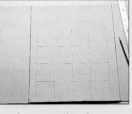

There's no need to go anywhere special to find interesting subjects to draw. It is quite possible simply to stay at home and pick out some of the objects around you to create a worthwhile composition.

Mapping size and position

Even experienced artists can have difficulty in accurately mapping the size and proportion of objects. One solution is to stand a sheet of white card with squares drawn on it behind your still life, then to rule a corresponding grid onto your drawing paper. This makes it easier to plot the height and volume of different objects.

Another plus point is that the white backdrop encloses the objects, aiding concentration while making a clear surface for any shadows to fall on. In this project however, it is the outline of the objects, their place within the grid and their 3-D form that is important.

Using a charcoal pencil

The outline is drawn using a 2B pencil, which is easy to rub out in case of mistakes; but the shading is done with a charcoal pencil to create strong, dark lines. In fact, because charcoal handles so differently to a graphite pencil, it's a good idea to get a feel for it first.

On a scrap piece of paper, move your charcoal pencil freely from side to side. Press lightly at first, then harder, and note the difference in the strength of the impression. Then go over your initial strokes with further strokes in different directions and check the varied textures you create. You will soon become familiar with the way that charcoal pencils work.

▲ It is much easier to draw a still life if you plot the position of the objects in it against a grid.

HOW TO MAKE A GRID SCREEN

1 Mark a vertical line about 20cm (8in) from each end of the pliable white card. Cut along these lines, then tape the severed pieces of card back in place with masking tape. This creates the moveable side flaps that will allow the screen to stand upright. Then use a 2B pencil to mark out the limits of the grid, making sure its base is positioned as close as possible to the bottom of the card.

2 Continue ruling horizontal and vertical lines on the card to complete the grid. The version shown here has 16 squares, each 8 x 8cm (3 x 3in) in size. Then arrange your still life group at eye level and stand the grid screen behind it. You are now ready to start drawing.

HOW TO USE THE GRID METHOD

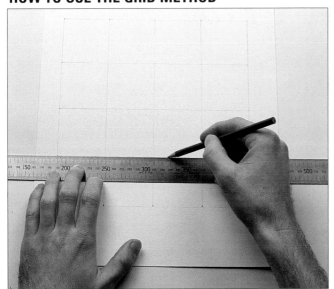

1 ▲ **Draw a corresponding grid on to your paper** Using the 2B pencil, draw another grid onto the drawing paper. You will need to divide it up into the same number of squares as appear on the card screen – although they do not have to be the same size as those you drew previously. The squares shown here measure 6 x 6cm (2.5 x 2.5in).

3 ▶ **Check as you draw** Continue drawing the bottle, including its stopper, referring frequently to the grid lines behind the object. Use a series of small strokes rather than a single line.

EXPERT ADVICE
Paper for charcoal

Charcoal, being a powdery substance, works best on slightly textured paper, which gives it something to 'grip' on to. If you use smooth or shiny paper, you will see the charcoal slide all over the place. Once you are familiar with how it handles, you can try using charcoal on paper with a highly textured surface. As the grain on this type of paper is prominent, it adds a distinctive character to the drawing.

2 ▲ **Start drawing the bottle outline** Start with the bottle because it is the tallest object in the group. Study where and how its outline crosses the squares on the grid behind it. Then start drawing in the bottle's outline using the 2B pencil. Make sure that you place each individual line in the corresponding grid square on your piece of paper as you draw.

ADD IN THE OTHER ITEMS IN THE GROUP

Once you have established the position of the first object in your still life – in this case, the bottle – you can add the other items around it. By continuing to follow the grid lines, you will ensure that the objects relate to each other as in the original.

4 ▲ **Sketch the outline of the glass** Again using the grid lines for reference, draw in the outline of the glass. The glass is positioned just in front of the bottle, so it appears slightly 'lower' in relation to the bottle's rounded base.

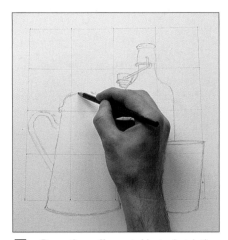

5 ▲ **Draw the coffee pot** Next, sketch the outline of the coffee pot, once again following the grid lines. Study the shape carefully and thicken up the lines slightly where the contours seem more intense – for example, on each side of the lid. If you use the rubber to correct any errors, you are likely to rub out the grid lines as well. Make sure to pencil these back in.

6 ▶ **Complete the pencil sketch** Add the details on the coffee pot. You have now achieved your initial sketch – a well-proportioned group of objects ready for developing with the charcoal pencil.

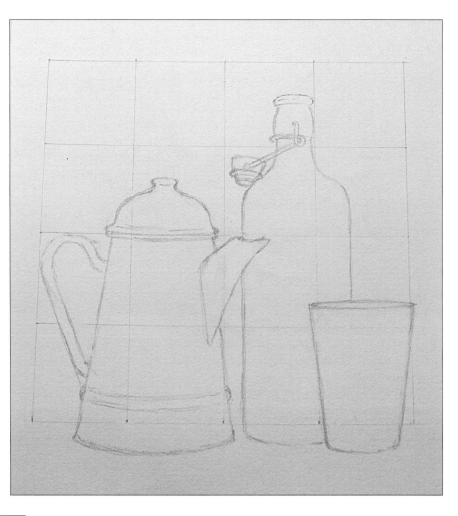

A FEW STEPS FURTHER

7 ▲ **Shade the bottle** Study how the light falls on the group of objects that you have just been drawing. Then use the sharp charcoal pencil and a combination of intense and lighter strokes to shade the bottle, building up areas of light and dark tones and leaving the highlights bare.

8 ▶ **Give form to the glass** Use the sharp point of the pencil to give form to the bottle's stopper. Then turn to the glass. Use heavy strokes to create the shaded areas along its right-hand edge and around the lower half; then medium strokes to give form to the other areas. Leave the highlights on the left and near the top of the glass untouched so that the white paper shows through.

9 ▶ **Work on the coffee pot**
Place a sheet of paper over the finished parts of the drawing to prevent them smudging as you work. Then start to shade the coffee pot, leaving the main highlights as wide, vertical strips.

10 ▶ **Build up the tones on the coffee pot** Gradually work up and darken the shading on the coffee pot. Reduce the main highlights to a few narrow bands, where the light bounces most intensely off the shiny, curved surface of the object.

THE FINISHED PICTURE

A The grid
The way the objects in the picture relate to their surrounding grid lines should mirror the way in which the original still life is positioned against the grid on the card screen. You can rub out the grid on the paper to complete the picture.

B Use of charcoal
The lines made with the 2B pencil, which was used to create the initial sketch in case of error, are completely hidden by the subsequent shading with the charcoal pencil. The charcoal produces darker tones and gives a softer finish.

C 3-D form
Once the shapes and arrangement of the three objects in the still life had been established on the grid, the artist then created the 3-D quality of their curved surfaces. This was achieved by the use of shading, and by creating highlights.

USING WATER SOLUBLE COLOURED PENCILS

If you would like to introduce some colour into your still life, you can achieve a very different effect from that in a charcoal drawing by using water-soluble coloured pencils. These pencils are extremely versatile, as you can begin by drawing your subject with them and then, as your drawing progresses, add water with a brush to soften the outlines and blend the colours in the drawing. The final result is similar to a watercolour painting. At this point you can add further pencil strokes over the top of the blended areas once the paper is completely dry.

Discovering textures

Whatever type of paint you use, broken brushwork applied to the appropriate support can create some very exciting textures.

Texture is an important element in painting. Some artists achieve this by adding texture to the paints, in the form of gels and thickening pastes (see pages 43–48). Others rely on using different brushes and adapting their brush strokes to create texture. The third approach is to work on a textured support, which shows through paint and is visible in the finished painting. Our artist has experimented with the two latter options and has come up with a number of imaginative and unusual possibilities.

Oils and acrylics

Finding 'something to paint on' is not a problem when using acrylics or oils as you can work on almost any surface you choose. However, canvas, canvas-covered boards and hardboard are ideal – and all of these have a characteristic surface texture that can contribute to the completed picture.

When working in watercolour and gouache, the texture of the picture surface is normally determined by the texture of the paper. This may be very smooth as with Hot-pressed (HP) paper, or coarse, as with Rough and Not (not Hot-pressed) paper. In addition, there are many handmade papers, including exotic ones from India, Japan and many other countries. These tend to have unusual surface textures, most of which are suitable for water-based paints (see Specialist Papers, pages 75–77).

However, there is no need to confine your choice of support to these rigid categories. Defying convention by choosing a painting surface that is more usually associated with another medium can achieve exciting results.

Ring the changes

Oil and acrylic sketches done on paper and cardboard are very common. These supports are easy to come by, and the resulting sketches are more spontaneous than those done on canvas that has been specially prepared.

There is no reason why a painting in either oils or acrylics cannot be done on sturdy watercolour paper. The coarser the paper, the more effective the texture

TEXTURAL POSSIBILITIES

These samples are painted on a variety of supports to create a range of unusual textures. Our artist worked in both watercolour (top row) and acrylic (bottom row), applying them to fabrics as well as to an assortment of papers and cards. Try these, then go on to experiment and develop your own repertoire of textures, using various supports with your favourite media.

The consistency of the colours and the way in which they are applied will affect the final result. Some of these textures were achieved with dilute colour, others by using thicker paint directly from the tube. Colours were laid with various brushes and tools, including a painting knife for some of the acrylic samples.

WATERCOLOUR EFFECTS

Applied with a 25mm brush to pastel paper.

Applied with a 25mm brush to corrugated cardboard.

Applied with a 12mm brush to smooth layout card.

ACRYLIC EFFECTS

Applied with a painting knife to primed card.

Applied with a 25mm brush to corrugated cardboard.

Applied with a 25mm brush to cotton duck.

will be. Embossed paper and corrugated card-board are also worth trying. Obviously, very thickly applied paint will obliterate the texture of the support, so you need to work with reasonably thin colour or use scraping-off techniques to reveal the texture underneath.

If you are using oil paints, the paper must first be given a coat of sealant, such as acrylic medium, to stop the oily colours from bleeding into the porous surface. This will also prevent the oil from rotting the paper in the long term.

Fabric supports

The traditional fabric support for oil paint is fine artist's linen. This is light brown in colour and stretches beautifully to form a taut, springy sur-face. Acrylics are more usually applied to cotton duck, which is softer and thicker than linen, and generally less taut when stretched. It is cream or off-white in colour. However, the two can be used for both types of paint.

Less common is the use of canvas and fabrics as supports for watercolour and gouache. Depending on how much water you mix with the paint, a fabric support can result in dry, broken texture or veils of thin colour. Try using these paint effects as part of a mixed media work, combining the watercolour textures with, say, pencil and pastel.

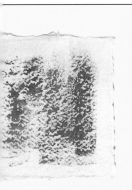

ed with a 25mm brush to made Rough paper.

Applied with a 25mm brush to khadi paper.

ed with a painting knife primed plywood.

Applied with a 25mm brush to jute.

BROKEN BRUSHWORK

Unlike oils and acrylics, watercolour doesn't give you the opportunity to build up texture with the paint. But if you let Rough paper show through broken brushwork, you'll get a strong sense of texture. Keep your mixes dry, so they don't flood the paper.

◄ ▲ LIGHT IN THE LEAVES
Broken brushwork is perfect for suggesting sunlight breaking through foliage. Hold the brush farther back from the tip than usual and work with a soft, loose arm action. Practise some brush strokes on scraps of paper first. Try to be spontaneous, letting the brush tail off towards the outer branches. A chisel-ended brush was used here with just enough pressure to splay the hairs.

▼ ► SUN ON THE WATER
In creating the shimmering effect of sunlight on water, broken brushwork comes into its own. Here, the artist laid an initial flat yellow wash in the centre of the paper, then applied broken blue brush strokes on top. Both the yellow wash and the white of the paper shine through the blue, creating a sense of radiant, dancing light.

Exploring watercolour

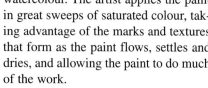

Exploit the fluidity and expressiveness of watercolour to the full in this painting of potted hyacinths.

Are you worried that your watercolour paintings look too 'timid'? It's worth trying some bold experiments now and again to inject excitement into your work and increase your confidence with the medium.

Learn to explore and exploit the fluidity of watercolour for all it is worth; you have to work with the nature of the medium and not against it.

This painting shows an obvious delight in the aqueous quality of pure watercolour. The artist applies the paint in great sweeps of saturated colour, taking advantage of the marks and textures that form as the paint flows, settles and dries, and allowing the paint to do much of the work.

Free movement

Use a large sheet of heavyweight paper, and paint standing up. This allows you to put more energy into your picture. Hold the brush near the end of the handle for freedom of movement. Use vivid colours and leave some areas of white paper to set them off to maximum advantage.

Be ready for accidents when controlling flowing washes of paint and learn to respond quickly to them. It's a great way of getting to know the qualities and quirks of this wonderful medium.

◄ **Dynamic brushwork and bold colours lend this image an exuberant quality.**

YOU WILL NEED

Piece of 640gsm (300lb) Not watercolour paper 61 x 51cm (24 x 20in)

Thin stick of charcoal

Soft cloth or paper tissue

7 watercolours: Magenta; Ultramarine; Rose doré; Cadmium yellow light; Cerulean blue; Cadmium orange; Yellow-green

Brushes: Nos.1 and 7 squirrel mops

Mixing palette or dish

Jars of water

FIRST STEPS

1 ▼ Make a drawing Use a thin stick of charcoal to make a light outline drawing of the hyacinths and pots. Suggest some of the individual blooms, but avoid putting in too much detail. Any loose charcoal dust on the surface of the drawing will dull your subsequent watercolour washes, so knock it back by lightly flicking (not rubbing) it with a soft cloth or a paper tissue.

2 ▲ Start painting the hyacinths Prepare a fluid wash of bluish purple mixed from magenta, ultramarine and a little rose doré. Touch in some of the individual hyacinth petals, using the tip of a No.1 mop brush and letting the strokes bleed into each other. Vary the hues by adding more blue or red to the mix.

Express yourself
White flowers

An interesting feature of this watercolour is the hazy, black outline defining the plant and pot. This was achieved by drawing with a dip pen and Indian ink on watercolour paper and then taking off most of the ink with a wet sponge. Before the paper dried out, washes of colour were applied wet-on-wet.

 EXPERT ADVICE
Versatile mop brushes

Squirrel mops come in a range of different sizes and combine an incredible paint-holding capacity with a very soft hair that has the ability to be moulded. Use the belly and heel of the brush for broad washes and wet-on-wet passages (right). The tip comes to a very fine point for rendering details and hard edges (left).

DEVELOPING THE PICTURE

As you continue with the step-by-step, you will be using large amounts of fluid paint. Leave plenty of mixing room in the middle of the palette and don't forget to change your water frequently to keep your colours fresh.

3 ▶ Paint the leaves and pots Mix a fluid wash of cadmium yellow light with a little cerulean blue. Fill in the hyacinth leaves with lots of juicy colour. Use pure cadmium orange to paint the terracotta pots. While this is still wet, brush in the shadows on the pots with vertical strokes of ultramarine. Leave the painting to dry.

4 ▼ Start on the background Prepare a big wash of cadmium yellow light with a tiny amount of cerulean blue. Change to a No.7 mop brush and, working quickly, make broad, sweeping strokes that surround the hyacinths. Use plenty of wash and work with the belly and heel of the brush, holding it near the end of the handle for maximum freedom of movement.

5 ▶ Add more washes to the background Work some of the same wash down into the spaces between the three hyacinths, leaving a rough border of untouched white paper around the group as a whole. Add yellow-green to the wash to make a zingy, acid green. Fill in the outer edges of the paper with broad sweeps of the brush.

6 ◄ **Develop the leaves** Fill more white space between the hyacinths with the acid-green colour, leaving a ragged 'halo' of white around each one. Now change to the No.1 mop brush and develop the forms of the leaves with transparent shadows mixed from varied tones of yellow-green and ultramarine. Add a touch of magenta to the mix for the warm shadows inside the leaves.

Master Strokes

Jorgan Roed (1808–88)
Vase of Flowers

Compared with the loose style of the brushwork in the step-by-step, the precision of this nineteenth-century oil painting is all the more striking. Each flower is described with botanical accuracy down to the last stamen. The elegant vase is placed centrally and the flowers flare out above it to form a graceful 'trumpet' enclosed by an arched border.

The dark background is a perfect foil to the brilliant colours of the spring flowers.

Subtle tonal variations capture the transparency of the glass vase, with white highlights suggesting light glinting off the surface.

Drawing with ballpoints

The everyday ballpoint pen, or Biro, is not usually considered an artist's medium, but this humble writing tool has much to recommend it.

▲ **A combination of ballpoint, rollerball and fibre-tip pens was used for this portrait.**

Ballpoint pens, invented in the 1930s by Hungarian journalist Lazlo Biro (1899–1985), make interesting, if slightly unconventional, drawing tools. They have many advantages, as they are cheap, easily portable, and can be used on most types of paper.

Black and blue

For the artist, black is probably the most useful ballpoint shade. It gives a strong, positive image, as you can see from this portrait. And it is also the least likely to fade.

Blue, although not quite as lightfast, makes a useful alternative colour for the artist, creating a brighter and perhaps more unusual effect. Experiment by trying a little sketching and drawing with both colours to see which you prefer.

Fine lines

Ballpoints produce fine lines of consistent width – you can't vary the character much by applying more or less pressure to the pen. The line has a wiry, mechanical quality and is ideal for hatching, cross-hatching, scribbled hatching and stippling. Even the broken line of a pen that is about to run out can be exploited.

In the portrait, the darker areas of shadow were applied with black rollerball and fibre-tip pens. These produce marks that are significantly bolder than the ballpoint lines, and so create a strong contrast of tone.

FIRST STEPS

1 ▶ Establish the left eye
Using the fine black ballpoint pen, locate the sitter's nearer (left) eye – this is the pivot for the entire portrait. Draw the edges of the lids and the line of the eye socket. Outline the iris and hatch shadows under the eye and beside the bridge of the nose. Sketch in the curve of the eyebrow.

WHITE IT OUT

TROUBLE SHOOTER

Ink from a ballpoint pen can't usually be erased, so check proportions and angles before you put pen to paper. If you do need to hide a mistake, you can cover lines with some bleedproof white gouache. Here, it is applied with a No.4 round brush.

2 ▼ Develop the eye Darken the iris, leaving a highlight to give sparkle to the eye. Develop the eyebrow and indicate the lower lashes. Start to build up the tone, using loose hatching.

3 ▼ Position the second eye Measure with your pen to locate the position of the right eye, which is partially hidden behind the bridge of the nose. Establish the upper and lower lids, the pupil, the iris and the curve of the eyebrow.

4 ▼ Draw the nose Use your pen to measure the length and width of the nose. In this view, the base of the nose looks broader than the eye. Add dark tone under the nose to make the tip advance and the underside recede.

DEVELOPING THE FEATURES

Continue working up the features to complete the face, then start to work outwards to establish the shape of the whole head.

5 ▶ Add the mouth
Lightly sketch the edge of the right cheek, using short pen strokes – these are easier to correct and look more natural than a single hard line. Draw the outline of the lips and the indentation between the nose and top lip.

6 ▶ Work on the face Finish drawing the mouth and plot the line of the chin. Add shadows on and around the lips and on the tip of the chin. Work across the drawing, developing the graduations of tone. The sitter has dark, well-defined eyebrows, so use small strokes of the ballpoint pen to add more texture and tone to these.

7 ▼ Plot the skull Add shadow under the right eye. Now outline the skull and ear. Notice how the skull is an egg shape, broader at the top. Note, too, how the top of the ear lines up with the eyebrow while the bottom aligns with the area under the nose.

8 ▲ Develop the skull Continue working on the head, adding the dark shadow at the back of the skull that helps to convey the volume and roundness of the form. Use regular hatched strokes for this.

9 ▶ Define the left eyebrow Use bleedproof white gouache applied with a No.4 round brush to tidy up the outline of the left eyebrow. Apply the white paint above and below the brow. Leave to dry.

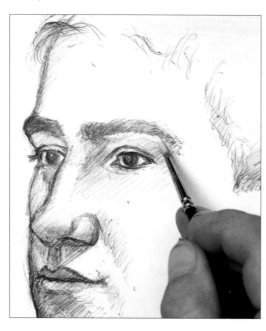

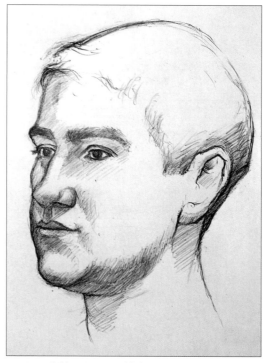

10 ▲ Add more tone Using regular hatched strokes, apply the shadow cast by the ear on to the neck, and the shadow within the whorl of the ear. Use a curving stroke for the shadow under the jaw to suggest the softness of the flesh. Add light shading across the forehead.

A FEW STEPS FURTHER

Stand back and review your progress. The likeness is excellent, and the head has a sense of solidity and volume. Study the way the light falls across the sitter's head and consider developing the tonal contrasts in the finishing stages.

11 ▶ Add more tone and texture
A black fibre-tip pen gives a darker, more emphatic mark. Use it to add definition to the shadow at the back of the head.

12 ▲ Suggest the hair Using a black rollerball pen, make loose, scribbled marks to indicate the hair on the top of the head. It isn't necessary to work up the hair over the entire head – simply indicate its texture at key points, such as the crown and around the ears, and the viewer's eye will fill in the areas between.

THE FINISHED PICTURE

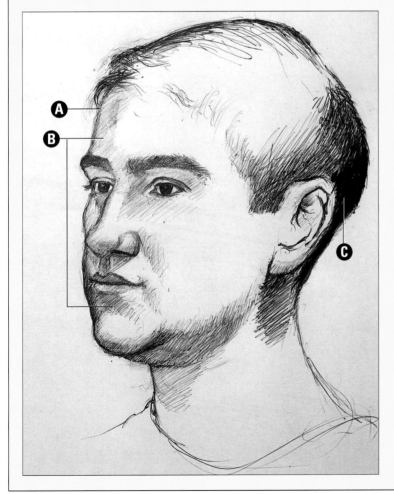

A Broken line
The outline was built up from an overlapping series of short lines applied with the fine tip of a ballpoint pen.

B Hatched tones
Mid and dark tones were created with closely laid hatched strokes – straight and regular on flat planes such as the forehead, and curving around more rounded surfaces such as the jaw.

C Fibre-tip for emphasis
The darkest darks – at the back of the head – were applied with a fibre-tip pen. This has a blacker line that is more fluid and less wiry than the marks of the ballpoint.

Painting with two colours

Restricting your watercolour palette has two great advantages: it makes paint mixing easier and results in paintings with wonderfully harmonious colour.

Successful watercolour painting depends to a large extent on knowing how to mix the colours you need. Experienced artists do this automatically with an ease and speed that makes the process appear almost effortless. Their secret lies in using as few colours as possible – the more limited the palette, the more harmonious and integrated the composition will appear.

The two-colour palette

As an introduction to working with a restricted palette, try painting a picture using just two colours. This sounds drastic, but you will be astonished at how much can be achieved with a pair of carefully selected colours, and at how realistic the result can be.

The selection is personal and depends very much on what you are painting, but a blue combined with a warm colour provides the maximum scope for most subjects. For the watercolour seascape on the far right, our artist chose ultramarine and burnt umber which provided a varied range of browns and greys. Combinations of the two colours created the dark neutral tone of the beach behind the breakwater; the subtle warm colours of the beach and rock face; and the cool blue-greys of the sea and sky.

Alternative pairs

To continue the two-colour experiment, try painting with different pairs of colours. Apart from burnt umber and ultramarine, other effective two-colour palettes are Prussian blue, cerulean blue or indigo with any of the warm earth colours – such as Indian red, Venetian red or burnt sienna.

For flowers, still-life arrangements and other subjects that contain bright colours, try working with a pair of complementaries – two colours that fall opposite each other on the colour wheel. It is surprising how many paintings are based on the use of opposites, and how effective the colours appear as a result. Depending on the subject, choose red with green, blue with orange, or yellow with violet.

The use of opposites produces a particularly brilliant colour reaction, and artists have long made use of this visual property. By laying a colour next to its opposite, the effect is to make both appear more vibrant and bright than when viewed separately. In addition, complementary colours produce a neutral tone when mixed in equal quantities, so greys, browns and other muted colours present no problem.

Black and white

Often the addition of black to two colours gives not only an additional repertoire of dark tones, but also extends the range of greys and neutrals.

TWO-COLOUR COMBINATIONS

The range of colours and tones that you can obtain from ultramarine and burnt umber are shown here. The limited range of colours available should help you think much more carefully about tone.

	Dark	Medium	Light	Very light
Ultramarine				
Ultramarine + a little burnt umber				
Burnt umber + a little ultramarine				
Burnt umber				

A TWO-COLOUR COASTAL SCENE

This coastal landscape was completed using only burnt umber and ultramarine. A wide range of the possible mixes is shown left. Six of these mixes – together with their exact position on the painting – are shown here.

As with any landscape, think about creating an illusion of distance through aerial perspective. Objects appear cooler in colour and lighter in tone in the distance. For instance, note how a dark mix of mainly burnt umber is used for the large cliff top in the middle ground, while the small cliff top in the far distance is rendered in a very pale mix of mainly ultramarine.

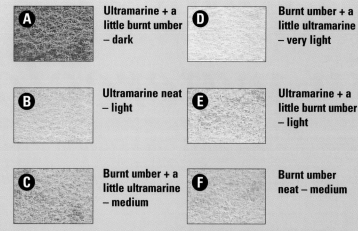

A Ultramarine + a little burnt umber – dark

B Ultramarine neat – light

C Burnt umber + a little ultramarine – medium

D Burnt umber + a little ultramarine – very light

E Ultramarine + a little burnt umber – light

F Burnt umber neat – medium

However, by choosing colours that are dark in tone, like the burnt umber and ultramarine used here, it is not really necessary to use black at all. You can create a near-black with a strong mix of the two palette colours – look at the breakwater in the painting above. For a paler shade of any colour, simply add water to the mixture. Areas of pure white are created by leaving the paper unpainted.

Using a limited palette is, in a sense, a return to the origins of the watercolour tradition. In the eighteenth century, watercolour was considered primarily a sketching medium – useful for making studies for oil paintings. One of the main aims of these sketches was working out the tonal arrangement of the final composition. To do this, you didn't need a full range of colours. Thus a limited palette was established early as one of the traditions of watercolour painting.

Paul Sandby (1725–1809), known as the father of watercolour painting, often worked in just two or three colours. He used this palette with great success to capture the diverse effects of sunlight and atmosphere.

A little improvisation

And if Sandby ever came unstuck with his limited range of paints, he was very imaginative in his use of other materials. For example, he once mixed a 'warm' black by combining the burnt edges of his breakfast toast with gum water!

Details and textures in watercolour

Although watercolours can be used in a free and loose manner, they can also be used to create intricate, highly finished paintings.

Using a simple pocket set of watercolour paints, the artist for this step-by-step created a sweeping rendition of a Scottish landscape – full of subtle variations of colour and texture.

In the foreground, features, such as the tree branches and intricate shadows, are brought into sharp focus using carefully controlled lines made with a fine brush. In contrast to these lines, lively elements have been created by applying the paint in unconventional ways.

Flicking paint

Sprays of seeded grasses, for example, were added in the foreground by gently flicking paint on to the paper. And outstretched, leafy branches have been implied by blowing small pools of wet paint across the paper. These details give the impression of wind blowing across the scene, playing on the grass and foliage as it passes.

In the background, however, little detail has been added. Instead, broad strokes have been used to create the smooth surface of the mountain in a harmonious range of greens, browns and blues. To create these colours, you need constantly to mix small amounts of different colours into your main washes.

It is, therefore, vital to wash your brush often to avoid muddy colours. Dry off the brush on a wad of tissues, or flick the spare water out on to a newspaper positioned on the floor.

▶ **The artist has used aerial perspective to create a sense of depth. The distant mountain is rendered in cool blues and greens, while the grassy areas are painted in warm browns. Note also that the figure in the reference photo (top right) has been omitted to create an unsullied scene.**

YOU WILL NEED

Piece of 300gsm (140lb) Not watercolour paper 40 x 60cm (16 x 24in) HB pencil Brushes: Nos.8, 6 and 2 flats; Nos.4 and OO rounds Large jar of water	10 watercolours: Ultramarine; Cobalt blue; Crimson; Burnt umber; Emerald green; Ochre; Orange; Forest green; Cadmium yellow; Black Large flat mixing dish Paper tissues

FIRST STROKES

1 ▼ Sketch out the scene With an HB pencil, sketch out the main features of your scene. In the palest areas, press only lightly with the pencil, capturing the faintest impression of the ragged outlines of the foliage. In darker areas, you can block in the shadows with a firmer scribbling action. These pencil marks are an important foundation on which to build your detailed composition.

2 ▲ Prepare the sky Use a No.8 flat brush and clean water to wet the sky area, making a neat edge along the line of the mountain. Do not let the area get too wet, or the paper might become wrinkled – but put on enough water to make the paper surface glisten.

3 ▶ Wash in the sky colours Put touches of ultramarine and cobalt blue into a pool of clean water on your mixing dish. Working quickly on the wet paper, boldly mark in the blue sky above the mountain. The water on the paper will make the edges of the colour blend into the white areas. Clean the brush. With tiny spots of crimson and burnt umber, colour a second pool of water and wash in the undersides of the clouds.

DEVELOPING THE PICTURE

Now that you have established the basic outlines and washed in the sky, you can begin work on the landscape itself. To achieve a range of lively textural effects, use various methods of applying the paint, from dabbing and hatching to spattering.

4 ▶ Block in the foliage With clean water, wet the paper in the main areas of foliage. Mix a wash of emerald green with touches of burnt umber and ultramarine. With a No.4 round brush, block in the foliage, using a dabbing action. Let the patches of colour overlap and run into one another, leaving patches of plain white paper in between.

5 ◀ Establish the foreground Wash the paper in the foreground with clean water. Mix a wash of ochre and burnt umber with a touch of orange, then use the flattened tip of the No.8 flat brush to sketch in the grass. Create strong, textural strokes to make these foreground features stand out. As you work, pull touches of other colours into your wash – emerald green, forest green, burnt umber, ochre and cadmium yellow.

6 ▲ Work into the shadows With a strong wash of ultramarine, forest green and a tiny touch of black, use a No.8 flat brush to work in the deep shadows under the bushes. Visually, this makes a strong line to draw the eye across the painting. Use tight hatching marks along the edge of the grassy area to give the impression of grasses growing up across the shadows.

Master Strokes

Robert Adam (1728–92)
Landscape with Bridge over a Stream

In this landscape, Scottish artist and architect Robert Adam has used a palette of colours similar to that of the step-by-step project, combining warm browns and ochres with a range of subtle greens and cool blue-greys. As in the step-by-step, the textures are varied – dabs and washes of colour contrast with meticulously painted details, such as the tree branches and the bridge.

The warm-toned bush on the right catches the viewer's attention. It offers a strong contrast to the more muted greens in the other areas of the landscape.

Cutting diagonally across the picture, the bridge leads the eye into the middle distance of the painting.

7 ▼ Establish the mountain Wait until the sky area is dry so that the edge of the mountain will remain crisp. The mountain is worked on dry paper with a wash of burnt umber, plus touches of cobalt blue and ultramarine to give it a cold, distant appearance. Use long, flat strokes of the No.8 flat brush following the contours of the mountain. Draw a touch more ultramarine into the mix for the darker (right) side of the mountain.

8 ▲ Develop the foliage Using a No.6 flat brush, dab emerald green with a little ochre and burnt umber on to the leafy areas. For a lively effect, identify pools of green paint around the edge of the tree. With your face close to the paper, blow sharply across the surface to throw spurts of paint outwards from the tree. Remove unwanted spots of paint with a tissue.

9 ▶ Mark in the twigs
Use a No.00 round brush and burnt umber paint to mark in the trunk and main branches of the tree. Some are visible between the green patchy areas. Others stretch out sideways to support external foliage. Refer back to your subject to ensure that your marks remain characteristic of the tree.

10 ▲ Work a foreground tree To create a light area, draw a wet brush along the line of the trunk. Dry the brush on a tissue, then draw it down the same line to leach out the colour. Use a mix of forest green, ultramarine and a little black for the shadows around the tree. Develop the foliage of the large tree and bushes, using the same colours as in step 8. Add ochre to help the foreground tree stand out.

TROUBLE SHOOTER

REMOVING PAINT SPOTS

If paint splashes on to a plain area such as the sky, it can be removed with some quick action. While the paint is still wet, press a clean paper tissue on top of the mark. Add a drop of clean water to the mark, blot with tissue and repeat until the mark disappears.

11 ▲ Enliven the foreground grass Add touches of orange and emerald green to ochre and use a No.6 flat brush to paint in coarse, grassy marks in the foreground of the composition. For a lively texture, make some flicking marks upwards from the base of the grass stems. To do this, load the brush with paint, then hold it in one hand close to the paper and pull the bristles back with the fingers of your other hand. Release with a flick upwards to spatter paint across the picture. Remove unwanted spots of paint quickly with a tissue.

12 ▼ **Develop the middle distance** Using a No.6 flat brush, mix a wash of cadmium yellow with a tiny touch of burnt umber to block in the field in the middle distance, behind the bushes. Put more burnt umber and a touch of orange into the wash, then use a stiff-bristled toothbrush to scrub the colour across the middle range of the grassy area. Mimic the textural lines of the grasses with your strokes.

13 ▼ **Deepen the tree shadows** Add a touch of black to burnt umber and, using the tip of a No.4 round brush, work in the deepest shadows on the trunk and branches of the tree. Use the black paint very sparingly, saving it for really striking details such as these.

EXPERT ADVICE
Indenting fine marks

Before you paint the finest twig lines in the tree structure, use the pointed wooden end of a paint brush to press indentations into the surface of the watercolour paper. These will make tiny 'rivulets', which will hold the dark paint neatly in delicate twig shapes.

14 ▲ **Strengthen the features** Stand back from the picture and judge the tonal balance between the different areas. Using the No.8 flat brush, strengthen the main features. Use a wash of ultramarine with touches of black and crimson to deepen the shadow areas on the mountain. Draw more ultramarine into the mix to establish the deepest shadows. Add ochre to emerald green in varying proportions to enliven the upper parts of the bushes.

15 ▼ **Add distance detail** Use the technique from step 10 to leach out colour from under one of the bushes. With a No.00 round brush, wash in a mix of cadmium yellow with a touch of burnt umber. Once dry, paint black trunk details.

16 ▲ **Finalize the balance** Using the No.8 flat brush and a mix of cobalt blue, ultramarine and emerald green, wash in the lower area of the mountain behind the distant trees. Add trunks and branches to the small tree on the left using the techniques from step 13. With the No.6 flat brush and a mix of forest green and ultramarine, use a dabbing action to develop the leaf detail of both the small and large trees.

A FEW STEPS FURTHER

The composition is now complete, but you might wish to draw out some of the character of the scene with more work on fine detail, such as the grass and branches.

17 ▲ **Develop the detail** With a strong mix of burnt umber and black, and using a No.2 flat brush, paint in more branches and twigs on the largest tree. Strengthen existing branches to the front of the tree, but leave the ones nearer the back more washed out, to give a sense of three dimensions.

Express yourself

Focus on texture

The chosen scene is characterized by contrasting areas of smooth sky, sculpted mountain surface and detailed foliage areas. To focus on these textures rather than the colours, discard your paints and take up a piece of charcoal or, as here, a burnt umber soft pastel. Working with a loose style on Not watercolour paper, capture the textures with a variety of strokes. Use soft, scribbling motions for the shadows, flowing marks for the contours of the mountain, and a hatching action for the grass. Use the charcoal or pastel on its side to block in larger areas of smooth shadow.

18 ▶ **Add sweeps of colour**
As a finishing touch, you could convey the impression of the sweeping movements of a strong wind. Make up a strong mix of burnt umber and ochre. With a No.4 round brush, make bold, slanting marks across the foreground area to suggest the blown and tumbled grasses.

THE FINISHED PICTURE

A Sense of distance
The cool blues and greens of the distant mountain recede, helping create a sense of depth. They contrast with the warmer ochres, oranges and browns in the foreground.

B Contrasting textures
Hatched brush strokes and spattered paint created a lively texture for the scrubby grass-land. This contrasts with the smooth sky and sculpted surface of the mountain.

C Strong diagonal
The line of trees and the slope in the middle distance helps create dynamic diagonals that cut across the picture. They provide a pleasing echo of the sloped profile of the mountain.

Painting in changing light

One subject painted several times from the same viewpoint can provide you with a series of entirely different images – it all depends on the effect of the light.

The more you paint and draw, the more sensitive you become to the way light describes your subject matter. In some types of light your subject may come alive with exciting colours and tones; at other times it may appear more muted and moody.

Indeed, if you work outdoors a lot, it really pays to spend some time looking at how your subject changes in various lighting conditions – at different times of the day, in different seasons and in different weather. You might even find yourself drawn into making a series of

paintings, such as the Houses of Parliament watercolours on the following pages.

Depending on the conditions, you may need to adapt your palette to suit the lighting and the time of day. A flexible approach really pays as it enables you to introduce different techniques to accommodate the changes in the subject.

Using photographs

Changes of light and colour are sometimes so gradual that the artist, engrossed in a painting, fails to notice

▲ Claude Monet's fascination with light led him to make 30 paintings of Rouen Cathedral from 1892 to 1894. In the examples here, you can see the radically different effects he achieved. On the left, the cathedral glitters in the sunlight, creating a rich canvas of golds, yellows and browns; on the right, it looks cool, pale and wintry in a hazy light.

the slow onset of an overcast sky or the arrival of dusk. It is therefore a good idea to take a photo before you start work, a reliable reference that can be checked later if the changes are so

MORNING GLORY

The artist made three paintings of the Houses of Parliament in London from three photos taken at various times of the day. Each photo makes a very different painting.

In the morning scene, above, the sun falls squarely on the buildings. This brings out the colour of the warm earthy stonework, which the artist captured with burnt sienna and touches of raw sienna. The sun and the shadows it throws also bring out the detail and texture of the buildings. The shadows were painted in burnt sienna and Payne's grey.

To preserve the crisp edges and straight lines of the buildings, the main shapes were blocked out with masking fluid before painting commenced. Doors, windows and ornamental stonework were picked out in detail using a small brush. For the darkest shadows under the bridge, a mix of Payne's grey and black was used.

 Palette: Ultramarine, cerulean blue, burnt sienna, raw sienna, Payne's grey, black.

great that it becomes impossible to finish the painting.

Better still, if your subject is close at hand, take a series of photos over the course of one, or perhaps a few days. Photos are more reliable than the human memory, and you can compare the pictures to see precisely the difference made by the altered lighting and then decide which conditions you prefer.

The one problem with this is that automatic cameras and film processors are likely to compensate for changes in light, making dark colours paler and vice versa. So try to supplement your photos with some quick sketches on site so you have a record of the tones and colours as you actually saw them.

Sunny days

The vivid colours and stark shadows of a sunny day are very prevalent in the morning and evening, and during the winter. At these times the sun is low in the sky, throwing long shadows – and these strong, dark shapes will play a central and positive role in the composition.

As a general rule, you need both warm and cool colours on your palette – warm ones to capture the effect of sunlight, colder ones for the contrasting shadows that this creates. In addition, you need dark colours for the deepest shadows – Payne's grey or combinations of blue and brown are useful. It is also worth noting that faraway objects appear closer on a clear, sunny day. Distant hills and buildings are often surprisingly sharp, with clearly visible details.

In dull weather, light is diffused and evenly dispersed. There are no sharply defined shadows, and distant objects appear hazy and out of focus. Colours are generally cool, and even warm local colours like that of the stonework on the

MIDDAY CLOUD

In early afternoon, with the sun behind the clouds, the buildings have a completely different appearance. The bold yellow stonework has changed to a subtler range of browns; the architectural details are much less clearly defined; and the range of tones is much smaller.

Without sunlight and sharp shadows, the whole scene has a diffuse, misty appearance. To achieve blurred outlines and soft shadows, the artist worked wet-on-wet to capture the buildings, the clouds in the sky and, in particular, the murky shadows under the bridge. Architectural features were suggested in loose brush strokes rather than depicted in detail.

As the range of tones and colours in this scene is much more limited, the artist used just three colours. The darkest tones – the shadows under the

bridge – are painted in Payne's grey and touches of cerulean blue without the addition of black.

 Palette: Cerulean blue, raw sienna, Payne's grey.

Houses of Parliament look cool and grey in an afternoon mist.

Although the sky contains little or no blue in dull weather, you will probably need to use a considerable amount of blue in the rest of the painting. For example, our artist added cerulean to burnt sienna and raw sienna to create a cool colour for the stonework in the 'midday' picture.

A misty atmosphere generally obscures some of the distant detail. Make sure you paint only what you can see – not what you know to be there. Usually it is more effective to suggest distant objects with a few brush strokes than to make fine renderings, which work against the illusion of haze.

Against the light

Working against the light – or *contre jour* as it is sometimes called – is traditionally used in evening landscapes when the setting sun provides a dramatic background to darker foreground shapes.

In *contre jour* paintings, the emphasis is on tone – the relationship of lights and darks. However, this does not mean a total absence of colour. As can be seen in the evening view on the right, the sky is streaked with blue and the reflections in the river contain traces of sky colour and raw sienna.

DARKNESS FALLS

This watercolour captures the Houses of Parliament in late afternoon. The sun is now behind the buildings and although it is hidden by clouds it still throws a strong backlight.

In contrast to the morning view, the emphasis is no longer on colour and detail, but on the drama of light and dark and the silhouetted shape of the buildings. The artist has deliberately

simplified and exaggerated the contrast of tones to heighten this effect.

Payne's grey is the dominant colour in the painting and – apart from splashes of blue in the sky, and raw sienna in the reflections – local colour is kept to a bare minimum.

 Palette: Ultramarine, cerulean blue, raw sienna, Payne's grey.

'Lost and found' edges

By defining objects clearly in places and more tentatively elsewhere, your paintings will not only look more beautiful but also more realistic.

An important aspect of painting is learning how to handle the edges that define objects and separate one element of a scene from another. Varying these edges between soft and hard, or 'lost and found', helps to convey the form and solidity of objects and the illusion of depth and distance. It is also the interplay of lost and found edges that lends beauty and sensitivity to a painting or drawing.

Selective focus

If an object is placed against an area of strongly contrasting tone, it tends to have a crisp, or found, edge; if it is surrounded by the same or similar tonal value, it will have a soft, or lost, edge. Likewise, an object might have one sharp edge, where it faces the light, and one soft edge, where it is in shadow.

Beginners sometimes fail to see this and portray everything with equal clarity, drawing a hard outline round each object and filling it in with colour. But too much sharp detail gives a hard, brittle look and is tiresome to look at. It robs the painting of its mystery and the viewer of a feeling of participation – filling in the missing details with the mind's eye.

Remember, the human eye can only focus on one thing at a time: if you hold up a pencil and focus on it, everything around it appears blurred. If you focus on the background, the pencil will be blurred. The trick is to mimic the way

◄ **Kunisada Utagawa's** *Prancing Horse beneath a Willow Tree* **(1830) is a simple but effective example of the use of lost and found edges. The bold, black outline of the horse is 'lost' around the tail, mane and parts of the face. This encourages the eye to move around the image. Imagine how static and crude the horse would appear if its outline had been one unbroken black line.**

the eye perceives things and employ selective focus – contrasting sharp detail with softness and suggestion. This will lend your pictures a sense of atmosphere and an altogether more painterly feel.

When drawing any subject, imagine the paper or canvas as a piece of clay from which you model form by pushing and pulling (exerting varying degrees of pressure on the pencil). Try to 'feel' the contours as you draw them: start with light strokes and then exert more pressure along those contours you want to emphasize – the swell of a cumulus cloud or the curve of a hip. This interplay of active and passive lines gives the drawing energy and suggests how the shape continues behind the image you have drawn.

If you are painting, first sketch in the composition lightly and avoid precise outlines. After blocking in the broad shapes with thin paint, you can start to use thicker paint and refine your brushwork, making certain areas more clearly defined – for example, developing more detail at the focal point and playing down everything else.

Avoid completing one area before

A STILL LIFE OF SHARP AND SOFT EDGES

Antoine Vollon's (1833-1900) *Still Life* has a wonderful array of lost and found edges. Some edges catch the light and jump forward, while others are lost altogether in the dark background. This helps encourage the eye to flit around the composition, resting on clearly defined objects and then searching for more obscure forms. It also helps to enhance the sense of recession.

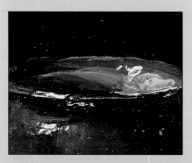

Although small, the thin, sharp highlights of white and yellow at the front edge of the rim are really telling. They bring the front edge forward while softer, broader strokes at the back edge recede.

Look at the variety of edges here. The knife handle is sharply defined, the edges of the glass are lost in places and found in others, while the outline of the vessel in the background is almost lost in darkness.

going on to the next. Instead, work constantly between background and foreground so that the two are unified. Where an object is in shadow, or in the distance, soften edges and contours by blending wet-on-wet or scumbling over the edge where it meets the background.

One way to create the illusion of spatial recession in a picture is by saving most of the hard edges for the foreground and gradually softening them as you move back in space. This applies even if you are painting a single object, such as a vase of flowers or a portrait head. Here, too, the illusion of light, atmosphere and three-dimensionality is achieved by reserving most found edges for the foreground, to bring them forward, while losing some of the edges at the back and sides so that they recede.

Observe carefully how the light strikes the forms in your subject and vary your edges accordingly. The human face, for example, is a complex

▲ **By losing edges in the eye sockets and around the outline of the figure, Théodore Géricault (1791–1824) adds a sense of mystery to his** *Portrait of an Old Man.*

mass of lost and found edges; bony areas like the bridge of the nose appear harder than the soft curves of the cheek and neck. Similarly, the light-struck contours of the face appear well-defined, while the contours on the shadow side are much less defined.

239

Creating emotional impact

*Tonal key tells us about the overall lightness and darkness of a picture –
and it's an invaluable tool for creating mood and atmosphere.*

The tones and colours in a painting are like musical notes – when pitched to a particular key, they produce a result that is not only rich and harmonious but also emotionally expressive. Music that is composed mainly of high-key notes can sound either light and cheerful or poignant and romantic. Low-key notes tend to produce a more melancholy sound. In the same way, light and dark tones in a painting can be 'orchestrated' to express a particular mood or atmosphere.

Tonal key

The term 'tonal key' is used to describe the range of tones within a picture. It tells us about its overall lightness or darkness. Imagine a bright, sunny scene. This subject is well suited to the lighter range of the tonal scale – a high-key painting. A dimly lit interior or a stormy seascape are obvious examples of low-key subjects.

Look at any good painting and you will see how the artist has deliberately orchestrated the tones to express a mood, to convey the character of a sitter, or to capture the atmosphere created by light and weather on a landscape. In short, sensitive control of tonal values can enrich the mood of a scene and make it 'talk'.

The Impressionists, for example, captured the shimmering light and the exuberant feeling of summer days with

▼ In a *Game of Tennis* (*c.* 1910), Spencer Gore (1878–1914) uses light tones to capture the carefree, sun-drenched atmosphere of summer in the park. Note how even the shadows are filled with light and colour.

brilliant high-key images. In contrast are the magnificent, low-key portraits by Rembrandt (1606–69) in which softly lit figures or faces emerge from the surrounding shadows.

High-key paintings

In a high-key painting, most of the tones are in the light-to-middle range. Depending on the intensity of the colours and the way you apply them, you can convey a mood that's cheerful and bright or quiet and restrained.

Take a beach scene, for instance. On a summer day, the light is intense and there is a lot of colour. To capture the bracing seaside atmosphere, you would use mostly light, bright colours, accentuated by a sprinkling of crisp, dark accents.

That same beach on a misty morning takes on a completely different mood. This time, let soft colours predominate. By keying most of your tonal values to the higher end of the scale, keeping contrasts to a minimum and blending edges wet-on-wet, you can convey a quiet, more poignant atmosphere.

In a high-key painting, watercolours can be applied in a series of transparent washes to create a delicate, subtle effect. Leaving flecks and patches of light-reflecting white paper breathes air into a watercolour painting – try it next time you paint a sunny beach scene.

Alternatively, try working on toned paper, using watercolours mixed with a little Chinese white; the colours take on a milky, semi-transparent quality that is well suited to romantic themes.

In oils and acrylics, colours can be lightened by adding lots of white to create delicate, high-key tones – as in the painting opposite. To keep the colours fresh

and lively, don't overmix them on the palette, and try using broken colour effects. Small strokes and dabs of pure colour will blend in the viewer's eye and give a vibrant, joyful effect.

In a low-key painting, tones from the darker end of the scale predominate – though a few telling accents of light will

▲ Rembrandt was the undoubted master of the low-key portrait. In this image, entitled *An Oriental* (1635), the shadowy tones underline the sitter's mood of melancholic contemplation.

enhance the drama. By choosing your subject carefully and picking colours in the mid to dark tonal range, you can use the psychological associations of darkness and shadow – mystery, suspense, sadness – to create powerful images.

As with high-key paintings, the effect depends on your choice of subject, composition and how you apply the paint. To convey a bleak winter landscape, you might accentuate the dramatic patterns of dark branches against a pale sky. But a low-key painting doesn't have to be sombre: an interior at evening, lit by a table lamp that casts a soft pool of light in a shadowy room, creates a low-key mood that is warm and intimate.

A change of mood

Try making a series of paintings of the same scene at different times of the day or under different weather conditions – similar to the Houses of Parliament series on pages 235–236. Choose a location that's convenient to get to – your own garden might be suitable as you can return to it quickly when the light changes. Notice the different moods created as the amount, direction and colour of the light changes, and communicate this observation by 'keying' your tonal values to fit the mood of the subject.

In the Houses of Parliament series, the evening scene is a low-key picture. The result is a rather ominous image that looks as if it could come from wartime. In contrast, the morning scene has a lot of pale tones, especially in the sky and water, creating a lighter, happier mood.

Creating foliage in watercolours

Trees, with their enormous variations in shape, colour and patterns of growth, are an important source of colour and texture in landscape paintings.

The flutter of leaves in a passing breeze is one of the most important elements in a convincing landscape painting. Using a few simple watercolour techniques, you'll soon be creating truly naturalistic effects.

When trees are in the foreground, you can make out the pattern made by the foliage and the shapes of some individual leaves. But you won't see every part of a scene with pinpoint accuracy, so don't paint every leaf. Instead, find a mark that describes the distinctive character of the foliage.

Study the subject carefully through half-closed eyes and put down the areas of tone. Gradually, a leaf-like pattern will begin to emerge. If you paint just a few leaves in detail, the viewer's brain will understand that the rest of the foliage follows the same pattern and will 'fill in the blanks'.

When a tree is further away, you can see only generalized leaf forms and the leaf masses around the boughs. And when trees are seen from even further away, only a broad silhouette of the leaves and trunk is discernible.

▲ The grey-green foliage of this gnarled olive tree is shown in enough detail to suggest the leaves without being too precise. The trees in the distance are treated as silhouettes.

FIRST STROKES

1 ▼ Draw the outlines Using a 2B pencil, establish the broad areas of the landscape. The branches and leaves of trees look complicated, so ignore the detail and concentrate on the underlying forms. Think about the composition – whether you are working directly from the subject or from references, adjust the drawing to create a pleasing arrangement.

YOU WILL NEED

Large piece of 300gsm (140lb) Not watercolour paper

2B pencil

Brushes: Nos.10, 6, 3 soft rounds

7 watercolours: Cobalt blue; Sap green; Sepia; Yellow ochre; Payne's grey; Cerulean blue; Black

Mixing palette or dish

Natural sponge

▼ A mix of sepia, sap green and yellow ochre makes a good foliage colour.

2 ▶ Block in the sky Using a No.10 brush, mix a wash of cobalt blue and lay it in for the sky. Remember that, in watercolour, the paper is the lightest colour available, so leave patches of paper unpainted as clouds. Leave to dry.

4 ▲ Soften the sponged effects The stippling created by sponging can be too unsubtle, so apply more colour and roll the No.10 brush through the wash to create a variety of edges to modify the sponged effects.

3 ▲ Apply background greens Make a wash of sap green and, using a natural sponge, apply this broadly and loosely in the grassy foreground area. Use sweeping, diagonal marks that suggest swaying grasses. Mix sap green and sepia to create a lighter green for the trees in the distance, and dab it on with a sponge.

5 ▲ Add texture to the foreground Mix sap green, sepia and yellow ochre to give a vivid grass green colour. Using a No.6 brush and making vigorous diagonal strokes, add more colour to the grassy area in the foreground. Leave the painting to dry.

6 ▼ Paint the trunks and branches Make a wash of sepia and Payne's grey for the tree trunks. Using the No.6 brush, apply flat colour, thinking about the way a tree grows: the boughs come out of the main trunk, and the branches and twigs grow out of each other in a logical pattern, becoming gradually thinner towards the edge of the tree. Allow to dry.

DEVELOPING THE PICTURE

The background and the main silhouette of the tree are established, so it is now time to create the foliage. The patches of leaves are built up gradually in three stages by layering a light, middle and dark tone of the same basic colour. This technique creates a sense of movement, suggesting light catching fluttering leaves.

7 ▲ Start to apply foliage to the olive trees Mix Payne's grey, sap green and cerulean blue to make a pale blue-green for the first foliage tone. Use a small No.3 brush to apply this wash, pushing and pulling the colour with the tip of the bristles to create random clusters of leaves. Try not to space the marks too evenly, and vary the tone of the wash by adding differing amounts of water.

EXPERT ADVICE
Adding gum arabic

Gum arabic is the medium that carries the pigment in watercolour paint. Adding extra medium intensifies the colour and gives a slight sheen, as in the darkest foliage colour shown below. You can buy gum arabic in bottles from most art supply shops.

8 ▲ Add shadows on the tree trunk Using a more concentrated wash of the sepia/Payne's grey mix and the No.3 brush, lay in the shadows on the trunk and branches of the main olive tree. These shadows give form and solidity to the tree, and also help to describe its gnarled surface.

9 ► Finish adding the first tone Using the Payne's grey, sap green and cerulean blue wash and the No.3 brush, complete the first application of tone to the foliage. Take care to keep the marks a similar size as you work across the painting. Leave the paint to dry thoroughly.

10 ▲ **Add a second tone to the foliage** Mix a darker tone of the foliage colour and use the No.3 brush to apply another layer of leaves. Screw up your eyes to isolate the main masses of foliage. Notice that the tops of each mass, especially those on the side from which the light is coming, are lighter than the undersides. Work as before, creating patches of wash and then painting detailed leaf shapes around the edges. Leave to dry.

11 ▲ **Paint shadows on the trunk** Mix a darker tone of the sepia/Payne's grey wash and apply dark shadows to the left side of the trunk and the branches that are turned away from the light. Use the same wash to 'draw' some thin branches and twigs amongst the foliage. Allow to dry thoroughly.

Master Strokes

Gustav Klimt (1862–1918)
Roses under the Trees

The Austrian painter Gustav Klimt developed a highly decorative style. In his treatment of these trees in an orchard, the foliage is painstakingly built up dab by dab using a pointillist technique, until the surface glows with hundreds of different shades.

The painting is dominated by the vibrant foliage of the tree which fills the picture area, creating a decorative, almost abstract effect.

The ridged texture of the tree trunks is described in detail, using broken, curved lines. Patches of green lichen enliven the grey surface.

12 ▶ **Give texture to the bark** Prepare a third, dark tone of the basic foliage wash used in step 7. Add gum arabic to intensify the colour (see Expert Advice on the opposite page). Apply a final layer of this colour, painting clusters of leaves as before. Mix a wash of black and, using the No.3 brush, apply dark tone on the darkest side of the trunk. Use the same wash to describe fissures and textures in the bark of the tree.

13▲ **Apply texture and shadows** Using a wash of sap green and the No.3 brush, apply wide brush marks to the grassy area in the foreground. Allow this to dry thoroughly and then use sepia with a little sap green to paint the shadows cast by both olive trees. These attached shadows help to 'fix' the trees to the horizontal surface of the ground.

Express yourself
Band of gold

The same olive tree has been given an arresting treatment here with the addition of bright orange and green bands dividing the composition in two. These are applied as a collage of coloured paper and represent the nets used to catch the harvested olives, which have been rolled up and tied. This unusual device not only adds a splash of almost fluorescent colour to the neutral grey-green background, but also acts as a counterbalance to the vertical trunks and branches that predominate in the painting.

A FEW STEPS FURTHER

Applying the foliage as layers of washes gives the tree canopy depth and form. This area of the painting can be considered complete – it is convincing and has textural interest. You could, however, add more texture to the foreground – this will add eye-catching detail and increase the sense of recession. Consider adding to the background by painting in a line of simple silhouetted trees.

14▲ **Add texture to the grass** Mix sap green with sepia and paint vigorous diagonal marks with the No.3 brush to create grassy textures in the foreground. Spatter the wash over the area for varied textures.

▼ **Use increasingly concentrated mixes of sepia and Payne's grey for the bark.**

15 ▲ **Develop the textures in the bark** Mix black and sepia and, using the No.3 brush, work across the trunk adding a variety of textures. The bark of this ancient olive tree is twisted and gnarled, so you can use a range of brush marks to describe its surface.

16 ▲ **Add trees in the background** Mix Payne's grey and sap green to create a dark green. Use the No.3 brush to paint a row of trees in the middle distance. These trees add interest to the composition and create a sense of recession. However, at this distance you cannot see details of the foliage, so reduce the trees to simple silhouetted shapes.

THE FINISHED PICTURE

A Textured bark

The rough texture and fissured surface of the tree trunk is one of the interesting features of this subject. The textures were applied gradually, working light to dark.

B Foreground textures

Vigorous brush marks in the foreground capture the appearance of wild grasses. The foreground texture also helps to create a sense of space and recession.

C Simple leaf shapes

Simplified, shorthand marks capture the character of the foliage. These have been applied in layers to build up the volume and depth of the tree's canopy.

Painting cloudscapes

There is an art to rendering cloudscapes, whether you are painting a sky full of picturesque 'cotton wool' clouds or a moody blanket of grey.

Clouds take many forms, from the fleecy skeins strung across a summer sky to the towering, anvil-shaped formations that predict a storm. Study clouds in a range of weather conditions and explore the way different media allow you to capture their forms, tones and colours – you will soon see improvements in your landscape painting.

Using different media

On the following three pages, the same sky study, which features a view over the River Thames, is tackled in three different media: soft pastel, watercolour and acrylics. Each medium offers a different approach to rendering the dramatic cloudscape, but the results all capture the contrast between the brilliance of the white clouds and the dark tones of those that threaten showers.

With watercolour, work light to dark and leave the white of the paper to stand for the clouds in sunlight. Wet-on-wet washes allow you to capture their swirling forms and soft edges. Acrylic paint provides the semi-transparent washes and scumbles that are ideal for creating the depth and complexity of cloud forms, while touches of opaque white impasto capture the light-reflecting white of sunlit clouds. Smearing the paint produces thin veils of colour that suggest the barely-there quality of the thinnest clouds. Soft pastel offers a similar combination of broken and smeared semi-transparent veils of colour and dense passages of solid colour.

Modelling clouds

As clouds are simply made up of water vapour, they can sometimes appear amorphous and insubstantial. However, some types of cloud, cumulus in particular, have definite shape, volume and perspective. So try to think of these as you would any other three-dimensional form that must be modelled with light and shade.

Often the top of a cloud is in sunlight while the base, which is turned away from the sun, is in its own shadow.

CLOUD FORMATIONS

The three main cloud types – cirrus, cumulus and stratus – are shown below and are easily identifiable by their shape, colour and altitude. Practise sketching them so that you become familiar with their different characteristics.

▶ Composed of ice crystals, cirrus are the highest and most delicate clouds. They form tufts and plumes that often appear to converge on the horizon. In the charcoal sketch (far right, top), the sky is shaded around the shapes of the clouds.

◀ Cumulus are the typical 'cotton wool' clouds of a fine summer's day. Fluffy and heaped, they are brilliant white on top and have a flatter, darker horizontal base. In the sketch (centre right), their forms are defined with tonal shading and their curved outlines emphasized with linear work.

▶ Stratus, the lowest-lying clouds, form a grey, semi-transparent blanket and sometimes produce a light drizzle. In a landscape, they give a flat neutral background, depicted in the sketch (far right, bottom) by light shading worked with the side of the charcoal stick.

CLOUDY SKY IN SOFT PASTEL

Soft pastel allows you to build up the form of the cloud masses in this dramatic skyscape by scumbling one colour over another. Use your fingertips to blend the pigment in order to achieve a hazy, amorphous effect. For this exercise, you'll need light grey pastel paper and six soft pastels: blue-grey, Prussian blue, dark grey, white, cobalt blue and raw umber.

1 ▲ Scumble in clouds Use the side of a piece of blue-grey soft pastel to scribble on a loose layer of colour that follows the broad shape of the main cloud. Blend the colour lightly with your fingertips to create a filmy effect.

2 ▲ Build the dark tones Work Prussian blue over the darkest area of cloud and blend with your fingers. Apply dark grey to the undersides of the clouds and soften the colour with your fingers, especially at the shadow edges.

3 ▲ Add light areas Use a white pastel for the bright highlights where the clouds are lit by the sun. Apply the pastel firmly to build up a thick covering – see how the white leaps out from the grey of the paper.

4 ▲ Apply blue sky Use a cobalt blue pastel for the patches of sky glimpsed between the cloud cover. Soften it with your fingers.

5 ▲ Draw the landscape Use dark grey and raw umber to depict the buildings on the horizon. Work freely, using scribbled marks that do not distract from the cloudscape.

▲ Thin veils of pastel create the shapes of the billowing clouds without making them look too solid.

Again, this is especially noticeable in flat-bottomed cumulus clouds – their heaped meringue-like tops appear brilliant white, while their shaded bases are grey. If you are working in oils or acrylics, try using impasto techniques to capture the sunlit tops of clouds, as this really brings out their fluffy forms. With watercolour, leave the paper unpainted to create the brightest white.

Also, don't forget the effects created by atmospheric perspective which applies as much to the sky as to the land. Clouds above you, and therefore closer to you, appear more sharply defined than those near the horizon.

Cloud types that are less well defined require less modelling. These include cirrus clouds – thin, wispy plumes made up of ice particles – and stratus clouds, which form a thick blanket across the landscape and let little sunlight through.

Work the sky as a whole

Treat clouds as an integral part of a composition, not as features to be added once the rest of the sky has been established. Note how in the three step-by-step exercises here, the artist has continually worked across the entire sky area, rather than concentrating on one section at a time. Think in terms of establishing general tonal variations rather than individually rendering each billowing form. When using wet media, employ blending and smearing techniques to suggest amorphous clouds.

Another aspect to consider when painting heavily overcast skies is colour. At first glance, leaden skies may appear uniformly grey, but look more closely and you might pick out shades

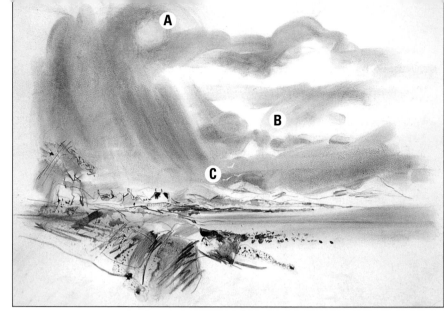

such as brown, purple, yellow and indigo. Indeed, these are all colours employed by the artist in the step-by-step exercises. Make sure, though, that you are subtle about it. Unless you are intentionally going for an expressionist approach, don't use pure alizarin crimson or pure cadmium yellow. In wet media, use these colours in mixes to neutralize their impact; in dry media, use them in semi-transparent veils.

A sense of movement

To really bring a cloudscape to life, also think about conveying the movement of the clouds. Cumulus clouds might look impressive when they are sharply defined, but to convey the turbulence of a stormy sky work more loosely.

Look at the cloudscape worked in graphite powder, on the right. The artist has applied the powder with swift, sweeping strokes, creating the impression of a strengthening wind and the imminent arrival of a heavy rainstorm.

▲ Applying graphite powder with the fingers is a great way to create a fast-moving, stormy sky. The powder can also be removed to create special effects in the sky. Here, graphite powder provides a light grey colour for the large masses of cloud. By contrast, the 8B pencil, charcoal and ink used in the foreground give much denser tones, suggesting the solidity of the land against the insubstantial nature of the clouds.

Ⓐ The flat side of a craft knife, rubbed over the paper surface in a circular motion, removed powder to create a pale sun. (It is best to use thick paper for this technique.)
Ⓑ Small, individual clouds were added by pressing pigment on to the paper with the finger or thumb, forming prints.
Ⓒ The sharp corner of a putty rubber was used to lift off the powder to create the three seagulls in the centre of the picture.

Clouds as washes of watercolour

You can create atmospheric cloudy skies very successfully with dilute watercolour washes. For this exercise, you'll need watercolour paper, a No.12 round brush, a No.6 Chinese brush and five watercolours: indigo, alizarin crimson, raw umber, cobalt blue and ultramarine.

1 ▶ Apply a wet-on-wet wash Load the No.12 round brush with water and work it over the upper part of the sky, leaving some areas dry. Mix a wash of indigo and flood this into the wet area, painting in different directions.

2 ▲ Add sky While the paint is still wet, mix alizarin crimson and raw umber and blend it in on the right, working down to where the paper is still dry. Leave to dry. Mix cobalt blue and ultramarine and, using a No.6 Chinese brush, add slivers of blue sky.

3 ◀ Describe the landscape Mix a dark, warm grey from alizarin crimson, indigo and raw umber. Working freely with the tip of the No.6 Chinese brush, sketch in the church tower and townscape.

▶ **Wet-on-wet areas of hazy cloud at the top of the picture contrast with crisper-edged clouds closer to the horizon.**

TEXTURAL CLOUDS IN ACRYLICS

With creamy textured acrylics, you can manipulate the paint by hand as well as with a brush. This creates subtle blendings of colour that are ideal for an overcast sky. For this exercise, you'll need a piece of canvas board, 25mm (1in) and 6mm (¼in) flat brushes, and five acrylic colours: titanium white, cadmium red, ultramarine, cadmium yellow and brilliant blue.

1 ▲ Apply base colour Mix a slightly muted blue-violet from titanium white, cadmium red, ultramarine and cadmium yellow. Use a 25mm (1in) flat brush to scumble the colour loosely over the support.

2 ▲ Paint warmer tones Add more titanium white and cadmium yellow to the base mix. Using sweeping gestures with the brush, apply this greyish mid tone to the underside of the clouds.

3 ▼ Add white clouds Apply creamy white paint straight from the tube for the lightest clouds. Smear the paint with your fingertips to smudge and blend the colours.

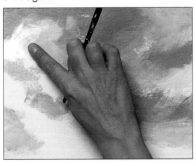

4 ▲ Use impastoed white With the 6mm (¼in) flat brush, apply touches of impastoed white to stand for the sunlit highlights.

5 ▲ Create blue sky Apply brilliant blue to suggest glimpses of sky between the clouds. Smear white across the blue with your fingertips.

6 ▲ Paint the landscape Use the 25mm (1in) flat brush and a mix of cadmium red, cadmium yellow and ultramarine to indicate the landscape.

▲ Here, thickly applied paint, manipulated by hand or with brushes, captures the diffuse character of the clouds.

Capturing reflections

The distorted reflections of two houses near Venice help to create a wonderfully vibrant image – perfect for coloured pencils.

Reflections in water are fascinating to draw. Unless the surface of the water is absolutely mirror-still, the reflected image will be distorted.

In this scene, the water has been disturbed by the swell of a passing boat. The reflection of the houses is clearest near the bank, where the water is calmest, but it becomes gradually more distorted by the ripples, especially in the upper window and roof areas.

▼ **The low evening sun brings the façades of the waterside houses to life, creating a bold, brightly coloured image.**

In the two waves created by the swell, an unusual effect has occurred – two narrow slivers of the reflection can be seen, as though they have broken off the main image. The shapes found in these thin strips of colour are so distorted that the reflections have become an abstract pattern.

Coloured pencils are versatile drawing tools, ideal for capturing watery effects. Use them for linear work and for layering to give a rich depth of colour. Make broken marks where the reflections are distorted to create an impressionistic interplay of different colours.

Piece of textured cartridge
paper 43 x 50cm (17 x 19¾in)

19 coloured pencils: mid grey; pale
blue; pale lilac; vermilion; Venetian
red; orange; cerulean blue;
deep olive green; Naples yellow;
very pale sap green; Prussian
green; dark Prussian green; raw
sienna; pale olive green; dark
blue-grey; burnt umber; deep
rose; cobalt blue; black

Scrap paper

Putty rubber (to erase mistakes)

Craft knife (to sharpen pencils)

FIRST STEPS

1 ▶ Sketch the scene
Using a mid grey
coloured pencil, put
in the line of the
bank, then draw
the houses and
outbuilding. Roughly
indicate the trees.
Now draw the
reflections of the
houses and trees
directly underneath,
describing the
reflected windows
with zigzag lines.
Mark in the diagonals
of the boat's wake
in the foreground.

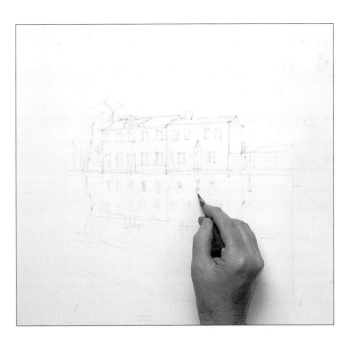

2 ▼ Introduce colour With a pale blue pencil, shade lightly
over the sky and down into the water. Change to a pale
lilac pencil and work across the sky to suggest clouds.
Strengthen the sky above the houses with more pale blue.

EXPERT ADVICE
Realistic reflections

If a house is set
back from the
water's edge, only
its top part is
reflected. Similarly,
because the roof
slants backwards,
only the front
edge is visible.
Make sure
you capture
these effects to
create a sense
of recession.

DEVELOPING THE DRAWING

As you begin to add colour, take care to show
the differences between the houses and their
reflections. In the reflections, the solid colours
and firm lines of the façades are broken up,
giving a feeling of movement to the water.

3 ▶ Work on the red house
Use a vermilion pencil to
colour the wall and gable of
the red house, working
neatly around the windows.
Take the same colour down
into the reflection of the
house, but this time use
loose, hatched lines.

4 ▶ Layer some reds Continue shading the vermilion reflections, including the chimney, making looser marks where ripples of water break up the colour. Work, too, along the sliver of reflection visible in the boat's wake. Now create a more accurate colour for the house wall and its reflection by layering Venetian red, orange, then more Venetian red over the vermilion.

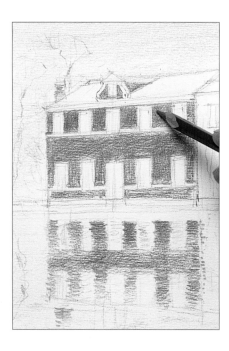

5 ▼ Colour the roofs Darken the water with cerulean blue, making loose, diagonal marks in the foreground. Now use Venetian red and deep olive green for the roof tiles. For their reflections, make broken marks to suggest the disturbed water. Show the tree on the left and the bank with deep olive green, then add their reflections.

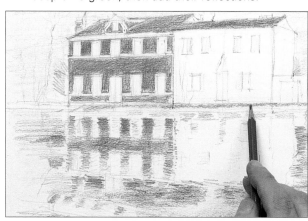

6 ▼ Work on the cream house Shade Naples yellow across the cream house and outbuilding, then layer very pale sap green on top. Work Venetian red on the roof of the outbuilding. Use the same colours for the reflections, making short, horizontal dashes of colour where the moving water distorts the image.

7 ◀ Put in some darks Strengthen the reflection of the cream house with more Naples yellow. Darken the shadowed side and reflection with deep olive green. Blend Prussian green and dark Prussian green to create an near-black shade for the doors and dark windows on both houses – use hatched lines for their reflections. Add a porch roof to the right-hand door with Venetian red.

8 ◀ Complete the windows On the right, work up the bank, trees and their reflections in raw sienna. Block in the upper windows of the cream house with pale olive green. Now hatch in the reflections of the lower windows, door and porch, using the two Prussian greens and Venetian red. For the distorted reflections of the upper windows, alternate bands of pale olive green and Prussian green.

9▲ **Define the trees** With raw sienna, roughly indicate the trunks and bare branches of the trees on the far left. Then, using dark Prussian green, draw the diagonal branches of the conifer. Work up the reflections of the trees beyond the houses, using the same colours.

10▲ **Darken the water** Shade dark blue-grey across the whole water area. When you reach the boat's wake in the foreground, work over a strip of scrap paper to achieve straight edges along the shadows here. Layer cerulean blue over the dark colour, again using the paper strip along the wake.

THE FINISHED PICTURE

11▲ **Add details** Strengthen the reflections along the wake with Naples yellow and vermilion. Edge the bank with burnt umber, using raw sienna for its reflection. Draw a tree in front of the cream house, adding a reflection with dots and wavy lines, then hint at trees in front of the outbuilding with deep olive green. Decorate the eaves of the red house with burnt umber dashes.

A Rippled surface
Dashed and dotted coloured pencil marks suggest the broken-up reflections of the roofs in the disturbed water.

B Abstract effect
The reflections along the line of the wake have been filled in with patches of colour that form a decorative, abstract pattern.

C Moving water
Diagonal, rather than horizontal, pencil lines in the foreground give the impression of movement in the water.

PROJECTS

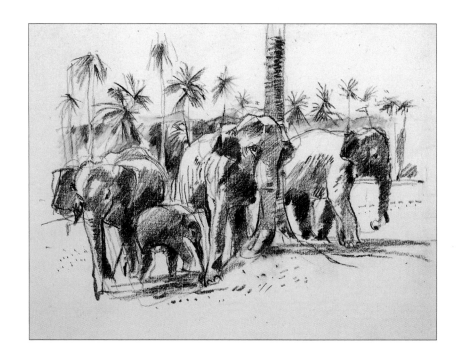

The projects which follow have been put together to help you practise and develop the skills learned in previous chapters. Each one includes step-by-step instructions and a full materials list, plus expert tips and advice. They're arranged in groups, according to the media used and are ready for you to follow or use as inspiration for your own, original works of art.

Seed pods and pebbles

Draw these fascinating shapes and reproduce their subtle textures and understated hues in graphite and coloured pencils.

N atural objects are an obvious choice for a still life. Here, the artist has put together unusual seed pods and pebbles, selected for their interesting shapes and textures.

You should always consider your subject matter carefully before choosing a medium to work with. In this case, graphite and coloured pencils have been used because they pick up the precision of the texture so well and because they are ideal for conveying the strong linear patterns and understated colours that characterize the composition.

You will notice that, although the outlines and patterns have been drawn with precision, the pencil strokes used for colouring and shading are

extremely varied. In places, they are purposely bold, with the intention of creating a textural rather than a smooth effect.

Drawing techniques

You will be able to put into practice a variety of drawing techniques, using hatching, cross-hatching, stippling and scribbling. The project will also give you the opportunity to explore the different effects created by simply varying the density of the lines and the distance between them. By doing this, gradations of tone can be introduced and the fascinating shapes of the pods and pebbles are brought to life on paper.

▲ **Hard rather than soft lighting was used for the still life. This emphasized the markings and textures on the pebbles and seed pods, making them more interesting to draw.**

257

1 ▶ Draw the objects
With golden brown and HB pencils, draw the long pod, then hatch over it. Draw and shade tone on the pebbles, using (from left to right) the HB pencil, red-violet lake, imperial purple and golden brown. Draw the curly pod with deep chrome and golden brown.

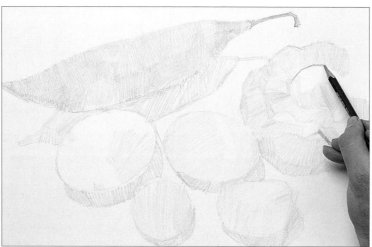

2 ◀ Put in cast shadows
Change to a blue-grey pencil and lightly hatch in the cast shadows – don't be afraid to make them definite. Colour both pods with Naples yellow, then deep chrome; leave white showing through. Define the stalks in raw umber, shade in with brown ochre and define the tips with the 3B graphite stick. Outline the curly pod in brown ochre.

3 ▼ Develop the pebbles Use burnt sienna, brown ochre, red-violet lake and blue-grey on the pebbles (from right to left), marking in their patterns. Vary the strokes, leaving light patches for highlights and shading more heavily to create shadows and roundness.

DEVELOPING THE PICTURE

The underlying colours and tones are now in place. Once you are satisfied with these basics, you can start to concentrate on building up the patterns and textures.

4 ▲ Colour the long pod Use burnt sienna and raw sienna round the neck and top of the long pod. Work over the underside with burnt sienna, scarlet lake and a B pencil. Use the B pencil and imperial purple to add the linear pattern, then take off some colour with a rubber to create a highlight.

5 ▶ Pattern the stones

With a 9B graphite pencil, work up the texture and shading on the large pebble. Work over the lighter areas with a B pencil and draw in the veins with the rubber. Hatch the shaded areas with imperial purple and cross-hatch a little blue-grey on the right. Colour the speckled pebble in imperial purple and blue-grey. Stipple on dots in imperial purple.

EXPERT ADVICE
Masking the band

You can achieve a clean edge on a pale band, without compromising the pattern of the stone, by making a mask. Tear off a piece of paper and match its curve to that of the band. Hold it in place while you continue to work.

6 ◀ Add more pattern

Scribble scarlet lake on the stippled stone. Mask the band on the striped pebble (see Expert Advice) and use a 3B graphite stick to add texture. Put in the shadow at its base in blue-grey and deep chrome. Add the markings to the last pebble in deep chrome and burnt sienna. Use red-violet lake for the shadow and deepen this with the 3B graphite stick.

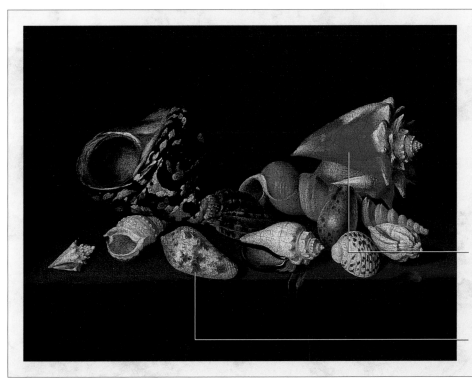

Master Strokes

Louis Hubner (17th century)
Shells on a Ledge

The fascinating shapes of shells are revealed in all their diversity in this striking still life. Their spirals, whorls and spikes create a wonderful array of forms and they are thrown into stark relief by the dark background.

The bright vermilion shell brings an element of colour contrast into the otherwise muted palette.

Dabs and dots of brown and black create a speckled texture on the shells in the foreground.

7 ▶ Develop the curly pod Use burnt sienna to build up texture and definition on the curly pod. Hatch over scarlet lake. Work golden brown over the upper part and add detail and shadows with imperial purple and blue-grey. Use a 3B graphite stick to work up the deep shadows and redefine the outline. Colour with burnt sienna in places.

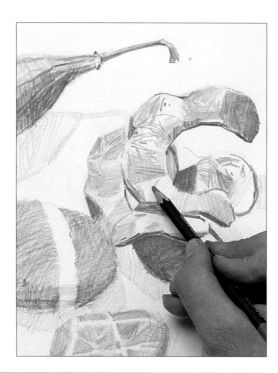

8 ▲ Create a crinkly surface To give the illusion of the pod's crinkly texture, use burnt sienna to make random marks on its surface. Use both the tip and the side of the pencil lead to create thick and thin lines.

9 ◀ Deepen shadows Use cobalt blue to work up the cast shadows. Work loosely and allow the white of the paper to show through. Introduce purple hues into the shadows by going over the blue with imperial purple. Assess and touch up the shadows on the pods and pebbles.

Express yourself
Pebble collection

In this still life, the artist has concentrated on pebbles and used only three graphite sticks – HB, 3B and 6B. The sheer variety of tones and textures of the pebbles creates an interesting image, and it has called for a range of mark-making techniques. The dark pebble in the top left corner, for instance, has been created with small, tick-like marks with the blunt end of the pencil. The side of the lead has been used elsewhere especially on the stripes, while a very fine point has been scribbled on the second largest pebble (bottom right).

A FEW STEPS FURTHER

To sharpen up the drawing, work over the composition, tightening up the textures and redefining the outlines.

10 ▼ **Assess the detail** Using the 3B graphite stick, add dotted and scribbled texture to the stone with the white band. With a variety of strokes, work up the shadows on the curly pod.

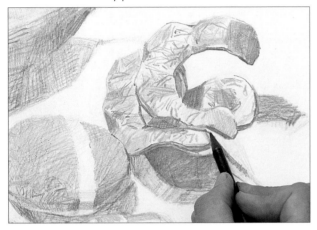

11 ▲ **Tighten up the shadows** Use the 3B graphite stick to stipple over the purple pebble and to sharpen up the large pebble. Redefine the grooves of the long pod. Darken the cast shadows, firming up the edges of the objects as you do so.

THE FINISHED PICTURE

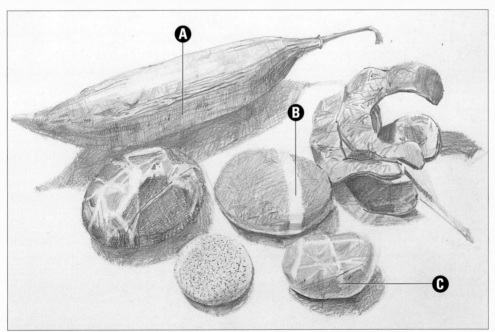

A Cross-hatched colour
Cross-hatching was used to build up texture and tone and also to introduce subtle colour harmonies. By laying one pencil colour over another, an illusion of blending was created.

B Pure white
As with watercolour, leaving the white paper to show through is an important device in coloured-pencil work. Although colour can be erased to some extent, the paper gives the purest white.

C Curved forms
The dark shaded areas at the base of the pebbles suggest their curved forms and give them a three-dimensional appearance. These dark areas also help to lift pebbles off the paper.

Churchyard in the snow

If you enjoy doing detailed work, try your hand at this pen-and-ink drawing of memorial stonework in an old cemetery.

▲ The loose, lively penwork for the foliage provides a pleasing contrast to the more considered drawing of the gravestones.

This peaceful graveyard scene, with its fine lines and stark tonal contrasts, has the quality of a black-and-white illustration in a Victorian book. The 'etched' effect was achieved by using a fine dip pen and black Indian ink on a hard, smooth paper.

Plenty of detail is evident in the drawing, especially on the carved urn, the ornate railings and the inscribed plinth. There are also interesting textural and tonal variations.

Making your mark

A wide variety of pen marks is used in this drawing to capture the textures in the scene. These range from neatly hatched lines that describe the smooth, shadowed surface of the stone, to energetic directional strokes that hint at a mass of thick foliage. There are also blots of ink to denote individual leaves against the sky.

As well as showing different textures, pen marks can create a range of tones. Closely applied hatching – as on the far gravestones – suggests deep shadow, while lightly hatched lines on the plinth give a pale tone. Very dark tones can be made by using cross-hatching or applying more pressure with the pen. Quite subtle tonal variations can be achieved with these techniques.

Piece of hard, smooth cartridge paper 47 x 36cm (18½ x 14¼in)

5B pencil

Putty rubber (for erasing mistakes)

Dip pen with fine nib

Black Indian ink

FIRST STEPS

1 ▼ Map out the composition Use a 5B pencil to make an initial sketch. Start with the urn, plinth and railings, then outline the gravestone in the foreground and suggest those in the distance. Jot in a few marks to represent foliage.

2 ▲ Begin using pen and ink Mark the position of the lettering on the plinth. Now change to a dip pen and black Indian ink and work over the urn, plinth, gravestones and cast shadows. Using lively strokes, hatch in foliage behind the urn and put dark tone on the drapery. Outline some of the foreground bushes.

BRINGING IN TEXTURE

At this point, bring more variety into the picture surface by starting to describe textures, such as the foliage, the stonework and the snowy ground.

3 ▼ Put in more darks Hatch in different depths of tone on the gravestones in the background by varying the density of the pen marks. Define the urn's drapes and border. Now develop the foliage with textural marks – use heavy hatching for dark areas and scribbled outlines for individual leaf sprigs.

4 ▲ Extend the foliage Complete the dark tone on the far gravestone with diagonal hatched lines. Using energetic pen marks, describe the background shrub, showing the main thrust of the branches. Jot in a few leaf details at the top and deepen the tone at the bottom with denser patches.

5 ▶ **Develop the plinth** Draw in the railings and the two finials (decorative tips) at the corners. Hatch a mid tone over the shadowed side of the plinth and over the railings beneath it (see Expert Advice). Develop the foliage around the plinth and add some of the cast shadows on the sunlit surfaces. Darken the base of the plinth.

EXPERT ADVICE
Tonal variations

With pen and ink, variations in tone can be shown very effectively with hatched lines. To create a mid tone on the shaded side of the plinth, make well-spaced, long, parallel strokes. Closely hatched or scribbled lines, such as those on the gravestones in the distance, produce darker tones.

6 ◀ **Work on the lettering** Hatch a little texture on the snowy ground around the plinth. The inscription is best put in with abstract marks that suggest the letters – these create a good impression of words seen from a distance.

7 ▶ **Add more foliage texture** Outline some simple leaf shapes to the left of the urn. Draw long branches in the background and hatch heavily into the shadows here. Jot in a few leaves against the sky and blot them with your finger to soften the pen marks.

8 ▲ **Put in details** Hatch shadows across the gravestones – work over a strip of paper to create the straight edge on the large stone. Add more leaves to the bushes and to the creeper on the plinth. Show the mottled effect of lichen on the plinth with dabs of ink.

A FEW STEPS FURTHER

There are still a few adjustments you can make at this stage. Ink lines can be softened by scratching away, and lights and darks can be emphasized.

9 ▶ **Scratch off some ink** If some of the ink lines seem too hard, you can soften them by scratching away the ink with the blade of a craft knife. Make sure you use this technique only on a hard, smooth paper, as the surface of a softer paper can get damaged.

10 ▲ **Accentuate the leaves** Work back into the dark foliage to throw the lit side of the large gravestone into relief. Fill in shadows behind the snow-covered leaves and twigs, leaving their shapes showing as white paper.

THE FINISHED PICTURE

A Elaborate centrepiece
As the centrepiece of the drawing, the urn was drawn with precise pen lines showing the decorative markings, the ornate curved base and the folds of the carved drapery.

B A sense of depth
Leaves in the foreground were picked out in more detail than those in the background to enhance the feeling of recession in the scene.

C Precise edges
A crisp edge to the shadow on the gravestone was achieved by working the hatched lines up to and over a strip of scrap paper held in position with the other hand.

Mother and child

A sensitive pencil drawing with delicate watercolour washes is the perfect way to capture the affection of a mother for her baby son.

This portrait of a mother carrying her baby is a pleasing, natural composition. The woman holds the child in her arms and gazes down on him lovingly, while the baby looks out of the picture, full of curiosity. His outstretched arm seems to invite the viewer into the scene.

Check your proportions

When you are establishing the pose, first work out how the mother's weight is distributed and look at the main angles and proportions of the figures (see Expert Advice, opposite). As you make your initial sketch, check that your proportions are accurate by measuring from one part of the body to another and comparing distances.

Adult and baby

Also, be aware of the differences between an adult's body and that of a baby. Notice how the baby's head is large in proportion to its body. The height of a one-year-old child is roughly four times the length of its head, whereas for an adult the ratio is about 7:1.

A baby's face is rounded and smooth compared to an adult's, and its limbs are chubby with creases at the ankles and wrists. In this picture, the difference between adult and baby is further underlined by the contrast between the dark, heavy clothing of the mother and the light, delicate baby clothes.

▶ The artist chose an oval format, which seems to emphasize the closeness between mother and baby.

Piece of 190gsm (90lb) cartridge paper 35 x 25cm (14 x 10in)

7B pencil

Putty rubber (for erasing mistakes)

Scalpel or craft knife (to sharpen pencil)

10 watercolours: Light red; Burnt umber;

Payne's grey; Vandyke brown; Ultramarine violet; Cobalt blue; Cerulean blue; Sap green; Chrome yellow; Yellow ochre

No.5 round brush

Mixing palette or dish

Jar of water

FIRST STEPS

1 ▶ Sketch the figures
Using a 7B pencil, start by putting in guide lines to show the stance of the mother's body (see Expert Advice). Draw her head and the shape of her hair, then lightly mark in her facial features. Moving downwards, position the mother's shoulders and draw the baby within her encircling arms. Complete the mother's figure, working down to the tops of the legs.

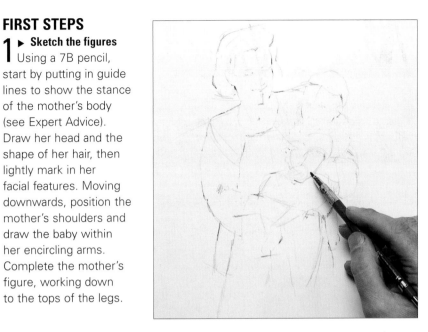

2 ▼ Strengthen the mother's features Darken the hair with decisive, directional pencil marks. Put a little shadow on the ear. Develop the eyes – because they are looking down at the baby, they appear almost closed. Mark in the eyebrows, then refine the nose and mouth, adding a small shadow under the lower lip.

EXPERT ADVICE
Analysing the pose

Before you start any figure drawing, it's a good idea to make a quick sketch showing how the weight is distributed and how the body is angled. Here, the mother is supporting the weight of the baby on her left hip, which is thrust out to one side. Her shoulders follow a similar angle, while her head and spine are on a tilted axis that crosses at right angles. Her body weight is mainly on her left foot.

3 ▶ Work on the baby's face Add shadows on either side of the mother's mouth and neck. Work up creases on the left shoulder of her jacket. Outline the tops of the baby's eyes and darken the irises and pupils, then put tone in the eye socket. Dot in the nostrils and draw the mouth with sensitive lines. Develop the ear, showing the baby's soft hair above it.

DEVELOPING THE TONES

Start to add depth to the drawing with a range of tones, from the lightest shadows on the faces and limbs to mid tones and darks on the mother's clothing.

4 ▼ Develop the limbs Work up a dark tone on the mother's T-shirt, then put in shadows and creases on her jacket and the baby's rompers. Redefine the mother's and baby's arms and draw their hands. Shade lightly under the baby's foot and draw his toes, showing the crease where foot joins ankle.

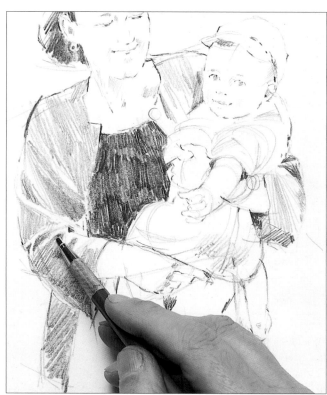

5 ▲ Suggest fabric creases The tone of the mother's jacket is lighter than that of her T-shirt, so use less emphatic pencil shading here. On the right sleeve, follow the direction in which the fabric is being pulled, but leave the paper untouched where the folds catch the light.

6 ▼ Develop the tonal shading Hatch dark and medium tones over the mother's jeans and left shoulder. Work very lightly over her face and neck, then refine her facial features and darken her hair. Hatch in some tone to suggest the background.

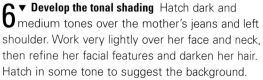

A FEW STEPS FURTHER

The pencil drawing is now complete, but you could take it further by adding light washes of watercolour. Don't flood it with too much water, as the paper will cockle.

7 ▶ Paint the flesh tones Make a dilute wash of light red watercolour. Using a No.5 round brush, apply it over the shaded part of the mother's face and neck. Paint the same wash over the baby's face, with slightly stronger colour on the eye sockets, cheeks and hair. Work this flesh tone over the limbs, too, keeping the baby's left arm pale.

8 ▼ Mix more washes Mix burnt umber, Payne's grey and Vandyke brown, and wash over the dark areas of the mother's hair. Paint her jacket with a wash of ultramarine violet.

9 ▲ Warm the background Darken the T-shirt and jeans with a mix of burnt umber and Payne's grey. Paint the baby's clothing with a light wash of cobalt blue and cerulean blue. Mix sap green and chrome yellow for the background, adding Payne's grey for the shadows.

10 ▼ Model the faces Mix a slightly stronger flesh tone from light red with a little yellow ochre. Use this to bring out the contours of the faces, taking it down on to the shaded part of the mother's neck.

THE FINISHED PICTURE

A Pencil texture
The pencil marks are still visible under the light washes of watercolour, adding texture and detail to the image.

B Baby face
The baby's face has been painted with a relatively even tone to convey his smooth skin and softly rounded features.

C Fabric folds
The pull of the fabric on the jacket sleeves is shown with directional pencil hatching. Light-coloured negative shapes stand for the folds.

On the waterfront

Clusters of houses jut out into the river, while boats form a disorderly line along the waterfront in this charming pen-and-ink drawing of a village in Vietnam.

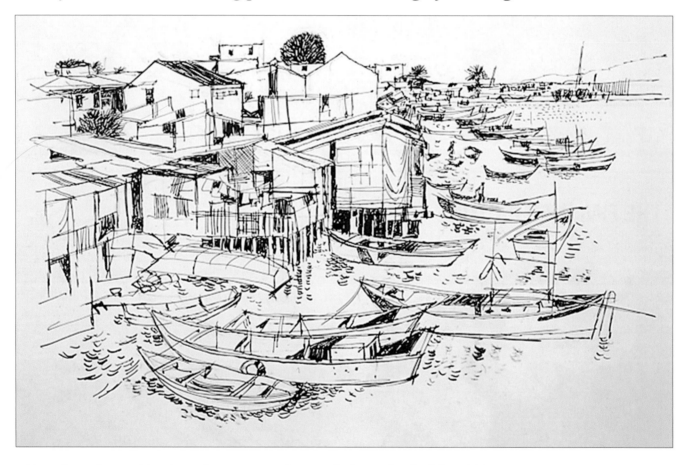

▲ **This pen-and-ink drawing captures the flavour of the busy scene without attempting to put in every last detail.**

At first glance, this view of a Vietnamese waterfront settlement seems an impenetrable jumble of houses and boats, but it's not difficult to reduce the scene to its bare bones if you treat the various elements as a pattern of shapes. It's best to make a simple pencil underdrawing before you begin the pen work, as you can then make adjustments with a putty rubber if necessary. Rub back the pencil lines slightly and use them as a guide for your ink lines.

Move from background to foreground when drawing the cluster of houses in pen, so that you don't smudge the ink lines you've just made. As you build up the houses, put in doors and windows as simple blocked-in rectangles. Once the ink is dry, return to the distant horizon from time to time and suggest the intricate detail here with a few abstract marks.

Drawing textures

Add interesting textures, such as the corrugated iron, woven matting and tarpaulins that cover some of the walls and windows. Touches such as the washing line outside one of the houses and the figures of fishermen in the middle distance introduce a human element.

When you work on the boats, leave those in the distance as simple curved outlines, but develop those in the foreground to show their structure and shadows more clearly. By jotting in texture on the water, you can create an impression of a rippled surface and put the boats in context.

FIRST STEPS

1 ▶ Make a preliminary pencil sketch
Working lightly with a 6B pencil, outline the main buildings and mark in the horizon. Put in a series of curved lines to show the position of the boats in the foreground and middle distance.

2 ▶ Begin the ink drawing Change to a fine dip pen and black Indian ink. Starting at the top centre, begin working over the pencil lines. Outline the houses on the skyline, filling in the simple shapes of windows and doors as you go. Draw the horizon out to the right, then mark in the spiky tree shapes.

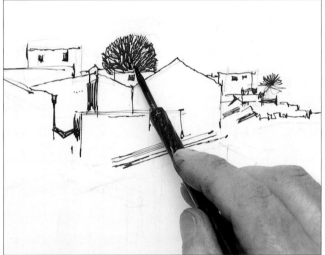

DEVELOPING THE DRAWING

Gradually move down the paper as you continue drawing over the pencil lines. Check the reference photo as you go and add any details that you think will lend character to the picture. Suggest textures with hatching and other pen marks.

3 ▼ Draw another building Draw the sloping roof of the building on the waterfront. Add its tarpaulin-covered walls and the stilts that raise it from the water, then outline the boat moored in front of it. Mark a few details in the jumble of houses in the background.

4 ▲ Extend the group of buildings Draw the large building at top left, shading the roof with hatched lines and adding the dark windows. Put in the sloping roofs in front of and next to this building, then outline the near house and the line of washing in front of it.

5 ▼ **Build up the scene** Continue working on the house with the washing, adding shadows and cross-hatching on the wall. Draw its fence and stilts. Show the textures of the tarpaulin and the corrugated iron on the building to the right. Mark in hills and cranes on the horizon and some boats in the distance. Move to the foreground to draw the upturned boat.

6 ▼ **Blot texture on the water** Outline the boats that stretch off into the distance. To show ripples on the water, jot in some small curved marks and blot them with your finger while the ink is still wet to give a softer effect.

7 ▲ **Work on the boats** Draw the roof and walls to the left of the washing line, hatching the sheets of corrugated iron. Put in the pile of rocks under the upturned boat. Outline the boats in the foreground, adding more ripples in the water around them. Then develop the shadows under the buildings and in the boats.

8 ◀ **Develop detail and texture** Suggest the boats in the far distance with simple marks and build up texture on the horizon. Place two figures in the middle distance. Mark and blot more texture on the water. Now develop the final buildings and trees on the left of the picture. Darken the shadows under the buildings on stilts and also behind the washing line.

A FEW STEPS FURTHER

There is such a wealth of detail in this scene that you can't hope to capture it all. However, you could work up more texture and shadow on the some of the houses and boats.

9 ▼ **Work up detail** Add more detail to the left-hand roofs and work up shadow under the building on the far left. Draw horizontal bars on the fence below the washing.

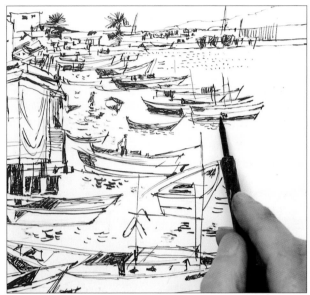

10 ▲ **Improve the boats** Emphasize the negative shapes of the stilts under the buildings by strengthening the shadows around them. Put in extra details and shading on the far right boat, then give the boats in the middle ground a more solid appearance with dark tone.

THE FINISHED PICTURE

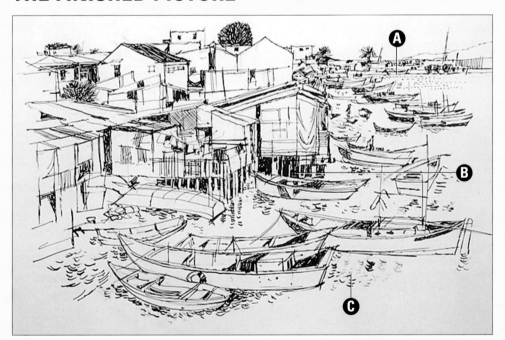

A Busy horizon
The line work used for the distant elements was kept simple, but still successfully conjures up the jumble of closely packed houses and boats on the horizon.

B Black and white
The shadows under the houses were worked around the vertical wooden stilts. This makes the stilts stand out as white negative shapes against a dark background.

C Water texture
Dots, dashes and small curved marks suggest the rippling surface of the water. They also create graduations of tone depending on how densely drawn they are.

Horse in motion

A beautiful combination of power and grace, the movement of a galloping horse makes a compelling subject for a drawing in coloured pencils.

Until the late 1800s, artists depicted galloping horses as having outstretched legs – front legs forwards and back legs backwards. Horses moved too fast for the naked eye to capture an isolated moment, so no one was actually certain how they ran.

Sequence of movements

It took the British-born photographer Eadweard Muybridge (1830–1904) to get to the truth. In 1872, in order to discover whether a horse in motion ever has all four feet off the ground at once, he set up a line of 12 cameras to record the sequence of actions that made up a horse's stride. As the horse ran, it triggered trip wires, which operated the cameras' shutters. The resulting photos, as well as proving that all four feet do leave the ground at times, also illustrated the individual movements made by the horse. Today, with the split-second shutter speeds of modern cameras, such knowledge has become commonplace.

Muscle structure

This study was inspired by one such photograph, showing a galloping horse at the moment in its stride where its legs are drawn up under its body. The artist's main aim was to describe the muscular form of the animal, while at the same time creating a feeling of great speed. The lines of horse's rippling muscles were indicated with precise areas of hatching and cross-hatching, while to give an impression of the horse's swift movement, the background was drawn as a blur of horizontal lines with no attempt at detail.

▼ **Energetic lines in pencil and coloured pencil give a feeling of movement to this beautifully observed study of a horse.**

FIRST STEPS

1 ▼ Draw a grid Attach tracing paper over your photo. Using an HB pencil, mark off eight equal sections down and across. Join the marks to make a grid of 64 equal rectangles. Now draw diagonals through all the rectangles.

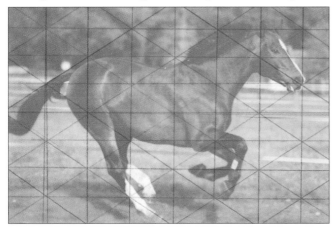

2 ▼ Transfer the grid The drawing is planned at 26 x 42cm (10 x 16½in), so on your paper rule up a rectangle with these measurements. Now draw a grid within the rectangle to match exactly the one drawn on the photograph in step 1.

3 ▶ Start on the hindquarters
Looking closely at your squared-up photo, use the HB pencil to map the outline of the horse, working from left to right. Draw its tail, hindquarters and back legs, making sure each element is in the same position on the grid on your paper as it is on the photo's grid.

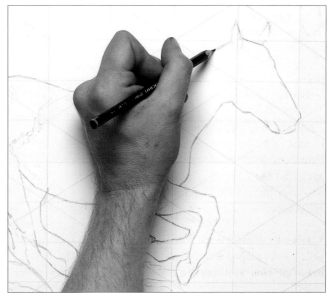

4 ▲ Complete the outline Draw the curve of the abdomen and the front legs. Continue up around the neck, the muzzle and the forehead. Now put in the long, gentle slope from the ears down to the withers (where the neck joins the shoulders).

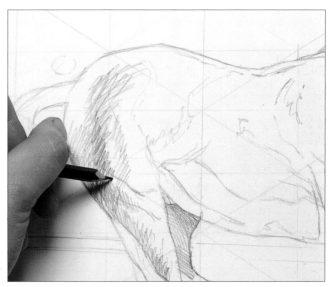

5 ▲ Hatch some darker areas Once the basic outline is in place, start putting in some shading, following the forms of the horse's muscles. Use hatched lines on the inside back leg and around the rump and thigh, pressing your pencil down harder to create the darkest areas.

6 ▼ Add detail to the head Lightly draw the features of the head, shading the cheek and the area around the white marking on the face. With darker, cross-hatched lines, create the mane and the contours of the long, powerful neck.

7 ▼ Work on the shading Switching to a 6B pencil, continue shading the muscular form of the body with hatched lines. Firm up the outline and add detail to the neck and front legs.

START WORKING IN COLOUR

So far, the contours of the horse's powerful muscles have been described with graphite pencil shading. It is now time to introduce colour by hatching coloured pencil over the marks you have already made.

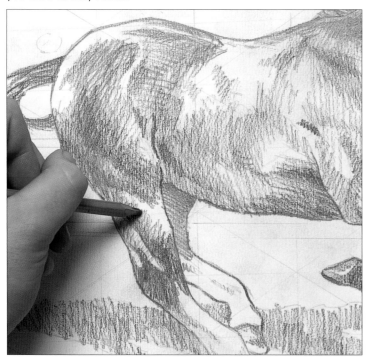

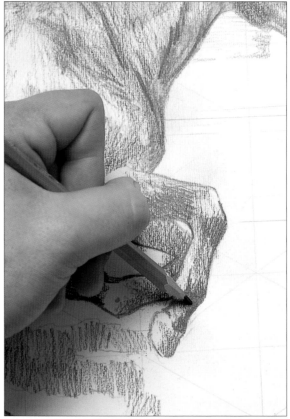

8 ▲ Introduce colour Complete the pencil shading on the body, then block in the cast shadow below the horse. Now, with an Indian red coloured pencil, hatch over the dark areas of the horse's abdomen and hindquarters, adding some shorter strokes on the upper leg.

9 ▲ Overlay blue and grey For areas of shadow on the front legs, put in a few strokes of Prussian blue, then hatch mid grey over the blue. By overlaying different colours, you'll generate a richer tone than working with a single colour.

10 ▼ **Build up the body tones** Hatch Prussian blue and mid grey over the back legs, as in step 9. Return to Indian red and develop the tonal shading on the horse's face, following the bone structure of the head. Draw a few emphatic lines on the cheek. Hatch curved lines on the body to emphasize its rounded contours.

EXPERT ADVICE
A sense of movement

The horse is galloping and yet appears perfectly still, frozen in time on the paper. To give a sense of speed, lay horizontal lines around the image, as though the background is blurred while our eyes focus on the moving horse. Use a range of colours for this, overlaying them so that they appear to merge.

11 ▼ **Blur the background** To give a feeling of speed, shade horizontal bands behind the horse in viridian, mid grey, cadmium yellow and cadmium orange (see Expert Advice). Add areas of viridian cross-hatching to the background and around the nose. Scribble horizontal lines of orange over the body to increase the impression of speed.

12 ▲ **Draw more loose strokes across the body** Strengthen the horizontal lines of orange you have just marked across the horse's body with some darker strokes of burnt umber. By cutting across the shaded contours of the body, these further the illusion of movement.

A FEW STEPS FURTHER

Although the horse does appear to be galloping, the background remains somewhat flat and undifferentiated. Put in a horizon line to divide the ground and the rest of the background, and so create a greater sense of space.

13 ▶ **Define the background** Draw a bold line in Prussian blue to define the horizon line and to locate the horse more clearly in a three-dimensional space. Smudge some of the colours in the background with a putty rubber to make them look out of focus.

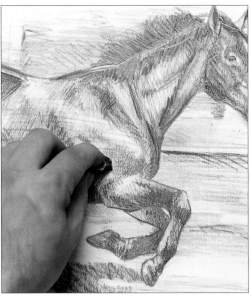

14 ▲ **Accentuate highlights** Finally, use the putty rubber to lift some of the colour off the horse's body to accentuate the sheen on its coat as it gallops by. The skin looks positively glistening from the horse's exertions.

THE FINISHED PICTURE

A Strong musculature
Hatched graphite pencil lines on the body, some overlaid with colour, follow the rippling contours of the main areas of muscle.

B Mane treatment
The bold, directional lines used on the mane, some pointing up, some to the left, add to the sense of swift movement.

C Blurred background
Loosely drawn and smudged horizontal lines create a blurred effect in the background, suggesting the horse speeding by.

Study of an exotic bird

Capture the proud bearing and beautiful, well-defined plumage of this crested screamer by using a watercolour wash over a crisp pen drawing.

▲ **Both the drawing and the washes were limited to tones of sepia to convey the muted shades of the bird's plumage.**

The bird study in this step-by-step was worked up after a sketching session outdoors. Sketching birds and animals from life draws on similar skills to those required for drawing people on the move. As your subject is unlikely to be still for long, you'll have to work quickly, simplifying your lines to capture the essence of each pose. At the same time, you'll need to memorize as many details as possible.

Observing birds on the move

There are many opportunities to observe birds and other animals moving, feeding and grooming themselves in zoos and urban farms. Children's zoos are ideal, as they keep a range of small creatures in accessible surroundings where you can view them at close quarters.

The artist spotted the bird in this drawing – a crested screamer – in a popular children's zoo in London. Its long, attractive grey feathers appealed to him and he made a number of rapid sketches to capture the bird's main characteristics, such as the large, rounded body supported on spindly legs, the striped face and the jaunty crest on the head. The artist took a selection of colour photographs to provide himself with additional reference material.

Back in the studio

For the final composition, the artist chose a sketch and a photo showing a side view of the bird. The photo was a source of feather details, while the sketch had a more pleasing head pose.

The bird's plumage suggested a pen-and-wash approach for this study. Fibre-tip pens are ideal for detailed texture, while a watercolour wash adds depth and softness.

STARTING WITH SKETCHES AND PHOTOS

SKETCHING BIRDS

On a visit to a zoo, take a camera and a sketch book. Watch different birds and make quick sketches of their movements. Even if they are very active, they'll tend to return to the same postures, so you can complete any unfinished sketches. The more you observe them, the more you'll develop a visual memory to fill in details.

FIRST STEPS

1 ▼ Make a pencil sketch Using a 7B pencil, sketch the shape of the large, rounded body and the projecting wing tips and tail. Position the legs and feet. Outline the head, adding the eye, beak and crest. Rough in the main oval groups of feathers (see Expert Advice opposite).

2 ▲ Begin drawing in pen Change to a 0.5 sepia fibre-tip drawing pen and work over the pencil lines. Outline the eye, then hatch in the ring of dark feathers around the neck, adding a few tufts above it. Using the oval shapes as a guide, start to draw the large, overlapping feathers on the top of the wing and the smaller ones on the neck.

3 ▶ **Draw more feathers** Complete the overlapping feathers on the top of the wing, then draw those on the front part of the wing, fitting them inside the oval shape drawn earlier. Move on to the body feathers – these are smaller and more pointed.

EXPERT ADVICE
Grouping feathers

When confronted with a mass of overlapping feathers, it is a good idea to simplify these by isolating the main shapes within the plumage. Here, the wing feathers and larger body feathers form several ovals, echoed by large single tail feathers.

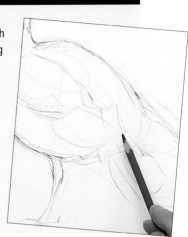

DEVELOPING THE FEATHERS

Now that the basic arrangement of the plumage has been set up, you can develop individual feathers by describing their regular structure. Don't fill in every feather, as this would make the drawing appear laboured.

4 ▼ **Develop feather detail** Continue working on the body feathers, making small, delicate marks to show the soft texture on the neck and chest. Hatch an area of dark shadow under the tail feathers. Now develop detail in some individual feathers, drawing lines radiating out from a central spine.

5 ◀ **Describe the downy feathers** Darken the eye stripe with light cross-hatching and emphasize the eye itself. Extend the fine, soft feathers down the chest and show the fluffy texture on the head and neck with more feathery marks.

6 ▶ **Complete the drawing** Develop the feather details all over the bird's head and body, darkening the shadow under the tail and wing. Outline the legs and feet, adding hatched texture. Finally, suggest grass with blocks of hatching – this dark area gives the bird a firm base. Rub out the pencil lines.

A FEW STEPS FURTHER

The crisply defined pen drawing can be softened by putting a loose wash over some of the bird's feathers and across the background. Make sure you leave plenty of white paper showing for a contrast of tone.

7 ▼ **Paint on a sepia wash** Build up the grass with more hatched lines. Then mix a wash from burnt umber, burnt sienna and alizarin crimson watercolour. Apply it over the bird's darker feathers and the grass with a No.6 flat brush.

8 ▲ **Darken the background** Apply the sepia wash loosely to the background around the head, chest and underbody. This throws the image of the bird forwards, adding a feeling of depth to the picture.

THE FINISHED PICTURE

A Bright eye
The eye of a bird is always bright and watery. Here, the eye was emphasized with a dark surround, but a clear white spot was left at the centre.

B Loose washes
The sepia wash adds form and solidity to the bird's body. Loosely applied, it contrasts pleasingly with the more precise pen drawing.

C Feather detail
Linear detail was applied to the mid-toned feathers on the wing, tail and underbody, suggesting both tone and texture here.

Portrait of a whippet

Bring out the character of this energetic breed of dog with lively lines drawn with water-soluble coloured pencils and blended for a painterly effect.

YOU WILL NEED

Piece of 300gsm (140lb) smooth watercolour paper 40 x 34cm (16 x 13½in)	Raw umber; Cobalt blue; Black; Violet; Cadmium red; Light blue; Burnt umber; Phthalo blue; Purple; Mauve; Crimson
F pencil	
Ruler	
14 water-soluble coloured pencils: Green ochre; Orange; Lemon yellow;	Brushes: 25mm (1in) flat; No.4 round
	Jar of water

Water-soluble coloured pencils have several advantages over other drawing and painting media. They are cheap, portable and versatile and, in addition, they allow the artist to work very quickly and, more importantly, to achieve the effects of line and wash with a single medium. This facility gives you scope for achieving a great variety of textures and effects, as you can see in this handsome portrait of a whippet.

Squaring up

In order to get the proportions of the whippet correct in the initial drawing, the artist decided to square up the reference photograph and then transfer the grid on to the support. In theory, the more detailed the grid, the greater the potential accuracy, but in practice a fairly simple grid works for most people as too many squares can be distracting.

If your photo is precious enough to turn into a painting, you probably don't draw directly on to it. In this case, either take a colour photocopy of it or, if you have access to computer equipment, scan the photograph and print it out in colour. Alternatively, you can draw a grid on a sheet of acetate or tracing paper and then attach this to your photograph. Remember that you need to draw the same number of squares vertically and horizontally on your support as you did on your original – although the scale is likely to be different.

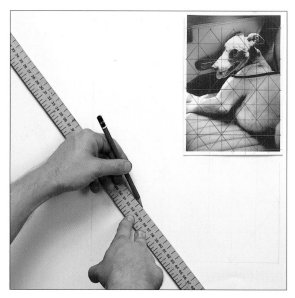

▲ The hatched and feathered pencil marks in this painting are softened by washing over them with a wetted brush.

FIRST STEPS

1 ▲ **Draw a grid** With an F pencil and ruler, draw a squared grid over your photocopied image. Then, for greater accuracy, draw a series of diagonal lines over the top of the grid, crossing through two corners of each square. Repeat the pattern of squares and diagonals on a piece of watercolour paper, using the same number of squares and diagonals but on a larger scale. Draw lightly, as you don't want the grid to show through the finished picture.

2 ▲ **Start from a corner** Working with a grid is a bit like doing a jigsaw puzzle – it's easiest if you start from the corners. Moving inwards from the top right-hand corner, start by drawing the whippet's ears, then develop the head and neck. Add the outlines of the trailing lead.

3 ▼ Make the drawing detailed With the help of the grid, you can make your drawing accurate and detailed. Note elements such as the door handle and the stitching on the seat, but also draw in more subtle details such as the creases in the dog's short-haired coat, and the areas of light and shadow.

DEVELOPING THE PICTURE

With an accurate drawing established, begin to develop the picture using water-soluble coloured pencils. Build up subtle colours and interesting textures with hatched marks, then blend the pigment in some areas by washing over it with a wetted brush.

4 ▼ Start with the light colours Hatch closely spaced diagonal lines around the dog's head, using a green ochre water-soluble coloured pencil. In spite of its name, this colour is more of a mustard yellow than a green.

5 ▼ Cross-hatch in brown For a richer background tone, add a variety of colours. Working in the same direction, add first orange and then lemon yellow coloured pencil. Now, with raw umber, hatch over the colours in the opposite direction.

6 ▲ Wash over some water With a wet 25mm (1in) flat brush, wash over the coloured pencil lines. Be careful not to use too much water or to overwork an area, or the pigment might lift off completely.

7 ▼ **Look at the negative shapes** Colour in the dark area behind the dog's ear by hatching across it first with cobalt blue pencil, then with black and violet. The individual colours can be seen quite clearly at this stage.

8 ▲ **Continue filling in the background** With the No.4 round brush, wash over the three colours to blend and diffuse them. Now indicate the dark tones below the dog's mouth with hatched lines of cobalt blue and black. In the photograph, this area appears virtually black, so darken it by cross-hatching more black coloured pencil over it.

Express yourself

Focus on tone

Look at the way the light falls on the dog's head in the reference photo on page 283. There is a very sharp divide between the rather brightly illuminated muzzle and top of the skull, and the deep shadow of the left side of the face. Emphasize this strong contrast in tone by working up a small study of the head with black Indian ink and a No.4 soft round brush. After making a light pencil sketch, gradually build up the form of the head with a range of pale to mid grey tones – dilute the ink with distilled water to mix these. Then use the ink undiluted for the darkest shadows around the head, on the collar and nose, and inside the mouth.

9 ▼ **Work around the dog** Wash over this area with the No.4 brush. Now fill in the collar with lines of cobalt blue and cadmium red. Colour the seat fabric above the dog with light blue and his lead with overlaid red, cobalt blue and burnt umber. Finally, define the shape of the lower body with a line of burnt umber, and use burnt umber overlaid with red to outline the dark shadow beneath him.

11 ▼ **Outline the head in blue** Again with the No.4 round brush, wash over the seat with gently curving strokes, keeping within the parallel lines. Describe the door handle with black, cadmium red and phthalo blue. Now outline the dog's head in cobalt blue, and hatch more blue to the right of his ear.

10 ▲ **Use curved lines for the car seat** To depict the rear seat, lay short marks of phthalo blue to form parallel lines of stitching. Fill the spaces between these by hatching strokes of purple, following the curve of the fabric.

12 ▲ **Start on the face** With the No.4 brush, wash over the cobalt blue hatching you have just applied. Now start to develop the dog himself. Begin by colouring in the tongue and mouth area with cadmium red.

13 ▼ **Blend fur colours** Add a little black to the tongue and inner mouth and wash over it. Do the same above the eye to create a pale brow. Now, for the dog's extended front leg, hatch areas of green ochre, raw umber and mauve. Follow the direction of the fur as you do this and then gently blend the colours with a wetted 25mm (1in) flat brush.

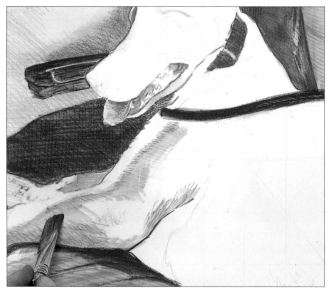

14 ▼ **Develop the head** To create the shadow under the dog's front leg, wash over feathered strokes of cobalt blue, cadmium red and black. Returning to the head, use black to develop the muzzle and nose. Mark short strokes of green ochre and burnt umber along the line of the muzzle and around the eye; add longer strokes in burnt umber to show skin folds. Work around the eye and inside the ear with crimson.

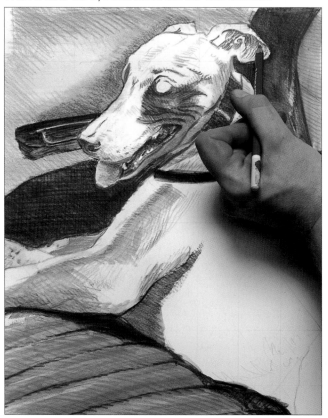

DEVELOPING THE PICTURE FURTHER

In the next few steps you will be developing the character of the dog by completing its features and building up the marks that describe its fur. Use feathered pencil strokes in a range of colours for the fur, softening the effect with a wet brush.

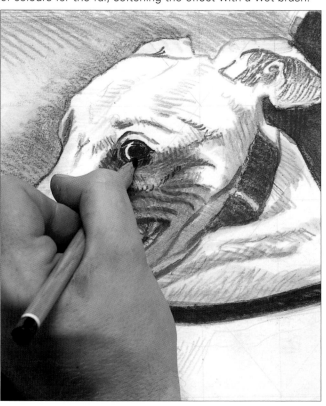

15 ▲ **Add the eye** Use black to form the shape of the eye and fill in the dark pupil. Notice how the addition of this small detail transforms the appearance of the dog.

EXPERT ADVICE
Vary your strokes

Alter the size of your hatched lines to suggest a sense of recession. For instance, make your pencil strokes noticeably longer on the hindquarters – which are near the viewer – than on the head, which is slightly further away.

Master Strokes

Elisabeth Frink
(1930–93)
Dog

British artist Elisabeth Frink is best known for her large, bronze sculptures, often of horses and other animals. This unusual, energetic lithograph of a dog has a certain sculptural quality – its dynamic pose and its solid, rounded forms with smooth outlines give it a distinctly three-dimensional feel. The only details are supplied by a few dark lines that help to shape the body and indicate the features of the head.

Simple lines in a slightly darker brown than the fur define the ear, eye, nose and cheek with great economy.

Two tones of reddish brown give the fur an interesting, mottled texture and a suggestion of highlights and shadows.

The three legs on the left side of the lithograph, set at dramatic diagonals, give the picture much of its impact. The head and tail continue these diagonals in the top right corner.

16 ▼ **Focus on the fur** Hatch long strokes of light blue over the shadowed areas of fur on the body, then feather raw and burnt umber, mauve and violet over them. Use the 25mm (1in) flat brush to blend the colours.

17 ▶ **Build up the fur** Build up the colours on the fur but leave the paler areas white. Then wash over the body with the 25mm (1in) flat brush so that even the white areas take on a hint of colour. Add detail to the mouth with cadmium red and to the ear with raw and burnt umber and purple.

A FEW STEPS FURTHER

Thanks to the grid, everything in the picture is in perspective and the foreshortening of the body appears accurate. However, parts of the coat could benefit from a few finishing touches.

18 ▼ **Hatch on some blue** Mark short strokes of light blue on the dog's neck just beneath the collar. Add a touch of blue to the eye.

19 ▼ **Enrich the colours of the fur** To create a greater contrast in tone between the dog's head and his body, loosely hatch the main fur colours – green ochre, mauve, violet and raw and burnt umber – all over the body. Darken the shadows with cobalt blue. Wash over these colours with the flat brush.

THE FINISHED PICTURE

A Areas of white
The highlights on the dog are simply the white of the paper showing through. No colour or water has been applied here.

B Multi-colours
The dog's short fur is developed with lively pencil strokes in a whole range of colours that add impact to the drawing.

C Padded seat
The curved strokes of blended blues and purples, arranged in bands, mimic the curved ridges of the upholstered back seat.

Female nude in charcoal

Charcoal is generally regarded as a broad medium, suitable for sketching and for bold, expressive work. However, as this drawing shows, it is also capable of producing an extremely subtle and delicate effect.

I n this nude study, the artist has developed the subtle contours of the figure with fine lines and subtle modelling, but using only a minimum of blending. He worked methodically from dark to light, developing the mid tones and shadows with a series of finely hatched strokes. The result is a rich diversity of tone that brings out the soft textural qualities of hair and skin, and captures the play of light on the face and figure.

Although the drawing is carefully worked, there is nothing static about it. While solid and stable, the impression given is that the girl could get up or change position at any moment.

This effect is due in part to the way charcoal marks break up slightly on the rough surface of the paper, giving them a feeling of energy, but it is due mainly to the artist's skilful draughtsmanship. Nothing is overstated, and there are no hard lines or contours to freeze the pose. There is a 'lost-and-found' quality to the drawing – the hands and feet, for instance, are barely stated – and this gives an impression of air, light and space surrounding the sitter.

Composing the drawing

The artist has positioned the head and torso of the figure to the right of centre, to give her more space in front than behind. This provides the sitter with space to 'move into' and emphasizes her gaze. It also opens up the image, helping to produce a relaxed and natural feel. However, if a figure is placed too close to the edge of the support, it can create a feeling of tension and imbalance.

PRELIMINARY SKETCHES

Just as you might move from place to place to find the best viewpoint when drawing a landscape, so you should also sketch a figure in different poses and from different angles before deciding which one to use for the finished drawing. Simple sketches like these will free up your drawing hand and help you to get to know the personality of your sitter.

FIRST STEPS

1 ▲ Position the figure on the paper With the tip of a charcoal stick, start to plot the main outlines of the figure. Use very light strokes so that you can easily erase mistakes with your fingertips. Observe your subject carefully, looking for the major lines and angles and how they relate to each other. Establish the position of the head and remember that it fits into the rest of the body roughly 7½ times.

2 ▲ Develop the body and head Draw the outline of the legs and arms and then suggest the shadows under the breasts. Change to a short piece of charcoal and use it on its side to put in the first tentative shadows that define the facial features and also to model the form of the head.

3 ▶ Draw the chair Continue working on all parts of the figure, always double-checking the angles and proportions. If a leg is too short, for instance, it can easily be adjusted at this stage, when the lines are light enough to be rubbed out. Sketch the outlines of the chair; if drawn accurately, it will give you something to measure the various parts of the figure against. Sketch the foot and put in the cast shadow on the floor.

DEVELOPING THE PICTURE

Once the proportions of the figure are correct, you can start to develop the outlines and to model the form and volume with shading.

4 ▶ Begin to add shading With a little more pressure on the stick, flick in the model's dark eyebrows, the shadow between the lips and the shadow that defines the hair curving back off the brow. Use both the tip and the side of the stick to establish the shadows on the limbs. Look for details, such as the bone of the knee and the shadow where the thigh muscle is pushed up by the chair seat.

EXPERT ADVICE
Check proportions

Look at vertical, horizontal and diagonal alignments to check that the proportions and relationships between different parts of the figure are correct. Note where these line up with other parts and lightly draw lines to check your accuracy.

5 ▲ **Add detail to the face** Snap off a short piece of dark brown hard chalk or pastel and use a corner of it to draw the facial features. This requires a delicate touch – the eyes, mouth and nose must be drawn accurately, but should not be overstated. Mould the corner of a putty rubber to a point and use it to soften and lighten the lower lip, which catches more light than the upper lip.

6 ▲ **Work on the hair** Look for the highlights and shadows on the hair. Put in the mid tones with soft side strokes of charcoal and increase the pressure where the hair is darker – for example, behind the model's neck and where it is pushed up by her left shoulder. Use your fingertip to soften some of the strokes, but leave some crisp lines for definition.

7 ▶ **Add the chair fabric** Begin to suggest volume with some light hatching on the arms. Use a featherlight touch and smudge the lines in places. Model the breasts and put in the nipples. Use the side of the charcoal stick to suggest the fabric folded over the chair, behind the figure. Model the torso with the faintest smudges of charcoal.

8 ▼ **Add more shadows** Strengthen the shadow that runs down the back of the arm, making it lighter where reflected light bounces into the shadow (just beneath the elbow). Define the folds and shadows on the fabric a little more. Put in the shadow cast by the arm on to the upper thigh, and strengthen the shadow under the thigh, so that the leg 'sits' convincingly on the chair. Start to model the lower leg, laying on some chalk or pastel and blending it into the charcoal marks with your fingertips.

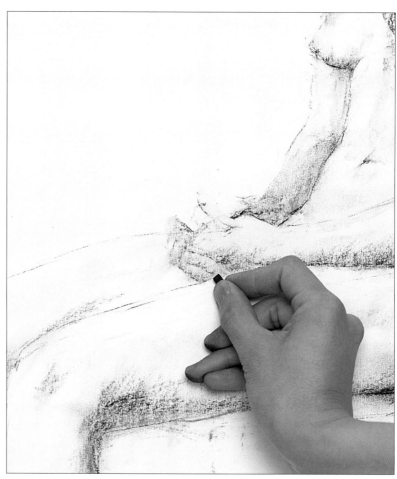

9 ▲ **Draw the hands** When drawing hands, suggestion is the key; if you draw them in outline, they look clumsy. Look carefully for the main shapes of light and shadow and put them in very lightly and sketchily, barely suggesting the individual fingers. It's amazing how mobile and lifelike the hands will look!

10 ▶ **Sketch the right foot**
Redefine the model's right leg, using soft strokes with the charcoal. Keep measuring the right leg against the left to ensure that it sits in the correct position and is in perspective. Sketch in the foot, avoiding the temptation to outline it too carefully.

▲ Thin sticks of charcoal are ideal for the delicately hatched and feathered strokes in this drawing.

11 ▶ Strengthen shadows Build up the forms of the model's legs and feet by using lightly hatched strokes for the shadows and half-tones. Suggest the toes of the left foot, but leave the right foot relatively undefined so that it gives the impression of receding into space. Strengthen the shadows underneath the left foot (to anchor it to the ground plane) and the left knee.

12 ▼ Suggest volume and weight Refine the highlights and shadows overall, but don't overwork the darks. Add highlights with white chalk or pastel to reinforce the volume of the figure. Draw the chair seat and hatch in some shadow to suggest the weight of the figure.

13 ▶ Refine the hair Introduce the more subtle tones in the hair and define its soft texture and sheen. Deepen the darkest shadows by smoothing the marks, and then use the putty rubber with firm pressure to pull out the lightest highlights.

14 ◀ Assess the work Step back from the drawing and assess it tonally; consider whether any of the shadows need to be darkened or if any of the highlights need sharpening.

A FEW STEPS FURTHER

The seated figure is now looking very realistic and requires only a few subtle touches to finish the drawing.

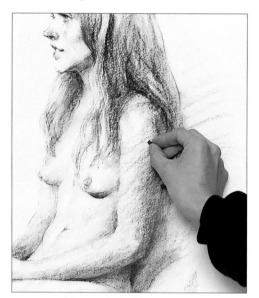

15 ▲ Add more darks Work over the upper arm with hatched strokes to darken the tone of the shadow. Also, deepen the tone of the hair where it drapes over the shoulder. This brings the nearer part of the body forward in the composition and adds depth and richness to the drawing.

16 ▲ Create some highlights Mould the putty rubber into a point and use it to pull out the highlights on the prominent bones of the tops of the knees.

THE FINISHED PICTURE

A Textured hair
Soft, smudged strokes combined with crisp lines and erased areas help to build up an impression of the sheen and texture of real hair.

B Subtle modelling
The softly rounded contours of the figure are modelled with featherlight hatchings that are built up layer by layer.

C Simple background
The chair is merely suggested in the drawing. It gives the figure a context without competing with it for attention.

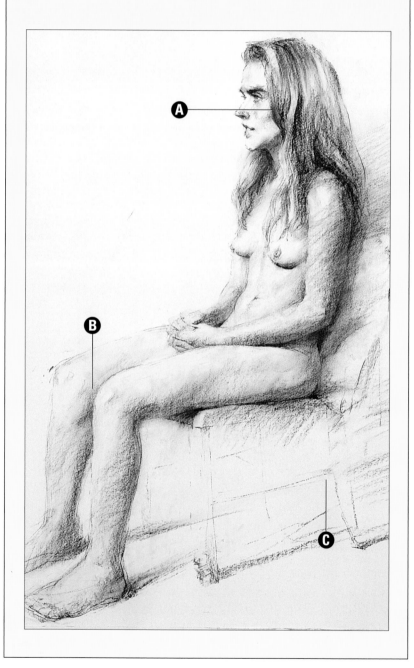

Standing stones

Be prepared to get your hands dirty when using charcoal to capture the rugged textures of these huge rocks.

These massive stones form part of Avebury Ring in Wiltshire, UK, which dates back to prehistoric times. Centuries of weathering have given the stones a craggy, mottled surface marked by indentations and fissures.

The aim of this step-by-step is to find ways of capturing the variety of rough textures. Charcoal, in its various forms, is the ideal drawing medium because you can use it in different ways to make a wide range of textural marks.

With willow charcoal, you can build up an irregular surface by hatching or jabbing on dark spots of pigment to give a speckled effect. By holding a charcoal stick on its side, you can block in shadow and develop form. For details, change to charcoal pencils sharpened to a point with a craft knife. The more marks you

▲ **Using charcoal, you can create a wide range of tones, from dense, velvety black to just the slightest hint of grey.**

make, the more solid the stones appear. You can use your fingers to smudge pigment and transfer it to other parts of the paper, such as the sky. Fix the picture as you progress, so that you don't smudge completed areas.

YOU WILL NEED

Piece of 150gsm (70lb) cartridge paper 56 x 76cm (22 x 30in)

Soft charcoal pencil

Thin and thick willow charcoal

Spray fixative

Putty rubber and vinyl rubber

Hard charcoal pencil

Scrap paper

White chalk

FIRST STEPS

1 ▶ Establish the composition Using a soft charcoal pencil, outline the shapes of the huge stones and the main areas of shadow. Draw in the horizon and indicate the trees very simply.

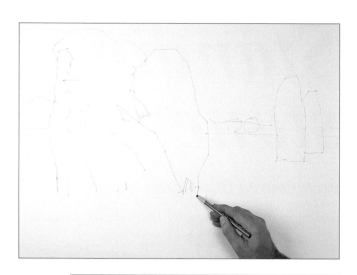

2 ▼ Block in the trees Change to a stick of thin willow charcoal and block in the distant trees with heavy, dense black strokes. Use a little artistic licence and continue the trees across to the right-hand side to balance the composition.

3 ▲ Smudge tone on the sky Using your fingertips, smudge pigment between the trees to create a mid tone on the horizon. Spray with fixative. Apply more charcoal to the trees and smudge some of it across the sky.

4 ▶ Put in the darkest shadows Using a putty rubber, work over the whole sky to lighten the grey tone and then fix the drawing once more. Continuing with thin willow charcoal, block in the darkest shadows on the large foreground stone with heavy black marks, smoothing the pigment with your finger in places.

5 ▼ **Develop mid tones** Using your finger, pick up charcoal from the dark areas and smudge mid tones on the large stone to give it form. Work up dark and mid tones on the background stones, too. Using the putty rubber, work over some of the smudged pigment to lighten it, then fix again. Change to a hard charcoal pencil and make textural marks.

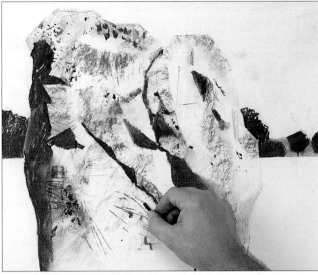

6 ▲ **Build up texture** Using thin and thick sticks of willow charcoal, make a variety of marks to create an interesting stone texture. For example, drag a short stick on its side across the paper to give a grainy effect, or make lines with the tip while varying the pressure. Add dots of charcoal to represent the pitted rock surface.

DEVELOPING THE PICTURE

As well as using a putty rubber to lighten tone, you can 'draw' light lines into dark areas of charcoal with the tip of a harder, vinyl rubber. This is a useful technique for developing texture and for describing blades of grass.

7 ▶ **Lift off pigment** Put in a lot of dark texture at the bottom left of the large stone with a thin stick of willow charcoal. To the right of this, use a thick stick to rub on some pigment, smoothing it with your finger. With a vinyl rubber, erase some linear marks from this mid-toned area – a vinyl rubber gives sharper marks than a putty rubber.

8 ◀ **Develop lighter tones** Using a soft charcoal pencil, hatch over the paler areas of the large stone with light, fine lines. Rub over some of these areas with the vinyl rubber to vary the tone and texture. Build up texture on the distant stones with charcoal marks similar to those used for the foreground stone.

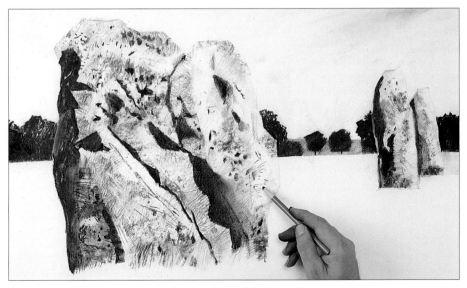

9 ▼ Hatch in the grass Change to the hard charcoal pencil and hatch short vertical blades of grass across the distant part of the field. As you work gradually towards the large stone, make the marks longer to suggest that these blades are nearer the viewer.

10 ▼ Work into the foreground Change to a thick stick of charcoal to make bold marks in the foreground. With your finger, smudge the base of the stone, then create pale blades of grass with the vinyl rubber.

EXPERT ADVICE
Masking off bands

A quick way to make a well-defined band of dark tone is to mask off the surrounding paper. Roughly tear off two lengths of scrap paper and hold them down on the drawing a short distance apart. Scribble between them, working up to or over the torn edges.

11 ▲ Create shadows Using the soft charcoal pencil between masks of paper (see Expert Advice), scribble in the dark shadow cast by the foreground stone. Move to the right and place the masks closer together to create the shadow of the distant stone.

12 ▶ Add detail to the grass With the soft charcoal pencil, scatter some dots across the grass, then rub them gently with your finger. Work boldly across the foreground with the vinyl rubber to create light blades curving gracefully across the darker grass behind them.

A FEW STEPS FURTHER

The charcoal drawing is now complete and shows the stones as highly textured, solid objects. Bring in a touch of contrast by using white chalk to make marks on the stones and trees.

13 ► **Draw white marks** To add contrast to the stone texture, work around the dark marks with a stick of white chalk. Draw a few crisp lines across some of the darkest areas.

14 ▲ **Add 'sky holes'** As a final touch, dab white chalk on to the dark trees to suggest gaps in the foliage where the sky shows through. Fix the drawing.

THE FINISHED PICTURE

A Horizontal divide
Strongly silhouetted against the pale sky, the line of trees forms a pleasing horizontal that contrasts with the vertical thrust of the massive stones.

B Solid stone
Diverse textural marks, areas of blocked-in shadow and contrasting pale areas create a fascinating surface on the stones that gives them a real feeling of solidity.

C Far horizon
The grass in the foreground is well defined and full of contrast. Compare it to the distant part of the field which is lightly hatched to create a diffuse grey.

Indian elephants

Use charcoal to capture the characteristic bulky shapes of these Indian elephants sociably gathered in a group.

Everyone loves elephants, and this family group, complete with a baby, is particularly endearing. The group forms a natural and attractive composition, the palm trees add interest in the background and the distant hills lend a sense of space.

Expressive charcoal

Charcoal gives wonderfully expressive lines and is ideal for quickly and loosely drawing the overlapping shapes of these elephants. It is also good for building up the areas of light and dark tone on the animals' bodies.

Charcoal comes in a variety of forms, so you can change from one type to another throughout the drawing, depending on the effect you want to achieve. Use a well-sharpened charcoal pencil for the initial sketch, then change to compressed charcoal for chunkier lines and for medium-toned shading. To achieve really dense shading, use willow charcoal. A rolled-paper stump is handy for smoothing out pigment and you can create light, hazy shading by using the tip to transfer pigment from one part of the picture to another.

Sharp tips

So that you don't lose detail, keep a pointed end on your charcoal pencil by sharpening it with a craft knife. You can keep the compressed charcoal stick sharpened by rubbing it on glasspaper whenever it gets blunt. As you move around the drawing, rest your hand on a piece of scrap paper to avoid smudging areas at the bottom of the paper. And remember to fix the drawing with a spray fixative when it is complete.

▼ **Charcoal is a great medium for creating very dense areas of tone and wonderfully loose, expressive lines.**

FIRST STEPS

1 ▶ **Sketch the group** Holding a charcoal pencil loosely, make a rough sketch of the elephants. As well as looking at the shapes of the individual animals, observe their relative sizes and how their bodies overlap within the group. Mark in the horizon on the left and outline the cast shadows.

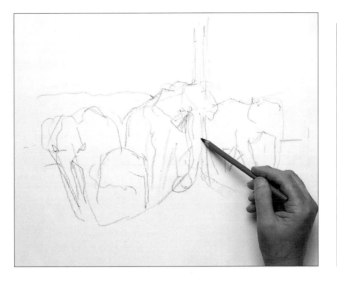

YOU WILL NEED

Piece of white Ingres paper 38 x 48cm (15 x 19in)	Putty rubber (for erasing mistakes)
Charcoal pencil	Craft knife (to sharpen pencil)
Compressed charcoal stick in clutch holder	Glasspaper (to sharpen compressed charcoal stick)
Scrap paper	
Stump	Spray fixative
Willow charcoal	

2 ▼ **Make stronger marks** Complete the composition by drawing the tall verticals of the palm trunks and by positioning fanned-out palm leaves between them. Redefine the elephants with stronger charcoal lines, drawing in their eyes and indicating skin folds on the central animal.

▼ **With just a small range of materials, you can create a wide variety of lines and tones in your drawing. From left to right: glasspaper, putty rubber, willow charcoal, charcoal pencil, compressed charcoal in clutch holder and stump.**

DEVELOPING THE PICTURE

Once you are satisfied with the position and shapes of the elephants, start to develop a sense of solid form with tonal shading, using various types of charcoal.

3 ▼ **Start to add tone** With the charcoal pencil, strengthen the shape of the baby elephant, marking its eye and ear. Now start to darken the tone on and around the elephants.

4 ▼ **Draw palm fronds** Add more tone to the elephants, then change to compressed charcoal and shade in the thick palm trunk – rest your arm on scrap paper to avoid smudging the lower part of the drawing. Draw in more palm fronds.

5 ▶ Work up the tone Develop the shadow on the elephants – you can cover the paper rapidly with the chunky compressed charcoal. Increase the pressure on it to make some areas look darker.

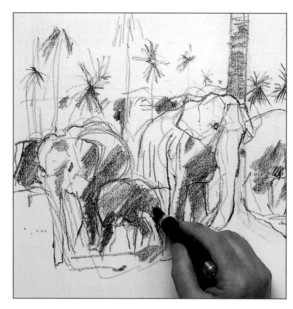

EXPERT ADVICE
Textural effects

Take advantage of the texture of Ingres paper when you are shading tone on to the elephants. With a light covering of charcoal, the lines of the paper show through and help to suggest the wrinkled look of the elephants' tough, leathery hide.

6 ▼ Add texture Describe the texture of the palm trunk with a series of short horizontal strokes. Work up more tone on the heads and trunks of the two right-hand elephants, then indicate the shadow cast on the ground on the right.

7 ▶ Rub soft tone on the horizon Add tone to the right-hand elephant's front leg, then blend some of the charcoal on its legs with the tip of a stump. With the pigment picked up on the stump, you can now rub a mid tone on to the far hills.

8 ▼ Develop tone and detail Return to the charcoal pencil to darken features such as the ears and trunks and sharpen up the eyes. Use descriptive textural marks to suggest the wrinkled hide (see Expert Advice, top). Work back into the palm leaves, adding harder, darker marks to contrast with the softer ones made previously.

A FEW STEPS FURTHER

The picture will have more impact if you increase the tonal contrast.
Change to willow charcoal to add some areas of deep, velvety pigment.

9 ▼ **Strengthen the darks** Work over the darkest areas, such as the chest of the central elephant and the neck and back leg of the right-hand elephant, with willow charcoal. Press hard for solid coverage.

10 ▲ **Add foreground detail** Changing to the charcoal pencil, put in any missed details such as the toes of the right-hand elephant. Add interest to the expanse of foreground by darkening the cast shadows and jotting in some texture. Finally, fix your drawing with spray fixative.

THE FINISHED PICTURE

A Palm patterns
Although only loosely drawn, the sunburst shapes of the palm fronds create a feeling of place and form interesting patterns across the background.

B Varied group
The elephants face different directions, allowing their body shapes to be drawn from various angles and making a pleasing composition.

C Shadow play
The shadows cast by the elephants are important in anchoring the animals in space and adding a feeling of solidity to the foreground.

The big picture

Make a dramatic statement by drawing on a very large scale.
This coastal scene lends itself perfectly to the big treatment.

One simple method to produce radically new and different results is to work on a large scale. To create this coastline scene, a piece of watercolour paper measuring well over a square metre was used.

Energy and expressiveness

With a support of this size, you have to stand, kneel, move from one side to another, and work from the shoulder and elbow rather than the wrist. The process is extraordinarily exhilarating, and the end product will have an energy and expressiveness that is rare in smaller works.

Remember, the size you work at will be dictated by practical considerations. Assess the space you have to work in and measure the wall you are going to attach the paper to. Also check at your art-supply shop to see what size of support is available – you can order large rolls of watercolour paper but these are expensive.

From little to large

It is a good idea to start from a photograph or, better still, a very small drawing of a location with which you are familiar. Because a small drawing or a photograph can contain only a limited amount of information, you will be forced to rely on memory and experience. Eventually the drawing takes on a life of its own and you'll find that you are having a dialogue with your own creation, the marks you have already made indicating your next move.

When you are working on a large scale, it is important to find a composition that works. Start by making a series of thumbnail sketches in which you analyze the distribution of lights and darks, and explore the underlying geometry of the image. If your composition is solidly constructed, the elements will slot together easily and the final image will hang together well.

The drama of darkness

The step-by-step project on the following pages is based on a photograph of cliffs jutting into the sea. The cliffs are in shadow and this emphasizes the drama – they are seen as dark shapes looming against the lighter areas of the sea and the beach it washes on to.

The artist decided to crop sections from both sides of a wide-format photograph (above, left). This focuses attention on the cliffs and gives an approximately equal division between light and dark areas. It also places the top of the farthest headlands roughly halfway up the picture area, while the edge of the nearest headland splits the picture area in half vertically.

The dark clouds and sheets of rain are not in the reference photo, but the artist felt they would give the image a slightly unsettled, threatening atmosphere and improve the composition. They create a progression from light to dark at the top of the painting that helps lead the eye. The slanted rain also echoes the slant of the cliffs.

Versatile charcoal

Charcoal is a wonderfully responsive medium and ideal for working quickly and on a big scale. You can use the side of a chunky stick to apply broad swathes of colour and build up tone at speed, while a thin stick of willow charcoal can be used to make more precise marks.

Charcoal can be blended and softened to give a veil of pale grey or built up to create passages of velvety black tone. It is also a very forgiving medium – you can knock it back with a cloth or sponge or lift it off with a putty rubber to reveal the crisp white of the support. Furthermore, the medium can create rich textures and deep, dark calligraphic lines.

▲ Charcoal is the ideal medium to render a dramatic sweep of a stretch of shoreline. The broad, deep velvety tones used for the rain clouds and shadowy cliffs create a brooding atmosphere, while the finer marks used for the grass add textural interest.

Piece of 300gsm (140lb) Hot-pressed watercolour paper 1.5 x 1.2m (5ft x 3ft 10in)

Willow charcoal in assorted thicknesses

Long ruler

Cloth or tissue

Graphite powder

Natural sponge

Black and grey compressed charcoal

Putty rubber

Stump

Fixative

MARKING KEY POINTS

When you are working on a large scale, start by establishing some key points so that you have some reference marks within the picture area – otherwise the composition may go adrift. Use a ruler to take some measurements from the reference picture and plot them accurately on the drawing, ticking them in with a thin piece of charcoal.

FIRST STROKES

1 ▼ Sketch the outlines Pin or tape a large piece of paper to a wall to give you a firm working surface. Place your sketch or photograph close by for reference and take some key measurements. For example, the base of the far cliff lies halfway up the picture area and the horizon is about a quarter of the way down from the top of the picture. Using thin willow charcoal, tick in the horizon and the shapes of the cliffs.

2 ▼ Develop the underdrawing Complete the underdrawing, indicating the grass and rocks in the foreground. The slope of the near cliff provides an energetic lead-in to the composition, while the uninterrupted horizon provides a barrier that prevents the eye from wandering out of the picture space. If necessary, make adjustments by rubbing out with a cloth or tissue.

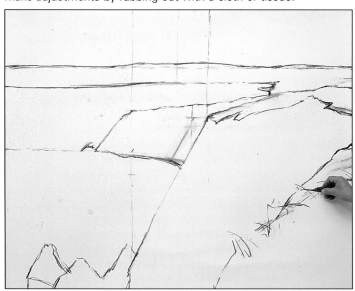

3 ▼ Apply graphite powder Graphite powder is useful for quickly blocking in large areas of light, even tone. It is grey rather than black so is less dominating than charcoal – use it in the early stages, before you want to commit yourself. Put some graphite powder on a plate, dip a sponge or tissue paper into it and apply the powder with a bold, sweeping gesture. Block in the main areas of dark tone on the shaded cliff face.

4 ▲ Darken the cliffs Once you are satisfied with the shapes of the cliffs within the picture area, make them more emphatic by applying charcoal. First, use a thick stick of willow charcoal on its side to block in the near cliff – make strokes that follow the fissures in the rock face. Notice that the charcoal picks up the dimpled texture of the watercolour paper.

5 ▶ Blend the charcoal Use a small natural sponge to soften and blend the charcoal on the near cliff. Work lightly with sweeping strokes that follow the form of the rock face, creating a rugged texture.

6 ▼ Complete the cliffs Now block in the far cliff with charcoal and soften it with the sponge as before. The dramatic shapes made by the two headlands are the focus of the image. Stand back and study them carefully, then, if you are satisfied with them, block in the rocky outcrops at the foot of the near cliff.

7 ▲ Suggest the grassy foreground Use your fingers to draw with the charcoal powder. Working from the edge of the blocked-in cliff, pull and flick out strands to suggest the edge of the grassy area in the immediate foreground.

8 ◀ Continue blocking in The narrow band of land in the distance links up with the cliffs in the foreground to create a single shape that encloses the light sea. Using a thick stick of charcoal on its side, fill this area with sweeping horizontal marks – for the moment, keep it darker in tone than it actually is to link it to the foreground and draw attention to the shapes and patterns within the subject.

9 ▶ Rough in the vegetation The area of coarse grass in the foreground draws the eye and creates a sense of recession. Lay the charcoal on its side and suggest clumps of grass by passing the stick lightly over the paper surface in the direction of growth. The broken character of the pigment introduces an impression of light into the image. Use the tip of the charcoal to add linear marks that suggest individual stems of grass.

10 ▼ Establish the sea Apply charcoal over the sea with the side of the stick, blending the pigment with your fingers as you go. Use undulating marks that establish the horizontal plane of the sea. Add tone to the beach.

11 ▲ Apply tone to the tops of the cliffs To ensure that the separate parts of the image knit together, keep the entire picture progressing. Apply a light tone to the sandy area in the distance and to the top of the cliffs – they immediately become part of the landscape rather than abstract shapes. Crisp up the cliff edges and define the ridges in the rock with linear marks.

Express yourself
Reducing the scale

The same composition is rendered here in water-soluble coloured pencils and on a much reduced scale – it measures only 17 x 23cm (7 x 9in). This picture has an entirely different impact. At this size, the marks are more subtle and less expressive. There are no rain clouds and most of the tones are lighter. Bright colours give a summery feel and the blue sky lightens the mood. Notice how complementaries – purple and yellow – liven up the cliffs and how the lightly blended blue and green make the sea's surface shimmer.

DEVELOPING THE PICTURE

Once you are happy with the balance of the composition, start to add details and adjust tonal relationships to create a sense of space. Stand back frequently to view details in the context of the drawing as a whole.

12 ▼ **Indicate the sky** With the sponge you used in step 5, suggest the sky – the charcoal powder picked up when you were softening the tones on the cliff will provide enough tone for the sky. Work in all directions and vary the pressure to create the effect of clouds.

13 ▲ **Work on the cliff face** Using the side of a stick of compressed charcoal, work over the far cliff to create a velvety black shape. Then use the same stick to work over the near cliff face with a mix of line and tone. Use free, linear marks to explore the surface of the rock, indicating some of its fissures and ridges.

14 ◄ **Develop the foreground textures** Using black and grey compressed charcoal sticks, build up a web of lines and marks to suggest the intricacy of the rock face and the tangled vegetation. Don't draw every crack in the rock or every blade of grass, but use a generalized texture that will read at a distance.

15 ▲ **Lift out the foam** Where the waves break on the shore, apply a clean putty rubber to the surface of the support and pull off the charcoal by exerting pressure on the rubber and then twisting and lifting it. This creates white foam and spray at the water's edge.

TROUBLE SHOOTER

CHANGE DARK TO LIGHT

You can lighten dark areas of charcoal by using a putty rubber. Here, the rubber is pulled gently across the cliff face to lighten its tone. Twist the soft rubber to give a point for fine work. If the rubber gets clogged with charcoal dust, rub it on scrap paper or slice off a sliver with a craft knife.

16 ▾ **Add more details** Use the rubber to pull out more whites around the two bays. Darken the horizon. Use a thin stick of willow charcoal to draw tide marks around the far bay and add details to the cliff top and fields, then develop the cliff face richly with black compressed charcoal.

17 ▸ **Add lights to the foreground** Use the putty rubber to draw light into dark in the foreground vegetation. Using a clean point or edge of the rubber, press it on to the paper and pull it with a flicking gesture, following the growth patterns of the grasses and twigs. Turn the rubber to present a clean surface to the paper and repeat.

Master Strokes

Ivon Hitchens (1893–1979)
Landscape, Bracken-Fringed Path to a Wood

This scene by British landscape painter Hitchens borders on the abstract, evoking – in a highly personal way – the feel of a walk through the woods. The path, trees and bracken are treated as loose blocks of cheerful colour that convey a sunny, uplifting feeling, and plenty of the white support is left showing through to lighten the mood further. The wide format is typical of Hitchens's style.

© Jonathan Clark Fine Art

Shapes can convey mood – here, gently curved blocks of colour convey a feeling of peace and tranquillity.

Four vertical marks break through the horizontal bias of the composition, adding an element of contrast.

Paint scratched off to reveal the white support creates graphic lines and textural effects in the foreground.

18 ▼ **Work into the headland** Indicate foreground grasses with a thin stick of charcoal. With the putty rubber, refine the rough ground on top of the cliff, using light pressure to create mid tones.

19 ► **Add more foreground detail** Twist the putty rubber to form a point and add more light details in the foreground. The calligraphic lines are both descriptive and decorative.

20 ▼ **Soften the tones** Some of the charcoal marks are too emphatic and leap forward unnaturally. Use a stump to blend them, so that they sit comfortably with the rest of the drawing.

21 ▲ **Draw more rocks** Using black compressed charcoal, draw the rocky outcrop behind the pointed rocks, then darken the rocks themselves with strong lines.

22 ◄ **Scumble in the sky** The sky encloses and completes the landscape, and also sets the mood. The clouds are an important part of the composition, leading the eye across the painting. Using the black compressed charcoal stick, make the sky on the right dark and overcast, becoming gradually lighter on the left.

23 ▼ **Soften and blend the sky** Work over the scribbled sky with the putty rubber, softening and blending so that the individual marks disappear.

24 ▲ **Suggest rain** Place a thick stick of charcoal on its side and make a series of dragging downstrokes to indicate rain slanting across the distant countryside.

25 ◄ **Add tone to the sea** Lightly skim the charcoal over the surface of the sea to add texture and create shadows of the rain clouds above. The waves breaking in the bay are distractingly white – soften them by smearing charcoal over with your fingers and the stump.

26 ▼ **Add distant details** With the putty rubber, indicate roads and buildings on the far side of the main bay. Use a light touch – you need only the slightest suggestion here. The details enliven this area and provide tonal links with the rest of the image.

A FEW STEPS FURTHER

Add finishing touches to bring the drawing into sharper focus – but resist the temptation to overwork the image. Drawing on a large scale forces you to make bold marks and to invent what you can't see in the original. Retain the freshness of this approach by being selective about the final adjustments.

27 ▲ **Develop the shore** Use compressed charcoal to make marks that describe the successive surges of water being sucked back over the shingle in the small bay. Be aware of the arc-like patterns they make.

28 ▼ **Add background detail** Add some lightly scumbled tone to the dark cloud to bring it across to the left of the image. Use a thin stick of charcoal to add more bushes around the fields and to suggest parallel cultivation lines.

29 ▲ **Lighten the hills** Lift out lines of charcoal on the hills with the putty rubber. Use the rubber, too, to hatch a pale area on the crest of the hills. These pale streaks suggest light skimming over the countryside, beyond the rainstorm. Once the drawing is complete, prevent the charcoal from smudging by spraying with fixative.

THE FINISHED PICTURE

A Lifting out lights
A soft putty rubber was used to pull out the white of the breakers in the small bay. The ripples of foam near the beach were created with the edge of the rubber.

B Directional marks
Tones and textures were built up by working lines of charcoal up and down the cliff face. These emphasize the steepness and height of the cliffs.

C Complex textures
A complex mesh of light-against-dark and dark-against-light marks captures the cliff-top vegetation. The detail here brings this area forward in the picture.

Steam power

A vintage locomotive, belching steam and smoke and set against a lively sky, presents a rewarding subject for a pastel study.

▶ A combination of blended and directly applied pastel is ideal for this atmospheric study of a steam engine leaving Fort William in the west of Scotland.

Steam trains hold a fascination for the artist as well as for the dedicated train buff. Spewing steam and smoke, they conjure up a sense of power and speed, and evoke the romance of travel in a way that their diesel and electric successors can never match.

Take the right track

The approach to painting a subject as big and complex as a steam train is the same as for any other. You need to look carefully, simplify if necessary and get the tonal values right. Feel free to make any adjustments that are necessary to create a composition that works.

In this project, the landscape provides an appropriately majestic setting for the steam locomotive – the hills form an imposing backdrop, which serves to enclose the scene. The station buildings and the picket fence frame the train on either side.

A sense of depth is created by exaggerating the tonal contrasts and textures in the foreground. The distant hills, by contrast, are rendered with smudged layers of pastel. Linear perspective also has a part to play in creating an illusion of space. Start by plotting the horizon line. When you sketch the train, the track, the station buildings and the picket fence, check that perspective lines, extended from the roof lines and ground lines, vanish somewhere on the horizon. If you get these basics right, the buildings, train and other elements will sit convincingly in the picture space.

Also use colour to create a sense of distance. Note how the warm browns of the carriages and the earth in the foreground advance from the cooler blues and greens of the hills. And, the reference photo is black and white, so you have licence to use colour creatively.

Mood and atmosphere

In a landscape, the sky sets the mood as it reflects the weather and light conditions. Consistency is important, so establish the location of the sun and make sure that highlights and shadows are placed accurately. In this study, the artist created a bright summer sky with cumulus clouds billowing behind the hills.

As the image neared completion, he adjusted the mood, creating a dark cloud on the left – both to balance the dark plume of smoke on the right and to introduce a sense of drama. The cloud is emphasised by applying a glaze of bluish light in the shadows on the left.

FIRST STEPS

1 ▲ **Lay in the sky** Use a short length of Naples yellow pale pastel on its side to scribble loose marks for the clouds. Apply burnt sienna pale lightly to the lower part of the sky, then use a small piece of cobalt blue to scumble in the blue of the sky, making it more intense at the top.

EXPERT ADVICE
Marking key points

Start by drawing a frame for the picture area, leaving a broad border. Use the margins to plot key points such as the location of the sun (A); the points at which the station buildings on the left (B) and the distant hills on the right (C) meet the picture's edge; the vertical centre of the picture (D); the horizon line (E); and horizontal centre (F).

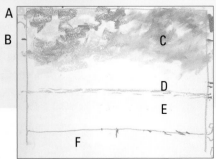

2 ▶ Blend the pastel Blend the pastel colours with your fingertips, using light pressure and swirling gestural marks to capture the vaporous effects of the billowing clouds.

3 ▼ Block in the hills Block in the rolling hills with the side of a grey pastel, then soften and blend the colour with your fingertips.

4 ▼ Develop the hills Build up colour on the hillsides, using strokes of Prussian blue, cerulean blue, blue-green and phthalo blue and allowing the marks to follow the contours. Blend the colours lightly so that they melt together. Use Hooker's green to indicate the trees among the foothills.

5 ▼ Establish the foreground Apply yellow ochre and yellow ochre pale over the hills on the right and leaf green pale below them. Scumble in the foreground with yellow ochre, adding areas of Hooker's green and grey. Use burnt umber to block in the fence on the right and the buildings on the left.

6 ▼ Build the tones Use grey to knock back the area of white in the middle of the image. You now have an underpainting on which to build up tones and develop details – the reference image is in black and white, so the tonal variations in the subject have already been simplified. Use sepia to indicate the structure of the picket fence and to suggest, very loosely, the forms of the station building and far telegraph pole.

7 ▲ Develop the station and fence Draw in the near telegraph pole in sepia. Apply strokes of Prussian blue over the buildings, fence and distant telegraph pole. Develop the building and fence with yellow ochre, leaf green pale and phthalo blue.

Express yourself
Further down the line

The diagonal slant of the railway line creates a dynamic composition for this alternative pastel painting of a steam locomotive. Notice the strong sense of perspective as the tracks and carriages recede into the distance. Clouds of steam trail behind the funnel, implying the steady forward motion of the train.

As in the main project, the pastel is built up in layers and lightly blended in areas such as the sky. Details on the engine and carriages are applied with sharp marks and foreground texture is added with crisply drawn blades of grass.

8 ▶ Lay the tracks Develop the right-hand fence with Prussian blue, phthalo blue and yellow ochre pale. Use leaf green pale, moss green, Prussian blue, blue-green, grey-green and sepia for the foreground grass. Plot the angle of the tracks in sepia and black, lightening the ground around them with bistre. Putting in an outline of the carriages in burnt umber helps give a sense of scale for when you draw the locomotive.

DEVELOPING THE PICTURE
The scene is set, so now you can introduce the star of the show – the magnificent old steam engine and its carriages.

9 ▼ Begin on the engine Sketch the front of the locomotive with Payne's grey and black. Use the tip of the pastel and light, exploratory strokes to 'find' the shape and size. Look for alignments to key the image against – for example, where the engine aligns horizontally with the station building.

10 ▲ Develop the train Apply swathes of lemon yellow to the sky. Block in the train with black and sepia, using a pastel to find the angle at which the tops of the carriages recede towards the horizon. Using the tips of the pastels, build up a tracery of lines: vertical strokes for the carriage sides and circular ones for the wheels and undercarriage.

11 ▶ Develop the engine Start to sculpt the cylindrical form of the engine, making curving strokes with the black pastel. Work into the black with phthalo blue to suggest the gleam of metal. Apply touches of Naples yellow for the highlights.

12 ◀ Work on the carriages Using black, raw umber and bistre, describe the carriages, noting the band of light-coloured paintwork, and the way the curving roof catches the light. Add more detail to the engine and tender (the carriage in which fuel and water are stored).

13 ▲ Add detail Add shadow to the carriages with black and Payne's grey, then gently stroke white and cobalt blue on to the engine to capture the sheen on the flat and curved planes. Use black to sharpen up details and put in slivers of Naples yellow for the highlights. Use vermilion for the plate at the front.

Master Strokes

Alfred Sisley (1839–99)
The Goods Station

The simple lines and bright colours in this oil pastel painting give it a vibrant, almost childlike quality. The trains themselves are little more than blocked-in rectangles, but because of their billowing clouds of steam, they convey a strong sense of activity. The horizontal emphasis of the composition is broken dramatically by the verticals of the trees.

The steam is scribbled in with white and pale touches of blue, green and yellow.

Cool blue shadows contrast with the warm pink in the foreground.

14 ▼ **Apply more highlights** Break off a piece of Naples yellow and use the sharp edge to draw crisp highlights on the engine. Apply the ribs of the boiler with black, curving strokes. Brighten the engine with touches of cobalt blue.

15 ▲ **Add detail to the carriages** Build up colour on the carriages, using Indian red for the red paintwork, Naples yellow for the cream band and grey for the roof. Touch in the highlights along the top of the carriages and around the windows with the tip of the Naples yellow pastel.

16 ▶ **Indicate the steam** Use the white pastel for the steam escaping from the vents under the engine. Press the pastel into the paper to get a good application of pigment.

17 ▲ **Tighten up detail** Mark the window in the driver's cab with leaf green pale; use vermilion and yellow ochre for the driver's head. Brighten the highlights with Naples yellow. Work over the ground with Payne's grey and burnt sienna; add texture to the grass with Hooker's green and cadmium yellow.

18 ▲ **Create the plume of steam** Like clouds, the plumes of smoke and steam are three-dimensional – the top, which catches the light, is lighter, while the underside is in shadow. Scumble on cobalt blue, then apply white, using the side of the pastel stick to make small curving strokes.

19 ◄ **Create the smoke** Introduce scribbles of Payne's grey and cobalt blue into the steam from the locomotive's vents. Apply loosely hatched strokes of Payne's grey for the cloud on the left. Define the fence posts with the black pastel, then hatch black smoke belching from the locomotive's funnel.

20 ▼ **Blend the smoke** Lightly blend the grey cloud on the left with your fingertips. Hatch phthalo blue into the smoke plume and blend into the black.

A FEW STEPS FURTHER

The painting is almost complete, so this is a good time to stand back and study it carefully to see what final touches are required. You'll need to adjust the light to be consistent with the dark cloud on the left. Also, bring a pair of figures into the foreground to give a sense of scale and create a splash of colour to draw the viewer's eye into the painting.

21 ▼ **Add highlights** Scribble crimson over the front plate. Use the tip of the Naples yellow pastel to add crisp highlights along the metal rails.

22 ▲ **Soften the shadows** Model the telegraph pole with burnt umber. Suggest cool shadow over the left side of the painting by drawing the cobalt blue pastel lightly across the area, creating a network of hatched marks.

23 ▼ **Add figures** Use Naples yellow, orange, cadmium yellow, vermilion, Prussian blue, cobalt blue and black to create the pair of workmen on the left. Work very simply and directly, putting down dabs of colour.

24 ▲ **Add touches of impasto** Spray the painting with fixative. Now that the pigment is firmly fixed, you can apply intense white highlights of thickly impastoed pastel on the clouds of steam.

THE FINISHED PICTURE

A Figure focus
Two railway workers in vibrant working gear emphasize the sheer size of the locomotive and provide a touch of accent colour.

B Lively sky
The sky is rendered very simply with direct applications of swirling pastel laid in with the side of the stick.

C A smoky frame
A plume of dark smoke frames the top right corner and emphasizes the recession from foreground to distant hills.

D Sparkling impasto
White highlights pressed on to the paper after fixing give the steam escaping from the vents a lively, sparkling quality.

Spring shower

This scene brilliantly conveys the atmosphere of a showery day with bursts of spring sunshine. Soft pastels are ideal for capturing the character of the weather and setting.

A sudden spring shower has brought a city street to life. The rain has stopped but has left a shiny, wet road surface that reflects sunlight, blue sky and the vivid colours of the shops and shoppers.

Because each colour is echoed elsewhere in the scene, the artist could not treat any area of this picture in isolation. Every patch of local colour also appears as a reflected colour, either on the watery road or in the shop windows.

The best approach is to develop the work as a whole rather than building it up one element at a time. In practical terms, this means that whenever you pick up a new pastel colour it should be a rule of thumb to use that colour wherever it appears in the scene.

The artist also resisted the temptation to start the drawing with the colourful figures – the most interesting bits! It is more important to concentrate on the overall composition and establish the perspective of the buildings before introducing the people in any detail.

Starting the drawing

The artist took an initial photo (above, right) before the shower to establish the basic composition. However, this was just a starting point. In the final picture, he introduced the rain effects that later appeared, and rearranged the shoppers. (Even if you intend to complete a work on site, it still pays to take photos and make sketches first. You never know when unforeseen events – such as rain – will mean you have to finish it at home.)

The preliminary drawing was done with thin willow charcoal. This is less

▶ Soft pastel is built up layer upon layer to create the highlights, shadows and reflections in this atmospheric scene.

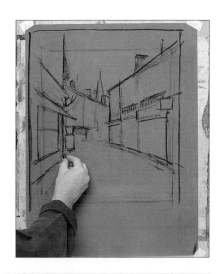

dense than pastel and it is therefore easier to rub back and make corrections. Empty space was left to the right of the picture area, allowing the composition to be altered and extended at any time during the early stages.

Transparent colour

Once the drawing was complete, initial colours and tones were blocked in using the broad sides of the pastel sticks. This allowed the colours to be laid transparently without clogging up the surface of the support in the early stages.

Layered colour gives an attractive finish and preserves the texture of the pastel marks. As traces of each colour show through subsequent layers, the surface develops depth and luminosity.

In addition, starting with thin veils of overlaid colour gives greater scope for using increasingly thicker marks in the later stages – especially for splashes of strong colour and highlights

Textured and toned

The toothy, slightly abrasive texture of the pastel board used for this project is created by tiny particles of pumice, which help the pastel pigment to adhere. The rough surface encourages a bold, lively approach, as it is difficult to work in too much detail. Once the painting is complete, give it a spray of fixative to prevent the pastel from smudging.

FIRST STEPS

1 ▶ **Make a charcoal drawing** Leaving some space on the right and to the bottom of the paper, make a line drawing of the subject using thin willow charcoal. Do not make the lines too heavy, otherwise the dust from the charcoal will affect the appearance of the subsequent pastel colours.

2 ▲ **Block in initial colours** Using the side of the pastel stick, lightly block in the sky with pale grey. Use random strokes, taking the colour neatly up to the edge of the rooftops and chimneys. Take a little of the same colour into the top of the awning and shop sign to indicate reflections.

3 ▲ **Develop the shop front** Still working with the side of the pastel sticks, start to block in the local colour of the shop fronts and chimneys with dark sap green and raw sienna.

325

4 ▶ **Introduce dark tone on the left**
Block in the shaded shop front with dark purple. Although it is important to establish the dark tones at this early stage, use the pastel lightly so that paler colours can be used on top if necessary.

6 ▲ **Suggest the reflections** Take a little mid purple into the shop windows on the right. Using a cool grey pastel, block in the reflections on the roofs, road and buildings.

**EXPERT ADVICE
Mixing neutrals**

In soft pastel paintings, blended neutral shades usually look more interesting than bought versions, which can look heavy and flat when used next to bright colours. Here, the artist is experimenting with mauve and raw umber pastel sticks, blending them to find a vibrant neutral that would look suitable on the road in the foreground.

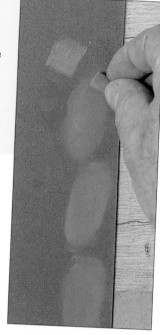

5 ◀ **Block in lighter areas** Establish the local colour of the shop front by applying mid purple over the dark purple of the shadow. Block in the background houses and the wet road in pale raw umber.

7 ▲ **Work into the sky** Using the side of the stick, work over the sky area in blue-grey. Take a little of this colour into the shop fronts and rooftops to depict highlights and reflections.

DEVELOP THE PICTURE

The scene is set and ready for some visitors. So far most of the colour has been lightly applied using the side of the pastel. It is now time to use some stronger colour, especially on the figures and the bright highlights.

8 ▼ **Introduce a brighter colour** Build up the distant figure in viridian and use the same colour on the hanging signs and shop fronts. Mark in the viridian reflections in the road.

9 ▲ **Add pale tones** Work flecks of pale viridian over the viridian you have just applied. With pale lemon, add blocks of reflected light to the background buildings, shop fronts and road. Use the same colour to highlight the shop sign on the right.

Master Strokes

Gustave Loiseau (1865–1935)
Fine Rain, Pont Aven

In this painting, as in the one in the step-by-step, the road is one of the main features, leading the eye right into the centre of the composition. In the same way, too, reflected light is shown bouncing off the road to give an impression of a wet surface after rain. Another feature of this painting is its textural finish. Creamy brush marks of oil paint in the foreground suggest a cobbled road, while thickly applied paint on the near roof is used to describe tiles covered in lichen. The artist has created a strong feeling of distance in the picture by simulating the effects of aerial perspective – the colours become paler and the details less distinct in the background.

Details are implied with minimal brush strokes. For example, a few marks are enough to convey the man on a cart.

The sky was painted in variegated greys to suggest shifting clouds and to avoid a dull, leaden appearance.

10 ▶ **Apply shades of Prussian blue**
Work into the shop fronts and windows in dark Prussian blue. Accentuate the detail and outlines in these areas in mid Prussian blue – this slightly lighter tone will look particularly vibrant next to the viridian.

11 ▲ **Develop the sky** Lighten the lower sky with very pale lemon; add strokes of pale ultramarine to the top. Use very pale lemon to lighten the reflections on the road and add highlights to the windows and figures.

Express yourself
Deserted street

A pastel picture of the same street but without the figures evokes a very different atmosphere. In this deserted scene, the mood is more subdued and the colours more earthy. The emphasis is on tone, the shadowy buildings on the right contrasting with the reflected light on the left. There are just a few splashes of bright colour in the shop fronts.

12 ◀ **Block in the foreground**
With loose strokes of a mauve pastel, work right across the foreground. Use the side of the pastel, pressing quite hard to get a good strong colour. Apply patches of raw umber over the mauve – these colours will blend together to create areas of cool grey.

13 ▲ **Strengthen deep tones** Use dark purple to strengthen the shadows and deep tones on the buildings. Take the same colour into the reflections on the road.

14 ▶ **Add more colour** Start to build up the colours and tones in the shop window on the left. First use the cool grey pastel, then add orange overlaid with pale orange.

REMOVING PASTEL

A stencil brush with cut down bristles is excellent for removing unwanted colour. It is also useful for getting rid of the thick pastel that tends to clog the surface of the paper.

TROUBLE SHOOTER

15 ▼ **Block in the figures** Working in bold strokes, block in the shop front on the right with orange and then pick out the highlights in pale orange. Use the dark purple pastel to block in the figures as dark silhouettes.

16 ▲ **Define the figures** Use strokes of brown for the figures' reflections on the wet road. With very pale lemon, define the outlines of the figures.

▲ These patches of mid purple, permanent rose and ultramarine have been given a three-dimensional appearance by overlaying them with pale tones of the same colours. The figures in the picture are worked in a similar way – they are blocked in with a single colour and a paler version of the same colour is then used for the highlights.

17 ◀ **Add local colours to the figures** Block in the jackets of the four central figures in ultramarine, burnt sienna, mid purple and permanent rose respectively. Build up the form of each figure by adding a highlight in a pale version of the main colour. For example, the figure on the right is blocked in with permanent rose, so the highlight on that figure is pale permanent rose.

A FEW STEPS FURTHER

Complete the picture with a few more details. For instance, you could develop the figures with touches of colour on the flesh and hair. Also, the bright foreground colours have made the pale sunlight appear weak in comparison. Strengthen this with more very pale lemon.

18 ▼ **Add flesh tones** Start to develop the figures using brown, purple madder and pale raw sienna for the dark, medium and light flesh tones.

19 ▲ **Develop the reflections** Continue to build up detail on the figures using touches of bright local colour for the skirts, bags and hair. Use pale versions of the local colours for the bold highlights. Remember to add a little of every colour you use to the reflections in the road. Here, the artist is adding a reflection in pale permanent rose.

20 ▼ **Develop the light** Take very pale lemon around the central figures, so that they stand out as dark shapes against the pale tone. Use the same colour to dot in sharp highlights on the remaining figures and the reflections.

21 ▲ **Add bright red detail** Generally strengthen the light tones in the background and road reflections by working across the whole picture with pale raw sienna. Use the same colour to add highlights and detail to the shop fronts and to define the edge of the pavement. Add touches of cadmium red to the left of the picture, including the edge of the advertising board.

22 ▼ **Tidy the shadows** Define the straight vertical edge on the reflected building in pale purple overlaid with very pale lemon.

23 ▲ **Add final details** Use raw sienna, cadmium yellow and very pale lemon to strengthen the gilding on the shop sign. Suggest the lettering over the awning in pale raw sienna. Finally, give the work a spray of fixative to prevent smudging.

THE FINISHED PICTURE

A Distant haze
Rainy days exaggerate aerial perspective, so the distant steeple is rendered in a very pale, hazy colour.

B Focal point
A foreground figure was placed in front of the sunlit buildings and surrounded by reflected light to create an eye-catching focal point.

C Pale sunlight
The palest shade of lemon conveys the impression of sunlit reflections.

D Mirror images
The reflections are rendered as mirror images of the figures and buildings.

Colourful landscape

Let your sense of colour run riot in this project that conjures up the vivid hues of a Greek summer.

Often, the most unusual landscapes are inspired by many different elements – photos, sketches and memories – brought together with a large helping of imagination. Here, the artist has created a painting from a series of photos that caught her interest on holiday in Greece, in particular the three on the left. The hillside, the limpid blue sea, a church, a whitewashed house, and cypress and olive trees were married together to generate a picture that is more interesting than its constituent parts.

Working in this way allows you to assemble your composition as you choose and to adapt it as you work. For example, in this landscape, the focus of the painting started out as the little

▼ Heightened colours are a striking feature of this landscape in oil pastel. The vibrant hues help capture the heat and the quality of light typical of the Mediterranean.

church in the top photo, but gradually, as the work evolved, it was balanced by the bright white house from the middle photo. This photo also provided much of the background reference while the bottom photo provided the source material for the dark trees which help to break up the foreground.

Blending oil pastels

Artistic licence was taken with the colours as well as the composition. The artist deliberately exaggerated and invented colour to help capture the hot and sunny Mediterranean atmosphere. Using oil pastels, which give bold, saturated colour, was perfect for the task. The artist blended them into smooth areas of colour using white spirit on kitchen paper. If you have particularly sensitive skin, wear surgical gloves or put petroleum jelly on your hands when you are working with white spirit.

FIRST STEPS

1 ▼ Draw with a pastel Use a purple oil pastel to map out the composition of hills, trees and buildings – purple is relatively unobtrusive and can be cooled down or warmed up at a later stage.

YOU WILL NEED

Piece of smooth cartridge paper 35 x 50cm (14 x 20in)

21 oil pastels: Purple; Orange; Azure blue; Indigo light; Lemon yellow; Red violet; Golden yellow; White; Deep yellow; Medium green; Rose madder pale; Flesh ochre; Olive green; Alizarin blue lake; Turquoise blue; Light blue; Naples yellow hue; Cobalt violet light;

Barite green; Phthalo green light; Yellow grey

Kitchen paper

White spirit

Surgical gloves or petroleum jelly (optional)

Scalpel blade

Masking tape

5 coloured pencils: Deep red; Pink; Mid green; Prussian blue; Brown

2 ▼ Start blocking in colours Scumble orange over the hillside and the side of the church. Work loosely – you are not painting, simply laying down colours in order to blend them later.

3 ▲ Smudge the orange Crumple some kitchen paper and dip it into white spirit. Working with loose strokes that follow the orange pastel lines, use the kitchen paper to smudge the pastel into areas of smooth colour.

4 ◄ Add some blues Apply loose horizontal strokes of azure blue over the sky and indigo light over the sea. Blend the marks with kitchen paper dipped into white spirit as before, smoothing out the colour in broad horizontal sweeps.

5 ▼ Fill in the trees Still using indigo light, describe the thin cypress trees with upward strokes and fanned-out, spiky strokes on the olive trees and large tree. Smooth out the colour with kitchen paper and white spirit, following the direction of the marks.

6 ▶ Build up colour in the foreground Apply lemon yellow oil pastel over the large tree in the foreground, followed by red violet to darken the tone. Use the red violet to fill in the tall cypress tree by the church. Now blend the colours on the large tree with white spirit and kitchen paper, as before.

7 ▶ Work on the trees Brighten the foreground and the trees in the middle distance with lemon yellow. Now return to the red violet pastel to build up the structure of the olive trees and cypresses. The contrast between the violets and greens makes the colours shine out.

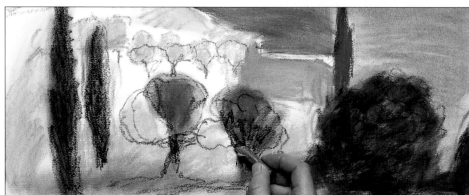

Express yourself

Inspirational sketch in watercolour

Here, the artist has taken an entirely different approach to the Greek landscape. For a start, she has focused on one headland and composed it in a panoramic format. The medium this time is watercolour and she has made use of its delicacy to brush in the sky with one pale wash. In contrast, the sea has been built up in several layers to give it a sense of solidity. The headland itself is described mainly in yellows and greens, giving an exciting warm-cool contrast. A dab of hot orange provides a bright focal point.

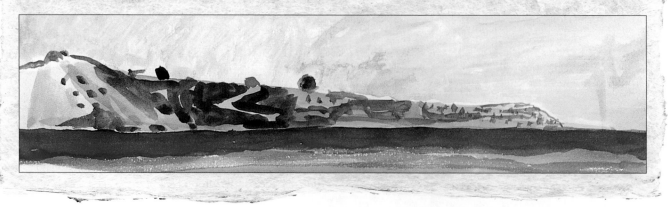

Master Strokes

Paul Sérusier (1863–1927)
Landscape

The French artist Paul Sérusier was inspired by Paul Gauguin's (1848–1903) expressive use of colour – as is evident in this oil painting, in which greens and oranges predominate and set up strong contrasts. The solid, block-like shapes of the cottages and hayrick and the well-defined areas of grass give the composition an almost abstract feel.

Layers of scumbled colours create a wonderful variegated texture on the roofs of the cottage. The colours leap out from the recessive blue-grey of the mountains behind.

Patches of coral pink and bright white immediately attract the eye – making the rock on the grass an important focal point.

Areas of pale earth break up the dark greens of the grass, helping to contribute to the lively chequerboard of tone that enlivens the whole picture.

8 ▾ Use a coloured pencil Add a line of azure blue oil pastel along the horizon and where the sea meets the distant land; smooth out as before. Now switch to a well-sharpened deep red coloured pencil to define the roof of the church.

DEVELOPING THE PICTURE

The main areas in the landscape are now blocked in and blended to a smooth finish with white spirit. Develop texture by scumbling and layering colour or scraping back with a scalpel blade.

9 ▴ Make the hillside glow Cover the remaining white areas with the golden yellow pastel. Pick out the house in the middle distance with white pastel and give it a deep yellow roof. Smear a little medium green into the hillside, then blend some rose madder pale over it. The resulting pinkish colour shines out against the strong blue of the ocean.

10 ▼ **Heighten the contrasts** Use flesh ochre on the church roof and strengthen the walls with orange. Fill in the middle row of olive trees with olive green. Return to the cypresses and squiggle alizarin blue lake over them to add visual interest.

11 ▶ **Add white on the trunks** With the deep red coloured pencil, block in the door on the church. In Greece, olive trees are sometimes painted white along the base of the trunks to deter insects. Suggest this effect by picking out the trunks of the two olive trees in the foreground with a thick layer of white oil pastel.

12 ▼ **Scratch back the pastel** To create texture on the shorter cypress tree, use a scalpel to scrape away some of the pastel colour, making branch-like marks in the process. So as not to damage the paper, work with the shaft of the scalpel rather than the blade – but cover the sharp edge first with masking tape to protect your fingers.

13 ▲ **Vary the blues** Strengthen the foreground by blending some strong alizarin blue lake along the base of the scene. Now build up the colour of the sea behind the church with turquoise blue and light blue. Blend these colours as before.

SHARPEN THE HORIZON

After darkening the sea in step 13, you may find that your horizon has lost definition. Lay a piece of paper over the sea so that the top edge is on the horizon. Work light blue pastel into the sky and blend it with white spirit, going right up to the edge of the paper.

TROUBLE SHOOTER

14 ▲ **Modify the church** With oil pastels you can lift colour with the shaft of the scalpel blade and rework it. If the church seems too dominant against the yellows of the hillside, knock it back by scraping away some of the orange on the walls and going over them with Naples yellow hue.

15 ▼ **Scumble some pink** Refine the roof of the church, too, scraping away some of the colour and going over it with Naples yellow hue and white. Next, scumble rose madder pale over the foreground.

16 ▶ **Rework the other cypress** Using the corner of the scalpel blade, carefully scrape away some of the alizarin blue lake pastel from the cypress tree next to the church, revealing the pink hue underneath. (Scratching back in this way is a technique called sgraffito.) Make linear marks that suggest the network of branches.

17 ▼ **Heighten the perspective** Work over the hill on the left with cobalt violet light pastel. Use a pink pencil along the sliver of land. Dot in some tiny trees with a mid green pencil.

18 ▼ **Add more trees** Put a few slashes of white pastel across the lower hillside to suggest terraces. Use an olive green pastel to dot in more olive trees.

19 ▼ **Stipple some green** Continue dotting olive trees over the hillside. Stipple barite green pastel into the four trees just beyond the church. This strong, acidic colour makes the row stand out and lends definition to the middle distance.

20 ▲ **Build up the greens** Using a Prussian blue pencil, draw more trees to the left of the house, building them up with the indigo light pastel. Then scumble alizarin blue lake pastel over the top. Stipple and scumble barite green, phthalo green light, medium green and yellow grey into the foreground olive trees.

A FEW STEPS FURTHER

There is a good sense of contrast and variety in the picture – hot pinks and yellows set against cooler blues and greens, and the straight lines of the buildings against the curved lines of the hillside. A few crisp architectural details will complete the picture.

21 ▼ **Put in architectural detail** Resting your hand on a piece of scrap paper so you don't smudge the colours, define the bell tower on the church with a brown pencil. The sharper the point, the crisper the detail.

22 ▲ **Pick out the roof** With the same pencil, define the edge of the church roof. Finally, pick out the highlights on it in white pastel so that it really stands out against the blue of the sea.

THE FINISHED PICTURE

A Hot colours
The vibrant pinks and oranges of the distant shore make it glow against the backdrop of the bright blue sea and sky.

B Focal point
Densely applied white pastel on the wall of the little house – together with the bright orange on the roof – takes the eye into the painting.

C Sgraffito
The underlying purples and pinks glimmer through the scratched-back lines on the cypress tree. These colours echo those used elsewhere in the landscape, adding to the harmony of the picture.

House plants in watercolour

This striking, close-up composition of three different conservatory plants shows that you do not need a grand subject or broad view to capture the beauty of nature.

P lants offer a particular challenge to the artist. The variety of forms, colours and textures require close observation and a careful choice of colours.

A painting like this inevitably includes a lot of greens. Although green might appear to be quite a cool, fresh colour, the painting nevertheless manages to evoke the sun-drenched, humid atmosphere of the conservatory.

A range of greens
The trick is to observe the colours to be found in the light and shadowed areas. The artist has captured a wide range of greens, both warm and cool. Occasionally, he used a wet-on-wet style to let the colours run together and gain smoothly blended tones.

Visual editing
When re-creating a scene such as this, you continually need to edit the still life, simplifying the information from the original into something that can be reproduced. You are not trying to make a botanical rendering. What is important is that your painting looks believable, with an accurate representation of the shapes and light. If the composition needs a bit of help, feel free to rearrange the plants or leaves.

▲ The reds and greens that predominate in this carefully observed study of plants provide an exciting complementary colour contrast.

FIRST STROKES

1 ▼ **Draw in the pencil outline** Use a 2B pencil to sketch the basic picture on to the paper. Pay special attention to the shapes of the leaves and the overall forms of the plants, as they are the main focus of the composition. Close observation at this stage will pay dividends as the painting progresses.

3 ▼ **Begin adding colour to the leaves** Look for the bluish reflections on the leaves and, using a No.9 round brush, apply a very thin mix of cerulean blue to these areas. Use the same colour to block in the rounded plant at the front of the picture, as well as the view through the leaves and out of the window. Leave to dry.

2 ▲ **Lay a thin background wash** Leaving the highlights and the brighter parts of the composition blank, apply a very thin wash of yellow ochre and Payne's grey over the entire picture using a No.10 round brush. Leave the wash to dry.

4 ▲ **Paint the light areas** Add a little lemon yellow to your blue mix to make light green. Apply the paint from top to bottom of each leaf on the large plants. The paint will be most concentrated at the bottom of the leaves, giving the impression of light shining through the paler parts. Develop the rounded plant. The cerulean blue applied in step 3 will show through the green in places, creating a denser colour that contrasts with the translucent blue-lemon mix.

5 ▲ **Block in the floor and pots** Mix a light terracotta colour, adding a lot of Indian red and a little more yellow ochre to the original ochre mix used in step 2. Changing to a No.7 round brush, block in the floor and pots. You will need to use this smaller brush in order to cut in around other areas of colour, as it is important that the terracotta shade does not 'bleed'. Darken the terracotta mix with a little more Indian red and some burnt umber. Apply to the lighter areas of the stems, using a No.3 round brush.

Master Strokes

Mark Gertler (1891–1939)
Agapanthus

This still life of a pot plant in bloom is painted in oils rather than watercolours, giving denser, less translucent colouring than in our watercolour step-by-step project. However, Mark Gertler – a British-Jewish painter, who was influenced by eastern European folk art – has captured the same interplay of light and shade on his subject. The almost black shadow areas at the heart of the plant act as a foil to the light and mid tones, where the foliage catches the light.

The background is plain and unfocused. The band of black at the top enables the beautiful blue of the flowers to sing out.

Both cool blue-greens and warm yellow-greens are apparent on the long, strap-like leaves. The paint is carefully blended wherever the two colours meet along the length of a leaf.

DEVELOPING THE PICTURE

Now that you have put in the palest tones of the leaves, pots and floor tiles, you can begin to build up the medium and dark tones on top. Work wet-in-wet so that the colours run into one another for a natural effect.

6 ▲ **Apply the main leaf colour** Mix sap green and lemon yellow to make a more intense lime green. Using a No.5 round brush, start to develop the detail of the lighter parts of the leaves where the sun catches them. Be very careful to render the shapes accurately.

7 ▲ **Introduce the darker areas** Mix lots of sap green with burnt umber and a little Payne's grey for a rich leaf colour. Add some gum arabic to intensify the colour and enable you to re-wet it once dry. Next, mix a dark stem colour with a little brown madder alizarin and lots of burnt umber. Work across the picture, painting the green mix wet-on-wet over the lime green to create the dark leaf areas. Drop brown colour on to the stems as you work across the painting.

341

8 ▲ **Continue adding definition to the leaves** Carry on adding the darker colours to all the plants. On the rounded plant, dab on the colour to show the smaller leaves. This adds density to the plants – until now, the painting has been very light and fresh. This stage takes a long time, but do not rush it, as the effect of the wet-on-wet technique is central to the whole painting. Work methodically across the picture, as you did before.

9 ▲ **Add colour to the pots** Mix burnt umber, a little yellow ochre and a little Payne's grey to make a medium brown for the soil and the insides of the pots. Apply with a No.6 round brush. Add some Indian red to the mix to warm up the shady side of the pots, paying close attention to where the areas of light fall. The warm colours of the pots contribute to the bright, sunny atmosphere of the painting.

Express yourself
Pattern of leaves

Leaf shapes and the patterns they create are endlessly fascinating. In this pencil drawing, the artist has focused closely on the foliage of a rubber plant so that the leaves fill the paper. The pattern of leaves is more important here than the structure of the plant itself. A hint of tone and texture is achieved by the lines drawn on the foreground leaves.

10 ▲ **Define the areas of shadow** Mix sap green, Payne's grey and just a little burnt umber. Use this for the very dark green leaves and stems. As before, work methodically across the paper, introducing the dark brown colour from step 7 occasionally to add variety – use the colours together wet-on-wet.

11 ▲ **Complete the areas of shadow** Continuing with the dark brown and green mixes, work into all the shadow areas. Stand back and look at your painting. Remember that you are trying to create a believable, evocative picture, not a slavish re-creation of the original, so you can use a bit of artistic licence if necessary. If you feel the painting needs some more areas of shadow, add them, but keep it looking natural.

12 ▲ **Embellish the background** Mix Indian red with a little brown madder alizarin. Block in the floor tiles, using the No.9 round brush – these will make sense of the composition spatially. Add a little ultramarine, and use this mix to add detail to the pots. Make a thin mix of yellow ochre, Payne's grey and brown madder alizarin for the window frames. Paint these in as simple straight lines.

▼ **Adding Payne's grey to the sap green creates a dark green for the shadow areas on the foliage.**

13 ▲ **Finish off the background** Complete the lines that form the window frames – these provide a suggestion of the setting, but do not detract from the main focus of the composition. The painting is now a very believable rendering of plants in a conservatory.

A FEW STEPS FURTHER

All the main areas of light and shadow are now included, but you can improve the picture further by adding more colours to the shadows and intensifying the background.

14 ◄ **Sharpen the picture**
Make a more intense mix of the dark green used on the leaves in step 10. This mix should be almost black. Using the No.3 brush, cut in around the leaf shapes, adding more definition and sharpening up the picture. Add further accents to the pots to emphazise the light and dark areas and to strengthen the effect of bright sunlight. Make sure that you have represented all the areas of intense shadow, even the very fine ones. For close work, change to a No.3 flat brush.

15 ▲ **Suggest the background** Mix sap green and cerulean blue. Apply using the No.6 round brush to give a suggestion of foliage outside the conservatory. This increases the sense of depth in the picture and helps the painting to look more complete.

THE FINISHED PICTURE

A Wide tonal range
To convey the impression of strong sunlight filtering through the window and plants, a wide range of tones was used, both on the leaves and the pots.

B Simple background
In contrast to the busy subject matter in the foreground of the picture, the background was kept uncluttered – the windows and floor tiles are suggested very simply.

C Dark shadows
The areas of deepest shadow on the plants were painted during the final stages of the picture. The dark colour crisply defines the lighter shapes of the leaves.

Watercolour portrait

To ensure success in portraiture, concentrate on painting only what you see, not what you think the subject should look like – and you'll find that a good likeness will gradually emerge.

When you are painting a portrait, the ultimate aim is to achieve a good likeness. However, don't let this distract you from other important aspects of the painting process. Indeed, a sure-fire way of failing is to be overly obsessive about getting a likeness right in the early stages of the painting.

Jigsaw of shapes

Start by deciding where the head will go on the paper and how big it will be. Look, in particular, for the angle of the tilt of the head. Then, starting in the middle of the head, indicate the elements in an orderly and analytical way, looking for areas of light and dark tone and for the shapes of shadows and features. Measure everything by eye, checking proportions with your pencil or brush if necessary (see Introducing figure drawing, page 151).

When you are satisfied with the broad outlines of the drawing, start to apply washes of paint, treating the head as a jigsaw of abstract shapes.

Leave the eyes until the later stages of the painting. If you put them in too early, the portrait tends to come to life too soon and you may feel disinclined to make any further changes. Some artists delay putting in the eyes until the very last minute, because once they're in, they say, they seem to follow you around accusingly!

Transparent watercolour

Watercolour has many qualities that recommend it to the portrait painter – its transparency is unmatched by any other medium and it lends itself to rendering the subtlety and luminosity of flesh tones. On the other hand, it is quite an unforgiving medium – it is difficult, though not impossible, to rework a dark area, unlike oil paint which can easily be scraped back and redone.

Plan the painting carefully, noting where the light areas will be. Generally, you should start with the palest areas, building up washes to create the dark ones. This gives you the opportunity to make adjustments. However, it is sometimes useful to establish an important area of deep tone, such as the dark background here, because this gives a key to the range of tones you'll need to show.

YOU WILL NEED

Piece of 300gsm (140lb) Not watercolour paper 57 x 39cm (22½ x 15½in)

Brushes: Swordliner; Nos.10, 20 and 4 rounds; 13mm (½in) flat

9 watercolours: Davy's grey; Burnt sienna; Burnt umber; Ultramarine; Raw sienna; Indian red; Alizarin crimson; Phthalo blue; Winsor violet

Mixing palette or dish

Jar of water and paper tissue

▲ The warm skin tones of this sitter are created using a palette based on earth colours varied with a range of reds and blues.

FIRST STEPS

1 ▼ **Map out the head** Using Davy's grey and the swordliner brush, plot the broad dimensions of the head, checking its width and depth, and the location of key features. Work from the middle out to the edges to allow space for making changes. Strengthen the outline of the cheek and jawline.

2 ▼ **Apply a basic wash** Mix a wash of burnt sienna. This earth pigment, with its golden flesh colour and transparency, is an ideal basis on which to build flesh tones. Using a No.10 round brush, apply the paint over the shaded side of the head. Take the colour into the left eye socket and the shadow below the cheek.

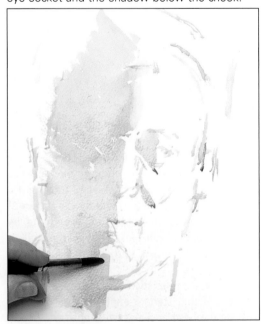

DEVELOPING THE PICTURE

With the basic division of light and shade established on the face, you can now develop the flesh tones using warm and cool mixes applied in translucent layers.

3 ▶ Block in a dark background Add a small amount of burnt umber to ultramarine and indicate the shadow on the sitter's right shoulder. Mix a warmer wash by adding more burnt umber to the mix to give a warm neutral. Load a No.20 round brush and loosely apply the colour over the background on the right of the picture and down over the sitter's left shoulder.

4 ▲ Add warm tones Using a No.4 round, apply a mix of raw sienna and Indian red to the left eye socket. With an Indian red/alizarin crimson mix, paint warm tone on the forehead, nose and under the mouth. Working wet-on-wet, add darker mixes of alizarin, raw umber and phthalo blue.

5 ◀ Add dark tones Dab the Indian red/alizarin mix on the right cheek, chin and mouth. Change to the No.10 round; mix burnt umber and phthalo blue and darken the eye sockets, the lower face and around the jaw. Add Davy's grey to the mix; paint a dark patch on the hair and behind the left shoulder. With the No.4 brush, darken the shadow on the chin.

6 ▲ Develop the light side of the head Using the No.20 round brush, wet the left side of the head, then apply a pale wash of burnt sienna.

7 ◀ Block in the left background Apply a dilute mix of burnt sienna and ultramarine with the No.20 brush to knock back the white background on the left-hand side of the painting. This will help you to assess the tones more accurately. Block in the sitter's shirt with a wash of ultramarine, then knock it back with burnt umber.

8 ▶ Develop the darks Mix burnt umber and ultramarine and, using the No.4 round and a ruler, draw the straight edge of the board on the left. Define the shirt collar, then lay in the hair with sweeping strokes from the parting to the tips. Wash the dark mix over the right-hand background with the No.20 round.

9 ▼ Add facial details Using the No.10 round, wash a mix of Indian red and alizarin crimson over the shadow on the nose. Sweep dilute burnt sienna over his right cheek. Mix burnt sienna and Winsor violet to give a rich, dark tone. Use the No.4 round to add the darkest shadows under the nose and within the eye sockets.

Master Strokes

Hercules Brabazon (1821–1906)
Head of Goya

Although he is better known for his watercolour landscapes, Brabazon was also an excellent portrait painter. His skills are evident in this interesting study of the Spanish artist Francisco de Goya (1746–1828) as a young man. Goya's black clothing and dark hair blend into the deep charcoal grey background, bringing the focus directly on to the pale oval of his face. The simplicity of the composition and the casual angle of the head give this portrait an informal feel.

Loosely worked brush strokes of grey, brown and blue create a wonderful sense of the colour and texture of the hair.

The eyes are described very simply – with dabs of paint for the pupils and small arcing brush strokes for the eyelids.

10 ▼ **Make adjustments** Darken the shadow tone mix from the previous step and add the pupils. These details bring the image into focus and suddenly the likeness begins to emerge. Develop the lips with mixes of Indian red and alizarin crimson and define the line in the middle with the dark burnt sienna/Winsor violet mix from step 9. Use a mix of alizarin and cadmium red, applied with a 13mm (½in) flat brush, to warm the forehead. Flood in burnt sienna wet-on-wet along the hairline.

THE FINISHED PICTURE

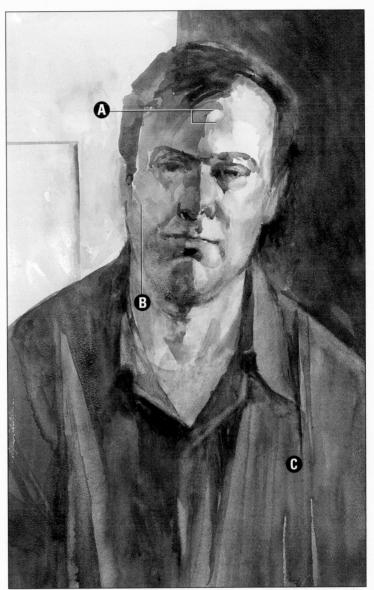

A Hard and soft edges
Wet-on-wet and wet-on-dry techniques give a variety of textures to the patches of flesh colour on the face.

B Warm undercolour
An underpainting of burnt sienna modifies the later washes, adding warmth and depth to the shaded side of the face.

C Broad brushwork
The shirt is loosely painted in broad brush strokes so as not to distract from the focus of the painting – the face.

11 ◄ **Work on the shirt** Using the No.4 round and the full range of flesh tones in your palette, make adjustments across the head – for example, adding warm tones on the neck. Use pure ultramarine and ultramarine mixed with burnt umber to build up the local colour of the shirt and to paint the folds in the fabric.

Sunlight and shadows

Watercolour is an ideal medium for capturing the subtle colours and shapes of shadows created by sunlight filtering into an interior.

What brings an interior to life? The subject matter certainly does – the room needs to have interesting objects, decoration and furniture and these should complement each other well. The composition is also crucial – everything you choose to include should sit pleasingly within the frame. However, one of the most often overlooked aspects of interiors is the lighting.

Light and dark

In this painting, direct sunshine creates an interesting play of light and dark with strong shadows and bright highlights. It illuminates the right wall yet leaves the far one in darkness. The artist has exaggerated this contrast of tone and also the contrast of colour it creates – the warmer browns of the sunlit areas beautifully offset the deeper bluish shadowed areas.

Capturing shadow areas

The key to achieving interesting, variegated shadows is to layer the washes, smudging the paint while it is still wet to give a soft, uneven look that mimics the effect of shadows in real life.

As you progress with the layers of colour in the darkest area of the room – the alcove – the paint will become thicker, but you can add drops of water to dilute the wet paint already applied and thus make sections of the wall less opaque. A similar effect can be achieved with some well-judged rubbing back with damp cotton wool. Varying the tone in this way creates lively and realistic shadows but, remember, you have to work quickly.

It is important to alter the colours as well as the tones in the shadow areas – for instance, half way down the alcove, the artist added more brown to capture light reflected from the warm table.

Before building up the shadow areas, however, it pays to establish the small details you wish to retain, such as the pictures and the items on the table, in the initial stages. This then enables you to focus on the bigger picture – the overall sense of light and shadow in the room. You can return to the details in the very last stages of the painting.

▶ Soft wet-on-wet washes in the shadows contrast with the crisp lines of the furniture in this atmospheric painting of an interior.

YOU WILL NEED

Piece of 300gsm (140lb) Hot-pressed watercolour paper 38 x 27cm (15 x 10½in)

4B pencil

11 watercolours:
Carmine; Cadmium scarlet; Indigo; Aureolin; Yellow ochre; Ultramarine; Payne's grey; Cadmium yellow pale; Cadmium red light;

Monestial green; Prussian blue

Watercolour brushes:
Nos.4, 2, 8, 1, 0 rounds

Mixing dish or palette

Jar of water

Masking fluid and an old No.4 round brush

Cotton wool and cotton bud

White gouache

FIRST STROKES

1 ▶ Sketch the room
Using a 4B pencil, mark the outline of everything in the room. (Note that to attain a strong sense of recession, the artist used a slightly different viewpoint than the one in the photo on the left.) Delineate the shape of the alcove carefully, as this area is a major focus of the painting. The other key objects that should be well defined are the chair and table. Draw the items on the table carefully too, marking in the clock face.

2 ◀ Paint and mask the poppies Mix carmine and cadmium scarlet to create a bright, warm red. Fill in the poppies using a No.4 brush – don't worry about definition at this stage. Once the red paint has dried, apply masking fluid over it with an old No.4 round brush. This will protect the flowers against being affected by the other colours you will be using around them.

3 ▶ Paint the small objects Using a No.2 brush, mix an indigo/aureolin wash for the vase and poppy leaves. Smudge the leaves with damp cotton wool. For the bottles, mix yellow ochre with ultramarine. When dry, lighten the far bottle with aureolin. Mix cadmium scarlet, ultramarine and yellow ochre to outline the clock. Add ultramarine and Payne's grey for the picture frame.

▲ The artist worked from a portable, self-contained watercolour set which is ideal if you're painting on-site.

4 ▼ Wash the right-hand wall Mix yellow ochre and cadmium yellow pale. Using a No.8 brush, wash over the floor and right-hand wall. While the paint is still wet, rub back the light area above the chair with damp cotton wool.

5 ▶ Paint the alcove Add cadmium red light and ultramarine to the mix used in step 4 and paint the top of the right-hand wall wet-on-wet. Create an aubergine colour by adding carmine and a little more ultramarine to this mix. Work over the alcove. Add indigo, Payne's grey and more carmine to the mix and drop it on to the wash with a watery brush. Where the wall joins the alcove, smudge the paint with damp cotton wool.

DEVELOPING THE PICTURE

Complete the main washes by lightly blocking in the table and rug. Then focus your attention on the chair and table, applying paint and then smudging it with damp cotton wool.

6 ▶ Define the chair Paint the skirting board in a pale wash of ultramarine with a little carmine. Make a dilute wash of ultramarine and yellow ochre and wash this pale shade over the table. Then mix carmine and yellow ochre and fill in the rug. Allow to dry. Mix a dark brown from indigo, cadmium red light and yellow ochre and, using the No.2 brush, start to define the chair.

7 ▶ **Smudge the paint**
Use a more dilute dark brown wash for the lower part of the chair. Add cadmium scarlet and yellow ochre to the mix and apply this warmer brown to the chair-back where the light hits it. With damp cotton wool, gently smudge the paint on the chair.

8 ◀ **Add the chair's shadow** Use the dark brown mix to paint the table top and legs. Rub back with damp cotton wool, allow to dry and re-apply the paint. While still wet, gently rub back once more. Mix ultramarine and yellow ochre and, with the good No.4 brush, paint in the shadow of the chair. If the colour looks too dark, rub back with a piece of damp cotton wool.

9 ▼ **Add detail** Mix Payne's grey and cadmium scarlet, then define the far frame with the No.2 brush. Warm the mix with cadmium red light and paint the clock rim; soften any hard lines with a damp cotton bud.

10 ▶ **Build up shadows** Use monestial green for the perfume bottle lid. Wash an ultramarine/ yellow ochre mix over the clock face. Mix Payne's grey with cadmium scarlet and a little ultramarine. Using the No.8 brush, wash over the top of the alcove, thinning the colour as you work downwards. Squeeze a few drops of water from a piece of cotton wool over the wet paint on the wall.

Express yourself
Paint another room

This corner of a bedroom, casually strewn with clothing and jewellery, has been treated in the same way as the step-by-step picture. Diffused dark grey on the shadowed wall contrasts with pale ochre on the lit back wall, the two colours merging where the walls meet.

11 ▼ **Add more detail** Apply a mix of cadmium red light, yellow ochre and Prussian blue to the top of the right-hand wall. Smudge with damp cotton wool. Wash the area around the table with a mix of yellow ochre and ultramarine, then smudge with damp cotton wool. Make various brown and beige mixes of yellow ochre, cadmium scarlet and ultramarine and, using the No.4 brush, define the main features of the two paintings.

12 ▶ **Strengthen shadows** Using a mid-beige mix from step 11, strengthen the tone on the floor. Paint the wall behind the chair too, leaving the area above and to the left of the chair unpainted. Dip the brush in water and tap a few drops on to the painted area to add visual interest.

BLOW GENTLY

TROUBLE SHOOTER

Using a small hair-dryer is a great way to speed up the drying process. It allows you to overlay wash on wash without fear of the colours running together. But be sure to use a low setting – if the force coming from the dryer is too strong it could accidentally blow paint across the paper.

13 ▶ **Refine the shadows** Using the No.2 brush, paint the shadows in the folded cloth on the chair with a weak mix of ultramarine and a touch of carmine. Mix indigo, yellow ochre and cadmium red light and use the No.8 brush to wash over the shadowy area under the table. With a weaker mix, paint the shadow of the chair on the floor and strengthen the wall shadow. Mix yellow ochre and ultramarine to create dark brown; using the No.2 brush, define the edges of the table and chair.

14 ▲ **Apply greens** Mix aureolin, indigo and a little cadmium red light and paint over the vase with the No.4 brush. Add a touch of indigo to make a darker green and apply to the foliage. Dilute this colour with water and apply around the foliage to create a halo-like shadow.

15▲ **Add finishing touches** Mix yellow ochre, cadmium red light and a tiny speck of Prussian blue and apply with the No.8 brush to the large picture frame. Leave to dry. Mix Payne's grey and cadmium red light to make a near-black and go over the picture frame again.

THE FINISHED PICTURE

A Coloured shadows
By using a palette of deep purples applied in layered washes, a very effective sense of late-afternoon shadow has been built up on the alcove wall.

B Focusing the eye
The crumpled fabric lying on the chair was left unpainted. Its dazzling whiteness creates a compelling focal point among the deep shadows that engulf the room.

C Spattered paint
The finishing touches of spattered and dripped red and yellow paint add a sense of excitement and drama to what might otherwise appear a rather sombre scene.

16▲ **Enhance the details** Mix indigo, yellow ochre and carmine and use the No.8 brush to darken the rug. Rub away the masking fluid from the poppies with your fingertip. Mix carmine and cadmium scarlet and paint over them with the No.4 brush, but don't cover the original colour completely. Use dilute Payne's grey and a No.1 brush to show the markings on the chair-back.

Leaping salmon

The flicker of silver as salmon leap up a cascade of water provides one of nature's most thrilling wildlife spectacles – and a great subject for a loose, lively watercolour.

Water tumbling down falls and churning over a boulder-strewn riverbed simply demands to be recorded in paint. But how do you capture the lightness and brightness of the broken water without making it look too solid or laboured? Watercolour, with its potential for spontaneous effects, is the ideal medium for such a dynamic and free-flowing subject.

Spattering techniques

Spattering, for instance, is easily done with watercolour. It creates a speckled or mottled surface ideal for depicting subjects such as foam, spray and turbulent water, which are too intricate to render in any other way. Soft-fibre brushes are the best for flicking colour.

Spattering with masking fluid was also used in this painting to preserve the white of the paper for light areas such as foam and spray. To avoid damaging the bristles, you should try flicking and dribbling the fluid from the handle of your brush (or use an old brush).

Masking fluid is available in two forms: colourless or tinted (yellow or grey). The advantage of using tinted fluid, as here, is that you can see exactly where the masked areas are.

Establishing the focus

Confidence is the key to success in this painting. Rather than working from light to dark in the usual watercolour way, the artist began by establishing the dark forms of the salmon. It is important that they are introduced early on as the composition pivots around their sinuous bodies. Use bold, assertive brush strokes – you don't want to have to rework or modify them. (If necessary, practise painting on scrap paper first).

Continue working in this confident, uninhibited way throughout the painting. Use dilute paint and gestural strokes to capture the tumbling water. Vary the colour of your washes and let them blend spontaneously – remember water picks up reflected colour from its surroundings and from the sky above. In short, try to bring something of the drama of the subject to the way you paint it.

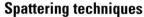

▼ **Spattered paint, vigorous brush marks and bold contrasts of tone help to capture the drama of salmon leaping in foaming water.**

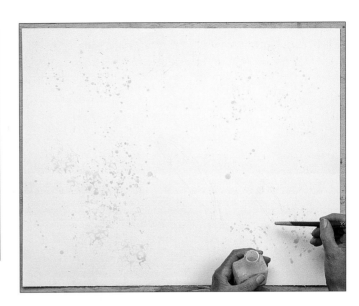

FIRST STEPS

1 ▲ **Spatter masking fluid** Use a B pencil to plot the location of the leaping fish. Dip the handle of a brush in masking fluid and flick and dribble the fluid on to the surface of the paper. Build up an area of dense spattering on the left to balance the fish on the right, then apply spattered masking fluid to the foaming water below the fish.

2 ▲ **Block in the first fish** Mix Prussian blue and cerulean blue. Using a fairly dry 13mm (½in) flat brush, describe the back of the fish with a sweeping stroke. Drag the brush over the pitted surface of the paper so that the wash breaks up in places to create a slightly speckled effect. While the first wash is still wet, charge the same brush with a mix of neutral tint and sepia and use this to describe the underside of the fish. Leave the stripe and eye area white, but allow the two washes to blend and fuse where they touch.

3 ▾ Work on the second fish Using the same brush, paint the second fish. Use neutral tint for the upper body and light red for the belly of the fish. Add the fins in neutral tint and light red.

4 ▸ Spatter around the tail Paint the fish's tail with the neutral tint and light red, then drag the handle of the brush through the wet paint to suggest its ribbed pattern. Load the brush with a dark mix from your palette and lightly spatter across the spray around the tail.

5 ▴ Start to paint the water Apply vigorous strokes of cobalt blue with the 13mm (½in) flat brush, then ultramarine with a touch of violet, followed by raw umber. Use gestural brush marks that trace the movement of the water. Allow the paint to flow together and puddle.

Master Strokes

Gustave Courbet (1819–77)
The Trout

Courbet was the leader of the Realist school in the nineteenth century. This picture highlights his powers of observation and bold style. The fish is not idealized as a wild creature but is shown captive and bleeding from the gills as it is hooked by an angler.

Dark tones surround the fish to define its form and bring it forward in the picture.

To create shimmering scales, dabs of blue-grey, green, pale pink and white have been loosely added over the brown ground.

6 ▼ **Develop broken water** Start to apply colour over the heavily spattered area with broad strokes. Use washes of neutral tint, sepia, ultramarine, violet and Prussian blue, allowing the colours to mingle.

DEVELOPING THE PICTURE

The painting is broadly established and this is a good time to stand back and see what else needs to be done. With a subject such as this, the reference photograph is a jumping-off point only – after a certain point the painting takes on a life of its own. The marks that you have made and the colours that you use will dictate your next moves.

8 ▶ **Add warm colours** Mix a wash of raw sienna, adding a touch of raw umber, and scumble this colour loosely over the lower part of the painting. This will warm the area of the painting, providing a contrast with the predominantly cool palette.

9 ▲ **Add textural marks** Mix Prussian blue and raw umber and work this into the dark area on the left. Use gestural flicking marks that suggest the splashing water. Spatter the same mix across the painting.

7 ▼ **Add more colour to the water** Still using the 13mm (½in) brush, apply a raw umber wash to the dark area in the lower left corner of the picture with vigorous brush marks. Work a pale wash of cobalt blue into the top left of the picture area.

▶ **A range of blues and browns was used for the wet-on-wet washes and spattering to create subtly shifting tones and splashes of colour in the turbulent water. The colours include (from top to bottom): Cerulean blue; Cobalt blue; Ultramarine; Violet; Sepia.**

10 ▾ **Spatter more colours** Wash emerald green across the lower right corner and spatter over it, creating texture with the brush handle (see Expert Advice, opposite). Add raw umber and apply loosely at top left. Spatter this mix and cerulean blue over the entire painting.

11 ▴ **Remove the masking fluid** Make sure the painting is completely dry, then remove the masking fluid by rubbing it gently with your fingertips. As the mask is removed, the sparkling white paper is revealed as foam, spray and swirling water, making sense of the brushed and spattered colour.

A FEW STEPS FURTHER

With the masked areas revealed, the painting assumes its final appearance. The energy of the surging water has been effectively described and the composition is nicely balanced with the dark forms of the fish silhouetted against the foaming water. At this point you could consider emphasizing the tonal contrasts by adding highlights and touches of dark tone.

12 ▴ **Suggest the scales** Drag a piece of white chalk over the surface of the fish. The powdery chalk will be deposited on the raised surface of the paper, suggesting silvery scales.

Express yourself

Fish studies

The streamlined bodies of fish form wonderful, sinuous shapes as they flash through the water or leap up the rapids. To familiarize yourself with their movements, it is a useful exercise to make pencil sketches of fish viewed from different angles. Notice the positions of the fins and the curves of the tails as they power the fish along.

These sketches will help you when making an initial drawing for a fish painting. In the step-by-step, the bodies of the salmon are implied with just a few sweeping brush strokes, so it is important that your underlying drawing is in proportion and accurately reflects the leaping motion.

13▾ Contrast tones Scumble chalk across the darker areas of water. Mix a wash of neutral tint and Prussian blue and, using a No.9 round brush, spatter on this dark tone.

EXPERT ADVICE
Drawing out paint

To create linear texture in spattered areas, draw out the wet paint into squiggly strands and tendrils of colour with the tip of the brush handle. Here, raw sienna and raw umber provide texture over an emerald green wash.

THE FINISHED PICTURE

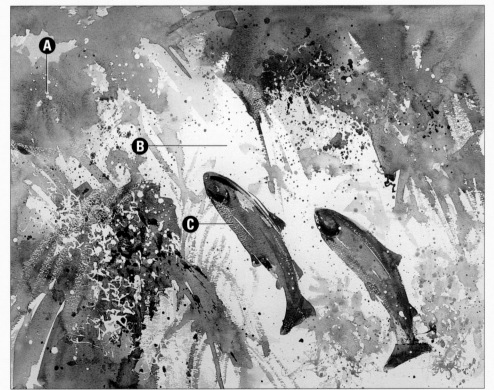

A Masked spatters
The patterns created by masking fluid spattered on to the support at the start read as foam and spray when the mask is removed.

B White paper
Extensive areas of unpainted white paper stand for the sheets of white water cascading down the waterfall.

C Scumbled chalk
Chalk scumbled over the pitted surface of the paper adds a bright, sparkling effect and lends texture to the solid washes.

Sunflowers and bamboo leaves

Contrasting colours and shapes give an exuberant quality to this simple but striking arrangement of flowers and leaves.

Watercolour has a translucency that is perfect for interpreting the delicate, filmy quality of flower petals. The secret to achieving this effect is to work in a logical progression from the first pale areas of wash to the final subtle details.

At first glance, this flower painting looks complex and highly finished. Closer inspection, however, shows that it is actually painted quite simply but with careful attention to modulations of tone and colour.

Building up washes

Working with watercolour washes can be tricky. If you allow the paint to dry between each wash, the colour acquires a hard outline. Applying a wash to a still-wet area, on the other hand, can produce lovely effects, but you risk losing control and creating a mess. The best method for painting flowers is to apply a second wash while the first is still just damp; in this way the colours merge softly to produce subtle effects.

The time factor

Flowers are living things and will not stay still when placed in a vase. Blooms will open or close depending on the light, leaves may droop and petals fall – as happened during the course of this painting. The changes should not be too great, but it's important to make an accurate drawing of the group and leave it unchanged as the painting develops.

▶ **This arrangement exploits the contrast between elegant, sword-like bamboo leaves and full, rounded sunflower heads.**

FIRST STEPS

1 ▼ Make an outline drawing Using a sharp 2B pencil, draw the sunflowers and bamboo leaves in outline, but don't attempt to suggest shading or texture. Extend the image right out to the edges of the picture area.

2 ▼ Begin the first sunflower Mix a wash of cadmium yellow pale, warmed with a hint of cadmium orange. Working on dry paper, start to paint the individual flower petals with a No.3 soft round brush. Add a touch of Winsor violet to the mix for the shaded petals.

3 ▲ Develop the petals Continue to paint the sunflower petals, looking for the subtle changes of tone and warmth or coolness created by light and shadow. When you have painted in all the palest petals, strengthen the wash with more cadmium orange and then put in the deeper tones and the shadows beneath and between the petals. Leave the painting to dry.

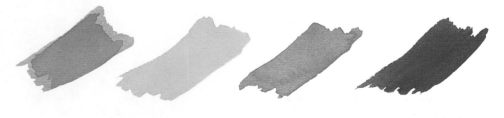

▶ The palette for the petals was based on cadmium orange and cadmium yellow pale with cadmium scarlet and alizarin crimson added to darken some tones.

4 ▼ **Paint the centre of the sunflower** Make a thin, loosely mixed wash of burnt sienna, Vandyke brown and a touch of ultramarine violet, and fill in the flower centre. Don't overwork the paint – let it puddle in places. Because the individual colours are only partially mixed, you will get a subtly variegated effect rather than a flat wash of colour.

A quick impression

Speed and spontaneity are the keynotes in this very different version of the sunflowers. A rapid pencil sketch is overlaid with equally rapid brush strokes and the fluid watercolour washes are allowed to fuse while wet. The aim is to capture the exuberant 'personality' of the flowers and leaves. Elements on the left of the arrangement are half-suggested, allowing the viewer's imagination to complete the image.

5 ◄ **Add darker browns** When the base wash is almost dry, darken it with more ultramarine violet. Then, with the tip of the brush, make small, broken brush strokes and stippled marks to suggest the texture of the closely packed seeds.

6 ► **Bring in some greens** Mix a dilute wash of sap green, enriched with a touch of cadmium orange. Use the brush tip to paint the greenish sepals surrounding the petals. Darken the wash with a hint of ultramarine to suggest the way the sepals curl over into shadow. Use the same colours to fill in the bamboo leaf. Leave to dry.

▶ **For the leaves, sap green is warmed with cadmium lemon and cadmium yellow pale, and cooled with ultramarine.**

Sap green

Cadmium lemon

Cadmium yellow pale

Ultramarine

7 ▼ **Paint the second sunflower** Return to the yellow and green mixes used in steps 2, 3 and 6 to paint the petals and sepals of the next sunflower. Leave to dry. Add a little alizarin crimson or cadmium scarlet to the deepest yellow mix and go over some of the darker petals again.

8 ▲ **Add more leaves** Fill in the flower centre as in steps 4 and 5. Then paint more bamboo leaves. Use sap green as the base colour, adding a little ultramarine and cadmium lemon for the stronger, cooler greens, as on the large vertical leaf. For warmer, yellower leaves, mix cadmium yellow pale with the sap green. For the faded leaves, add a hint of Vandyke brown. Vary the tones of the leaves by adding more or less water to the paint. Leave to dry.

EXPERT ADVICE
Sharp-edged leaves

Bamboo leaves have clean, sharp edges. To capture these, fill in the leaf with colour and then, while the paint is still wet, rinse your brush and stroke a little clean water on to the centre of the leaf. The water will carry some of the pigment to the edges of the leaf, where it will dry, leaving a dark outline.

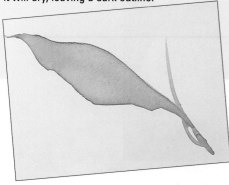

9 ▲ **Complete the third flower** Fill in the chinks of the blue background showing between the flowers and leaves with a wash of ultramarine. Build up the petals on the third sunflower with the mixtures used in step 7, then fill in the centre with tones of brown as before. Add cast shadows to the bamboo leaves with a mix of sap green and ultramarine.

DEVELOPING THE PICTURE

The flowers and leaves are now almost complete and it is time to work on the other elements in the composition – the vase and background. These should be more loosely painted, so as not to compete with the main subject.

10 ◄ **Work on the background**
Loosely brush a watery wash of ultra-marine over the upper right of the picture to give a suggestion of background. Make the wash deeper near the flowers, fading out towards the edges of the paper.

11 ◄ **Paint the vase**
Mix sap green, cadmium lemon and cadmium orange and paint the vase, leaving flecks of white paper for highlights. While the wash is damp, drop in a tiny bit of ultramarine at the top of the vase, letting it bleed.

12 ▾ **Paint the fallen petals** Cut flowers may shed some of their petals, especially on a warm day, but you can use this to your advantage. They add interest to the bottom half of the composition, often a rather 'dead' area, and they also provide a natural colour echo of the flowers themselves. Paint the petals with different shades of yellow, just as you did for the petals on the flowers.

13 ▾ **Finish the vase** Complete the leaves on the left as in step 8. For the unglazed base of the vase, mix burnt sienna and chrome yellow. Dab on Vandyke brown and alizarin crimson for the darker tones on the left, suggesting the vase's rounded form. Let these colours bleed together wet-on-wet.

14 ▾ **Add more background wash** With a No.5 soft round brush, fill in the background on the left-hand side of the picture with a wash of ultramarine – make it slightly stronger than the wash on the right-hand side. Brush the colour on loosely, leaving a few tiny flecks of white paper to give it some sparkle.

15 ▴ **Complete the background wash** Take the blue wash down into the foreground area and into the lower right of the picture. While this is still damp, float on a few small strokes of dilute cadmium yellow pale here and there, just to the right of the flowers and also just beneath the vase.

A FEW STEPS FURTHER

The yellow sunflowers are almost complete and are enhanced by the blue background. Just add some final shadows and details to give the image more depth.

16 ▶ **Add a cast shadow** While the blue wash is still damp (but not wet) mix ultramarine, ultramarine violet and a hint of Vandyke brown and put in the sliver of dark shadow underneath the vase. Let the shadow edge bleed softly into the surrounding blue wash.

17 ▲ **Create dappled light** Work over some of the leaves with very dilute ultramarine applied with criss-cross strokes. This gives the effect of shadows with tiny chinks of light in between.

18 ▲ **Complete the sunflowers** Mix cadmium yellow pale, cadmium orange and alizarin crimson. Add touches of this warm yellow to the petals and dot a few highlights on the flower centres.

THE FINISHED PICTURE

A Transparent washes
Delicate washes of watercolour allow light to reflect back off the paper and suggest the translucent petals.

B Exciting shapes
The bamboo leaves were extended right to the edges of the picture to create lively positive and negative shapes.

C Blue background
A blue background wash contrasts effectively with the bright yellow flowers while harmonizing with the greens.

Going underground

Most of the time, travelling on crowded trains might seem a bit of a chore. But remember, there's a potential painting in every carriage and on every platform.

Although painting from real life has much to commend it, there are occasions when working from a photographic reference is useful, and sometimes essential. This step-by-step is a good example. The scene at a London Underground station would be almost impossible to render working from real life. Instead, the artist has photographed it and painted it later in the comfort of his home. Remember, a compact camera can fit into a pocket or handbag and – if used with an eye for the potential of everyday situations – can provide a wealth of painting material.

A painterly subject

In choosing what to photograph, the artist's eye for colour and composition led him to focus on a man sitting alone on his suitcase, oblivious to all around him. The subject is naturally framed by the wall on the left, and by the rail tracks on the top right-hand side. The colours in the photo also work well – the red of the jacket immediately throws the subject to the fore, while the muted clothes of the other figures help them to recede.

When it came to translating the photo into a painting, the artist tweaked colours and details. The figures and objects surrounding the seated man were reduced to simple planes of colour and restricted to a palette of blues and greens in order to emphasize the solitary figure in his red jacket.

▲ **Dabbing cotton wool on damp washes of paint has helped to create the wonderful array of textures, tones and edges in this picture of a traveller on the London Underground.**

FIRST STROKES

1 ▼ Sketch the main outline Using the photo as a guide, sketch the image with a 4B pencil. The key elements to capture are the strong diagonal lines of the tracks in the top right-hand corner, the seated man in the foreground and the outlines of the figures behind him.

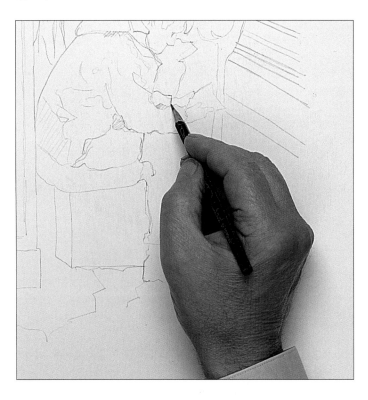

2 ▼ Block in the clothes Mix a dilute wash of cadmium scarlet and ultramarine; apply to the jacket, using a No.6 brush. Mix Prussian blue and cadmium yellow pale to paint the bag next to the face of the seated figure. Using dilute yellow ochre, wash the jacketed figure at upper left. Add a little Prussian blue to the wash to make a green for the trousers of the figure on the right. Now mix Prussian blue and Payne's grey and paint the trousers of the seated figure. Dilute the wash and apply to the figure's shoe.

EXPERT ADVICE
Special effects

To achieve areas of lighter tone just after you have applied a watercolour wash, gently rub out sections of paint with a small piece of damp cotton wool. Here, a pale patch has been lifted from the seat of the dark blue trousers, and another area is being removed from the green trousers.

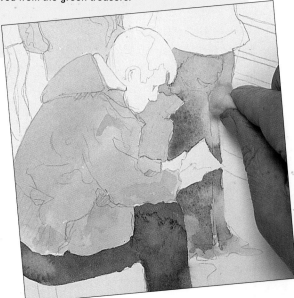

3 ▼ **Continue blocking in** Mix yellow ochre, cadmium yellow pale and a dot of Prussian blue; paint the undefined figure on the left. Mix ultramarine and Prussian blue and wash the jacket of the figure on the right. To this mix, add cadmium scarlet, yellow ochre, and a little more ultramarine to creaate a black-brown for the suitcase. Use a dilute wash of ultramarine to fill in the small area behind the seated figure.

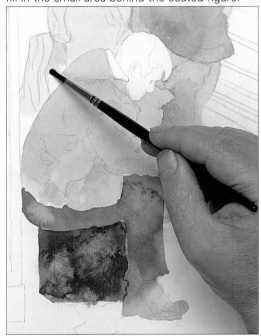

4 ▶ **Paint the platform** Mix yellow ochre and cadmium yellow to 'draw' the line on the platform. Add cadmium scarlet to make a skin tone for the face. Mix indigo, ultramarine and yellow ochre; paint the tracks, using a No.8 brush. Wash dilute cadmium yellow pale, Prussian blue and ultramarine over the platform, and dilute ultramarine on the wall. Mix cadmium red light and Payne's grey for the background.

5 ▶ **Add tracks** Using a No.4 brush, apply a yellow ochre/ultramarine wash to the back of the hair. Then paint the tracks with the blue trouser mix and allow to dry. Wash yellow ochre across the tracks. Add ultramarine and Payne's grey and define their contours.

6 ▼ **Silhouette head and hands** Define the hood with Payne's grey. Make an ultramarine/yellow ochre mix and wash over the jacket at upper left. Mix indigo and yellow ochre to darken the green trousers, adding small dabs of pure yellow ochre and indigo while the paint is still wet.

7 ◀ **Build up tone** Mix Payne's grey and ultramarine and, using the No.6 brush, apply this to the dark blue trousers. Leave the knee section lighter, and rub back the whole area with damp cotton wool. Mix ultramarine and cadmium yellow pale and wash over the platform with the No.8 brush. Squeeze damp cotton wool so that a few drops of water fall on to this area and rub gently to give a mottled effect to the paint surface.

DEVELOPING THE PICTURE

The basic areas of colour are now blocked in and it is time to develop the forms with tonal shading. Continue using damp cotton wool or a cotton bud to rub back any hard edges.

8 ▲ Add texture to the platform Returning to the No.6 brush, overlay a wash of ultramarine and Payne's grey on the platform area in the bottom left-hand corner.

9 ▲ Build up tone With a cadmium scarlet/yellow ochre mix, vary the tone on the red jacket. Define areas of the green trousers with indigo and cadmium yellow pale. Mix cadmium yellow, scarlet, yellow ochre and cadmium yellow pale; paint the hands. Now mix indigo, carmine, cadmium red light and yellow ochre, and apply to the suitcase. Wash an ultramarine/yellow ochre/Prussian blue mix over the blue jacket and bag.

10 ▶ Add detail Return to the jacket, mixing Payne's grey and cadmium scarlet and dotting under the arm with the No.4 brush. Use the brush to smudge the colour from under the arm to the edge of the jacket. Draw a curve at the side of the jacket to indicate a fold line.

Express yourself
Single or return?

Another familiar scene at an Underground station, this composition is full of graphic linear elements, such as the ticket-office window, the noticeboard and the bands on the wall.

11 ▲ **Add features** Use cotton wool to smudge any hard red edges. Mix yellow ochre, cadmium scarlet and a little ultramarine. With a No.2 brush, define the ear, nose, forehead and cheek. Rub back the cheek with a damp cotton bud. Apply a mix of yellow ochre and ultramarine to the hair.

▼ **Cadmium scarlet/yellow ochre (left) and cadmium scarlet/ultramarine (right) are the two basic mixes used for the red jacket.**

12 ▶ **Vary tones** Mix cadmium yellow, ultramarine and cadmium scarlet, then wash along the platform edge with the No.8 brush. Darken the rails with a Payne's grey/ultramarine mix.

A FEW STEPS FURTHER

Finish off the picture by working some additional surface interest to give the painting character.

13 ▲ **Add foreground interest** Mix indigo and aureolin and wash over the platform area. Flick a few drops of water on to the wet paint. Allow to dry, and wash roughly over the top with dilute cadmium yellow, using the No.8 brush. Rub back with a piece of damp cotton wool.

14 ▲ **Spotting and dribbling** Using the No.4 brush, apply dilute washes of cadmium yellow, cadmium red light and ultramarine to the wall. Using the No.2 brush, draw an ultramarine border on the wall and platform. To create a lively picture surface, dribble a line of cadmium yellow pale on the left and then add dots and lines of cadmium red light.

THE FINISHED PICTURE

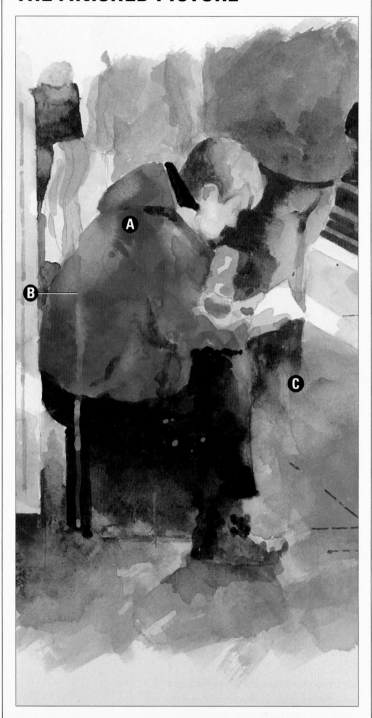

A Textured paint
The red jacket is the focus of the painting. It has been given a deep, textured appearance through the layering of colour and rubbing back of the paint with pieces of damp cotton wool.

B Distressed finish
By purposefully adding dribbles and spots of brightly coloured paint to the darker areas of the finished composition, the artist has given the painting a lift and a feeling of immediacy.

C Abstract shapes
The washes of colour around the central seated figure have been intentionally kept loose and abstract. They are represented as blocks of toned-down colour with little detail.

Cubist cathedral

Architecture is a great subject for Cubist painting. Try rearranging the walls, roofs and buttresses of this cathedral to create an explosion of planes and colours.

In this unusual interpretation of Winchester Cathedral in southern England, the artist was struck by the patterns of light and shadow playing across the building. The sunlit walls glowed warm in contrast to the cooler shadows – and these geometric shapes of contrasting colour and tone inspired the artist to make a painting in the Cubist style.

A radical approach

In Cubism, the artist is free to view the subject from every possible angle – from the side, front, above and below – so several aspects can be shown at once. Angles and proportions can be exaggerated and the light source varied to enhance the geometric structure of the painting.

The idea is to create a picture which is not a 'view' in the conventional sense, but which is a personal interpretation of the subject. Most importantly, the painting is treated as an entity with its own inherent qualities. The subject is less important than the abstract elements of colour, tone, line and shape, and the arrangement of these elements within the picture space.

Magnificent scale

Architecture lends itself readily to Cubism, and in this painting the gables, buttresses, arches and rooftops of the cathedral are fragmented into planes of colour and pieced together to form a pattern of abstract shapes. Through a subtle arrangement of diagonals and tilted planes, the cathedral rises up to the top of the picture, evoking a sense of its magnificent scale.

To create the painting, the artist first made a sketch, using a much steeper, more dramatic viewpoint than the one in the photograph. He also used artistic licence with the colours, emphasizing the golden glow of the sunlit walls. These contrast well with slanting shadows of cool grey-green.

YOU WILL NEED

300gsm (140lb) rough watercolour paper 56 x 38cm (22 x 15in)

13 watercolours: Davy's grey; Raw sienna; Winsor green; Yellow ochre; Cobalt blue; Burnt umber; Payne's grey; Ultramarine; Raw umber;

Burnt sienna; Gold ochre; Cobalt turquoise; Indian red

Brushes: No.1 rigger; 19mm (¾in) flat; Nos.2, 6 and 12 rounds

Mixing dish or palette

Metal ruler and blotting paper

▲ The beautiful surface texture of this watercolour has been built up using printing, blotting and scumbling techniques.

FIRST STEPS

1 ▼ **Put in the main lines** Draw the main lines of the composition with dilute Davy's grey applied with the No.1 rigger brush. Davy's grey does not stain the paper so you can lift out lines and make adjustments.

2 ▼ **Add more lines** Continuing with Davy's grey, emphasize the straight lines, using the imprinting technique (see Expert Advice, opposite). Add more lines with raw sienna and the rigger brush.

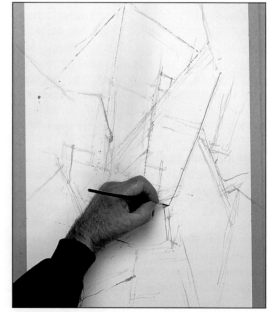

3 ▼ Paint lights and shadows Make a dilute wash of raw sienna for the light areas, and another of Winsor green mixed with yellow ochre for darker ones. Using these two washes and the 19mm (¾in) flat brush, add blocks of light and shadow on the tower. Work inwards from the edge, allowing the colour to fade out as you go – this accentuates the sharp-edged, angular form of the church. Leave to dry.

4 ▲ Indicate the sky Mix a dilute wash of cobalt blue, and suggest the sky by making a straight line with the edge of the flat brush and then dragging the paint across it. Gently blot the inner edge with blotting paper to soften it (right).

EXPERT ADVICE
Imprinting lines

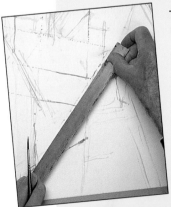

There are lots of straight lines in this painting and you don't want them to be too obvious. For unobtrusive lines, brush a small amount of paint along the edge of a ruler. Hold the ruler with the fingers of both hands and press down on to the paper, lifting it off to reveal a straight but broken line.

▲ A mix of cobalt blue and cobalt turquoise is used to capture the summer sky. The warm tones of the stone walls are made from mixes of gold ochre, raw sienna and burnt umber.

DEVELOPING THE PICTURE

You have now created a strong, geometric structure, upon which you can build up the planes and facets of colour with carefully applied washes.

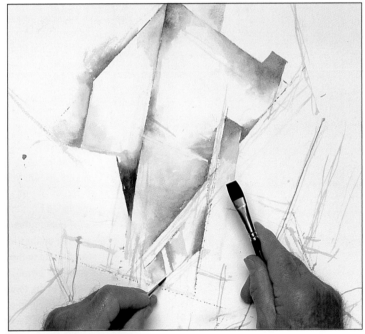

5 ▲ Develop shadows Build up the shadows on the stone walls of the cathedral, using the same colours as in step 3 but adding burnt umber for the darker parts. Work around the windows with raw sienna, alternating between the No.2 round brush (for the outlines) and the 19mm (¾in) flat (to fill out blocks of colour).

6 ▶ Add the roof and buttresses Using the No.2 round and 19mm (¾in) flat, define the grey roof with diagonal lines and strokes of Payne's grey and cobalt blue. (You can achieve straight lines by steadying the ferrule of the brush against a ruler held just above the surface of the paper.) Outline the buttresses with mixes of raw sienna, burnt umber and ultramarine, then add shadows around them with raw umber and burnt umber.

7 ▼ Fill in the walls Mix a dilute wash of raw sienna and use the 19mm (¾in) flat brush to fill in the planes of the cathedral walls. Gently blot the colour with blotting paper to soften it.

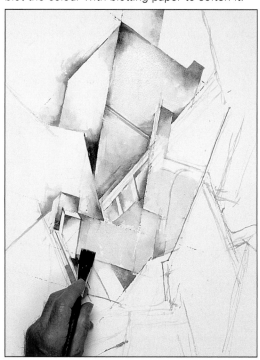

8 ▼ Use washes and scumbles Just above the buttresses on the left, use the No.2 round to draw two angled lines in burnt sienna to form the lower edge of the roof. Fill in the resulting area with a flat wash of dilute Payne's grey. Mix Winsor green, gold ochre and a hint of cobalt blue. Pick up a small amount on the No.6 round and roughly scumble it over the upper part of the tower, and the triangular shape to the right of it, to give a suggestion of texture.

Express yourself

Light fantastic

In this picture of Lyndhurst church in England, the composition is more conventional than our step-by-step – but artistic licence has been taken with the lighting. The church tower appears to be lit not from the outside but internally – which seems appropriate for a 'House of God'. Our eye is led from the solid colour of the angular shapes in the foreground to the luminous, jewel-like planes of the tower. The low viewpoint and the imposing vertical add to the mood of religious awe.

Master Strokes

Maurice de Vlaminck
(1876–1958)
Village and Church

Just as in the step-by-step project, this painting is full of strong diagonals and unexpected tilted planes. The liveliness of the composition is underlined by the exciting use of light and dark tones – look at the way the roofs and the walls create a chequer-board effect. The village appears almost to be alive, as if some great event is about to happen here.

A simple pale line in the sky suggests a ray of sun shining out from behind the clouds.

Sharp, jagged brush strokes in the sky echo the shape of the spire and rooftops.

© ADAGP, Paris and DACS, London 2002

Delicate dabs of paint used for tree blossom contrast with the strong, angular brushwork in the rest of the painting.

The diagonal road at bottom right leads the eye towards the focal point of the painting – the church tower.

9 ▲ Work on the right Use the No.2 round and the 19mm (¾in) flat to outline and fill in tonal areas on the buttresses and pillars. Use raw sienna for warm tones, ultramarine with a burnt umber wash for grey tones, and a stronger mix of ultramarine and burnt umber for dark areas. Echo the sky colour with cobalt blue.

10 ▲ Introduce greens Suggest more walls, cornices and buttresses by adding lines and washes of raw sienna, burnt sienna and cobalt blue. Mix a warm green from Winsor green, raw sienna and a hint of burnt umber, then fill in the large shape on the right with the No.12 round brush. Leave to dry.

11 ▼ **Outline some windows** Apply a thin wash of gold ochre over the parts of the tower already painted. While this dries, pick up some Winsor green on the rigger brush and outline arched windows on the green area you painted in step 10. Then, using raw sienna, paint simple lines and graded washes to suggest the tall arched windows at the top of the tower.

12 ▶ **Deepen the tones** Using the 19mm (¾in) flat and washes of ultramarine, complete the sky area. Leave to dry, then apply a wash of cobalt turquoise over the left-hand part of the sky. Block in the triangular shapes at top right and bottom centre with a greenish wash of burnt sienna, Winsor green and raw sienna. Next to the triangle at the bottom, use raw sienna and Payne's grey to paint more Cubist shapes and draw in the small arched windows. Darken the tone of the wall in the centre of the picture with a thin wash of Indian red.

13 ▼ **Paint smaller shapes** Add slanting lines of cobalt blue to the sky. Block in shapes at bottom right with gold ochre, raw sienna, Payne's grey and cobalt blue. Blend a wash of gold ochre wet-on-wet over raw sienna to fill in the angled wall on the left, then add a shadow of Payne's grey to the roof above it.

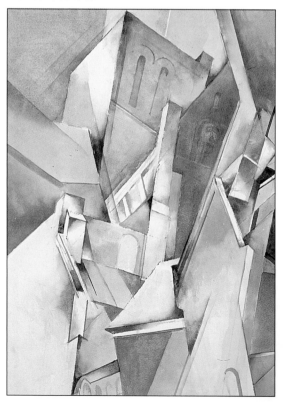

A FEW STEPS FURTHER

You have now successfully developed the interplay of colour between the soft, warm yellows and the cool blues and green-greys of the stonework. All that remains is to complete the arched windows.

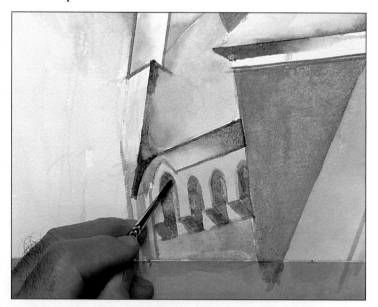

14 ▲ **Fill in the lower windows** Use gold ochre for the stone corbels jutting out from the wall beneath the arched windows at the bottom of the picture. Mix a greyish-brown from raw umber, cobalt blue and gold ochre and fill in the windows with the No.2 round brush.

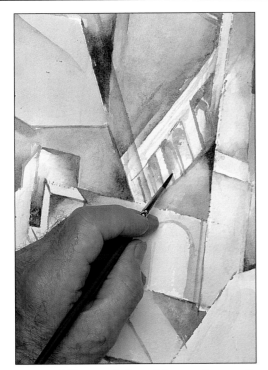

15 ▲ **Add more windows** Mix raw sienna with a touch of burnt umber and fill in the row of arched windows in the middle of the picture, allowing the colour to fade out at the edges.

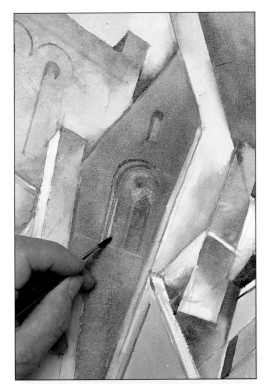

16 ▲ **Define the stained-glass window** Create highlights on the large stained-glass window by lifting out some colour with the edge of a dampened flat brush. Redefine the darker outlines, using the No.2 round brush and the raw sienna/burnt umber mix from step 15.

THE FINISHED PICTURE

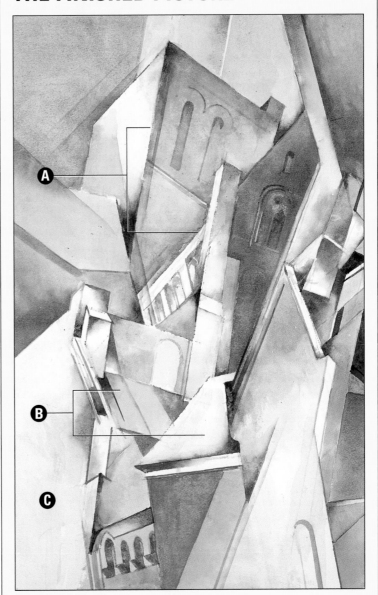

A Varied viewpoints
The eye is kept on the move, directed up and down along the strong diagonals of the rooftops and buttresses.

B Sense of space
The overlapping facets of the cathedral suggest volume and a sense of space, creating a three-dimensional look.

C White paper
Areas of untouched paper provide a contrast to the earthy colours of the painting and suggest air and light.

Tree-lined road

Transform a bleak, monochrome winter scene into a warm, atmospheric watercolour by adding a little sunshine and touches of colourful autumn foliage.

The two stately trees dramatically outlined against the sky are a major feature of this village scene. The reference photograph was taken in the winter – a good time for artists to study trees, as, devoid of foliage, their shape, structure and proportions are easier to see. What you learn from painting winter trees will reap rewards when you come to paint trees in summer and autumn.

With his long experience of observing and painting trees, the artist felt free to add some clumps of autumn foliage to the bare winter ones in the photo to give them added colour and interest.

By using warm colours throughout and adding a blue sky, the artist has created a lively interpretation of the subject.

To enliven further the colours and emphasize the contrast, the artist added sunlight to the overcast scene. In the painting, the sun is low and off to the right, throwing long shadows across the road. It also brings out the cylindrical form of the trees and the angular form of the cottage.

Using a rigger brush

The branches of the trees were painted with a rigger brush. This has extra-long hairs and can make very expressive marks. If you've never used one, make some practice strokes first to learn how to control the brush.

Try sketching some simple trees. Hold the brush near the ferrule to make small marks, but if you want to exploit the flexibility of the brush for creating elegant, tapering lines, hold it lightly, nearer the end of the handle. Keep your hand still and move the brush with your fingers, letting the long hairs twist and bend to make delicate strokes.

▼ **Warm, sunlit areas contrast with cooler shadows and an expanse of blue sky in this picturesque study of a tree-lined road.**

FIRST STEPS

1 ▶ **Sketch the scene**
Using a 4B pencil,
make an outline drawing
of the scene. You might
find it helpful to mark the
horizon line lightly and
visualize the lines of the
cottage roof and walls
receding to the vanishing
point. Feel free to omit
ugly details such as
the street light and
road markings.

2 ◀ **Lay down the initial wash**
Tilt up your board slightly.
Using a 38mm (1½in) flat
brush, dampen the paper,
except for the cottage area,
with clean water. Change to a
19mm (¾in) flat and mix a pale
wash of raw sienna – make
the colour a little stronger than
you need, as it will dilute on
the damp surface of the paper.
Brush the wash across the
lower part of the sky and the
foreground.

3 ▼ **Add warmth to the sky** While the paper is still just damp,
sweep a band of thinly diluted cadmium red across the lower
sky, just above the band of raw sienna. Allow it to melt softly into
the raw sienna to give a touch of autumnal afternoon warmth.

DEVELOPING THE PICTURE

These initial blushes of colour will establish the overall
warm tonality of the scene, as they will glow through
the overlaid washes of colour to come.

4 ▲ **Paint the upper sky** Mix a wash of ultramarine and a
little cobalt blue. Still using the 19mm (¾in) flat brush,
sweep this across the upper sky, letting the colour drift
gently down the damp paper in a graduated wash.

5 ▶ Finish the sky
Lighten the wash with more water as you work down the paper. Make flicking diagonal strokes at the edges of the picture to give some movement to the sky (as long as the paper is still damp, these will dry as soft shapes). Leave the mid-section of the sky untouched.

6 ▲ Block in the background Use some of the ultramarine sky colour to make an underwash for the line of trees glimpsed in the far distance. Make a series of short, vertical strokes with the tip of the brush.

7 ▼ Underpaint the trees Lightly place a few broad, vertical strokes of burnt sienna around the tops of the trees, keeping the brush almost dry. Pick up a little more raw sienna on the brush tip and paint the tree-trunks with short, horizontal strokes.

8 ▶ Paint the cottage roof Add some cadmium red to the raw sienna on your palette to warm it. Change to a No.14 round brush and paint the roofs of the cottage, leaving flecks of white paper to stand for the branches of the small tree on the right.

9 ▼ Paint the chimneys Darken the mix slightly with a hint of ultramarine and, using a No.6 round brush, paint the chimneys and chimney pots. Leave slivers of bare paper for the flashing at the top and base of the chimneys.

10 ▲ Put in the windows Use a very dilute mix of ultramarine and cobalt blue to show the sky reflected in the window panes, varying the tone to suggest light and shadow. Leave the glazing bars white, but blur them slightly so that they are not over-defined.

11 ◀ Paint the garden wall Mix together cadmium red, light red and a touch of ultramarine to make a slightly cooler red than that used on the roof. Paint the garden wall with the tip of the No.14 round brush, leaving flecks of white here and there. Paint around the posts in the foreground. Mix a green from lemon yellow and ultramarine and use this to suggest moss and foliage growing on the wall.

12 ▶ Return to the trees Mix lemon yellow and a little raw sienna to make a light, warm yellow. With the No.6 round brush, start to define the main clumps of foliage on the tall trees. Hold the brush almost parallel with the paper and work it with a sideways motion, letting the colour break up on the textured surface of the paper.

13 ▼ Paint dark foliage Add more raw sienna and some ultramarine to the wash. Put in the dark green clumps of foliage, again laying the brush almost flat to the paper and skipping it lightly across the surface with a sideways motion to make broken-edged marks, as before.

14 ◀ Paint the branches Use broken strokes of burnt sienna to suggest clumps of brown leaves, letting the colour blur into the green. Mix a near-black from ultramarine, raw sienna and light red and paint the branches with a No.1 rigger brush. Start at the trunk and pull the brush in the direction of growth, skipping in and out of the foliage clumps. Vary the pressure on the brush to make the lines swell and taper.

Express yourself
Pen and colour wash

This country scene has a similar composition to the one in the step-by-step. The curve of the road leads the eye into the picture and tall trees dominate the sky area. This time the scene is worked up in more detail. The initial line drawing is made with a dip pen and waterproof Indian ink and is then washed over with watercolour. The ink lines give structure to the image and sharpen up architectural features, while the freely applied washes create a fresh, lively feel. The pen has been used in a similar way to the rigger brush to suggest the tree branches.

15 ▶ **Put in distant trees** With the No.6 round brush, model the tree-trunks by painting their shadowed sides with a mix of ultramarine and light red (see Expert Advice, right). Suggest the slanting shadows cast on to the trunks by the branches. Paint the more distant trees with varied mixes of ultramarine and light red, leaving a broken glimmer of white paper along the top of the wall.

EXPERT ADVICE
Modelling the trunks

To suggest the cylindrical form of the tree-trunks, first dampen them with water and then put in the shadow colour down one edge with a slightly wavering vertical stroke. The colour will fade out softly on the damp surface, creating a tonal graduation from dark to light.

16 ◀ **Work on the foreground** Use the same colours and techniques as for the two main trees to paint the foliage and grass on the left (paint these slightly more freely – elements on the edges of the image should be understated, so as not to compete with the centre of interest). Mix lemon yellow with a touch of ultramarine and paint the grass verge on the right with loose strokes of the No.14 brush.

17 ▲ **Model the cottage** Suggest the kerb with light red and ultramarine. Mix a dilute wash of ultramarine and a hint of light red. Using the No.6 brush, paint shadows on the brick wall, roofs and chimneys. Clean your brush, then put in the shadows on the cottage.

18 ▲ **Add cast shadows** Indicate the kerb on the left with curved strokes of raw sienna greyed with ultramarine. Leave to dry, then use the ultramarine/light red mix to put in the shadows cast across the road by the small tree on the right. Darken the mix slightly for the broken shadow in the immediate foreground, cast by unseen trees to the right.

Relaxing inside the house

Cool blues, mauves, pinks and greys, enlivened with touches of brighter colour, create the right mood for this tranquil study.

This relaxed study shows off the versatility of the watercolour medium. Working with wet-on-wet washes, colours have drifted into each other to suggest the luxurious texture and the fall of the velvet throws on the sofa.

And these large expanses of colour contrast effectively with the more detailed study of the sitter. Moreover, the warmish pinks and purples of the sofa covers – together with the browns of the table and floor – also play off against the cool colours of the subject's clothes. This contrast helps to focus attention on the sitter. In terms of colour, the picture is further lifted by the lively pattern of blues and yellows on her blouse.

Looking at shape

Understanding how shapes work together is a major part of painting. The woman's pose – half lying, half sitting – creates an interesting, fluid shape. This is set off against the angularly shaped expanses of the velvet throws. The coffee table in the foreground helps lead the eye into the picture.

▲ Note how most of the detailed work in the painting has been reserved for the sitter and her clothes. The rest of the painting has been completed in relatively loose washes.

388

FIRST STROKES

1 ▼ **Sketch in the scene** Using a 2B pencil and light but legible strokes, sketch the model and the draped sofa, checking the angles and proportions of the figure (see Introducing figure drawing, page 151). Don't be afraid to erase parts of the drawing with a putty rubber and start again.

YOU WILL NEED

Piece of 300gsm (140lb) Not watercolour paper 28 x 38cm (11 x 15in)

2B pencil

Putty rubber

Brushes: Nos.10, 6 and 2 rounds

15 watercolours: Winsor violet; Naples yellow; Burnt sienna; Purple madder alizarin; Permanent rose; Payne's grey; French ultramarine; Raw sienna; Burnt umber; Sepia; Cerulean blue; Black; Emerald; Raw umber; Cadmium red

2 ▲ **Establish the back-drop** With a No.10 round brush, block in the background throw with light washes of Winsor violet. Now take up a No.6 round and work on some smaller areas. Begin on the face and hands with a very watery Naples yellow and the broad headband with burnt sienna. Throw the model's head forward by adding strong shadows in Winsor violet behind it.

DEVELOPING THE PICTURE

The main areas of your composition are now blocked in, and the pale and brighter colour registers are established. Progress by working with a range of other colours, right across the picture, using various paint thicknesses and techniques.

3 ▲ **Fill in the scene** With the No.10 brush, paint the foreground fabric in purple madder alizarin, and deepen the background fabric with mixes of purple madder alizarin and Winsor violet, adding permanent rose highlights. With a wash of Payne's grey and a touch of French ultramarine, paint the trousers, the fringed shawl, and the shadows on the blouse and wall. Use raw sienna over burnt sienna for the sofa, raw sienna on the sitter's headband, Naples yellow for the feet and French ultramarine for the mug.

4 ▲ **Add upper-body detail** Changing to a No.6 round brush, use the tip to pattern the blouse with watery raw sienna. Add a little more Payne's grey on the fringed shawl. Dot in the design on the headband in burnt umber and sepia.

5 ▲ **Brighten the blouse** Still using the pointed tip of the No.6 brush, lift the whole scene by painting in the blue parts of the blouse pattern with cerulean blue.

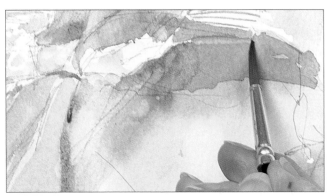

6 ▲ **Paint in the book** Now bring the model's book into the picture, balancing the right-hand side of the painting. Use the fine tip of the No.6 brush to sketch in an outline of the book cover in watery sepia. Put in the faintest suggestion of the pages in the same colour. Working wet-on-wet, use sepia and Payne's grey to block in the book cover. With a mix of purple madder alizarin and Payne's grey, paint the shadow of the book on the throw.

7 ▲ **Work on the large areas** Taking up the No.10 brush, start working up more depth and richness on the two throws. Use purple madder alizarin on both of them, laying thin washes over the dried colour to suggest the texture and sheen of velvet.

◄ Sepia (top), Winsor violet (bottom right) and purple madder alizarin (left) have been used extensively in the picture and help to set its overall colour key. They harmonize well with each other, creating an air of calm.

EXPERT ADVICE
Be complementary

By making use of complementary colours – opposites on the colour wheel – in a prominent part of the scene, you can really lift the whole. Here, placing brown-yellow and blue together in the blouse's pattern enhances the colours and brings a bright but balanced element to the picture.

8 ▲ **Define the facial features** Now turn your attention to the face. With a No.2 round, start to add some fine detailing with intense sepia paint. Wash a little watery burnt sienna over the lips.

9 ▼ **Intensify the darks** With the No.10 and No.6 brushes, use a mix of cerulean blue and black to define the feet and legs by adding shadows on and between them. Intensify the shadows across the blouse, too. Using the No.10 brush, wash strong Naples yellow across the table as a base colour.

10 ▼ **Work on some detail** Use the same blue-black mix and the tip of the No.6 brush to define the shawl's fringe, then dot ultramarine along its border. Mix up cerulean and emerald paints and wash this across the wall behind the sofa. Notice how leaving the pencil underdrawing in has created some surface interest and definition.

Express yourself

A different viewpoint

This painting, also in watercolours, creates a different mood to the step-by-step one. The high viewpoint – combined with the curled, sleeping body position – provides a highly original figure study. Note how the model's nightgown is beautifully described by controlled wet-on-wet washes. The contrast in tone here – from the white of the paper to the deep blue shadow in the middle of her curl – really brings out the form of the body. The teapot and cup and saucer in the corner pick up on blue of the nightgown and help balance the composition.

11 ▲ **Adding definition** With the No.6 round, sweep lines of dry sepia, burnt umber and raw umber across the table to suggest wood grain. Using a 'palette mud' mix of black, burnt umber and ultramarine, strengthen the shadows on the legs and next to the mug. Add sepia to this mix to build up the tone of the book. Paint a little sepia and burnt sienna on the feet and hands, and a touch more detailing on the fringed border of the scarf.

A FEW STEPS FURTHER

Now that you have worked hard on bringing up the detail on the reclining figure, even up the balance of the picture by giving a little more attention to the larger expanses of plain colour on the throws and sofa seat.

12 ► **Finish the drapes** Wash some plain water across the throws to give them more drama and depth. Using Winsor violet and the No.6 brush, strengthen the shadows on the background throw. Wash a little cadmium red lightly over the foreground throw.

13 ▲ **Bring up the sofa** Using the No.10 round, add the final touch by washing watery sepia across the front of the sofa seat. Now the drapes, table and model are all well-balanced, and the central figure retains its solidity, strength and interesting visual detail.

THE FINISHED PICTURE

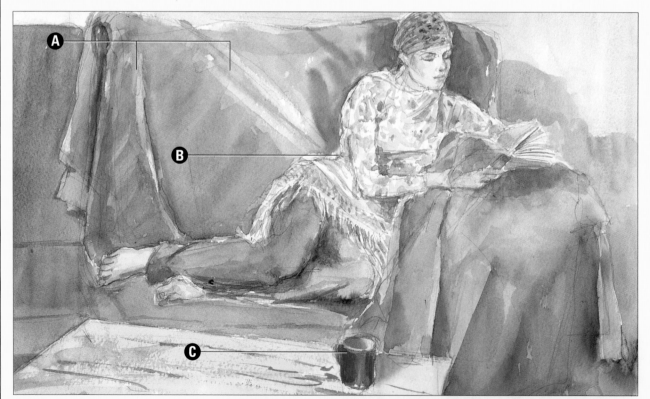

A White highlights
The tiniest flecks of unpainted white paper are sufficient to represent white highlights on the luxurious fabric.

B Central interest
Attention to detail by painting the pattern on the fringed shawl brings a point of interest to the centre of the picture.

C Drawing the viewer in
The artist has placed a strongly coloured object – the mug – in the foreground to help draw the viewer into the picture.

Orange lilies

Use watercolours and a touch of white gouache to help capture the exotic blooms and glossy leaves of these fabulous, showy flowers.

▲ **These lilies are painted with a light touch that emphasizes their fresh beauty.**

Watercolourists love painting flowers because the medium lends itself so well to the subject matter. Watercolour has a sensitivity and translucency that perfectly matches the delicacy of petals.

To get the best results when tackling flower studies, spend time on your initial sketch; if necessary, make colour notes or take a digital or polaroid photo. Flowers tend to wilt – particularly under strong lights – so work quickly, as your arrangement could look quite different a couple of hours into your painting.

Mixing or layering

When using watercolours, there are essentially two ways of blending colours – physically or optically. To mix them physically means combining two or more colours on the palette – mixing red and yellow to make orange, for example. The other method involves laying one colour over another dry one on the paper in transparent veils. For instance, if you paint yellow over red, the eye will 'read' this as orange. The artist in this project has primarily used this optical method, since it preserves the purity of the colours. Be careful not to overdo it – three layers is generally considered the maximum you can apply without muddying the colours.

In addition, to paint the lilies the artist has relied heavily on the use of complementary colours such as orange-reds and blue-greens. These are colours that lie opposite each other on the colour wheel and so set each other off to best advantage.

FIRST STEPS

1 ▼ Make an initial sketch The starting point for the painting is to make an accurate drawing. Use a 2B pencil to map the outline of the vase and the spray of lilies. Notice how the pointed leaves overlap one another.

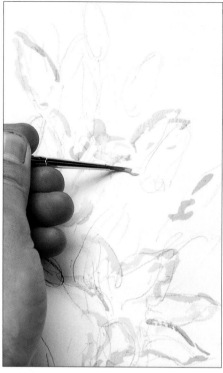

2 ▲ Start on the flowers Using a No.2 round brush, lay in the outlines of the flower-heads in cadmium orange.

3 ▶ Create hazy shadows Make two very watery mixes of cerulean blue and raw umber. Using a 25mm (1in) flat brush, mark in some of the creases in the fabric backdrop with cerulean blue. The way the flowers are lit creates a soft shadow behind them. Wet the left side of the paper with clean water and wash in the cast shadow, using cerulean blue and then, along the left edge, raw umber.

◀ Leaf and stem shapes were made by manipulating a 25mm (1in) flat brush. Practise the following strokes before tackling the painting:
Ⓐ Dry brush stroke, using the flat of the brush (step 15).
Ⓑ Wet brush stroke, using the edge of the bristles (step 4).
Ⓒ Wet brush stroke, using the flat of the brush (step 8).
Ⓓ Flourish, using first the edge and then the width of the brush (step 5).

Ⓐ　　Ⓑ　　Ⓒ　　Ⓓ

4 ▲ Draw the first leaves Block in some of the flower petals with cadmium orange and yellow ochre, then change to a No.2 rigger brush to start on the foliage. Draw in the stems and outline the leaves with differing strengths of Hooker's green.

DEVELOPING THE PICTURE

Continue building up the leaves and petals with descriptive brush marks. Create form and shadow by applying layers of darker paint wet-on-dry.

5 ▲ **Block in the leaves** Switch back to the 25mm (1in) flat brush and, with a watery olive green wash, start shaping the leaves. Manipulate your brush to use both the broad and the narrow edge of the hairs to create the tapering shapes.

6 ▲ **Create the illusion of glass** Watercolour is the perfect medium for suggesting glass, which combines the qualities of solidity and transparency. Mix a very dilute grey – mainly water with just a hint of ivory black – and apply this down the right-hand edge of the vase with a No.12 flat brush.

◄ The artist's palette shows how he avoided unnecessary mixing. The blue, greens and yellows, in particular, have been diluted and then used purely.

Express yourself
Flower miniature

This version of the lilies is on a much smaller scale than the main project, measuring only 15 x 11cm (6 x 4½in). Worked in opaque acrylics rather than translucent watercolours, its luminous appearance and delicate texture is achieved by building up shapes and surfaces with patches and dots of colour – a technique known as pointillism. Look, in particular, at the cast shadow – it is brought to life with dabs of blues and purples.

7 ▲ **Add form to the vase** Paint the base of the vase as an oval, following your initial pencil sketch. Now, switching to the No.2 round brush, define the left-hand edge of the vase in the same watery grey.

8 ▲ **Block in some lighter leaves** With the 25mm (1in) flat brush, block in some of the broader leaves in olive green. Use your sketch as a guide, but don't feel you have to follow it slavishly.

9 ▲ **Describe the tangle of leaves** Within the vase, the leaves fight against the confines of the glass. Allowed their freedom, they spread out in every direction. Working above and below the waterline, build up the tangle of leaves, using the olive green wash from step 5 and a No.4 round. Add cerulean blue to the olive green for darker areas.

10 ▲ **Enliven the orange** Add a touch of burnt sienna to cadmium orange to make a dark tone for the petals in shadow. Using the No.12 flat, paint single strokes that follow the curve of the petals.

11 ◄ **Paint the veins**
If you look closely at the reference photograph, you can just make out some darker ridges on the petals. Paint these with the No.2 round and a touch of purple.

12 ▲ **Create two-toned buds** Use the No.4 round and dilute Hooker's green to shape the buds. Make a stronger mix to define the darks and add cerulean blue to it to create some greenish-blue areas.

13 ▲ **Return to the stems** Add touches of burnt sienna along the flower stems to suggest the shadows on them.

14▼ **Emphasize the background** If the painting seems a little flat, you could emphasize the folds in the background fabric. Use the No.4 round brush and a watery cerulean blue to accentuate them.

EXPERT ADVICE
Well-defined stamens

To make sure that the prominent, dark-coloured flower stamens really stand out, use a strong mix of purple and check that the paper is completely dry before you paint them. If there is any moisture in the paper, the paint will spread and the stamens will lose definition.

15▼ **Adjust the colours** Add a few more leaves in places, using olive green. Edge the petals in cadmium red and add stamens in purple (see Expert Advice). Paint dilute cerulean blue over some leaves and apply a stronger mix along the vase rim. Darken the cast shadow with a cerulean blue/raw umber mix.

A FEW STEPS FURTHER

A common painting error is overworking a picture – that is, not knowing when to stop. So when you've got all the elements in place and adjusted the colours so that the balance seems right, put your brushes down. Wait until the next day before looking at it again. You never know, your picture might be perfect just as it is.

16▲ **Make the colours zing** Beef up the picture by adding strokes of strong colour among the flower-heads – use the No.12 flat and mixes of cadmium red and cadmium orange, as well as some of the blue-greens used previously.

17 ▲ **Pick out certain flower-heads** Having applied bold strokes of colour with a flat brush, move on to the No.4 round brush to paint stronger outlines around the petals with cadmium red and purple.

18 ▲ **Add highlights** Use permanent white gouache and the 25mm (1in) flat brush to paint a highlight on the top left of the glass vase. For a warm, radiant effect, apply cadmium yellow highlights on to and among the leaves.

THE FINISHED PICTURE

A Purple outlines
The petal outlines are much more pronounced than they are in reality and make the flowers really stand out.

B Blue shadows
The sense of the vase's volume and mass is heightened by the strong shadow cast on to the background.

C Line of body colour
A fine line of permanent white gouache was added within the vase at the end of the project to suggest the water level.

Boatyard

The jumble of boatyard paraphernalia and splashes of bright colour keep your eye on the move around this watercolour painting.

This study was inspired by one of the artist's favourite haunts, his local boatyard in Cornwall. What captured his imagination was the array of textures and patterns. In the densely packed yard are tools of all shapes, sizes and textures. There are the undulations of the corrugated iron walls and a jumble of

▼ Elements from two photographs were combined to develop this composition, which is packed with detail.

ropes dangling from the ceiling. The result is a tapestry of random shapes, in which even the figures of the men at work are just part of the overall design.

Working on gesso

The artist decided to work on a textured surface to heighten these effects within the painting. He covered graphic designers' line board – available at art shops – with acrylic gesso. Painting on a gesso ground involves a different

approach to traditional watercolour techniques. The gesso seals the board, so that the paint floats on the surface rather than sinking into the support, creating interesting pools when it dries. The paint takes longer to dry and you have to work carefully when building up layers, as the original colour tends to lift off the surface. Be prepared for some happy accidents, but don't worry about mistakes – unlike conventional watercolour you can alter areas when they have dried.

YOU WILL NEED

Line board 34 x 46cm (13½ x 18in) primed with white acrylic gesso

4H pencil

12 watercolours: Cerulean blue; Ivory black; Chrome yellow; Phthalo blue; Vermilion; Magenta; Payne's grey; Raw sienna; Ultramarine; Burnt sienna;

Phthalo green; Raw umber

Brushes: Small and large squirrel brushes; No.3 sable round

Mixing palette or dish

Putty rubber

Steel ruler

FIRST STEPS

1 ▼ Scale up the scene Prime your line board with acrylic gesso and let it dry. Using a well-sharpened 4H pencil, copy the scene on to the board, including as much detail as you can. As it is an intricate drawing, it's best to copy the grid below, shown in light blue, on to your support – that is, with a ruler lightly pencil in eight equally spaced lines down the support and five equally spaced lines across it. Then you can do the drawing accurately, square by square.

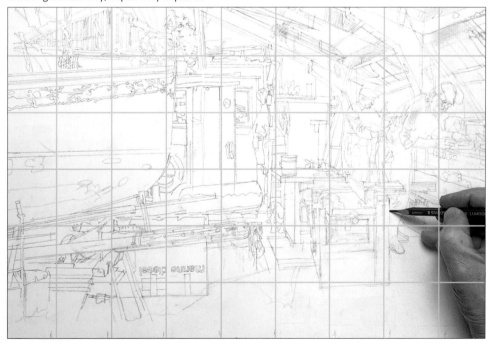

2 ▼ Begin with a blue Dilute some cerulean blue watercolour and, using a small squirrel brush, apply it along the rubbed-down paintwork on the boat. Then move on to other areas of blue. Add a little ivory black to the cerulean wash and make a subtle blue-grey to apply over the pale grey areas, such as details around the roof, workbench and on the window frame. When dry, feel free to use a putty rubber to soften the drawing so that it doesn't interfere with the painting.

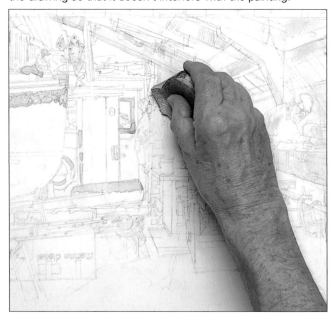

3 ▲ Test your colours Using the small squirrel brush and a dilute mix of chrome yellow, fill in the pale band along the hull and leave it to dry. Make a strong phthalo blue and try it out at the edge of the gesso board – testing colours is important when working on gesso, because it is difficult to modify them once they are down. Then use a large squirrel brush to apply this colour over the top half of the hull.

4 ▼ Work wet-on-wet Paint the base of the hull in a red mix of vermilion with a touch of magenta, working carefully around the drawn details. While the paint is still wet, drop some Payne's grey into it to suggest staining on the boat.

5 ▲ Work around the board Paint the overalls and oil drum in phthalo blue. Use the red mix to add bright details, modifying it with raw sienna and black where you need an orange tone, and ultramarine where you want a bluer effect. Now mix a very dilute brown from chrome yellow, phthalo blue and a hint of vermilion and wash this over the floor.

DEVELOPING THE PICTURE

Continue working up all the browns in the scene, varying their tones by making the mixes progressively stronger and darker.

6 ▶ Start on the background Mix a mid brown from raw sienna, burnt sienna and chrome yellow. Using a No.3 round sable brush, paint the background, taking care to avoid the various ropes and other items that cut across the area.

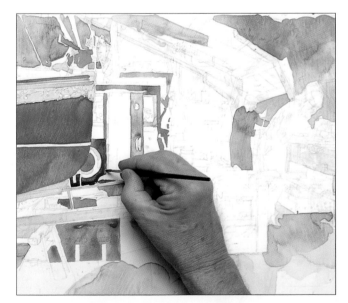

7 ▲ Add more browns Still working with the mix from step 6, paint other mid brown areas, such as the planks and door. Strengthen the tone and paint the box in the foreground. Then mix a dark brown from raw sienna, black and vermilion, and use the various brown mixes to paint lines along the top of the hull. Apply the dark brown to the door frame and behind the lifebelt.

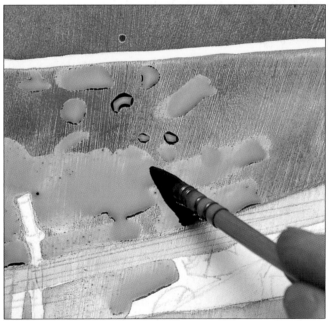

8 ▲ Suggest weathering on the hull To represent the weather-beaten appearance of the hull, apply a watery mix of magenta and Payne's grey with the large squirrel brush. Work carefully – if you paint the new colour on too roughly, it will lift off the colour underneath.

EXPERT ADVICE
Taking colour off

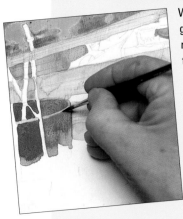

When working on gesso, it is easy to remove colour because the paint sits on the surface of the board rather than sinking into it. Here, the artist is using the tip of a brush dipped in clean water to take some blue off the top of the oil drum and suggest its metal lip.

9 ▸ Bring in some green
Using the small squirrel brush, paint the workman's jumper in ultramarine. Then mix a little black and raw sienna into phthalo green to make the muddy brown hues around the doorway. Overpaint some areas with black. Use phthalo green plus varying amounts of raw sienna and water for the small workbench in front of the figures – paint it wet-on-wet so that the colours pool together.

10 ▲ Add detail to the hull Paint a darker shade of blue over the weathered band on the boat's hull with a mix of cerulean blue and a little Payne's grey. Take care to avoid the pale patches as before.

11 ▸ Darken the man's overalls
Now give the men's clothes some texture. Using your original drawing to guide you, paint a layer of phthalo blue over the areas of the workman's overalls which are in shadow. Once the paint has dried, the texture of the board shows through, giving the appearance of tough denim fabric.

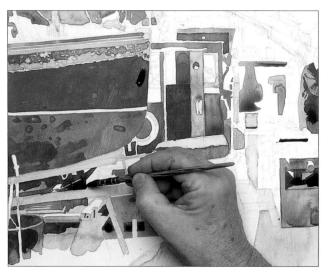

12 ▲ Paint under the boat Dilute the green mixes from step 10 and paint the trestle and other green details. Add shadows under the hull with a mix of black and varying amounts of ultramarine. It isn't necessary to know what every shape represents – just create a pleasing rhythm of patterns.

13 ▲ Add flesh tones Work up shadows on the right-hand man's clothes with mixes of phthalo blue or ultramarine and black. Paint pale skin tones on the faces with a watery mix of vermilion and raw sienna. Leave to dry, then use a stronger mix for the darker tones. Paint his beard with dilute raw umber.

14 ▼ **Fill in the background** Finish the figure in the foreground, painting his arms with the same light and dark skin tones as on his face. Now mix shades of grey from varying strengths of black plus phthalo blue and define the man's cap, glasses and watch-strap. Then, with a more dilute mix of grey, add areas of shadow to the structure above his head.

15 ▼ **Paint the cocker spaniel** Define the horizontal mast with bands of dilute Payne's grey and burnt sienna. Then paint the spaniel. Use Payne's grey for the shadows on his coat, burnt sienna on his face and ears, and black for his nose, eyes and the tip of his ear. Leave the surface of the board for the white of his fur.

16 ▲ **Add the final details** Paint the skylights above the workbench with a mix of Payne's grey and raw umber. Mark in the tools and shadows on and around the workbenches with dilute Payne's grey, black, phthalo blue and a raw sienna/burnt sienna mix. Now, for one of the final patterns, paint the triangle of beams in the top left of the composition with the sienna mix.

THE FINISHED PICTURE

A Textured surface
The painted gesso ground heightens the sense of texture on the side of the boat and on the tea-chest. Note how white ridges show through.

B Blocks of tone
The workmen, in their bold blue overalls, act as focal points in the yard's clutter. The masts in the foreground and the sloping roof help guide the eye to the men.

C Pools of colour
The tidemarks on the floor – painted wet-on-wet – add to the range and variety of textures. They work well against the geometric shapes elsewhere.

Riverbank reflections

Various watercolour techniques are used to great effect in this painting of a cool, shady stretch of river, with the sun filtering through the trees.

There are three main elements in this lovely river scene – water, grass and trees. Each element is treated separately and each is painted using a different technique. This jigsaw approach will enable you to complete the painting in simplified stages, and you will have the satisfaction of seeing how the pieces eventually fit together to make a realistic landscape.

Start by making the initial drawing on tracing paper. In this way you can experiment with the composition without spoiling the paper. The transferred image will always be clean and minimal – an ideal start for watercolour painting.

Grass and foliage

Spattering is the key to the fresh, grassy banks – first with clean water, then with colour, so that the paint finds its way into the wet shapes. The first spatter of colour looks like an explosion of tiny stars, but as the sequence is repeated the 'stars' eventually build up to form a perfect impression of grass and leaves.

To create perspective in the painting, make the foreground spatters larger than

those in the background by spattering with the brush held closer to the paper.

Watery reflections

Paradoxically, the fluid nature of water is effectively painted with precise brush strokes. Here, both vertical and horizontal strokes are used to create reflections in the river. Paint the reflections wet-on-wet; when dry, they provide a soft background for precise ripples and reflected shapes, overpainted in stronger colours.

▲ **Lively spattered texture on the foliage contrasts with the glassy surface of the river in this peaceful scene.**

FIRST STEPS

1 ▼ Trace the image Having sketched the image on to tracing paper, draw with a B pencil over the main lines on the reverse of the paper.

2 ▲ Apply masking fluid Transfer the image on to watercolour paper by turning the tracing paper the right way up and going over the lines with a sharp pencil. Use an old paint brush to dab masking fluid between the trees. Also mask distant horizontal reflections and the stumps in the foreground. Use an old toothbrush to spatter masking fluid across the background.

3 ▼ Block in the river bank Mask off the river with scrap paper. Using a No.6 round brush, spatter water on to the grassy bank on the left. Dab on cadmium lemon, allowing the colour to run into the blobs of water. At the top, blend the yellow with more water to create a wash of solid colour.

4 ▲ Continue blocking in Wet the right-hand bank and flood the area with cadmium lemon, leaving a broad band of white along the top of the picture.

Express yourself

Down the road

Here is another watercolour, painted with many of the same techniques as the step-by-step. Here, however, the river is replaced by a road. Note how the blues and purples of the wet tarmac surface contrast with the yellows and greens of the verge. The long, linear tree shadows across the road also make a pleasing contrast with the spattered detail on the verge.

5 ▼ Suggest the grass Mask out all the areas around the right-hand bank. Mix phthalo green and cadmium lemon and flick the mixture on to the wet cadmium lemon paint.

6 ▲ Suggest the background To suggest the distant trees on the right, lightly apply water to the paper, then spatter and dab the wet area with varying mixtures of cadmium lemon, turquoise light, indigo, burnt sienna and alizarin crimson. Allow the colours to run together on the wet paper.

7 ▼ Continue the background Paint the tree-trunks and branches in cadmium lemon. Moving to the left, lightly wet the paper, spatter on turquoise light and phthalo green paint, then blend the colours in the shady areas around the base of the trees.

DEVELOPING THE PICTURE

The main areas of grass and foliage have been initially blocked in with yellow and green and it is time to start work on the trees. There is a handy technique for painting them quickly and effectively.

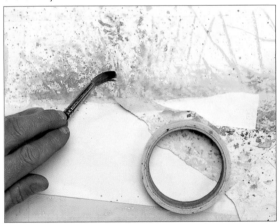

8 ▶ Paint the trees Change to a No.4 round and paint green bands across one of the tree-trunks in a dilute mix of indigo, turquoise light and Naples yellow. Define the trunk by dragging Payne's grey quickly down through the wet bands. The paint will run horizontally to suggest branches.

EXPERT ADVICE
Fine lines with a feather

In the nineteenth century, marine artists and architects often used a tail feather of a woodcock to paint fine, even lines. The feather, which is very springy and holds a surprising amount of colour, is used here taped to a brush handle to paint the long, thin branches of the trees. If you do not have a woodcock feather to hand, a No.1 rigger or fine liner brush does a similar job!

9 ▲ Develop the grass With the No.6 brush, develop the far bank, alternately spattering it with water and then with a mixture of phthalo green and indigo to create the light and dark greens. Use the tip of the brush to take the colour up to the edge of the water.

10 ▼ **Complete the trees** Use the No.4 brush and burnt sienna to paint the bank of trees on the right-hand side. But don't overdo it – work from the wrist to achieve natural curves on trunks and branches.

11 ▼ **Build up the grass tones** Moving to the left bank, spatter the grass with drops of water, then with dilute phthalo green. Repeat to build up textured colour, adding indigo for the darker foreground tones.

12 ▼ **Paint the water** Using the No.6 brush, block in the river in broad, horizontal strokes of ultramarine. Use deep colour in the foreground, diluting it as you move towards the distance. While the colour is wet, smooth out brush marks with water and a fan blender.

13 ▼ **Suggest reflections** Start to paint the foreground reflections into the wet blue paint, applying mixes of burnt sienna and indigo with vertical and horizontal strokes.

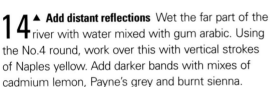

14 ▲ **Add distant reflections** Wet the far part of the river with water mixed with gum arabic. Using the No.4 round, work over this with vertical strokes of Naples yellow. Add darker bands with mixes of cadmium lemon, Payne's grey and burnt sienna.

15 ▲ **Remove masking fluid** Paint strokes of indigo mixed with burnt sienna between the bands of masking fluid on the water. Leave the painting to dry; rub off the masking fluid from the background and water. Paint a dilute mix of indigo, burnt sienna and phthalo green among the trees; add reflections in a mix of phthalo green, indigo and burnt sienna.

A FEW STEPS FURTHER

The picture is almost complete, but more can be made of the ripples and reflections on the river. So far, these are suggested with soft, wet-on-wet brush strokes. Now allow the painting to dry completely, so that you can add some crisper reflections to the surface of the water.

16 ▶ **Paint moving water** With the No.6 brush, paint the reflections of the trees in the foreground in a dark mixture of indigo, burnt sienna and phthalo green, adding touches of lemon yellow for the paler tones. Use squiggly, tapering lines to capture the movement of the water.

17 ▲ **Define the bank** Continue building up reflections, diluting the mix to make lighter tones. Use the No.4 brush for finer lines. Apply water along the edge of the riverbank and flood with mixes of cerulean blue, turquoise light and cadmium yellow.

18 ▼ **Add branches** Paint the reflections of the fine branches in mixes of indigo, burnt sienna and phthalo green. Our artist used a woodcock feather for the tapering lines (see Expert Advice on page 409), but a No.1 rigger or fine liner brush works well too. Apply water across the far ripples, then dab off some of the colour with a paper tissue.

19 ▲ **Paint the posts** Remove the masking fluid from the wooden posts and paint the tops in a mix of burnt sienna and cadmium lemon with the No.4 brush. Add the shadow in indigo mixed with burnt sienna.

THE FINISHED PICTURE

A Background sunlight
White sunlight filtering through the trees is established in the early stages of the painting with masking fluid.

B Grass and foliage
The riverbank is built up by spattering the paper with water and paint alternately to achieve a mottled, leafy texture.

C Wavy lines
The moving surface of the water is created by overpainting horizontal lines with squiggly and zigzag marks.

Poppies in a landscape

If your ideal landscape doesn't exist, why not create it from various sources and with a little artistic licence?

This glorious landscape with its jubilant poppies bordering a field of golden corn doesn't exist in reality. The painting is a fabrication – a work in which a still life set-up and a landscape photo, plus a dose of imagination, come together to create a totally plausible composition.

The photo of a luxuriant green field, a farmhouse and an ancient stone wall bordering the field (top right) formed the basis of the work, although it is considerably altered, both in content and in colour. Green fields became yellow cornfields; greyish hills became purple; stone walls vanished from view.

The poppies, which give a burst of red in the foreground, were based on a bunch of bought poppies (right). These provided an ideal visual reference.

▼ **The poppies and grasses that dominate the foreground contrast in scale with the distant cottage, setting up a strong feeling of recession in the scene.**

FIRST STEPS

1 ▼ **Plan the composition** Using a brown water-soluble pencil (it will wash out when you paint over it), sketch the distant hills and house. Place the poppies in the foreground, making them very large to give the sense of a receding landscape.

Piece of 300gsm (140lb) watercolour paper 36 x 46cm (14 x 18in)

Brown water-soluble coloured pencil

9 watercolours: Cerulean blue; Ultramarine; Alizarin crimson; Cadmium red; Cadmium yellow pale; Winsor green;

Lemon yellow; Yellow ochre; Burnt sienna

Brushes: Nos.16 and 8 rounds; No.2 rigger

Mixing palette or dish

Jar of water

Stiff card

Old toothbrush

2 ▼ **Start with the sky** Using a No.16 round brush, wet the sky area and then go over it with sweeps of cerulean blue, followed by ultramarine. Use loose, curved brush strokes rather than broad, horizontal strokes.

3 ▲ **Mix a purple** Combine alizarin crimson with ultramarine to make a purple, and use this both within the sky and on the furthest hill. Although the hill appears blue-grey in the photo, you can adapt the colours if you wish. To create some warmer accents, wash areas of cadmium red into the landscape.

▼ **To prevent the red and purple mixes (left) from accidentally running into the blues and greens (below), the artist used two palettes.**

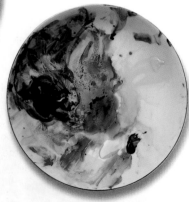

4 ▼ **Paint with water** Move forward in the scene, painting the distant fields with mixes of cerulean blue, cadmium yellow pale and Winsor green. To create a hazy effect, dip the brush in clean water and use it to slice across the sky and hills, lifting and blending the colours as you do so.

5 ▼ **Establish the cornfield** Transform the grassy field of the photograph into a cornfield by washing lemon yellow over the foreground area. Use the No.16 round brush for this, taking care to avoid the poppies.

DEVELOPING THE PICTURE

With the broad areas of the landscape blocked in, turn your attention to the details in the scene – the house, the clumps of trees and the poppies in the foreground.

6 ▲ **Paint the farmhouse** Switch to a No.2 rigger and cadmium red to outline the farmhouse and paint the windows. Now, with a No.8 round brush, paint the roof and side of the house. Brush clean water on to the side wall, and draw some of the colour down from the roof to create a pale tone.

7 ▲ **Put in the trees** A line of trees spans the middle distance. Paint these with mixes of Winsor green and yellow ochre, varying the proportions of the colours to create visual interest.

8 ▶ Fill in the poppies

With the No.2 rigger, define the doorway of the house, the roof and the side wall in Winsor green. Then with the No.8 round brush, start painting the poppies. Use varying strengths of cadmium red for the flower heads, with occasional touches of lemon yellow.

9 ▶ Print with card

Using the edge of a strip of stiff card, print narrow lines to stand for the dried grasses – yellow ochre on the left, burnt sienna on the right. Bend another card strip to form a 'V'-shape and print the ears of corn, beginning at the top of each stem. Again, use yellow ochre on some of the stems and burnt sienna on others.

10 ▶ Print the fence

Using the No.2 rigger, strengthen the cadmium red roof of the house and add details to the windows, chimney and wall with burnt sienna and ultramarine. Then, changing to the No.8 round, block in the foreground fence-posts with burnt sienna. Print Winsor green outlines with a card strip.

Express yourself
Change of format

Within a landscape, real or imaginary, there are often various ways of cropping into the scene to produce new and equally interesting compositions. Here, the artist has focused more closely on the farmhouse in the middle distance by cropping off the sides of the original composition, creating an unusually tall and narrow format. The verticals of the poppies and grasses in the foreground fill the paper from top to bottom, cutting across the view and bringing the viewer even closer into the scene than in the conventional landscape format. The sense of distance created by contrasting warm and cool colours is, however, just as strong.

11 ▼ **Provide some dark accents** Use the No.2 rigger and Winsor green to dot in the dark centres on the poppies. Mix ultramarine and burnt sienna to define the background hills.

12 ▲ **Build up the foreground** With the No.2 rigger and a mix of alizarin crimson and ultramarine, define the brow of the hill in the centre by dotting dark accents along the ridge. To create visual interest in the foreground, print more hedgerow grasses, as in step 9. Use Winsor green for some and a dark mix of ultramarine and burnt sienna for others.

THE FINISHED PICTURE

A Visual reference
The device of showing just the top of the fence in the foreground makes us feel that we are actually at the scene – spectators within a real landscape.

B Central landmark
The inclusion of the farmhouse in the middle distance, a recognizable landmark dwarfed by the poppies and grasses, reinforces the vast scale of the countryside.

C Sense of space
The cool hues of the hills on the horizon create a powerful sense of recession, particularly when contrasted with the warm colours in the foreground.

Bay in Greece

This painting brilliantly evokes the sun-drenched atmosphere of a Greek island. Watercolour is the ideal medium to portray the vivid turquoise sea.

No single watercolour pigment can quite match the extraordinary clarity and depth of colour of the water in this Greek bay. To capture a similar effect in paint, you will need to use several colours ranging from deep blue to bright turquoise. The secret lies in building up the paint in thin layers, allowing the colours to dry between each application. The washes then act like transparent veils of colour, each one contributing to the final effect.

Clear mixtures

Some of the green and turquoise washes used here are mixed from blue and yellow. The blues vary, depending on the colour required. However, the artist stuck with one yellow for all the mixes – aureolin. As it is a very transparent yellow, aureolin can be used with other colours without creating cloudy mixes.

Simple composition

The composition in this painting is compact and deliberately simple. It is made up of three interlocking shapes – the sea, cliff and sky – and the emphasis is on flat pattern and vibrant colour rather than on a realistic seascape with an illusion of space and distance.

The artist devised a useful technique to help choose the most effective composition. He cut a cardboard mount to the size and proportion of the envisaged picture. He then worked the painting on a piece of paper larger than the cut mount. At various stages during the course of the painting, he moved the mount around on the paper looking for the best arrangement.

▶ **Looking through the layers of paint that make up the sea in this painting is rather like peering down into deep, clear water.**

Piece of 300gsm (140lb) Not watercolour paper 76 x 56cm (30 x 22in)

9 watercolours: Cerulean blue; Aureolin; Cobalt blue; Winsor blue; Winsor green; Ultramarine; Burnt sienna; Raw sienna; Ivory black

Brushes: 25mm (1in) soft flat; Chinese brush

Cardboard mount, cut to the required size of the painting

Mixing dish or palette

Jar of water

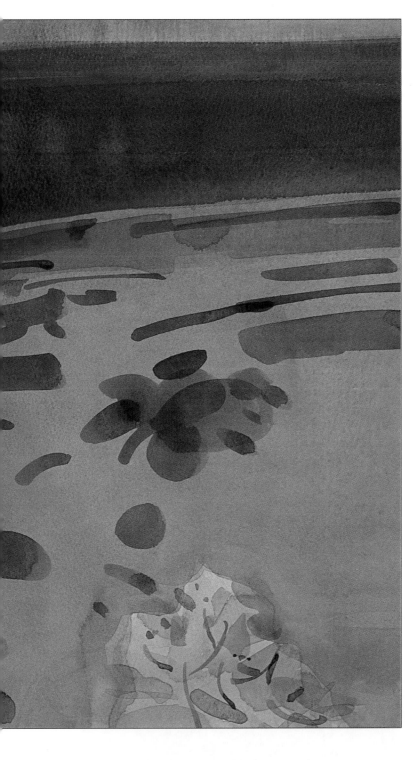

FIRST STEPS

1 ▼ Apply the first wash Turn the board upside down and tilt it slightly. Apply a graduated wash of cerulean blue and aureolin across the paper with a 25mm (1in) flat brush. Start with a weak wash and gradually add more colour to the mixture as you work down the support – the colour will run down into the sky. Allow the painting to dry.

2 ▼ Position the cliff Return the board to a level position and the right way up. With a Chinese brush and a dilute mix of cerulean and cobalt blue, define the shape of the cliff and lightly indicate the skyline. Work tentatively, correcting the lines by overpainting until you are happy with the composition.

◀ **Several shades of blue were used to bring out the vivid hues of the sea and sky, including cerulean blue (top left), cobalt blue (top right) and ultramarine (left).**

3 ▼ Wash in the sea Mix a wash from aureolin, Winsor blue and Winsor green. Using the 25mm (1in) brush, apply it to the sea with horizontal strokes. When the wash is dry, mix cerulean, Winsor blue and Winsor green and paint this over the first wash, working around the tree shape in the foreground.

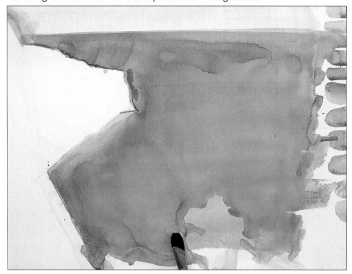

DEVELOP THE PICTURE

The sea and sky are now established as broad washes of colour. It is now time to change your approach and add some detail. Do this with the Chinese brush, using the tip of the bristles for fine lines.

5 ▶ Darken the horizon Apply a strong ultramarine wash, starting at the horizon and continuing downwards as far as the rocky peninsula. Work in broad, overlapping bands, tilting the board slightly away from you so that the darker colour collects along the horizon. Paint around the rock, defining the shape with a hard, crisp edge. Allow this to dry. (Remember to keep replacing the water so that you do not muddy the colours.)

4 ▲ Consider the composition Cut a cardboard mount to the envisaged size of the finished picture and place it on the painting. Move it around until you are happy with the composition. You can then concentrate on developing those areas that lie within the frame. Here the artist has decided to crop the sky to form a narrow band at the top of the painting.

6 ▼ Add rock patterns Working closely from the subject, look for the main shapes and patterns in the cliff face. Indicate vertical markings and diagonal strata in diluted burnt sienna and raw sienna.

TROUBLE SHOOTER

TESTING THE WASHES

Test the tone of each colour wash on the edge of the paper before committing it to the painting. Make sure the trial swatches are large enough to compare them easily with other colours already in the painting.

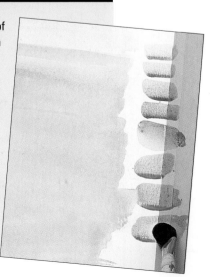

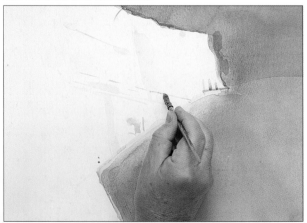

7 ▼ Paint a further wash Continue working into the cliff, blocking in sections of rock with broad strokes of dilute colour. Allow this to dry. Change to the 25mm (1in) soft brush and apply a further layer of colour to the lower area of sea in a dilute mixture of cerulean blue, Winsor blue and a little aureolin. Leave a margin of paler underpainting around the cliff to indicate shallow water.

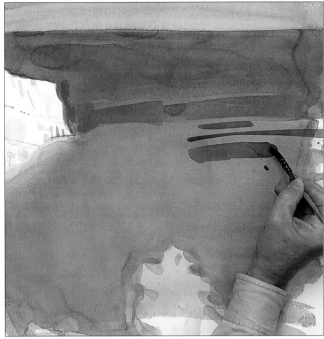

8 ▲ Darken the distance Mix a bright blue wash from Winsor blue and ultramarine. Use this to strengthen the sea below the horizon and to darken the sky. (Note: You need only paint the sky just above the horizon, because the rest will be out of the painting when cropped.) Add streaks of blue to the lower part of the sea to indicate dark reflections.

Master Strokes

Joan Eardley (1921–63)
Seascape

In this wonderfully expressive painting, the artist has applied the oil colours with a knife to attain an impasto finish. By changing the direction of the strokes on the sea and harbour, the artist has achieved a lively sense of movement, suggesting a sea-breeze and choppy water. To contrast with these textured areas, the sky is rendered with smooth glazes of thinner paint.

Thick layers of paint have been built up to make a textured surface streaked with many different colours.

The brilliant reflection on the water attracts the eye into the foreground and reflects the band of yellow in the sky.

9▼ **Develop the rock face** Using the tip of the Chinese brush, dot clumps of grass into the cliff face in a mixture of Winsor green and ivory black. Continue to block in darker sections of the rock face in a cool grey mixed from cerulean blue, ivory black and raw sienna.

10▲ **Paint the reflections** Radically darken the distant water using the 25mm (1in) brush and a strong mix of Winsor blue and ultramarine. Indicate the patches of underwater reflection and seaweed in short, broad strokes of Winsor blue mixed with a little ivory black and aureolin. Paint the tree in a pale mixture of aureolin and Winsor green.

Express yourself
Take a broader view

Although this marine view is slightly more complicated than the one in the project, the artist has used similar colours and techniques to depict the water and rocky landscape. The calm surface of the sea is shown with horizontal bands of paint, which become closer together as they reach the horizon, to give a sense of recession. The distant hills, which are paler and bluer than those in the foreground, add to this feeling of depth.

A FEW STEPS FURTHER

Allow the colours to dry and assess the work. The strong blue and turquoise washes on the sky and sea are now complete. However, the rock face could be developed further. In addition, you might wish to add the reflections around the bottom of the rock.

11▲ **Check the composition** Before continuing with the painting, place the mount on the picture once more. Check the composition and make sure that all the elements you want to include are inside the picture area, and that you are not left with unpainted areas around the edge.

13 ▾ Paint the reflections Finally, paint the pale reflections just below the water line in aureolin mixed with a touch of ivory black and Winsor green.

12 ▲ Add dark tones Paint the red iron deposits on the cliff face in burnt sienna. Add more shadows to the rocks with a dilute mix of cerulean, ivory black and raw sienna. With the tip of the Chinese brush, define the dark edge along the base of the cliff in a mixture of Winsor green and black.

THE FINISHED PICTURE

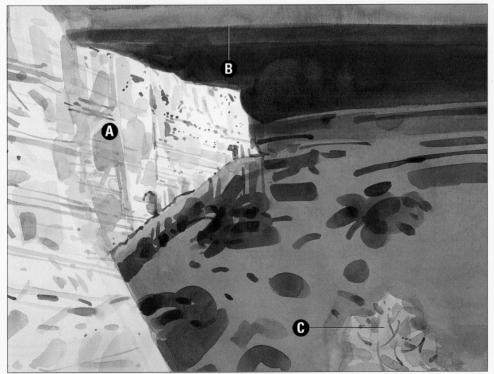

A Surface patterns
A variety of marks and lines were built up to form strong patterns on the face of the rock.

B Narrow sky
The sky was cropped to form a band of deep blue across the top edge of the painting.

C Tree texture
Linear brush strokes on the tree reflect the patterns and textures on the rock face.

Klee-inspired watercolour

In a rut with your painting? Looking at the world through the eyes of another painter can show us a fresh way of interpreting a subject.

Just for fun, why not try working in the style of a favourite artist? We chose the Swiss Expressionist Paul Klee (1879–1940), whose work includes oils, watercolours and prints. Klee often used a subject as a departure point from which he then went on to produce an abstracted image. He is particularly known for his beautiful watercolours, which have been described as 'mosaics of wash'. It was this aspect of his work that tempted our artist to try a similar approach.

Adapting the view
By occasionally copying the style of other painters, you can develop new ideas and discover ways of working that you might not have considered. Before you begin, take a good look at several works by your selected artist. Select the paintings that appeal to you most, and decide how you can adapt the style to suit your own subject.

This Venetian canal scene was chosen for its angular shapes and strong geometric composition, both of which are characteristic of much of Klee's work. Although Venice is famous for its earth colours, our artist liked Klee's vivid-coloured watercolours best. For this reason, earth pigments were banned from the palette, and the Venetian scene was depicted using bright overlaid washes instead.

Flattening the subject
The initial drawing simplifies the subject and flattens the shapes to form a two-dimensional pattern. However, as is often evident in Klee's work, the composition is not completely abstract. Buildings, boats and the bridge across the canal are all recognizable elements. The figure crossing the bridge is a final clue as to the identity and scale of the subject.

If you are wary of straying from what you can see in front of you, try to imagine the reference photo as a series of shapes, colours and tones – turning it upside down helps. Feel free to alter these shapes and tones as much as you like in order to make the arrangement look more attractive or balanced.

▶ **The houses and canal are represented as blocks of harmonious colour in this well-balanced painting.**

Piece of watercolour board 38 x 30cm (15 x 12in)

2B pencil

6 watercolours: Lemon yellow; Cadmium yellow;

Cadmium red; Viridian; Alizarin crimson; Phthalo blue

Brushes: Chinese brush; No.4 round

Scraperboard tool

FIRST STEPS

1 ▲ Block in the sunlight Make a drawing of the scene with a 2B pencil. Mix lemon and cadmium yellow and use a Chinese brush to block in the sunny areas of sky, background and reflections in the water.

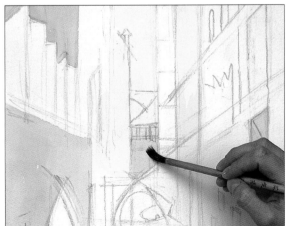

2 ▲ Develop the buildings Allow the yellow washes to dry. Mix a warm orange from cadmium red and cadmium yellow and block in the pink façades on the left and other areas on the right. Leave to dry.

3 ▶ **Continue with the blocking in** Mix a pale wash of viridian and block in some of the shaded areas and shutters, varying the tones of the washes. Try to keep a pleasing balance between the warm and cool areas. Allow the painting to dry. Now mix a wash of alizarin crimson and paint the façades of the pink stucco buildings and the archway on the left. As you apply the colour to the buildings, take the same colour into the reflections in the water.

4 ▲ **Develop the reflections** Continue blocking in the main shapes using washes of diluted colour. Here, a pale mix of phthalo blue and viridian is applied to the sky and to the bridge and its reflections.

Master Strokes

Paul Klee (1879–1940)
Castle and Sun

This glowing oil painting is typical of the distinctive style of Swiss artist Paul Klee and illustrates his wonderful powers of imagination. Klee's painting is much more abstract than the step-by-step project – the castle of the title has been converted into a series of rectangles, squares and triangles. Neatly aligned and separated by white lines, the interlocking shapes have a mosaic-like quality.

A layer of reddish-brown oil paint scumbled over the golden yellow sun creates a lively textured surface.

The rounded archway at the bottom echoes the circle of the sun and is the only other curved shape in the painting.

DEVELOPING THE PICTURE

Most of the white support is now covered with diluted colour. Continue building up the washes, applying one over another to create rich, dark tones.

5 ▶ Paint small shapes Mix a purple from alizarin crimson and phthalo blue and block in areas of shadow. Strengthen the arched doorway and shaded areas on the bridge. Using the cool viridian wash, pick out small dark shapes across the picture. Don't be too literal – choose areas that enhance the composition.

6 ▼ Vary the orange tones Carry on blocking in more small shapes, using warm mixes of cadmium red and cadmium yellow. Vary the proportions of red and yellow in the mixes in order to get a range of tones.

7 ▼ Add windows Mix a deep purple from phthalo blue and alizarin crimson and start blocking in the windows. Vary the tones by painting the top part of each shape, then diluting and spreading the colour with clean water.

Express yourself
Watery effects

Try this unusual combination of soluble felt-tipped pens and watercolour washes. Start by drawing the scene with the pens, then apply watercolour over the top. The pen lines will dissolve and run, giving the image a fluid appearance entirely appropriate for the water-based subject matter.

8 ▶ Darken the shadow Use the deep purple mix for the windows on the left. Then continue blocking in with red tones. Here cadmium red mixed with a little cadmium yellow is being used to strengthen the dark shadow on the lower part of the right-hand building.

9 ▶ Add drawn detail Wait for the painting to dry, then use the 2B pencil to add detail. Keep the drawing loose and decorative rather than being too literal. Mark in windows and a canopy above the bridge, and reflections in the water. Draw the ironwork on the bridge as criss-cross lines.

EXPERT ADVICE
Useful sgraffito tool

Any sharp implement can be used for scratching texture into paint. However, a scraperboard tool is particularly effective because it is very sharp and has a strong, rigid blade. Here, the finely painted lines that form the ironwork on the bridge are continued across the shadow area by scratching into the dark green paint with the scraperboard tool.

10 ▶ Paint the figure Mix phthalo blue, viridian and alizarin and strengthen the dark reflections and shadows around the bridge. Paint the shutters on the left and the windows drawn in step 9. Using palette mixes, keep blocking in shapes and adding details. Use scratched texture on the doors and window shutters (see Expert Advice). Change to a No.4 round brush and add the figure on the bridge in alizarin crimson with a touch of viridian.

11 ▲ Work into the boats Develop the two boats, adding a mix of cadmium yellow and cadmium red to the interior of the foreground boat; add dabs of viridian mixed with a little alizarin to the other boat.

A FEW STEPS FURTHER

You may want to carry the work further, adding more detail and strengthening colours and tones. A few touches of strong colour at the centre will draw the eye into the heart of the painting.

12 ▲ Add colour Mix a small quantity of brilliant orange from cadmium yellow and a touch of alizarin crimson. Use the No.4 round brush to paint the background above the bridge.

13 ▼ **Develop the dark tones** Work across the picture, darkening any tones that now appear too pale compared with recently painted areas. For example, strengthen the dark ironwork on the bridge with the green mixed in step 10 so that it stands out in front of the figure.

14 ▲ **Add linear details** A few more details complete the painting. Use the tip of the No.4 round brush to add any remaining linear features, such as the inside of the arch, which is painted in neat viridian.

THE FINISHED PICTURE

A Narrow view
The linear perspective of the buildings on either side of the narrow canal draws the eye towards the centre of the composition.

B Central focus
The silhouette of a figure on the bridge provides a strong focal point for the painting.

C Sgraffito marks
Scratched texture adds interest to areas of flat colour, such as the door and window, by creating pale lines on dark paint.

Shelf life

Familiar but often overlooked corners of your home can provide a rich source of subject matter for still-life painting.

This composition is a still life with a difference. Unlike conventional still lifes, it doesn't involve any setting up. It's just there – a cameo scene among many others in your home, waiting to be noticed. This approach to choosing a subject is all about finding beauty in the commonplace.

Master of realism

The original master of matter-of-fact realism was the French artist Jean-Baptiste-Simeon Chardin (1699–1779), who chose modest scenes from everyday life as his subject matter. Unlike his contemporaries, he was interested in the shapes, textures and colours of objects rather than any

symbolic or moral overtones they might have. He liked to work on a toned surface, as was used in this project, with minimal background detail.

A loose approach

The object of this exercise is to get the feel of the subject rather than make a faithful rendition of the items. Your palette – the three primary colours and white – won't allow for photographic realism, so you are forced to adopt a looser approach. Draw the shelf freehand and if your lines wobble a little, so be it – old shelves are rarely straight. Similarly, don't copy the decorative motifs on the china exactly – indicate them roughly with areas of tone.

▲ The range of colours in this painting was achieved with a very limited palette.

YOU WILL NEED

Piece of board 48 x 33cm (19 x 13in)

5 acrylic paints: Cadmium yellow; Titanium white; Prussian blue; Cadmium red; Cobalt blue

Brushes: Wide wash brush; 13mm (½in) and 6mm (¼in) flats; Nos.1 and 3 rounds

Propelling pencil

FIRST STEPS

1 ▶ Plan your composition Before you begin, paint the board with a mid-toned undercolour. Mix cadmium yellow with titanium white plus touches of Prussian blue and cadmium red to make a straw colour. Apply this evenly over the surface of the board with a wide wash brush and leave to dry. Then, using a propelling pencil, draw the shelf and its contents so that they span the central third of the board.

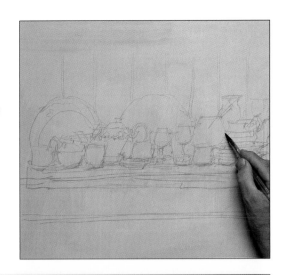

2 ▼ Block in the wood Mix a brown for the wooden slats from cadmium red and cobalt blue with a little cadmium yellow. Use a 13mm (½in) flat brush to block in these background tones, but don't blend the colours completely, so that when you apply the paint you can see occasional streaks of red or blue.

4 ▲ Mix darker brown Add more red to the brown mix to make a deeper shade and apply along the front edge of the shelf using a 6mm (¼in) flat brush. Mix in more cobalt blue to make a darker tone and paint the top surface of the shelf. Leave to dry. Add titanium white to the dark brown mix to create a greyer tone and paint around the base of the crockery.

3 ▶ Pick out some pencil lines Dip a No.1 round brush into cobalt blue and go over some of the pencil lines to give more shape to the forms. The blue is dark enough to be seen, but not so dark as to dominate the picture.

▲ Here are two wood mixes and two china mixes used in the painting. They are made from (left to right) red, blue and a touch of yellow; red with touches of blue, yellow and white; blue, white and a touch of red; and blue, yellow and white.

5 ▼ **Start on the crockery** Although the china appears white, pure titanium white would overpower the composition. Dull the white slightly by adding tiny touches of cobalt blue, red and yellow to it and apply these tints loosely with the 13mm (½in) flat brush over the various items of crockery.

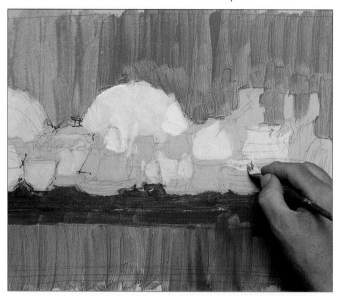

6 ▲ **Work on the cups** Using the 6mm (¼in) brush, define the edges of the crystal goblet in grey (white with a hint of blue, red and yellow) and paint the cocktail stirrer in the same colour. Now mix a dull purple (red, cobalt blue and white) for the cup on the left and a whitish-blue for its neighbour. Use some of the dull purple for the rim of the blue cup and mix a blue-grey to define the inside.

EXPERT ADVICE
Softening colours

If you want a softer or more subtle colour, apply the paint as you would normally and then, while it is still wet, blend it with your finger. Use this 'smudging' technique to create the somewhat distorted appearance of the glass cocktail stirrer inside the crystal goblet.

7 ▲ **Block in more shapes** Work backwards and forwards across your paper, filling in and adjusting the colours as you go. On the left, suggest the design of the yellow sunflower on the cup; block in the red and green cups in the centre and paint the tall-stemmed yellow and blue glasses next to it. Notice how just a few strokes of colour are needed to create the effect of glass.

8 ▲ **Define the edges** Using the No.1 round brush and cobalt blue, draw with the brush, defining the edges of the red cup and wine glasses to accentuate their form.

9 ▼ **Add bright highlights** Crystal has a high lustre. To make the reflections on the goblet and the cocktail stirrer really stand out, dab a few dots of pure titanium white on to them with a No.3 round.

10 ▲ **Suggest the china pattern** The plates and teapot have a leaf motif. Don't attempt a faithful reproduction of this – just suggest the pattern with touches of blue-grey, using the 13mm (½in) flat.

Master Strokes

Georg Hinz (*fl.* 1625)
Treasure Chest

A far cry from the homely objects ranged along the dresser shelf in the project, the objects on display in this cabinet are precious jewels and other rare treasures. Each is depicted in meticulous detail and the variety of textures is brilliantly captured – amber and pearls gleam, rubies and sapphires glisten, and carvings and metalwork have their own distinctive surfaces. The precision is deliberate – this painting belongs to the *trompe l'oeil* genre, in which the aim was to deceive viewers into believing they were actually seeing real objects, not a painting.

The skull, an object often used by still-life artists in the 1600s, symbolises death and the passing of time. No matter how beautiful the objects in this cabinet look, the viewer is reminded that they are but worldly vanities.

The rendition of the carving is a superb example of *grisaille* (literally 'painting in greys'). It was a technique first used in the Low Countries in the 1400s by artists such as Jan van Eyck.

11 ▼ **Add touches of pink** The little bowl in front of the teapot has tiny, rose-coloured flowers. Mix a pink from cadmium red and white and add a few dots of colour to the bowl using the No.3 round.

13 ▲ **Continue outlining forms** Move to the right of the picture and fill in the spaces between the items such as the goblet and the milk jug, with the dark grey-brown mix. Once again, this edging lends solidity to the various forms. Take care not to eliminate all the background colour, as this golden tone lends vitality to the image.

12 ▼ **Fill in the negative shapes** To make the forms appear more three-dimensional, work on the spaces between and behind them. Mix a dark grey from your colours (using mainly red and blue) and start defining the small dark slivers in the background.

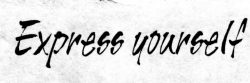

Express yourself

Cupboard love

In this pen and watercolour study, the artist focused on another corner of his dresser. The elegant sweep of the plate – defined with emphatic strokes of blue and grey – contrasts neatly with the detail of the foreground objects. A few dabs of pale opaque acrylic have been added to the foreground to break up the dense blue tone.

A FEW STEPS FURTHER

Despite the dark edges and shadows, the glass items appear rather flat. Add highlights to make the glass look more obviously translucent.

14 ▶ Paint reflections on the glass

Glass can present problems to the artist, particularly when it is colourless. The two wine glasses on the right side are barely discernible, so use the No.3 round brush to add some dots and vertical slashes of white to suggest light reflecting off the rounded surfaces.

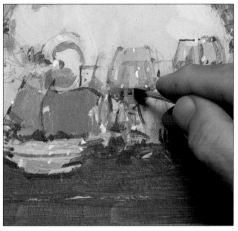

15 ▲ Heighten the contrasts
The two glasses in the centre could also do with some work. Dot more white highlights on to the bluish glass and add dark brown accents around the bowl of the yellow one.

THE FINISHED PICTURE

A Toned ground
The mid-toned straw undercolour is left unpainted to form the basic hue of the two central wine glasses, suggesting their translucent, coloured surface.

B Rough brush marks
Loosely applied brush marks are all that is needed to suggest the pattern on the crockery. Any more definition would draw too much attention to them.

C Shades of brown
The streaky mix of brown paint captures the varied tones of the wooden slats and helps describe their texture. The undercolour adds body beneath the thin mix.

Sweet selection

Bold acrylic colours are used to express the crinkled foil and cellophane wrappers of these shiny sweets.

At first glance, this painting looks like an abstract arrangement of bright colours and overlapping shapes, but closer inspection reveals a selection of sweets wrapped in foil and cellophane. If you compare the painting with the original photograph, you will see how the artist has communicated the busy nature of the composition, without getting bogged down in the reproduction of every single detail and pattern.

Abstract parts, lively whole

The painting was worked using small strokes of acrylic paints, which were mixed with matt medium in order to increase the flow and transparency of the paint. The artist has made use of varied directional brush strokes communicate the texture of the crinkled sweet wrappers.

The lively effect of the finished picture is hard to visualize when you put down the initial layer of paint, as this simply plots the sections of each sweet as semi-abstract shapes – it is accurate, but pretty flat. But once the pattern is set up, you can decide which sweets to emphasize and have fun developing their shiny surfaces.

▶ **Reflected colour, shadows and highlights create visual interest on these bright sweets.**

YOU WILL NEED

Piece of MDF 30 x 30cm (12 x 12in), prepared with four coats of gesso

HB pencil

13 acrylic paints: Cerulean blue; Deep violet; Titanium white; Phthalo blue; Lime green; Phthalo green;

Cadmium red; Naphthol red; Turner's yellow; Cadmium yellow light; Ivory black; Raw sienna; Yellow ochre

Acrylic matt medium

Mixing palette or dish

Brushes: No.2 flat; No.4 round

FIRST STEPS

1 ▶ Sketch out the composition Using an HB pencil, draw the outlines of the sweets on to the gesso-coated board. Then look for the main areas of tone within the sweet wrappers and mark these in too.

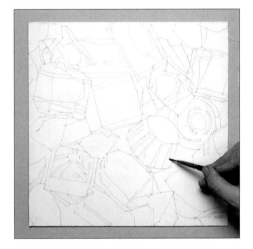

2 ▼ Begin with mid tones Pick out the blue stripes on the wrappers, using a mix of cerulean blue with a little deep violet and titanium white. Use a No.2 flat brush to describe the shapes, working within the pencil lines. Blend deep violet, a little phthalo blue and white to create purple and apply in the same way.

3 ▼ Paint the green shiny paper Blend equal amounts of lime green and phthalo green and paint the sweet wrapped in green foil. Allow the white gesso to show through between strokes to suggest the light catching the foil.

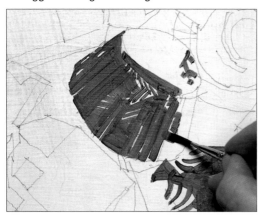

4 ▶ Echo the creases Mix cadmium red and naphthol red with a little Turner's yellow to make a vivid orange. Use directional brush strokes to describe the foil creases on the square sweet. Work up other areas of orange, including the reflections in the gold foil on the sweet next to the orange square.

5 ▼ Add more colours Dull the naphthol red with a little deep violet and block in the pink areas of the sweets at the top. Use a mix of cadmium yellow light and Turner's yellow to contrast with the purple stripes on the sweet at top left.

EXPERT ADVICE
Crinkled effects

On the crinkled surface of the gold sweets you can use the texture of the brush strokes to your advantage. Use the No.3 flat brush (with the hairs slightly splayed) to build up the surface with visible marks. Be careful not to brush the paint out flat, instead work in various directions.

6 ▶ Paint the gold sweets Blend ivory black, raw sienna, white and a little cadmium yellow light to form the gold-covered sweets as described in Expert Advice (see above right). Paint an extra gold sweet at the top right to balance the composition. Now lighten some ivory black with raw sienna and a little white and paint the dark areas of the wrappers.

7 ▼ Deepen the blue With acrylics, you can go back and rework an area with another layer of paint. To add a shadow to the blue and purple sweet, mix cerulean blue, deep violet and white, and use this mid tone to paint over the lighter blue underlayer.

DEVELOPING THE PICTURE

Now that you have blocked in the sweets as brightly coloured shapes, step back and see how you could develop the painting. It is time to make sure the sweets are seen as separate morsels rather than simply adjacent blocks of colour.

8 ▶ Crimping the wrappers Add more pigment to create darker versions of the blues and purples, and use angled brush strokes to describe the crimped surfaces and twisted ends of the sweet wrappers. Stick with one family of colours at a time, touching points all over the board with your brush. Then load up with the next colour and begin again.

9 ▲ Fill in a pink centre Mix naphthol red and deep violet with water. Use this translucent colour to narrow the white centre and modify the flat colour of the dark pink round sweet.

Master Strokes

Wayne Thiebaud (b. 1920)
Four Ice Cream Cones

Typically American processed foods – such as hamburgers, pies, cakes and ice creams – attracted artist Wayne Thiebaud during the early 1960s. He would often, as here, play on their regular shapes, arranging them in rows or other formal groupings. Thiebaud's everyday subject matter – together with his colourful, realistic painting style – led him to be categorized as a Pop Artist.

The texture of oil paint dragged across the paper conjures up the luscious quality of the ice cream itself.

Bright red and green lines edging the shelves contrast with the pastel shades used for the ice creams and add a strong horizontal element to counteract the vertical cones.

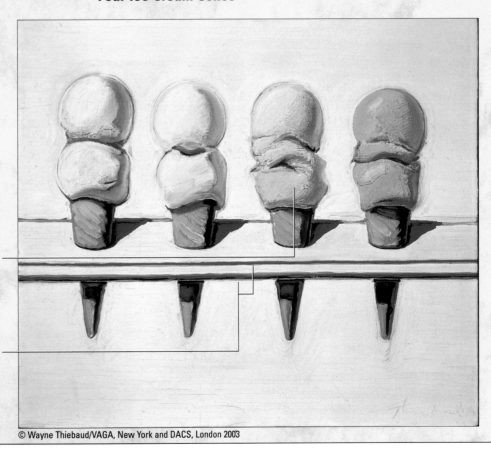

10 ▸ Show reflected colour Notice how the sweets next to the foil-covered ones are reflected in the shiny surfaces. Use a mix of naphthol red, deep violet and ivory black to darken both the square orange sweets, showing the reflections of the sweets around them. Then brighten the colour on your brush with a bit of cadmium red and vary the tones on the orange and purple sweet.

11 ▾ Deepen the folds Use phthalo green to paint the crinkles around the sides of the green sweet. Pull a dilute version of this over the red sweet to show the green reflection.

12 ▴ Add shadows Darken the browns on the golden sweets with a raw sienna/ivory black mix. Add yellow ochre and a little white and paint shadows on the gold cellophane. Now mix Turner's yellow with yellow ochre and a lot of water; brush shadows across the yellow sweets.

13 ▸ Texture the background Crisp up the sweets by painting a shadow under each with a mix of deep violet and ivory black. Show the green reflection on the central gold sweet with a mix of phthalo green and raw sienna. To add texture to the background, brush pure titanium white over the areas of white gesso, leaving your brush marks visible.

Express yourself
Sweets in pen and wash

Wrapped sweets with their shiny, eye-catching colours are fun to arrange and rearrange into different compositions. While still forming an interesting pattern across the paper, these sweets are treated in a more realistic way than the ones in the step-by-step project. They are drawn in pen and ink, with plenty of cross-hatching to build up tone and form and suggest the twists in the cellophane. Colour is added with water-soluble wax crayons, smoothed out by brushing on a little water.

A FEW STEPS FURTHER

The impasto background throws the 'cellophane' washes across the painting into relief. Just add some highlights and drawn details to make the sweet wrappers crackle into life.

14 ▼ **Dab on some white** Dilute some white with a little water. Using a No.4 round brush, mimic the sharpest highlights in the photograph by using bold dabs in the centre of the painted sweets.

15 ▲ **Tighten folds** Use the tip of the HB pencil to define folds in the cellophane sweet wrappers. Emphasize the edges of some of the earlier, twisting brush strokes.

THE FINISHED PICTURE

A Twisted ends
The purple and yellow brush strokes at the end of this sweet interlock with each other to suggest the twist of cellophane securing the wrapper.

B Mirrored colours
The shiny wrappers reflect the colours of the surrounding sweets. The green and orange reflections on the gold sweets are striking examples of this.

C Simplified design
The artist deliberately included the orange and purple sweet wrapper as the lines and vivid colours create plenty of excitement. Elsewhere he ignored a lot of the wrapper patterns as he thought the composition was busy enough.

Still life group in natural light

Two jugs and two bottles on a window sill can make a great painting – full of bold shapes, sinuous curves and a rich range of warm and cool colours.

A ccessible and small scale, still lifes are probably the most convenient subject for the painter. And they offer the added advantage of complete control over the composition.

The creative process

Some still lifes are 'found' – objects on a mantelpiece or window sill, for example. But most are 'composed' or put together by the artist, so that selecting and arranging the objects becomes part of the creative process. If you look around your home, you will find plenty of fascinating material.

Sometimes objects suggest a narrative – a collection of personal objects or an unfinished meal, perhaps – leading the viewer to speculate about the events surrounding the creation of the still life.

Arranging the objects

Often, however, objects are selected for purely formal qualities, such as colour or shape. This was the case in this painting – the artist chose to contrast two tall and rather austere bottles against the curving shapes of two jugs. He also liked the contrasts of tone and colour: the dark bottle

against the light jug, the warm ochres of the amber bottle and the brick of the window-sill contrasting with the cool tones of the white and blue jugs.

Changing your viewpoint

Take some time over the arrangement of the objects in your still life, creating either a casual appearance, as here, or organizing them more formally. It always pays to walk around any still life you have set up, viewing it from high and low, and from close to and farther back. Make thumbnail sketches to see how the various arrangements and viewpoints work and then choose the best composition. The artist here deliberately chose a high viewpoint, which emphasizes the sinuous shapes of the jug mouths.

Lighting is another important aspect of any still life. It creates shadows that give clues about the direction and intensity of the light, and the solidity of forms. Cast shadows anchor objects to the surface on which they are resting.

Lighting the objects

In this case, the artist placed the objects on a window sill because he liked the quality of the light. Natural light changes throughout the day, altering the appearance of the set-up, so the artist took a photograph to freeze one light effect. Although he worked directly from the subject, he had the photograph as reference.

▶ **These familiar, everyday objects offer a wealth of interest in terms of shape, colour and texture. The high viewpoint allows them to be seen from a slightly unusual angle.**

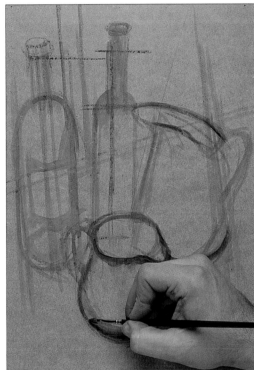

FIRST STROKES

1 ▲ Drawing the set-up Study the set-up, then load a No.1 short flat brush with a thin wash of phthalo blue and start to sketch in the main outlines. Try to visualize the objects as simple geometric shapes: the bottles as a series of cylinders, the white jug as a truncated cone and the bottom of the blue jug as a sphere. Let your eye travel over the subject looking for vertical and horizontal alignments, using your brush held at arm's length to find these relationships. Include the construction lines – these will be helpful in the early stages, but will be lost under the subsequent layers of paint.

2 ▶ **Add the brick sill**
Draw the bricks that make up the sill – these introduce important diagonals into the composition and establish a ground plane and a sense of recession. Use your brush to check the slant of the diagonals and note where they intersect with the objects. Block in areas of medium tone, using a thin phthalo blue wash. Add a little titanium white to make a pale tone for the white jug.

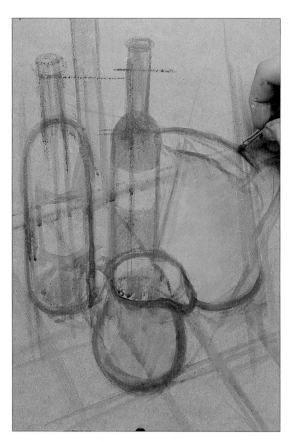

3 ▲ **Apply colour** Extend the pale tones on the white jug with a wash of phthalo blue, white and cadmium red. Use a lighter mix on the handle, and inside the blue jug. For the outside of the blue jug, make various mixes of phthalo blue, viridian, lemon yellow and white for a range of tones. For the light blues, mix phthalo, cadmium red and white.

4 ▲ **Block in the window sill** Use the darkest blue mix from step 3 to define the blue trim on the white jug and to paint the shadow of the blue jug cast on to the sill. Mix pale pink from lemon yellow, alizarin crimson, viridian and phthalo blue. With a No.6 brush, apply this colour to the sill, around the base of the blue jug, refining its shape as you go.

5 ▲ **Paint the dark bottle** Add a little more phthalo blue to the pink mix to darken the sill in the shadow of the white jug. Mix yellow ochre, viridian and alizarin crimson to give a range of green-greys for the dark tones on the large jug. Now mix dioxazine purple with viridian and alizarin crimson and apply this to the dark bottle with the No.6 brush. Add lighter tones on the sides where they catch reflected light.

6 ▼ Paint the light bottle Use cadmium yellow and yellow ochre to block in the amber tones of the left-hand bottle. Add alizarin crimson and viridian green to get a range of rich brown tones for the shadows and reflections. Allow the brush strokes to follow the surface forms – here the artist is working around the ellipse at the base of the bottle.

DEVELOPING THE STILL LIFE

The warm mid tone of the MDF support means that the image begins to emerge as soon as some light and dark tones are applied. Stand back and study the painting and subject to check that the balance of tones is correct. Then you can start to work up the background.

7 ▶ Develop light and dark tones Develop the tones on the bottles by modifying the basic mixes. For the labels, use an opaque grey mixed from yellow ochre, viridian, alizarin crimson and white.

Master Strokes

Patrick Caulfield (b.1936)
Untitled

Although the theme of this painting is the same as the one in the step-by-step painting – a still life on a window sill – the end result couldn't be more different. The image is reduced to simple black outlines and flat areas of intense colour with no suggestion of light and shade. While the focus of the step-by-step image is the sensitively modelled, curved forms of the objects, this image is about the abstract arrangement of shapes and lines.

Reduced to its bare essentials, the glass of water is a series of ellipses set within two slightly angled lines. The uncomplicated shape breaks into the flat blue plane of the sky.

The lines of the window and sill are cropped off at the edges, creating a series of interesting abstract shapes within the composition.

Don't show the lettering on the label in fiddly detail, which would be out of keeping with the style of the painting. Just make a pattern of marks – upright strokes for the large letters and horizontal strokes for the smaller ones.

8 ▲ Develop the sill Use some of the greys mixed in steps 5 and 7 to paint the pointing between the bricks. Work up more of the pink brick colour in between.

Express yourself
Monochrome study

Making a study in black and white with Conté crayons will encourage you to look hard for the tonal values in the still life. The grey tinted paper gives a mid tone. This is a useful exercise before you start working in colour and provides a striking drawing in itself.

9 ▲ Work the background Add the lettering to the label of the dark bottle (See Expert Advice, above) with the same mix you used for the rest of the bottle. With some of the greys mixed for the large jug in step 5, paint the glazing bars and mortar between the bricks. Add more white to this mix to paint the road in the background. Then paint in the outer sill and highlights on the bottles with white and just a touch of your grey mix.

A FEW STEPS FURTHER

The painting is now almost finished. The image is convincing and has a pleasing harmony of colour and tone. All it needs is a few touches to sharpen up the details of the bottle neck and to make the white jug look more solid.

10 ▼ **Add dark tones on the bottle**
Define the top of the amber bottle with a brown mix of dioxazine purple, viridian and alizarin crimson. Then switch to a violet made from dioxazine purple and a little palette mud.

11 ▲ **Develop the white jug** Use a range of warm and cool greys from your palette to convey the gradation of colour on the white jug. There is an area of cool grey where it picks up light reflected from the blue jug – elsewhere it is warmed by light reflected from the brick sill.

THE FINISHED PICTURE

A Toned ground
The naturally golden tone of the MDF unifies the image and provides a warm contrast to the cool greys in the background.

B Reflective surfaces
Touches of bright impastoed white on the bottle suggest the shiny, reflective character of the glass.

C Variations of tone
The gradation of light and dark and warm and cool tones around the blue jug helps to describe its smoothly curving surface.

Casual figure study in oils

The oil paints used to create this study of a young woman give the picture a distinctive, loose style, and a relaxed feel.

To do justice to a figure study in oils usually takes several hours – the painting here, for instance, took the best part of a day. During this time, sitters inevitably shift their weight slightly as they settle into a pose. Instead of ignoring these small changes, it pays to keep redrawing the figure as the painting progresses. This was the technique used in this portrait.

Keeping the painting alive

Frequent reassessments – boldly made in red and blue – kept the picture alive and lent a feeling of movement to the work. They also resulted in a more faithful rendition of the sitter – it is, after all, easier to paint the pose in front of you rather than the pose you remember.

A broad approach should start with the initial drawing. This need be no more than a few well-placed paint strokes to show the main directions of the subject. The positioning of the legs on the floor is particularly crucial. To get this correct, draw an imaginary square on the floor, linking the legs (see Step 1).

Flesh colours

Skin colours are kept simple. The subject is lit from the left, creating a strong bluish shadow down the right side of the figure. You will therefore need to introduce cool colours on this side while reserving warmer pink and brown mixes for the flesh tones that catch the light.

By using the traditional oil painting technique of working 'fat over lean', you will be able to build up the flesh tones in a loose yet controlled manner. The term 'fat' is normally used to describe paint that has been mixed with oil to give it a rich, thick texture. 'Lean' paint has been diluted with turpentine or other spirit to speed up the drying time. Hence the expression 'fat over lean'.

Start by blocking in washes of dilute, or lean, colour. As you develop the figure, introduce oil to your colours to create planes of bright colour in thicker, more opaque strokes. Then, by using less turpentine and more oil, gradually build up the image in progressively thicker layers until the work is complete.

▶ **Dynamic, broad brush strokes are a key feature of this study. Even the fingers and facial features are painted in this way.**

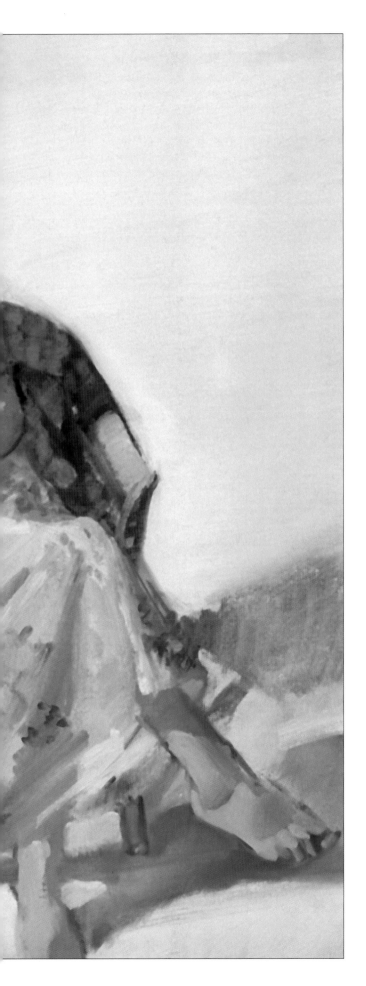

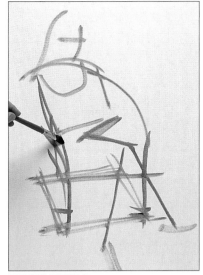

FIRST STEPS

1 ▲ **Make a brush drawing** Dilute raw umber and a little cobalt blue with plenty of turpentine and use this with a No.12 filbert brush to map out the position of the figure on the canvas. Paint with broad strokes, concentrating on the main lines and directions of the figure and chair. You may find it helpful to join the base of the legs into a square shape.

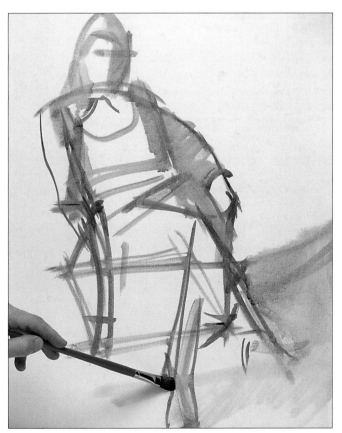

2 ▲ **Block in the shadows** Using the same dilute colour, loosely block in the shadow areas on the figure and indicate the shape of the thrown shadow on the floor.

3 ▶ Redefine the pose Add permanent mauve to the existing mixture and indicate the shadow on the clothing. Take the same colour into the shadow on the floor, paying attention to the cool, dark area between the feet. Change to a No.2 flat brush and redraw the figure. Make any necessary corrections and accommodate any changes that might have taken place in the pose by drawing over the existing lines using crimson lake.

A LARGE PALETTE

When working in oils, some artists prefer to mix their paints on an offcut of board, such as hardboard or marine ply. Unlike a conventional palette, the mixes can then be spread out and kept apart. This can encourage a looser, livelier painting style. A board measuring about 75 x 50cm (30 x 20in) is an appropriate size and can be rested on a table beside the easel.

4 ▼ Strengthen the shadow Returning to the No.12 brush, mix a dilute cool shadow colour from raw umber, permanent mauve and a little cobalt blue and use this to strengthen the shadow on the floor. Add a little yellow ochre to the mixture and block in the inside of the chair and the cool, dark shadows on the figure.

5 ▲ Paint the highlights For the pale flesh tones, mix yellow ochre, titanium white and a touch of crimson lake. Paint each highlight on the limbs as a single stroke. Add a little more white and crimson lake to the mix and block in the lit side of the face. Make a pale pink for the skirt with white, crimson lake and a touch of yellow ochre.

6 ▾ **Block in the background** Mix off-white for the background by adding a little of the palette mixtures to undiluted white. Working in bold, diagonal strokes, use a 25mm (1in) flat brush to block in the area around the figure. Vary the tone by adjusting the colours in the mixture – on the shaded side of the figure, the background should be slightly paler.

7 ▲ **Define the figure** Continue blocking in the background, cutting closely into the outline of the figure and using the thick off-white colour to redefine the form.

TROUBLE SHOOTER

BLOTTING THICK COLOUR

Oil paint that has become too thick too quickly, making the surface of the picture unworkable, can be blotted off with tissue, newspaper or other absorbent paper. A scrap of cotton fabric will also work well.

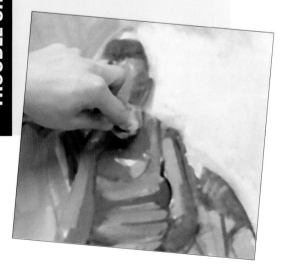

8 ▲ **Redraw in blue** Complete the background. Then change to the No.2 flat brush and finish blocking in the chair in yellow ochre and titanium white. Make sure the chair legs are accurately spaced. Paint the pink top in mixtures of crimson lake, permanent mauve and white. Finally, take in any adjustments to the model's position, using the cobalt blue.

DEVELOP THE PICTURE

The main areas of the chair and figure are now established. It is time to develop the features and add a little detail, carefully maintaining the broad, lively brushwork of the initial stages.

9 ▼ **Define the face and hair** With a No.4 flat brush, strengthen the cool shadows on the arms and neck in cobalt, white and a little raw umber. Mix raw umber, crimson lake, cobalt and white to paint the shadows on the face and define the features. Moving to the hair, paint the pale highlights in yellow ochre and white, and the dark shadows in raw umber.

10 ▲ **Paint the skirt tones** Using crimson lake and the No.2 brush, redefine the figure and reposition the legs and feet to accommodate any changes in the model's position. Mix light and dark versions of mauve, crimson, white and ivory black. Change to the No.12 flat and use the two mixes to strengthen the shadows and highlights on the skirt.

11 ▼ **Add pale flesh tones** Build up the flesh tones in opaque colour. Mix white, cadmium red pale, yellow ochre and a touch of lemon yellow and apply this thickly in short strokes to the illuminated side of the arms and face with the No.4 flat.

12 ▶ **Develop the chair** Add dark tones on the chair to match those on the figure, using the No.2 flat. The cushion is painted in ivory black and titanium white with a touch of cobalt blue. The structure of the chair and the dark interior of the seat are strengthened in a mixture of raw umber, burnt sienna and ivory black.

13 ▼ **Strengthen shadows** Suggest the skirt pattern with dabs of crimson lake. Change to the No.12 filbert and paint around the shape of the figure with the off-white background mix. Work into the shadow under the chair, using the background colour with added mauve.

14 ▶ **Describe the foot** Using the No.2 flat brush, describe the shape of the raised foot. Look carefully for the planes of light and shade and paint the pale areas in white, yellow ochre and cadmium red pale. For the shadow areas, darken this mixture with a little raw umber and cobalt blue.

Master Strokes

Thomas Wyck (*c.* 1616–77)
Young Girl Seated Before a Window

In this painting by the Dutch artist Wyck, natural light coming through the window illuminates the face of the young girl, leaving the room behind her in shadow. There is a lot of detail to be explored in the scene, but the girl's lit face and bright clothes serve as the focal points. Draped fabric plays an important part in the composition. The cloth on the cushion follows the shape of the girl's arm, while the curtain on the right echoes the curve of the body.

The rounded forms of the arms and the planes of the face are built up with creamy flesh colours blending into light grey shadows.

The precise rendition of light and shade on the red skirt and green apron describes how the fabric falls into folds and creases.

Express yourself
Sketching in paint

In this portrait, the artist is less interested in detail than in capturing the most important elements of the face. Like the main figure study, this approach is extremely valuable as a painting exercise – it discourages spending too much time on superficial pattern and detail, which can reduce the impact of the main structures and general composition.

EXPERT ADVICE
Improvised mahl stick

When wet colour makes it difficult to reach a particular area of the painting, you can use a large brush with a long handle as an emergency mahl stick. Hold the brush handle well clear of the wet surface and rest your painting hand on the handle to avoid smudging the wet oil colour.

A FEW STEPS FURTHER

The composition is bold and strong, but the face and body would benefit from a little more definition. Take care not to overwork the painting and bring in too much detail, as this would detract from the deliberately loose style.

15 ▲ **Complete the arms** Develop the skirt pattern in crimson lake and white, defining folds in mauve, white and raw umber. On the arms, pick out the highlights in yellow ochre, white and crimson lake. Suggest the shadows in yellow ochre, mauve and lemon. Take the light and dark tones into the face and hands, sculpting the wrists and fingers.

16 ▲ **Complete the head** Using mixtures of raw umber, yellow ochre and white, develop the highlights and shadows on the hair. Strengthen the shadows around the eyes, nose and mouth in mixes of raw umber, cobalt blue and yellow ochre. Paint the cheeks with yellow ochre and cadmium red pale, and the eyes with black and cobalt blue.

18 ▶ **Add final lights and darks** A few final details and the painting is complete. Define the chair legs in raw umber and yellow ochre. Sharpen the shadow under the chair, using a mixture of permanent mauve, cobalt blue and raw umber. Add highlights to the arms of the chair and on the patch of floor underneath it, using yellow ochre and white.

17 ▲ **Add chair texture** Work into the torso, using mixes of permanent mauve, crimson lake and white to define the stomach and chest. Darken the chair with raw umber, using directional strokes to indicate the wickerwork.

THE FINISHED PICTURE

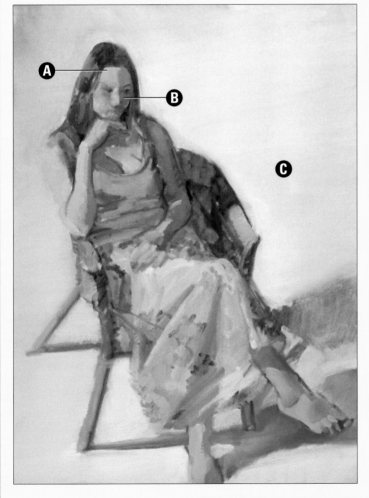

A Warm highlights
The pale, opaque flesh colours on the face catch the eye – they are mixed mainly from white with touches of red and yellow.

B Broad approach
The facial features were indicated as areas of light and shade with the minimum of detail, which complements the loose paintwork used for the rest of the figure.

C Integrated background
To create a colour harmony, the pale background was painted in white with small amounts of other mixes used elsewhere in the painting.

Seated figure in gouache

Soft, harmonious colours and an unusual pose make for an interesting study with the emphasis on modelling forms with light and dark flesh tones.

If a friend has agreed to pose for you, make the most of it – having a model is a great luxury. But at the same time don't abuse his or her generosity. Decide on a pose that is comfortable for them as well as interesting for you.

Bear in mind that your painting could, and probably will, take several hours. Don't expect your model, however flexible and well-intentioned, to hold an uncomfortable pose for too long. Also, whatever pose you establish, give him or her plenty of breaks. If, as in this case, it's a seated position, put a little masking tape on the ground to mark where the model's foot goes. Then she can return to her original position no matter how many coffee breaks she takes.

Paint with large brushes
The loose feel of this figure study is achieved initially by painting the outline with a large brush, rather than drawing it in pencil. Develop the form with flesh tints, again using a large brush. Gouache is opaque, so you can adjust the shapes and proportions as you progress, if necessary. Only change to a small brush for the final details of the facial features.

Stay-wet palette
To prevent your paints from drying out while you work, use a Stay-wet palette, which keeps paint moist for hours. This type of palette is made with quick-drying acrylics in mind, but is also useful for gouache paints if you are working on a project over a long period of time.

You can make your own palette from a polystyrene tray from a supermarket. Cut blotting paper to fit, then cut greaseproof paper to the same size. Place the blotting paper – the lining of the reservoir – in the tray and add a little water. Now put the greaseproof paper – the membrane – over it to form a surface to hold the paints. As the paints gradually dry out, more water is absorbed from the dampened reservoir paper below to keep them fresh.

▶ **The peachy flesh tones of this model are rendered with loosely applied gouache paint. The russet red cloth and pink slip add to the overall harmony.**

FIRST STEPS

1 ▶ Paint a loose outline Mix up a watery blend of burnt umber and cerulean blue to make a neutral tone. Using a No.12 round brush, start to map out the body, noting the relative positions of the limbs and head.

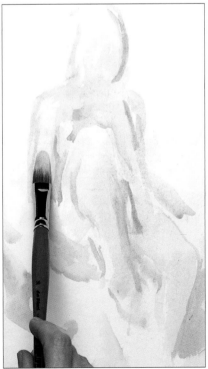

2 ◀ Start filling in the form Change to a No.16 filbert brush and mix combinations of titanium white, cadmium yellow and the two cadmium reds – deep and pale – to make a range of peachy flesh tones. Start filling in the body, applying the paints loosely.

3 ▼ **Add cool tones** Mix a cool blue from cerulean blue and a little burnt umber to paint the shadow along the side of the raised leg. With a more concentrated mix plus a little ultramarine and alizarin crimson, paint the triangle of the underwear.

4 ▶ **Balance the colours** Add a warm gold to the girl's left arm with a dilute mix of cadmium yellow and a touch of cadmium red deep. Suggest the sweep of her hair with burnt umber. Then use the No.12 brush to fill in the silk slip in a watery purple mixed from red-violet with a little cerulean blue and ultramarine. Balance this colour with a russet red shadow to the left of the raised leg – this is mixed from cadmium red pale, cadmium red deep, red-violet and burnt umber.

5 ▼ **Fill in negative shapes** Paint the russet triangles of fabric created by the position of the girl's legs. These negative shapes are important – get them right and the correct positive shapes will emerge. Now paint the varying tones on the girl's left arm, using the neutral mix from step 1 with cadmium red pale, cadmium yellow and white.

DEVELOPING THE PICTURE

Continue working up the flesh tones with pale pinks and peachy tints. As you are adding colour loosely, you'll need to define the edges of the limbs with darker lines of shadow in places.

6 ▲ **Develop flesh tones** Having completed the russet areas, mix pale pink for the girl's right arm where it catches the light, using cadmium yellow, cadmium red pale and white. Add a little cadmium red deep, burnt green earth and more white to the mix to describe grey shadows on the arm and left leg. Don't worry about being exact at this stage. Gouache is forgiving, so you can adjust colours and tones as you go.

7 ▶ Develop the tones For the shadows on the breasts, dilute the slip mix from step 4. Mix neutral grey, red-violet and burnt green earth to paint the stocking tops and a shadow beneath the foot. Wash a mix of cerulean blue, white and cadmium red deep over the wall. Now adjust limb tones, using the mixes from step 6 with more green earth for shadows and more white for lights. Put in the darkest shadows with neutral grey, cadmium red deep and ultramarine. Add a white highlight on the knee.

8 ▶ Model the face Paint the hair with a washy neutral grey mixed with burnt green earth. With the brush tip, pick up mixes from the palette to suggest facial features, using pale grey-browns for the eyes and a pinky-mauve for the mouth. Paint a slash of cadmium red pale mixed with white for the cheek, and cadmium red deep with white for the nose. Put a grey accent under the lower lip.

Master Strokes
Spencer Frederick Gore (1878–1914)
The Green Dress

In this oil painting by the British artist Spencer Gore, another pensive young woman is getting dressed. Gore's early work was strongly influenced by the Impressionists – which is evident here in the subtle play of light in the scene and in the sketchy application of the paint. The artist has used the device of a mirror to show the girl's face from two different angles – one as a three-quarter view, the other in profile. The palette is limited to a range of creams together with blue-greens and orange-browns – complementary colours that set up a strong contrast.

Dabs of thick, creamy paint are applied to the window panes to create an impasto surface that suggests sunlight filtering into the room.

The girl's face is modelled through the use of light and dark tones, with no attempt to capture the detail of her features.

9 ▶ Paint the fabric folds Extend the background shadows with a wash of red-violet, cerulean blue and white. For the chair leg, mix a light brown from burnt green earth and white; add the shadow in burnt green earth and neutral grey. Use the same browns on the girl's hair. Mix deep reds from red-violet and cadmium red deep to block in the folds in the draped fabric, defining the shape of the feet as you do this. Add more water and a little cadmium red light for the paler areas of the fabric.

REWORK PROPORTIONS

TROUBLE SHOOTER

Gouache paint is naturally opaque, which means it is ideal for overpainting areas and adjusting mistakes you might have made. Here, for example, one arm seems too broad, but it can be slimmed down by overpainting the edge in white.

Express yourself

Soft-focus figure

This smaller version of the figure study is worked in watercolour on a textured paper. Wet-on-wet washes produce soft passages of colour that run together where they meet, creating fuzzy, out-of-focus edges. Contrasts of light and dark tones give the face its form, and its features are just hinted at rather than clearly defined. Washy grey shadows form a hazy backdrop that enhances the rather ethereal feel of the composition.

10 ▲ Define the arm Edge the right forearm with a neutral grey/burnt green earth mix. Using a deep red from step 9, define the upper edge of the forearm, the slip and the lips. Finish the bottom right corner of the painting with a mix of red-violet with a little ultramarine.

A FEW STEPS FURTHER

Although the artist wanted the girl to have a dreamy look, the expression remains a little undefined. So revisit the face and suggest the features in greater detail.

11 ▶ **Work on the eyes** Use a No.4 round brush for the details. Paint the irises in cerulean blue with a touch of neutral grey, putting in black pupils and a white highlight. Then, with the very tip of the brush, draw the eyelids in a brown mixed from red-violet and ivory black.

12 ▲ **Complete the features** Paint the right eyebrow in burnt umber, and the left one in neutral grey. Use a peachy flesh tone from the palette to define the nose. With the red used for the lips in step 10, mark the nostrils.

THE FINISHED PICTURE

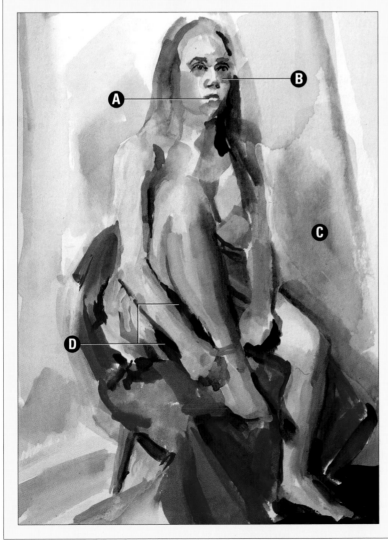

A Suggest the lip
The girl's bottom lip remains unpainted. It is suggested by the dark shadow beneath it.

B Distant expression
Subtle shadows around the girl's eyes, cheeks and jaw give a distant, rather melancholy feel to the picture.

C Anchoring the pose
The blue-grey shadows create a pleasing neutral background, as well as anchoring the pose.

D Dark outlines
Areas of deep russet red shadow surrounding the girl's forearms and legs were added to help define the forms of the limbs.

Sunlight and shadow

Use a variety of media to capture the moody atmosphere of a sunlit Indian interior.

This painting of the interior of a colonial mansion in Goa, south-west India, has an abstract quality to it, with much of the detail lost in areas of dark shade or bright light. Using a combination of media will help you to work loosely and capture these contrasts. Try to avoid searching for detail – instead, keep half closing your eyes so that the complex shapes are reduced to areas of light and dark.

First of all, use washes of Indian ink to create a loose tonal composition, blocking in the main shapes and areas of tone. Apply the acrylic colours in an impressionistic style until the overall picture begins to emerge. More Indian ink and charcoal are introduced, which helps to strengthen the dark tones of the painting and to mark in some of the detail.

Limited palette

Although a wide range of colours appears to be used in this rich painting, the artist actually worked with a fairly limited palette. Cadmium red, cadmium yellow, brilliant blue, alizarin crimson and white form the basis of many of the shades.

▲ **Sunlight streaming through jewel-coloured glass helps to evoke the exotic character of this Indian interior.**

1 ▶ Block in areas of dark tone Using a dilute wash of black Indian ink and a No.8 flat brush, block in the dark areas. Work very loosely and don't worry about achieving a uniform tone. With a No.6 round brush and less dilute ink, build up the darkest shadows (around the windows and on the furniture on the right), and outline the bureau on the left.

2 ▶ Introduce colour Still using the ink, deepen the shadows in the corners. Use a pale mix of titanium white and brilliant blue acrylics to edge the alcoves; make a stronger mix for the blinds outside the left-hand window.

3 ▲ Mix light tones Continuing with the blue mix, paint reflected light at the far end of the room. Add cadmium yellow for green glass on the left. Mix cadmium yellow and cadmium red for gold highlights on the floor; add lots of white for the pale cream areas on the furniture.

Express yourself

A snapshot view

Painting impressions of interiors provides very personal memories. Work in a handy, pocket-sized sketch book. This small watercolour shows a sunlit corner in the Goan mansion. Its features are described loosely, with some detail brought in for the chairs and balcony.

4 ▼ **Build up colour** Define the table with charcoal. Using dabs of alizarin crimson, cadmium yellow, cadmium red and white, suggest the highlighted chairs on the left. Paint the sunlight on the floor with the cream mix from step 3. Build up colour in the alcoves, using the cream mix with extra yellow, or the reddish chair mix. With a mixture of Indian ink and alizarin crimson, build up shadow on the bureau and wall.

5 ▲ **Draw out detail** Block in white lights on the windows and strengthen the shadow around them with ink. Use a brilliant blue/phthalo green mix to enhance the reflected blue light. Describe a chair leg on the left with a mix of alizarin crimson, yellow and white. Add gold tones to the furniture on the right, then use the ink to strengthen the dark tones here.

DEVELOPING THE PICTURE

Now that the main shapes are blocked in, introduce more colour, such as in the stained glass, and begin to add definition to the furniture with the charcoal.

6 ▶ **Add coloured panes** Using alizarin crimson, ultramarine and phthalo green, paint the stained glass. Blend ultramarine and ink for the darkest panes. With the inky brush, mix dark red-browns and mark in the table under the window. Add ultramarine panes to the left-hand window. Mix ultramarine, cadmium yellow, alizarin crimson and white to block in pinky-grey tones on the bureau.

EXPERT ADVICE
Broken lines

Use charcoal to roughly draw in the leading around the coloured glass in the far window. Don't draw an exact grid – use broken lines to create a more realistic image.

7 ▶ **Develop furniture detail** Use charcoal to delineate some of the furniture and ornaments. Changing to a No.3 round and the pale cream mix from step 3, add light touches between the chairs. Build up the chairs with mixes of alizarin crimson, red and cadmium yellow for warm tones; charcoal and ink for dark ones. Add mauve and more white to the pinky-grey mix for the side of the dresser.

Master Strokes

Patrick William Adam
(1854–1929)
Interior, Morning

A view through a doorway is a classic compositional device used by artists to frame a smaller scene within the main picture area. It has the effect of both intriguing the viewer, who can see only part of the room beyond, and offering an invitation to come inside. In this painting, the open window leading to the garden creates a third scenario. Dark tones in the foreground create a cool, shady hall, while the pale colours of the sunny room pull the eye into the picture. The palest tones are used for the sunlight that streams through the window, skimming across the objects on the table and the seat, and illuminating the floor.

The steep perspective on the open door leads the eye into the room beyond and gives the composition a convincing sense of depth.

The warm tones that dominate the painting are offset by small patches of blue for the sky and the flowers on the table.

8 ▲ Add warm tones Draw into the furniture on the right with charcoal. Mix alizarin crimson, brilliant blue, and cadmium red and yellow to paint the warm tones here.

9 ▲ Paint the floor Paint blue and white panes on the centre window. Mix grey-brown from alizarin crimson, cadmium yellow, brilliant blue and white; add to the walls and floor. Develop floor shadows with alizarin crimson and green mixes. Build up the tiles with dabs of alizarin crimson, blue, an orange palette mix and ink. Add mauve and blue-grey highlights on the right.

10 ▲ Build up detail Further define the furniture on the right with charcoal. Make a pale blue-grey with white, ultramarine and a touch of alizarin crimson to add highlights around the far and left windows. Using a dry brush, pick out the candlestick and touch in shadows on the table on the left. Use the grey-brown mix for the panes on the left.

A FEW STEPS FURTHER

With a loosely worked picture, it can be difficult to decide when to stop painting. At this stage, you only need to build up a little more contrast between light and dark tones.

11 ◀ **Build up the highlights**
Brighten the window alcove on the left, using the No.6 round brush. Use a pinky-white mix next to the window panes and a greeny-white one beside it. Strengthen the brilliant blue and white tiles on the edge of the alcove.

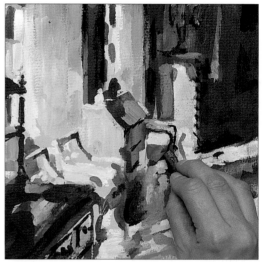

12 ▲ **Contrast lights and darks** Use charcoal to strengthen the shadows on the walls and to pick out some of the detail on the furniture. Add further details with ink and the No.3 brush.

THE FINISHED PICTURE

A Built-up colour
Complex shapes such as the elegant carved chairs were reduced to areas of light and dark tone. The actual image emerged gradually as dabs and longer strokes of colour were built up.

B Loose work
The pattern of the floor tiles was suggested rather than rendered in detail. Indeed, in the bright sunlight, the artist ignores the pattern altogether and simply builds up pale yellow tones.

C Charcoal details
Charcoal was used to tighten up areas of the painting by adding linear definition to the furniture and ornaments. Its matt texture contrasts with the slight sheen of the acrylic paints.

Moroccan market

Market scenes provide endless subject matter for drawing. Convey the life and colour in this bustling scene with a combination of media.

W hen drawing a vibrant, sun-baked scene such as this bustling market in Morocco, you'll be able to capture the atmosphere more effectively if you introduce some colour into the picture. For the painting here, the artist used gouache paints to convey the bright sunshine, exotic clothing and plentiful produce of this stimulating scene.

Brown paper
To make a change from white paper, the artist chose to work on a heavyweight brown wrapping paper – also known as kraft paper – which provides a warm background for the market scene painting. This pleasing tone shows through in between the painted figures here and there, and this echoing of colour helps to unify the composition.

Brown kraft paper is shiny on one side and matt on the other, and has a faint stripe running through it. Here, the matt side was used – it has a fairly rough texture, so you'll find that your pencils wear down quickly and will need frequent sharpening. As you'll be using a

fair amount of paint in this project, make sure you stretch the brown paper before you begin.

Pair of pencils
The drawing is worked in two different types of pencil, which gives you scope to make a variety of marks and tones. The red-brown colour and soft,

▲ Gouache paints complement a pencil-and-Conté drawing of traditionally dressed Arab women in a market.

chalky texture of the sanguine Conté pencil are ideal for the initial drawing, while the 7B graphite pencil makes heavy, black lines suitable for prominent details and areas of dense shadow.

FIRST STEPS

1 ▶ Map out the scene
Most of the main lines in the scene are gently curved – the draped awning, the edge of the shadow on the ground and the clothing of the woman in the foreground. Draw these on to the rough matt side of the brown kraft paper, using a sanguine Conté pencil.

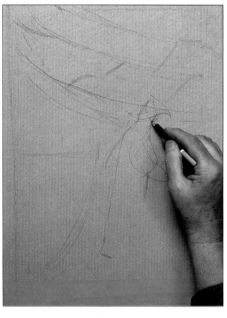

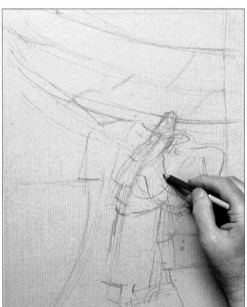

2 ◀ Work up the woman's figure
Rework the main lines to strengthen them. Complete the foreground by drawing the crates of produce and outline the bending figure on the right. Work into the figure of the woman standing in the foreground, describing her layers of clothing in slightly more detail.

3 ▼ Sketch the other figures Strengthen the lines of the bending figure on the right. Suggest the strolling figures on the left quite simply, marking in the draped fabric of their robes.

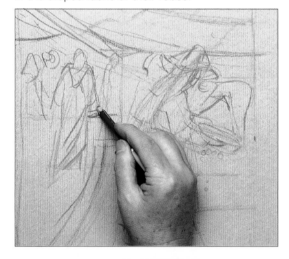

DEVELOPING THE DRAWING

At this point, change from the Conté pencil to a soft, black one to shade in the darkest areas in the scene. Use this pencil, too, to build up details on the clothing and market produce.

4 ▶ Look for dark tones Change to a 7B pencil and shade in the dark figure in the distance on the left, and the back of the bending figure on the right. In the foreground, draw the potatoes in the crate, then rework the main figure, outlining details such as her hands holding the bowl and the pattern on her blouse. Begin drawing in the stripes on her skirt.

5 ◄ Complete the pencil lines Finish drawing the stripes on the skirt, add the sash and darken the hatband and the shadow under the hat brim. Sketch in more vegetables. Now outline the row of figures in the centre and strengthen with black lines the awning above them. Work up the figures, indicating the main folds and shadows in their robes (see Expert Advice, right).

6 ▼ Paint on some pale colour Still using the 7B pencil, block in the shadows under the left-hand figures and scribble roughly over the shadow cast by the awning on the ground. Now mix a little burnt umber gouache with bleedproof white gouache to make a very pale beige. Working loosely with a No.4 squirrel brush, paint this over the awning and sunlit ground.

EXPERT ADVICE
Folds in stripes

When you are drawing the draped fabric of the skirt, don't just indicate the fold with a curved line. The draped fabric will look much more natural if you slightly curve the stripes along the length of the fold. To suggest the shadow formed under the fold, darken the stripes by pressing harder with the 7B pencil.

▶ **Burnt umber gouache (left), mixed with a little burnt sienna (middle) and bleedproof white (right), provides the brown and beige shades in the awning.**

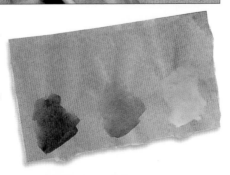

7 ▲ Paint the shadows Add more burnt umber and a little burnt sienna to the mix to make a grey-brown. Apply the colour freely over the shaded fold of the awning and across the path.

8 ▾ Bring in brighter colours Take the shadow colour over the robed figure to the left of centre. Then mix cerulean blue with white and fill in the patch of bright blue sky. Change to a No.5 round brush. Add a little scarlet to white to make a pale pink and brush this over the pink-robed figures, describing the fabric folds with the brush tip.

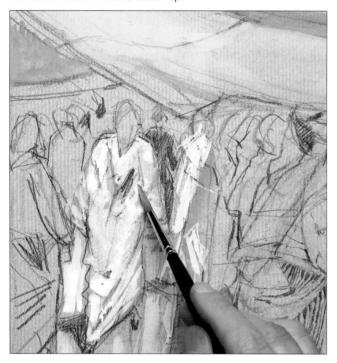

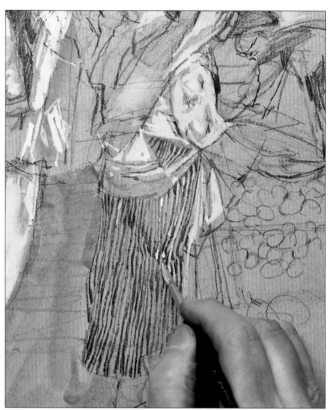

9 ▴ Put in the lights Mix bleedproof white with a little cerulean blue and scarlet, then work over the pale areas on the main figure's clothing.

10 ▾ Paint the vegetables Mix white with a little burnt sienna; paint the woman's hand and bowl. Change to the No.4 squirrel brush. Add olive green to lamp black and pick out the pattern on the woman's sleeve. Use it to put in shadows around the vegetables, too. Paint the peppers with a mix of olive green and a little burnt sienna.

11 ▴ Add warm colours Use the olive green/burnt sienna mix to paint the other box of peppers beyond the bowl. With pure vermilion, add splashes of red to the scene – the tomatoes, the robes and the patterns on the main figure's clothing. Paint the woman's face and ankle with the white/burnt sienna mix, adding more white for her shoe. Using pure bleedproof white, paint the headscarves of the women on the left. Mix yellow ochre and white to paint the potatoes and the main woman's hat.

12 ▾ **Paint the purple robe** Describe the purple clothing on the left with a mix of brilliant violet and white, then put in the shadows with a darker violet mix. Use white for the scarf and distant awning.

13 ▸ **Put in details** Shade under the main figure's hat with a mix of burnt umber and yellow ochre, then darken flesh tones with vermilion mixed with burnt sienna. Add the blue robes in the crowd with a cerulean blue/viridian mix; use black for the darkest robes and final details. Mark in the stripes in the awning with a mix of burnt umber and yellow ochre; for the lighter areas and the fringe, mix white with a touch of yellow ochre and vermilion.

A FEW STEPS FURTHER

The market scene is now almost complete and is full of life and colour. To bring the picture into sharper focus, return to the Conté and 7B pencils to add some texture and details over the paint, especially in the foreground.

14 ▸ **Put pattern on the clothing** Using the No.5 round brush, mix cerulean blue with a touch of black and dot in the spotted pattern on the woman's scarf. Suggest the butterfly pattern on her blouse with the brilliant violet.

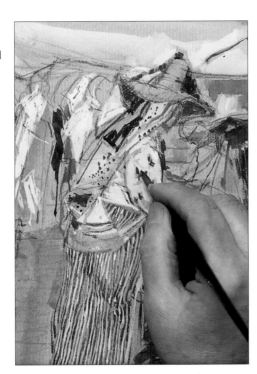

15 ▴ **Add drawn details** Complete the sleeve with a black/cerulean blue mix and cadmium lemon. With the 7B pencil, work up texture on the hat and on the bending woman. Draw shadows among the vegetables with the Conté and 7B pencils.

16 ▲ **Draw in shadows and texture** Use the 7B pencil to draw folds on the robes on the left and to darken the cast shadows. On the right, block in the hair of the bending figure. Draw fine lines to suggest the woven texture of the awning.

17 ▲ **Draw final details** Outline some of the peppers in the foreground, using the 7B pencil. Shade the front of the woman's leg with the Conté pencil.

THE FINISHED PICTURE

A Loose colour
Vibrant gouache colour was applied very loosely once the initial drawing was complete. In this way, the gouache complements rather than dominates the drawing.

B Pencil over paint
Pencil lines were added over the painted colour of the women's robes on the left. This describes the folds in the flowing garments and captures a sense of movement.

C Uncluttered space
The curve of the market awning at the top of the composition offers a large, uncluttered area of plain colour to offset the otherwise busy and detailed scene.

City architecture

Contrast old with new, light with dark in this exciting coloured pencil drawing of a street in the City of London.

▲ **A dramatic study of light and shade, this unusual cityscape uses coloured pencils in a painterly way.**

In the business areas of thriving cities, tall modern buildings spring up seemingly overnight and dominate the skyline, dwarfing the more traditional ones around them. In most cases, old and new buildings exist happily side by side, creating fascinating contrasts of shape and style.

Tonal contrast

In this scene, two striking examples of modern architecture soar above the conventional office blocks. While the narrow street is in deep shadow, the tall buildings emerge from the shade into the sunlight. The artist has heightened this tonal contrast by making the diagonal band of sky a strong, bright blue that shines out from the moody, dark colours of the street below.

Dark paper

As much of the scene is in shadow, the artist chose as a support a dark pastel paper with a honeycomb texture. This saves a lot of work, as you don't need to spend time shading heavily in order to create all the dark tones – lightly shaded colour allows the grey-brown paper to show through. For pale areas, such as the sky and the white features on the buildings, you'll find that light-coloured pencils cover the dark paper well, especially if you press hard as you are blocking in.

FIRST STEPS

1 ▶ Begin with the sky Using a bright blue coloured pencil, draw the sky as a negative shape defined by the buildings and the diagonal overhang at top right. Change to a white pencil and mark in key points such as the vertical pipes on the left-hand tall building. Return to the bright blue pencil to block in the sky.

STARTING ON THE DARK TONES

With the main light areas established, go to the other end of the tonal scale and begin blocking in the dark areas down at street level and on the shaded walls of the buildings.

3 ◀ Establish the darks Build up more white in the sky, then use the white pencil to outline the office buildings at the far end of the street. Changing to a black pencil, establish dark features on the tall buildings and mark in the road and the edge of the office blocks on the right. Hatch verticals on to the block on the left and begin shading this dark area.

4 ▶ Work on the dark tones With the black pencil, mark in the dark diagonals on the conical building and add details to the crane. Shade loosely across the left-hand office block with vertical strokes, darkening the tone on its right edge. Define the bottom of the exposed pipework.

2 ▼ Lighten the sky To make the distant sky paler, layer white over the bright blue undercolour, working carefully around the edge of the conical building and the crane next to it. Use strong pressure to fill in the texture of the paper. Mark in diagonals on the conical building and highlight its right-hand side.

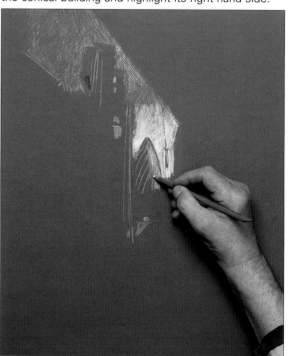

5 ▲ Develop the foreground Shade a mid tone across the road with the black pencil, then work up some architectural features on either side. For example, shade in some of the windows on the right and the negative shapes around the struts on the left. To add life to the scene, mark in the distant taxi and the figure as simple silhouettes.

6 ▼ **Warm up the picture** Work up the dark tone on either side of the street with the black pencil, varying the direction of your strokes to follow the lines of the buildings (see Expert Advice). Now change to a raw umber pencil and add warm colour to the sunlit tops of the buildings on the left. Shade the same colour over the pale stone walls at the end of the street.

7 ▼ **Emphasize the white detail** Using heavy pressure on the white pencil, define the light-coloured architectural details on the left-hand tall building – the vertical pipes, the balconies and the spiral feature. For the strongest whites, fill in the texture of the paper.

EXPERT ADVICE
Shading the walls

The buildings are best shaded with sweeping strokes that follow the direction of the flat plane. Here, the slant of the overhang is accentuated with diagonal blocking-in strokes.

8 ▲ **Develop the darks and lights** Complete the long white pipes on the left-hand building, then put in contrasting black areas of shadow between the white features. Highlight the office blocks on the right with the white pencil. Now deepen the black tone on the edge of the diagonal overhang and layer blue-violet and Indian red pencils to liven up the shadowy walls below it.

9 ▼ **Use more Indian red** With long, free strokes, shade more Indian red over the area on the right, moving up to the diagonal overhang. Work the blue-violet all over the office block on the left, then cross-hatch Indian red over the top – the colours mix optically to create a lively brown.

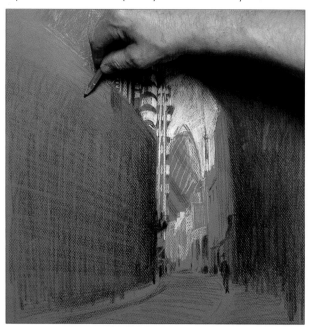

10 ▼ **Describe the left-hand façade** Working quite loosely, shade layers of Indian red and blue-violet where the sun hits the block at top left. Then drift black pencil lightly over it. Outline the windows in white, making the lower ones less defined. Block in the dark windows with black, the pale ones with white.

11 ▼ **Work on the conical building** Use the white pencil to lighten the sky around the conical building and intensify the highlight on the right-hand side. Then build up its diagonal framework with bands of white and bright blue.

12 ▲ **Strengthen darks and lights** Using the black pencil, outline the conical building with a fine line and fill in the darker diamond-shaped panes of glass. Sharpen up features on the other buildings, too. Make the shadow on the right even more dramatic with heavy black and blue-violet shading. Finally, lighten the top part of the sky with a layer of heavily applied white.

A FEW STEPS FURTHER

By indicating some of the architectural features, you can give the buildings on the right more character. Very loosely suggest a few more figures and some street furniture too.

13▶ Add architectural features Drift a little olive green over the stone buildings at the end of the street. Then use the white and black pencils to describe their architectural features in more detail, such as windows and cornices.

14▲ Darken the foreground Shade more black pencil over the road, emphasising the left-hand kerb edge. Suggest bollards and figures on the left. Now change to an indigo pencil and shade loosely over the foreground area, including the figures.

THE FINISHED PICTURE

A Leading the eye
The diagonal band of bright blue sky draws the eye into the picture towards the focal point – the conical building.

B Striking whites
The unusual architectural features of the tall, modern building have been emphasized with heavily applied white pencil to provide a contrast with the shadowy street below.

C Dramatic darks
The dark tones and dramatic angles of the buildings on either side of the road create a canyon-like space that guides the eye to the skyscrapers in the distance.

Birds in flight

Arctic terns give structure and scale to this energetic study of the churning seas off the remote Farne Islands in the North Sea.

You don't have to be a dedicated ornithologist to enjoy watching, drawing and painting birds. Apart from their variety and grace, they enliven a composition, leading the eye into or around a picture. They are especially useful in seascapes, where there are no sight lines and few other spatial clues. Birds wheeling over the sea inject a sense of scale into a marine study.

Emphatic shapes

There are other ways in which birds can contribute to a composition. In flight, birds create a series of emphatic shapes. The fully extended wingspan provides a strong horizontal which becomes a dynamic diagonal when tilted, while the beating wings make a series of V-shapes. These forms can become an important element within a composition, especially when the birds are placed to the front of the picture space.

Broad characteristics

When you are painting birds as part of a landscape, you won't need the same degree of detail as an artist dedicated to bird studies. It is more appropriate to capture their broad characteristics and sense of movement in a simple way. The birds depicted in this painting are Arctic terns, which are closely related to gulls, but are smaller and more slender in build with narrow, tapering wings, a forked tail and long bills. Most have whitish plumage with black caps.

The terns in the foreground were first sketched in silhouette, using light-coloured pastels. Simple tonal shading built up the birds' forms, which were then refined by adding the characteristic markings and bright orange bills and legs. The bird in the background was more simply drawn.

Find the right approach

When you are working on your painting, avoid the temptation to give more attention to the birds than to their

surroundings – if they become more resolved than the rest of the painting, then the picture will jar.

For example, if your style is loose and impressionistic, render the birds in the same way. If you tend to work in a tighter, more closely focused way, then apply that approach over the entire support, depicting the birds in more detail.

▼ **This image captures the graceful flight of Arctic terns as they dip and wheel above the surging waters of the North Sea.**

YOU WILL NEED

Piece of 300gsm (140lb) Not watercolour paper 56 x 76cm (22 x 30in)	Piece of thin plastic for scraping
	16 soft pastels: White; Sky blue; Putty grey; Light grey; Lemon yellow; Off-white; Light blue; Yellow ochre (light tint); Raw umber; Dark grey; Burnt orange; Pale yellow; Cobalt blue; Cerulean blue; Pale blue; Ultramarine (light tint)
Brushes: No.20 flat; 75mm (3in) hake; No.20 filbert; Nos.4 and 8 rounds	
9 gouache paints: Prussian blue; Burnt sienna; Marine blue; Winsor green; Naples yellow; Ultramarine; Permanent white; Ivory black; Indian red	Paper tissue and cotton cloth
	Putty rubber
	Strips of card to crop the image

PICK AND CHOOSE

Don't feel you have to take all your information from a single photograph or sketch. The photo above helped with the drawing of the far left tern, while the photo on the right was used for the sea and spray. Reference books can also be invaluable for establishing bird shapes.

FIRST STEPS

1 ▶ Block in the rocks
Mix Prussian blue and burnt sienna gouache to create a deep blue colour for the rocky promontory. Use a No.20 flat brush and big gestures to apply the colour. Work broadly and try to 'feel' your way around the looming bulk of the rocks.

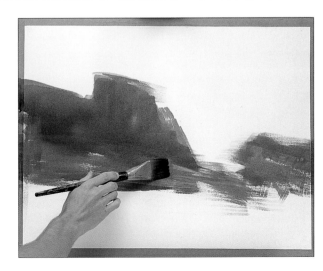

EXPERT ADVICE
Scraping back

By scraping paint from the support, you can create light tones and interesting textures and reveal underlying paint layers. This technique is very effective with gouache, which has more body than watercolour. The best scraping tools are slightly springy – a piece of scrap plastic, an old credit card or a plastic painting knife.

2 ▲ Block in the sea Using the same brush and a wet wash of marine blue, apply broad strokes of colour to the sea. Do the same with a thin wash of Winsor green. This transparent blue-green provides an effective base for the heaving sea.

3 ◄ Apply base colour to the sky Mix a wash of Naples yellow and block in the sky, using a 75mm (3in) hake to give broad coverage. The creamy yellow hue captures the sense of sunlight. Mix in a little marine blue on the right.

4 ▲ Add dark tones Mix ultramarine and burnt sienna to make a deep, almost black tone. Returning to the No.20 flat brush, apply this colour over the surface of the rocks, using broad, sweeping strokes.

5 ▲ Scratch through the paint Use a piece of thin plastic to scrape through the dark paint at the base of the rock (see Expert Advice, above). This lightens the area and restores the transparency of the paint layer. Work into the rock forms, using your scraping tool to reveal the planes of the rock surface.

DEVELOPING THE PICTURE

As both soft pastel and gouache are opaque and slightly chalky, they complement each other very well. Alternating one with the other as the painting develops gives a range of effects.

6 ▼ Apply soft pastel Start to work into the rocks with pastel sticks which allow you to make more precise marks. Apply highlights in white, sky blue, putty grey and light grey. Use the tip of the stick to make narrow lines and the side of the stick for broader swathes of colour.

7 ▼ Add highlights on the water Change to a No.20 filbert brush and apply washes of permanent white gouache at the base of the rocks, where the sea swells against them and breaks up into spray. Brush on the paint with a series of energetic marks.

8 ▼ Develop the rocks Take white gouache over the sky. Refine the silhouette of the rocks and apply brushy marks over their surface. While the paint is still wet, soften the marks with your fingertips to create a thin veil of scumbled colour. Where the paint covers the pastel marks, it becomes tinted with the pigments.

9 ▼ Apply pale pastel across the sky With the stick held on its side, work lemon yellow pastel into the sky. Then use the tip of the pastel to draw back into the rocks, highlighting some of the edges.

10 ▶ Block in the tern Sketch the silhouette of the tern in the centre of the composition, using a combination of off-white, light grey and light blue pastels. Look only for the main shapes at this stage – leave the details for later.

11 ▶ **Add details to the bird** Using a yellow ochre (light tint) pastel with a few touches of raw umber, add warm tones under the tern's body. Put in some dark grey shadow and white highlights. Use a No.4 round brush and ivory black gouache for the bird's characteristic black cap, the long curving beak and the legs.

12 ▼ **Work colour details** The Arctic tern has a distinctive orange bill and legs. Use a burnt orange pastel to apply colour to them.

Master Strokes

Winifred Nicholson (1893–1981)
Sandpipers, Alnmouth

In this simple, semi-abstract composition, the flock of birds together with the curved shapes of the seascape form a simple, graphic image. Note how the birds echo the curve of the inlet. The colours in the painting are restricted to shades of blue and honey brown, with a few emphatic strokes of dark grey and white for contrast. This gives an overall effect that is light, airy and harmonious.

Thickly applied oil paint leaves brush marks visible on the sea, giving an impression of its rippling surface.

A glaze of light brown applied over the water in the shallow inlet suggests reflections of the sandy banks.

Scattered over wet paint in the foreground, a sprinkling of sand creates a granular texture on the beach.

13▾ **Develop the sea** Add pale yellow pastel highlights on the tern's bill and legs. Apply dark grey pastel to the tern's head and to the rock behind the bird. Develop the sea, using cobalt blue and cerulean blue pastels, then soften the marks with your fingers or a tissue to create a film of colour.

14▾ **Add dark tones in the sea** Mix Prussian blue gouache with a touch of Indian red to make a deep blue tone. Using the No.20 filbert brush fairly dry, make a succession of vigorous, sweeping marks that follow the undulations of the waves around the rocks.

15▾ **Indicate spray** Scumble cobalt blue pastel over the sea and rocks, using the side of the stick. Make a pad from a piece of cotton cloth and work this over the surface of the pastel, spreading it thinly to produce a veil of pigment that suggests spray.

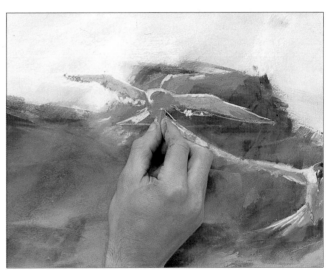

16▴ **Add a second tern** Outline the second tern with white pastel. Block in the shadows under the body and wings with light grey, dark grey, yellow ochre and raw umber pastel. Work broadly, looking for light and dark areas and warm and cool tones rather than details such as the feathers.

17◂ **Build up layers on the sea** Finish the second tern by indicating the black cap and burnt orange bill and legs. Add touches of pale blue to enliven the shadows on the bird. The sea in the foreground needs more texture and detail to pull it forward in the picture plane. Using the No.20 filbert and a wash of permanent white gouache, start to apply the colour with sweeping gestural marks that follow the shapes of the waves. Note that the white paint picks up the cobalt blue pigment from step 15 and tints the white to a very pale blue in places.

18 ▲ Add more blue Skim an ultramarine (light tint) pastel over the surface of the sea on the left. Blend and soften the pigment with your fingertips to add a further glaze of colour to the sea.

19 ▲ Paint a third bird Use off-white, white and light grey pastels to draw a third tern in the distance. With a No.4 brush, paint the bill and legs with burnt sienna gouache and the cap and wingtips in pale grey mixed from permanent white and ivory black. By showing birds at different sizes, you create a sense of recession in the painting.

Express yourself
Solo flight

If you are interested in birds, devote some time to making studies of different species in their natural habitat. Here, a gannet is depicted in mid-flight against an impressionistic sky. Seen in profile, the shape of the head and the characteristic long, pointed beak are clearly discernible, while the upstretched wings, poised for a down beat, give a sense of imminent movement. As in the main step-by-step painting, a combination of gouache and pastel provides soft passages of layered colour.

20 ▲ Create more texture Load a No.8 round brush with a thinned wash of permanent white paint and describe a few foam-tipped waves in the centre ground with linear marks. Draw more swirling lines with the white pastel. Using the tip of the brush, flick white paint across the sea and rocks to suggest spray.

A FEW STEPS FURTHER

Before continuing, tape strips of card over the painting to crop it to a wide format known as a 'marine' format (see The Finished Picture, below). This emphasizes the birds in the composition, but makes the left-hand rock look too dominant. Correct this by adjusting the rock's silhouette to fall below the bird.

21 ▼ **Overpaint the rock** Apply light grey pastel over the rock behind the left-hand tern, working carefully around the bird. Work freely over the rock to suggest waves breaking over it.

22 ▲ **Soften the pastel** Use a putty rubber to soften and smear the light grey pastel – this enhances the effect of water streaming off the rocky surfaces.

THE FINISHED PICTURE

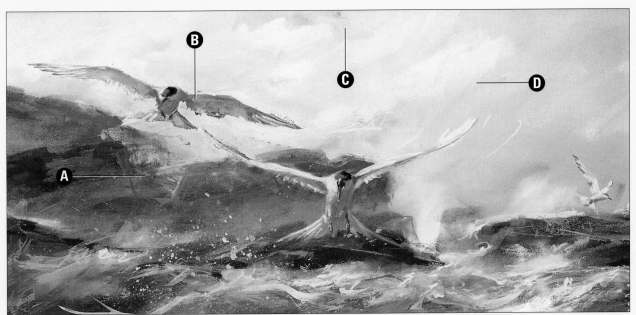

A Layered colour
The shifting mass of the sea was suggested with layers of scumbled and dry-brushed gouache, and with pastel applied as blended veils of thin colour.

B Selective editing
The left-hand tern creates a dark shape against the light background of the sky. This is in contrast to the other tern, which appears light against dark.

C Warm sky
An underwash of Naples yellow worked across the sky glows through subsequent layers, suggesting sunlight glimpsed through scudding clouds.

D Bright lights
Touches of opaque white pastel and gouache above the rocks capture the misty effect created by spray and foam thrown up by the crashing waves.

Fish pond with carp

Working on a large-scale project demands a bold approach and plenty of paint. Buy your materials at your local DIY store to create this mural-sized fish pond.

Koi carp are a wonderful sight in a garden pond, their streamlined bodies flashing to and fro beneath the surface. This large-scale painting focuses on several fish swimming in water overhung by leafy trees that create dark reflections. The moody, light-dappled water dramatically offsets the silvery grey and golden shades of the fish.

Photos and sketches

A selection of photographs of carp swimming in small groups (right) provided the initial inspiration for the painting. The artist combined the fish into a pleasing composition in a tonal pencil sketch (far right), omitting one or two to create a clean, unfussy look.

DIY materials

When working a large-scale project such as this – the picture measures 1.2 x 2.4m (4 x 8ft) – you will need plenty of room, so consider working outdoors on a dry day. You will also need lots of paint. Emulsion paints from DIY stores can look just as effective as artists' paints and are much cheaper than the equivalent artists' colours – especially if you use sample pots. These are available in a standard range of shades or can be individually mixed, giving you access to a vast array of colours. The project is painted on a piece of MDF (medium density fibre-board). This, too, is available from DIY stores, where they will cut it to size for you. MDF has a smooth surface and forms a rigid support for a large painting.

Emulsion paint is very versatile. It can be mixed on the palette and thinned with water, and it dries quickly so that you can overpaint it. This picture was initially worked with washy paint to establish the tones. This underlayer was applied with a 50mm (2in) flat brush, allowing the artist to cover the large support rapidly. Once dry, this was developed with thicker paint to give a richer surface.

YOU WILL NEED

Piece of 13mm
(½in) MDF,
1.2 x 2.4m
(4 x 8ft)
primed with
white emulsion

4B graphite stick

8 emulsion
paints (sample
pots): White;
Crimson; Bright
yellow; Dark blue;
Black; Pale stone;

Grey-green;
Dark grey

Brushes: No.4,
25mm (1in),
50mm (2in) and
13mm (½in) flats

Large palette
or tray

Jar of water

Kitchen paper

4B graphite pencil

▼ Emulsion paint applied with big brushes makes this larger-than-life composition easy to achieve.

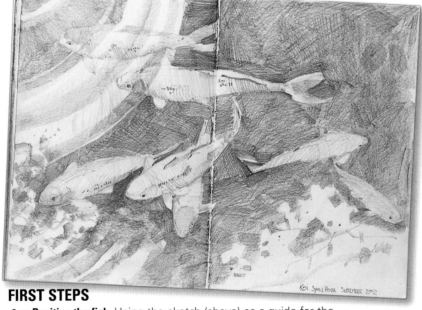

FIRST STEPS

1 ▼ **Position the fish** Using the sketch (above) as a guide for the composition, draw the shapes of the fish with a 4B graphite stick. Step back often to check that you have a balanced composition. Mark in the fishes' backbones, fins and eyes and add the curves of the ripples in the top left-hand corner.

2 ▼ **Start painting** Mix white emulsion with crimson, bright yellow, dark blue and black to make a mid grey. Using a No.4 flat brush, begin outlining the grey fish. Add pale stone to the mix, then paint the bodies using a 25mm (1in) flat brush. Returning to the No.4 flat, add further touches of dark blue, black, pale stone or white to the mix to create a range of dark and light greys for the tails, fins, backbones and underbodies.

3 ▲ **Bring in bright colours** Complete the grey areas on the fish. Mix crimson and bright yellow to make orange, then outline and block in the fish on the right. Add pale stone to the mix to vary the colour for the orange fish in the centre.

DEVELOPING THE PICTURE

By using a range of grey and orange tones, you have suggested the basic forms of the fish, ready to develop in more detail later. Now paint the background so that you can assess the overall tonal effect. The reflections of the overhanging trees makes the water look very dark.

4 ▶ **Block in the watery background** Mix a dark bluish grey from grey-green, dark grey and a little dark blue. Using the 50mm (2in) flat brush and varying the proportions of the colours, block in the background with lively strokes. Brush around the outlines of the fish, changing to the No.4 flat for detailed areas. Add more grey-green or dark blue to paint the ripples.

5 ◀ **Develop the water tones** Deepen the basic bluish grey mix with more dark blue and a little black. Continue blocking in the water, moving down and to the right. Paint lines and dabs of pure grey-green at the bottom, where the reflections are lighter. Add more dark blue to the basic mix for the top right-hand corner. Vary the direction of your brush strokes.

Master Strokes

Paul Sérusier
(1863–1927)
The Submerged Buddha

Many of the later paintings of French artist Sérusier showed evidence of religious symbolism. Here, a statue of the Buddha, surrounded by fish and underwater creatures, appears as a mysterious hazy form on the seabed. The application of the oil paint in dabs of colour is almost Pointillist in style and gives a soft overall texture to the painting.

Dabs of bright paint form a flurry of sunlit bubbles that illuminate the murky water.

Some of the fish are barely defined, creating a sense of depth in the picture.

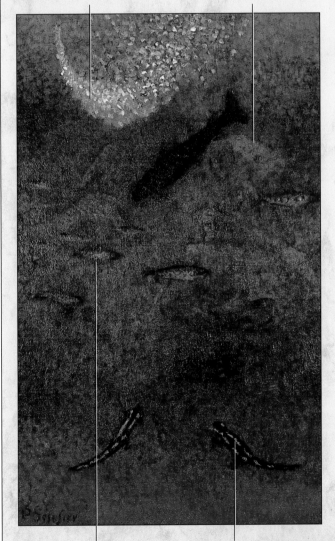

The fragmented colours of the fish give the impression of their swift movement through the water.

Brightly striped, newt-like creatures are placed at angles to help lead the eye towards the Buddha.

6 ▾ **Begin the detail** Mix a range of light and mid greys from pale stone and white, adding touches of dark blue or black. Use a 13mm (½in) flat brush to sharpen the forms of the grey fish. Paint bands on their bellies with hatched strokes of the No.4 flat.

7 ▾ **Develop the fish** Add white to the palest grey mix and highlight the grey fishes' backbones, fins and eyes. Next, using the 25mm (1in) brush, complete the water with mixes of white with a little dark blue. Define the tail of the top orange fish in grey-green. With the No.4 flat and varying amounts of crimson, bright yellow, pale stone and white, firm up the orange fishes' bodies in mid and light tones.

WIPING OFF EMULSION

TROUBLE SHOOTER

It is easy to correct mistakes when working with emulsion paint. While the paint is still wet, you can wipe off most of the colour with kitchen paper or a rag and then simply repaint the area. Wiping off areas of colour from the fishes' bodies also produces a good impression of water skimming over them.

Express yourself
Watery effects

If you want to work the fish pond on a much smaller scale, try this watercolour version which measures 28 x 38cm (11 x 15in). Sketch the shapes of the fish lightly with a 2B pencil, then paint their bodies with pale tints, working the herringbone pattern on their bodies wet-on-dry with darker tones. Create the mottled reflections in the water with patches of grey-green softened by spattered droplets of a pale wash. To suggest the ripples, sweep broad, translucent bands across the fish.

8 ▼ Intensify the background Mix more dark bluish and greenish greys from the colours used in steps 4 and 5. Starting at the top right, overpaint the water, using the 25mm (1in) flat brush to dab on broad patches of colour.

9 ▼ Paint watery effects Mix a washy dark bluish grey from grey-green, dark grey and a little dark blue. Using the 25mm (1in) flat brush, drag a thin layer of colour across the bodies of the fish on the left to suggest the ripples in the water. Wipe over the paint with kitchen paper or your hand to soften the effect in places.

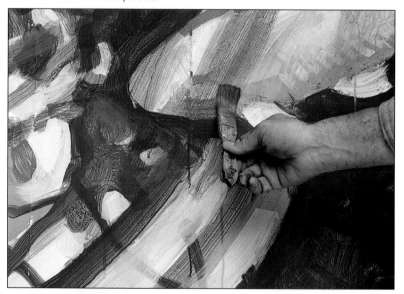

10 ◄ Complete the background Continue dabbing on dark greys as in step 8 to complete the reflections of the trees in the water. Pull some lines of grey across the light areas in the corners to suggest reflected branches and dab on grey patches for individual leaves. Deepen the tones of the ripples with mixes of grey-green, dark grey and dark blue. Finally, mix white with a little dark blue and dab on pale tones in the bottom left-hand corner where the sky is reflected in the water.

A FEW STEPS FURTHER

As the painting has been worked on such a large scale with broad brush marks, some contrasting linear detail would look very effective. You can easily draw over dry emulsion paint with a graphite pencil.

11 ▼ **Draw on details** Once the paint has dried, draw details on the fish with a 4B graphite pencil. With this fine linear work, you can create interesting texture on the underbodies, fins, tails and eyes.

12 ▲ **Heighten the contrast** Using the 25mm (1in) flat brush, dab thick white paint roughly on to the bottom corners. Work around the darker spots of colour.

THE FINISHED PICTURE

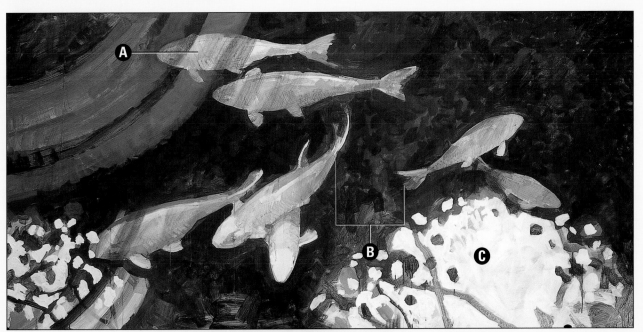

A Underwater effects
Washy paint brushed in broad bands over the fish and then wiped back with a rag gives the impression of looking down on them through the rippling water.

B Sense of movement
The lively arrangement of fish swimming in various directions keeps the eye moving around the picture area and creates an interesting, dynamic composition.

C Light and shade
Brilliant areas of white, where the sky is reflected in the pond, contrast strongly with the deep tones of the reflected foliage and enliven the lower part of the painting.

Power station at sunset

Capture the moody atmosphere of an industrial stretch of river at sunset, using tonal shading and muted watercolour washes.

Sunsets bring all kinds of interesting tonal effects into play. In this view of the River Thames, strong tonal contrasts create a dramatic skyline with equally dramatic reflections in the mirror-like surface of the water. The setting is reminiscent of the twilight riverscapes in the series of paintings known as *Nocturnes,* by American-born artist James Abbott McNeill Whistler (1834–1903). These are characterized by their low-key, harmonious hues.

▼ **Tall chimneys, pitched roofs and masts of boats break up the skyline in this tonal rendering of the River Thames.**

Lights and darks

The industrial buildings in the background have lost some of their detail in the fading light, but their silhouettes stand out crisply against the horizon. There is also enough tonal variation to be able to read the three-dimensional form of the buildings.

The boats in the foreground are lost in shadow, but you can still make out a few dim shapes. Darkest of all is the bridge, which makes a strong statement as it crosses the middle of the scene.

To counteract the shadowy areas, the sky is comparatively light in tone with a brighter patch to the left. This light distribution is directly reflected in the river. Bright spots of light catch the eye on the bridge and power station, shining out from the darkness.

Masking the edges

Once you have sketched in the main elements of the scene – the horizon, the bridge and the dark reflections in the foreground – establish the boundaries of the picture with masking tape. When you start adding washes of watercolour, you can then work up to and slightly over the tape. Remove it when the paint is dry – your picture will be left with beautifully straight edges.

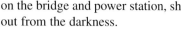

FIRST STEPS

1 ▼ Establish the picture area Using a 2B pencil, outline the buildings on the horizon, then sketch the bridge. Mark in the dark bulk of the boats and their reflections in the foreground. At this point, decide on your picture area and mask the edges. Jot in reflections of masts, chimneys and dark areas on the water.

2 ▼ Use masking fluid The spots of light shining out through the semi-darkness, as well as their reflections in the river, are important elements in the composition. Retain these as white paper by dotting tiny amounts of masking fluid along the bridge, on the power station and in a vertical line in the water. Use an old stiff round brush – you'll be picking them out in colour later.

EXPERT ADVICE
Drawing details

It is worth changing to a harder pencil when you are drawing in architectural details such as the windows. This helps bring interesting detail and definition to the otherwise shadowy shapes in the composition. Here the point of a B pencil is used to contrast with the surrounding tone drawn in with the side of a 2B.

YOU WILL NEED

Piece of 400gsm (200lb) rough watercolour paper 38 x 47cm (15 x 18.5in)	Old stiff round brush
	Spray fixative
2B and B pencils	Brushes: No.2 squirrel brush; No.6 round
Putty rubber (for erasing mistakes)	Jar of water
Craft knife (to sharpen pencils)	6 watercolours: Raw sienna; Light red; Ultramarine violet; Cobalt blue; Burnt umber; Cadmium yellow
Masking tape	
Masking fluid	

3 ▶ Block in the power station Working lightly with the 2B pencil, shade a light grey tone over the gasometer and the wall of the power station that is catching the setting sun. Now press harder to render a dark tone on the roof, chimneys and the shadowed side of the building.

BUILDING UP THE TONE

Apart from some windows, details on the horizon are barely discernible in the fading light. The buildings along the river are mainly just blocks of medium and dark tone.

4 ▲ Continue shading Shade the buildings on the horizon with a range of tones. Start to work up a heavy black on the bridge – the darkest tone. Use a B pencil for linear details on the left and mark windows on the buildings (see Expert Advice).

5 ▼ Develop the left-hand building Using loose strokes of the 2B pencil, block in the half-built flats on the left. Render dark tone where the bridge fades into shadow below them. Use the B pencil to define a tree shape beyond the bridge on the left and to mark horizontal reflections in the water.

6 ▼ Outline the boats The pale cabins of the boats moored on the left are just visible in the dim light. Using these as a guide, pick out the shapes of the boats with the 2B pencil and start to shade in the heavy shadow around them.

7 ▼ Mark the reflections Finish blocking in the bridge on the right of the picture with dark tone, then render pale grey on the water under the bridge and beyond it. Develop the reflections of the tall chimneys and the bridge piers in the water, using irregular horizontal hatching to show how ripples distort their shapes.

8 ▲ Work on the moored boats It is difficult to pick out all of the detail in the cluster of boats on the left. Choose a few of the more prominent boats and define their dark hulls, then block in the deep shadows around them with loose strokes, avoiding the verticals of the masts. Show the slightly distorted reflections of the masts and rigging with dotted lines.

9 ▼ **Draw ripples in the foreground** Still using the 2B pencil, strengthen the hulls of the boats with darker shading to further define their shapes. Complete the dark reflections of the boats in the lower left-hand corner with closely worked horizontal lines of ripples. Now extend the area of shadowy, rippling reflections over to the right.

10 ▼ **Add crisp details** Change to the B pencil and use heavy shading to define the wall and slanting roof of the low building just to the left of the tree. This marks it out from the mass of buildings behind it, creating a sense of depth. Indicate the windows on the ground floor of the block of flats, working up bands of dark tone that follow the curved walls.

11 ▼ **Bring in warm colour** Use some spray fixative to fix the pencil work. Then, with a No.2 squirrel brush, wash clean water over the sky and river. Mix a gold-coloured watercolour wash of raw sienna with a little light red and paint this wet-on-wet across the brighter areas of the sky and the river on the left.

12 ▲ **Add cool colour** The shadowy areas in the scene are a cooler, grey-blue colour. Mix this from ultramarine violet, cobalt blue and a little burnt umber and paint it wet-on-wet all over the right-hand side of the picture. Extend the same colour over the moored boats and across the lower part of the block of flats on the left.

A FEW STEPS FURTHER

The warm and cool colours in the sky and river blend subtly together to suggest the fading light giving way to shadow. Add some accents of colour by painting the bright lights in the distance and their reflections.

13 ▶ **Pick out the power station** Mix a grey from ultramarine violet and burnt umber. Using a No.6 round brush, paint the roof and chimneys of the power station. Then warm up the sunlit wall of the building with a wash of pure light red.

14 ▲ **Paint the lights** Wash over the shadowy water under the bridge with a raw sienna/violet mix. Scrape off the masking fluid with the tip of a craft knife or the end of a brush. Mix cadmium yellow and light red in varying strengths and dot in the uncovered spots. Remove the masking tape from around the picture.

THE FINISHED PICTURE

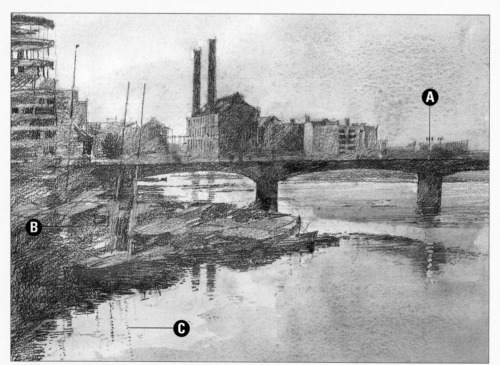

A Glowing lights
Pinpricks of light, painted in a mix of yellow and red, shine out from the shadow along the horizon, adding tiny focal points of bright colour to the muted palette.

B Textured paper
The rough surface of the watercolour paper shows through the large areas of pencil shading, giving a pleasing texture and avoiding a flat, uniform finish.

C Dots and dashes
Irregular dotted and dashed lines in the foreground show how the dark reflections in the river are broken up by the movement of the rippling water.

Hothouse plants

The graphic shapes and lush greenery of tropical plants are beautifully rendered in a pen and wash drawing.

I f you can't see exotic plants in their natural habitat, a visit to a tropical greenhouse is the next best thing. Here you can observe a wide variety of plants in a single location and marvel at their size and exuberant growth.

Character study

For this pen and wash drawing, the artist's aim was to bring out the character of the plants rather than attempt to create a meticulously accurate botanical study. He worked from three reference photos joined together, making a roughly square format. The composition encloses a balanced arrangement of leaves, with the large, spiky-leaved plant holding centre stage. The other leaves all have their own distinctive characteristics and together they make an exciting pattern of lines and colours.

A rough-textured Indian khadi paper was used as a support. This makes the black ink lines bleed slightly in places, creating textured edges on the leaves. The rough surface also breaks up the washes of coloured ink, which are applied with a brush. You can mix the coloured inks to create a range of luscious-looking, translucent greens.

▼ **A free and lively style brings out the essence and vigour of these dramatic hothouse plants.**

Piece of Rough Indian khadi paper 31 x 31cm (12 x 12in)

4B pencil

Putty rubber

Craft knife (to sharpen the pencil)

Dip pen with medium nib

8 acrylic artist's inks: Black; Turquoise; Lemon yellow; Ultramarine; Indian yellow; Indigo; Venetian red; Chrome yellow

No.6 round brush

FIRST STEPS

1 ▶ Set up a pattern of leaves Using a 4B pencil, draw the spiky leaves up to the top of the paper. Then, in the lower left-hand corner, draw the fanned-out shapes of the palm fronds. Outline the big, bold monstera leaf on the right and scribble small leaves in the top corners. Complete the sketch by drawing the leaf of the spiky plant that is bent forwards on the right.

2 ▶ Use the pencil lines as a guide With a dip pen and black acrylic ink, strengthen the outlines of the spiky leaves, describing wavy edges on some and smooth edges on others. Use short stabbing strokes for the out-of-focus leaves at the base of the plant. Now jot in the small leaves at the top and bottom.

3 ▼ Draw the palm fronds Complete the small ivy leaves trailing across the bottom of the picture. Then use long, closely spaced pen strokes to draw the thin, pointed palm fronds. Add a few leaves crossing in front of the first ones.

4 ▲ Build up a pattern Continue with the pattern of palm fronds, drawing the individual leaves with long, gently curving lines. Notice how they spread out in different directions and overlap one another, some covering the ivy leaves in the foreground.

AVOID SCRATCHY LINES

When you are strengthening the deep indentations in the edge of the monstera leaf, draw the pen smoothly and evenly around it without taking the nib off the paper. This rhythmic movement is reminicent of the one used for the elegant lettering of old-fashioned copperplate handwriting and avoids making scratchy lines with the nib.

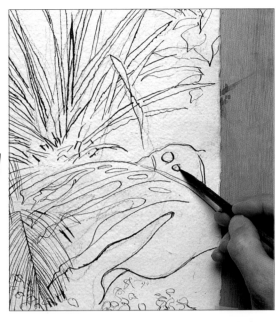

5 ◄ **Draw the large leaf**
Work the pen around the outline of the monstera leaf (see Trouble Shooter, left). This large, smooth shape – quite different from the spiky leaves of the other plants – brings contrast into the picture. Add the rows of holes in the leaf.

ADDING COLOUR

By laying down some washes of coloured ink, you can add depth and substance to the drawing. Don't just stick to naturalistic shades – bring the picture alive with cheerful lights and dramatic darks.

6 ► **Use coloured inks** Using a No.6 round brush, wash turquoise acrylic ink over the spiky leaves. Work with long, free strokes, overlapping the drawn edges. Now mix a bright lime green from lemon yellow and ultramarine. Wash this over the palm and the monstera. Where the lime is layered over the turquoise, a leaf green is created.

7 ◄ **Mix a warm green** Make a mixture of Indian yellow, indigo and lemon yellow inks to make a grass green. Working loosely, dab this mid-toned colour across the ivy leaves in the foreground. Don't worry if you go over the black outlines.

8 ▼ **Bring in a dark tone** Mix a dark green with indigo and lemon yellow and paint over the turquoise underlayer on the spiky plant. This time, work more closely inside the outlines so that the turquoise is visible around the edges.

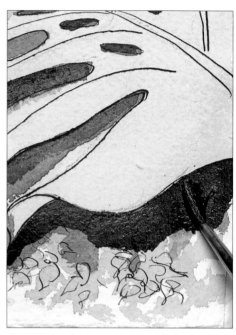

9 ▲ **Paint shadows** Using a dark olive mix of ultramarine and Indian yellow, paint the shadow visible through the holes in the monstera. Now extend it behind the monstera, working around the curves of the leaf.

10 ▲ **Mix a mid tone** Knock back the base of the picture with the dark olive mix thinned with water. Apply between the palm leaves with a dry brush to create texture. Mix more of the grass green from step 7 and paint the small leaves at the top. Now mix a bright green from lemon yellow with some indigo; add a mid tone to the monstera leaf and small leaves.

11 ▲ **Adjust the tones** Add more indigo to the bright green mix from step 10 and dilute with water. Wash this over the lime green of the palm – the underlayer will show through to create a lively green. Add indigo to the dark olive mix on your palette and use this deep green to strengthen the spiky leaves and darken the shadows behind the monstera and palm.

A FEW STEPS FURTHER

As greens predominate, add a few highlights here and there as a contrast.
You can also work back into the drawing using black ink for emphasis.

12 ▼ **Add warm touches** Dab touches of Venetian red ink around the palm fronds and small leaves on the left. Changing to chrome yellow, brighten the spiky leaves and monstera leaf with streaked highlights. Return to the pen and black ink; rework some of the leaves.

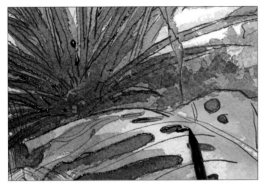

13 ▲ **Develop the darks** Add black to the olive mix and paint over the small leaves on the left. Spatter some of the mix across the palm. Brush on more black ink to darken the shadows behind the monstera and on the spiky plant.

THE FINISHED PICTURE

A Light undercolour
A loosely applied pale turquoise underlayer throws the leaves of the large, spiky plant into relief and hints at an unseen background.

B Lively lines
The pen lines, describing the shapes of the small leaves, are clearly visible under the wash of green ink. Note how the edges of the washes do not follow the pen lines exactly — contributing to the loose, lively drawing style.

C Wavy edges
Descriptive lines, added in black ink after the washes of colour were dry, exaggerate the wavy edges of some of the spiky leaves.

Using a painting knife

The simple shapes and vibrant colours of fruit provide a perfect subject for textural oil paint, applied in bold strokes with a painting knife.

If you have not used a painting knife with oil paints before, you will be amazed at the difference it makes to the finish of your work. Applying oil paint from a blade instead of the traditional brush is a technique that will immediately free up your painting style. This is because detail must be ignored in favour of bold shapes and lines, and these are well suited to the textural quality of oils.

Before you begin, practise making some marks on a spare piece of canvas. Don't overload your knife with paint, as it can be quite difficult to control. Try defining a sharp edge with the side of the blade, pressing it down on to the surface, then dragging it away from the line. In this way, you can achieve the effect of gradually fading colour. Also, try smoothing paint across an area with the side of the blade, then picking up a new colour and drifting it across the first, so that they mix on the canvas.

Working into the textures

Liquin, an oil medium, was added to each mix of oil paint throughout the progress of the project. This medium allows oil paint to be applied with a smooth flow and helps it to dry more quickly. It also enables textures scraped into the surface of the paint with the hard edge of the knife blade to retain their sharp definition.

When working with oils and a painting knife, it can be time-consuming to cover large areas of canvas with colour to lose the stark white of the surface. Here, the canvas was prepared by applying a pale brown wash of acrylic paint – a short-cut solution to this problem.

▼ **Bold applications of paint with a knife blade give a tactile surface to this painting.**

FIRST STROKES

1 ▶ Sketch the still life Using the 4B graphite stick, loosely sketch the outlines of the fruit and any prominent highlights and features on each. Mark in the edges of the shadows, and the most obvious grain lines in the wooden surface.

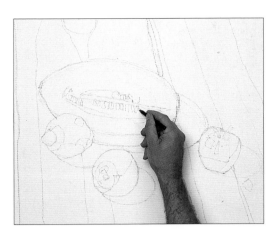

2 ▶ Begin the underpainting Mix a wet wash of cadmium red, raw umber and yellow ochre acrylic paint. Using a No.8 flat brush, work quickly and fluidly to block in the background. This will give an even wash of colour upon which to build your composition, avoiding the need to spend lots of time covering up the white expanse of canvas with the oil paints.

DEVELOPING THE PICTURE

Continue with the acrylic paints, using them to model the fruit and add their cast shadows. Then you are ready to start applying the oil paints with your painting knife.

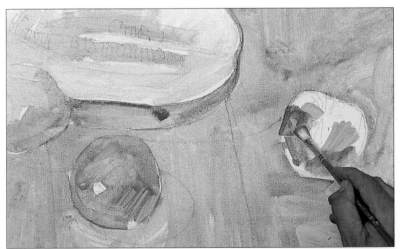

3 ▲ Underpaint the fruit Use lemon yellow acrylic paint and a No.6 flat to block in the lemon. Mix cadmium yellow with a little cadmium red acrylic to block in the orange. Dilute the mix and mark in the melon seeds and the shadows on the lemon. Draw titanium white acrylic into the mix to block in the melon's flesh. The melon skin and apple are worked in a mix of cerulean blue and cadmium yellow. Draw a little cadmium red and burnt umber into the mix to paint in the red areas of the apple.

4 ▲ Start painting with oils Complete the acrylic work with shadows in a mix of cadmium red, burnt umber and cerulean blue. Mix lemon yellow, cadmium yellow and titanium white oil paints and daub on to the lemon shape with a painting knife. Drag in more white for highlights.

5 ▶ Add texture Draw cadmium red into the yellow mix. Use the knife to model the orange and suggest melon seeds. Pull white into the yellow mix and drag over the melon flesh. Mix cerulean blue, lemon yellow and cadmium yellow and drag along the side of the melon.

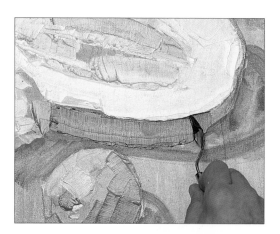

A FEW STEPS FURTHER

If you wish, you could develop the background and add texture to the wooden surface. Try adding grain lines with a graphite stick, and the plank edges with paints.

6 ▼ Define the seeds Dip the blade edge into the mix and apply a thin line along the top of the melon. Mix cadmium red and cadmium yellow and apply to the orange. Add more cadmium red into the mix and use the very tip of the knife to mark seeds on the melon.

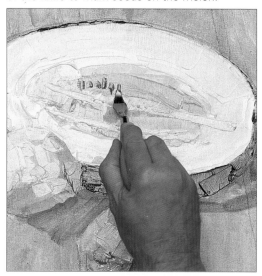

7 ▲ Paint the shadows Use the green mix from step 5 to paint the end of the lemon and the top of the apple. Complete the apple with the red mix from step 6. With a mix of cerulean blue and cadmium red, block in the shadows under the lemon and melon. Drag in some cadmium red for the orange's shadow and a little yellow ochre for the apple's shadow.

Master Strokes

Gustave Courbet (1819–77)
Still Life with Apples and a Pomegranate

The wonderfully rich colours of the fruit really leap out from the dark background. To prevent the composition becoming too static, Courbet placed a few items to the side of the bowl.

The pewter pot is subtly modelled, with tones ranging from bright white to black.

The use of reflected colour is particularly effective – red apples pick up the colour of adjacent green apples and vice versa.

9 ▶ Colour the wood Mix Payne's grey and yellow ochre with a little cadmium red. Use the edge of the blade to mark the plank edges. Drag more yellow ochre into the mix, thinning it with white spirit. Use the knife to drag this across the wood in the direction of the grain lines. Scrape grain lines into the paint with the knife tip.

8 ▲ Develop grain lines Drag the 4B graphite stick in bold lines down the painting to suggest the wood grain, letting the stick run right through the shadows. You can also use the graphite stick to define the melon seeds.

THE FINISHED PICTURE

A Texture of seeds
The melon seeds were depicted individually by picking up paint on the tip of the painting knife and dabbing it on in rows to make small raised shapes.

B Smooth surfaces
Relatively flat areas of colour were achieved by smoothing on the oil paint with the side of a painting knife.

C Scraped lines
An underwash of acrylic paint created a pale background. The painting knife was used to scrape textures into the oil paint, revealing lines of this pale colour.

Glossary

Abtract A style of painting where colour and form (and sometimes the materials and support) make up the subject of the painting rather than it representing objects or people.

Accent A detail, brushstroke, or area of colour placed in a painting for emphasis.

Acrylic paint A type of paint made with synthetic resin as the medium (liquid) to bind the pigment (colour), rather than natural oils such as linseed used in oil paints. It has the advantage of drying more quickly than oil paint and being water soluble.

Blending Creating a gentle and gradual transition from one colour or tone to another so that no sharp divisions are apparent.

Blotting An absorbent material such as tissues or paper towels, or a squeezed out brush, to pick up and lighten a wet or damp wash.

Binder The substance in a paint which holds together (binds) the pigment and makes the paint stick to whatever it's painted on.

Cool colours Blues, greens, and purples are considered cool colours.

Complementary colours Two colours on opposite sides of the colour wheel. Complementary colours are contrasting and stand out against each other.

Drawing grid A grid of squares made for transferring a sketch proportionately onto a large-scale support.

Dry Brush A painting technique in which, as the name suggests, a little bit of paint is put on a dry brush. When applied, it produces a broken, scratchy effect.

Easel A frame for holding a drawing while the artist works on it. A good sketching easel allows the drawing to be held securely in any position from horizontal to vertical.

Expressionism A movement of the early 20th century that started in Germany in which the artist aims to express their emotions through the use of vivid colours and strong, distorted lines.

Etching An illustration made by drawing through a wax covering on a metal plate, which is then put into acid to eat away (etch) the metal where it has been uncovered. The plate is then inked and printed. Also the process of creating such an illustration.

Eye-level The plane of vision from the viewer to the horizon, i.e. the horizontal line.

Flat colour A section of colour applied in a uniform tone and hue.

Flat wash Any area of a painting where a wash of single colour and value is painted in a series of multiple, overlapping strokes following the flow of the paint. A slightly tilted surface aids the flow of your washes.

Glaze The term used mostly for oils and acrylics for a thin, transparent layer of paint. Glazes are used on top of one another to build up depth and modify colours in a painting.

Gouache Water-soluble paints differing from watercolours in that gouache uses glue to bind the pigments and the lighter tones contain white pigment, which means they're opaque rather than transparent. The white in watercolour comes from the paper.

Graphite stick A thick graphite pencil, used for large-scale work.

Hard edge A hard edge is the term used when the edge of an object is painted in a well defined or definite way. A soft edge is when it is painted so that it disappears or fades into the background.

Half tone Any of the tones in a painting between the darks and the highlights.

Highlight Those parts of a painting that have the lightest tone. In watercolour painting, the white paper is left unpainted to create white highlights.

Horizontal line Where the land (or sea) and sky meet. A term used in perspective.

Hue The actual colour of something, such as red, green, or blue. What we generally, but less technically correct, call colour.

Impressionism A movement that started in France around 1870 which attempted to capture fleeting impressions, particularly the changing light on a surface.

Masking out A technique for leaving areas of paper unpainted when applying washes by first covering them with paper or masking fluid.

Mixed media A painting which combines different painting and drawing materials and methods. Any materials can be used, such as pages from magazines, newspaper, photographs, fabric, soil, or packaging.

Oil Paint A type of paint made with natural oils such as linseed, walnut, or poppy, as the medium to bind the pigment.

Palette The surface on which an artist lays out their colours (paints) as well as the range of colours an artist works with.

Pastel Ground pigment mixed with chalk and gum or oil, then shaped into drawing sticks. Pastels cannot be mixed on a palette like paints, but are mixed on the paper by overlaying or blending.

Primary colours The three colours – red, blue and yellow – that cannot be produced by mixing other colours.

Resist Any material, usually wax or grease crayons, that repels paint or dyes. Lithography is a grease (ink) and water (wet stone or plate) resist-printing technique. Batik is a wax resist fabric artform.

Scumbling Dragging a dense or opaque colour across another colour creating a rough texture.

Secondary colours Colours obtained by mixing two primary colours. For example, green, violet, and orange.

Sketch A rough or loose visualization of a subject or composition.

Sgraffito A technique in which dried paint or pastel is scratched or scraped off to reveal the colour below. Often used for textural effects.

Stippling A method of painting or drawing that involves the application of tiny spots of colour by stabbing and dotting with the tip of a brush or pastel to create an area of tone.

Texture The actual or virtual representation of different surfaces, paint applied in a manner that breaks up the continuous colour or tone.

Thumbnail Sketch Small tonal and compositional sketches to try out design or subject ideas.

Tone The light and dark values of a colour.

Vanishing point A term used in perspective to describe the point on the horizon where parallel lines appear to meet.

Viewpoint The height from which the artist sees the subject they're painting. It determines where the horizon line is.

Wash A transparent layer of diluted colour that is brushed on.

Wash-off Dislodging an area of water-soluble paint, usually with a bristle brush dipped in water or with a damp sponge.

Index

Page numbers in *italics* refer to captions.